THE FORGOTTEN VICTOR

GENERAL SIR RICHARD O'CONNOR
KT, GCB, DSO, MC

Frontispiece
Lieutenant General O'Connor, moving at his usual high speed, visiting Derna just after its capture by the Australian 6th Division on 29 January 1941.

(*Imperial War Museum*)

THE FORGOTTEN VICTOR

GENERAL SIR RICHARD O'CONNOR
KT, GCB, DSO, MC

John Baynes

BRASSEY'S (UK)

LONDON · OXFORD · WASHINGTON · NEW YORK
BEIJING · FRANKFURT · SÃO PAULO · SYDNEY · TOKYO · TORONTO

First edition 1989

UK editorial offices: Brassey's, 24 Gray's Inn Road, London WC1X 8HR
orders: Brassey's, Headington Hill Hall, Oxford OX3 0BW

USA editorial offices: Brassey's, 8000 Westpark Drive, Fourth Floor, McLean, Virginia 22102
orders: Pergamon Press Inc., Maxwell House, Fairview Park, Elmsford, New York 10523

Distributed in North America to booksellers and wholesalers
by the Macmillan Publishing Company, N.Y., N.Y.

Library of Congress Cataloging-in-Publication Data
Baynes, John Christopher Malcolm.
The forgotten victor: General Sir Richard O'Connor, Kt, GCB, DSO, MC/John Baynes. —
1st ed.
p. cm.
1. O'Connor, Richard Nugent, Sir, b. 1889.
2. Generals—Great Britain—Biography.
3. Great Britain. Army—Biography. I. Title.
U55.026B38 1989   355'.0092—dc20
89–33821

British Library Cataloguing in Publication Data
Baynes, John
The forgotten victor: General Sir Richard O'Connor Kt, GCB, DSO, MC.
1. Great Britain. Army. O'Connor, *Sir*, Richard
I. Title
355.3'31'0924

ISBN 0–08–036269–9

Printed in Great Britain by BPCC Wheatons Ltd, Exeter

Contents

v

Contents

List of Maps

List of Maps

The title *The Forgotten Victor* is taken, with its author's generous permission, from Correlli Barnett's book *The Desert Generals*, in which the term is used as a sub-title for the section describing General O'Connor's desert campaign of 1940–41.

Acknowledgements

In the first place, my thanks must go to General Dick's widow, the late Dorothy, Lady O'Connor, and his step-son, Jamie, lately Major, Queen's Own Highlanders (Seaforth and Camerons), for their approval of my long-felt wish to write his biography. Their support and interest has been unfailing.

Major James Nairne, a one-time Seaforth Highlander and more recently a Queen's Messenger, should really have his name recorded above mine as author of this book. It was through James's friendship that the General was persuaded to have his papers gathered together, and not only put in order, but bound and catalogued by James himself with enormous care and skill. Most of these have been lodged in the Liddell Hart Centre for Military Archives in King's College, London: some, however, have been retained for the family, and to these I have been given privileged access. Without all James's patient 'spade-work' the biography could never have been written.

Kenneth Startup, an American university lecturer at a college in Arkansas, was kind enough to give me his own Masters' degree thesis entitled 'General Sir Richard O'Connor, A Profile of His Life and Career' to use, and also much material collected while preparing it. This included records of personal interviews given when he stayed with the O'Connors in 1975.

The advice of many distinguished people has been of immense importance in trying to reach the truth. Field Marshal Lord Carver gave me an interview and read the two chapters on north-west Europe. The late Field Marshal Lord Harding gave me a long interview and read and approved the Epilogue. The Rt Rev Simon Phipps, lately Bishop of Lincoln, has also read two chapters, and given invaluable information about his period as O'Connor's ADC, and later MA, during his own soldiering years in the Coldstream Guards. Major General 'Pip' Roberts has also read the north-west Europe chapters, and he and his wife entertained me hospitably when I visited them in May 1988.

Others to whom I am indebted for interviews, and in several cases hospitality as well while visiting them, include Correlli Barnett, at Churchill College, Cambridge; Sir Alastair Blair, KCVO; the late Colonel Neville Blair; Mrs Janet Corrie; Mr and Mrs John Dent; Lieutenant Colonel and the Hon Mrs Michael Evetts; General Sir Victor FitzGeorge Balfour; the late Earl of Ranfurly and the Countess of Ranfurly; and Dr John Laffin.

Numerous people who knew the General at various times in his life have sent me useful letters and other material. Among them are Lady Aldington; Earl Haig, whose influence in Chapter 7 will be obvious; Brigadier F B B Noble; Lieutenant Colonel Charles Mackinnon; and Squadron Leader C E Roberts.

I am indebted to Lieutenant Colonel Bob Barnes and to my son William for production of the excellent maps.

Among the librarians and archivists my thanks must go first to Patricia Methven and her staff at the Liddell Hart Centre, who have been immensely efficient and courteous. Peter Liddle, whose superb First World War collection is now lodged, with himself as Keeper, in the Leeds University Library, gave me access to important material during his last months in his previous quarters at Sunderland Polytechnic. The staff of the photographic department at the Imperial War Museum demonstrated the amazing extent of their knowledge of all aspects of the Second World War. Mr J C Andrews and Mrs J M Blacklaw at the Ministry of Defence Library have been most helpful, as have Mr M G Sims of the Staff College Library, Camberley, and Mr A A Orgill of the Royal Military Academy, Sandhurst.

At Brassey's, Major General Tony Trythall, Brigadier Bryan Watkins, Jenny Shaw and Angela Clark have, as usual, been full of encouragement, and ready to help at all times.

Finally, there are several individuals with whom I have corresponded although we have not met, and in this group I would like to thank Conte Ottino Carraciolo di Forino; Professor The Rt Hon John Freeman; General Sir John Hackett; Mr J Ingolsby, lately Police Sergeant in Duns, Berwickshire, and, as a young Scots Guardsman, the General's soldier servant in the Desert; Mr Ronald Latham, one time librarian of the Pepys Library, Magdalene College, Cambridge, who wrote to me about Owen Morshead (Chapters 3 and 4); Mrs Sylvia Lewin; and Lieutenant General Sir

Acknowledgements

John MacMillan, who has followed in the footsteps of his father, General Dick's great friend 'The Babe', to become GOC Scotland.

Several ladies have typed parts of the book for me, in some cases the same chapter in more than one draft, and I would like to thank Miss Shirley Hare, Mrs Elizabeth Harvey, Mrs Caroline Jacobs, Mrs Lynne Kendall and Mrs Jayne Roberts for their neat and accurate work, which has caused Tony Trythall to praise the typescript of the book in glowing terms.

Quotations

I am indebted to the authors or publishers named below for permission to use long quotations from the following books in their copyright:

The Desert Generals by Correlli Barnett (George Allen and Unwin); *Disastrous Twilight* by Major General Shahid Hamid (Leo Cooper); *Decision in Normandy* by Lieutenant Colonel Carlo D'Este (Collins); *Farewell Campo 12* by Brigadier James Hargest (Michael Joseph); *Dilemmas of the Desert War* by Field Marshal Lord Carver (Batsford); *From the Desert to the Baltic* by Major General G P B Roberts (William Kimber); also Miss Rosemary Lewin for the long quotation in the Epilogue from the private papers of her father, Ronald Lewin.

Except where otherwise stated in the plate section, all photographs have kindly been provided by Major W J O'Connor and are reproduced with his permission.

Prologue

Long after the end of the Second World War, General of the Army, Dwight D Eisenhower, formerly President of the United States of America, wrote to the man whose name he had first heard 'spoken among my British friends, in tones of respect and admiration'. In a further letter written shortly after, he stated: 'You, of course, had a most interesting, not to say glamorous, career during the war. I trust that one of these days you will publish your recollections.'[1]

In fact, the idea of publishing his own memoirs was something that had little appeal to General Sir Richard O'Connor. This was partly due to his completely natural modesty about his own exploits. His modesty, however, never weakened his authority, for he possessed, in full, what the poet Edmund Blunden called:

> ... that harmony and whole,
> Of soldier creed, and act, and pride of place,
> The eye's shrewd humour, the lip's generous grace,
> The stirring zest, the power to make and give ...

His reluctance to go into print on his own account was also reinforced by observing the results of doing so in the case of some of his contemporaries, especially Alexander and Montgomery. Of the former he commented, in notes written in his later years, 'that he should never have written a book',[2] while the unfortunate consequences of the publication of the latter's *Memoirs* in 1958 demonstrated how much offence could be taken in high places around the world at relatively mild criticism.

Montgomery was to be a particularly important person in O'Connor's life and appears frequently in this biography throughout a span of over fifty years. How the fate of each of them might have unfolded had O'Connor not become a prisoner of war in 1941 becomes one of the great 'ifs' of the history of the Second World War.

Other figures who achieved fame in that war and were friends of O'Connor's were four future Field Marshals: Wavell, Auchinleck,

Harding and Slim. With each he had a happy relationship of mutual trust and respect and, at different stages, he was particulary close to the first three. From the other services, his special friend was the great sailor known as 'ABC', Admiral of the Fleet Viscount Cunningham of Hyndhope. He also earned the respect of that famous airman, Marshal of the Royal Air Force Lord Tedder, whose affection for the Army was not among his better known attributes.

Returning to the matter of O'Connor's dislike of self-advertisement, it is undoubtedly one of the reasons why he was so rightly described by Correlli Barnett in *The Desert Generals* as the 'forgotten victor'. It was also something ingrained in people of his background and class, of whose best qualities he was such a sterling example. He was a gentleman, and he did not advertise. As John Keegan has written of Wellington, he was 'the embodiment of the gentlemanly ideal', and 'the values on which it rested—reticence, sensitivity, unselfseeking, personal discipline and sobriety in dress, conduct and speech, all married to total self-assurance'.[3]

From his mother he learnt to admire the qualities mentioned above and, in addition, he was taught the Christian faith which sustained him throughout his life. She also taught him to respect the feelings of others. This latter quality was occasionally at variance with the calls of military leadership, though more often gave him added stature in the eyes of those he commanded.

When his great moment came in 1940 with his command of the Western Desert Force, and his annihilation of the massive Italian Tenth Army, he was ready to excel in what Barnett has described so well as 'the most complete human activity, since generalship involves all the intellectual, physical and moral power in a man'.[4]

The martial attributes which were so strongly present in him owed much to his own long study of his profession, and, perhaps even more, to the grounding he received in his early years of service, spent in his much loved regiment, The Cameronians (Scottish Rifles). Here he was lucky to come under the influence of several officers of unusual distinction, some of whom will appear again in the pages which follow. His devotion to his regiment and to the British Army never wavered during a long and exciting life, which had its full share of 'triumph and disaster'.

1

Childhood and Schools

Richard Nugent O'Connor was born in Srinagar, the capital of Kashmir, on 21 August 1889. His father, Major Maurice Nugent O'Connor, was serving at the time in the 87th Royal Irish Fusiliers, into which regiment he had transferred from the Royal Scots in order to serve abroad after his marriage. By doing so, he could live less expensively than at home, an important consideration at the time, as he was not well off. Mrs O'Connor had been a Miss Lilian Morris, daughter of Sir John Morris, KCSI, of the Indian Civil Service, who finished a distinguished career as Governor of the Central Provinces. Lady Morris, O'Connor's grandmother, was the daughter of Colonel Cheape, a member of a well-known family in Fife, who also owned a property on the west coast of Argyllshire. This was to have great significance for the young Richard (or Dick as he was always known from early years), as in due course his grandmother inherited from her family this Argyllshire estate called Killundine, which lies near Morven on the east side of the Sound of Mull.

However, good fortune did not shine at first for the O'Connor family, for in the same year that Dick was born his father had an accident which necessitated a return to Britain: in 1891 he was put on half-pay, and in 1894 retired from the Army. From that date, until his death in 1903, the O'Connors lived in his family home in Ireland. This was at Ballybrock, near Killeiney, in the county now known by its ancient name of Offaly, but on those days called Queen's County. With only a small pension and little private means, the family found shortage of money a constant problem. His ailing father appears to have had little influence on the young Dick, leaving his mother and his nurse, Christina MacInnes, to be the ones who guided him in his early years. Christina had entered

1

service with the Morris family at Killundine in 1883 and joined the O'Connors as 'nanny' on their return from India in 1890. As will be told later, she spent the rest of her life with them.

The two women who were left with the task of rearing the young Dick carried it out with total devotion. Mrs O'Connor, a formidable lady, though fundamentally kind, was determined that her only son should not be spoiled, and took on the responsibilities of a father as well as a mother. Christina, the West Highland nurse with a softer, gentler nature, supported her wholeheartedly. The most significant lessons implanted into the mind of the young boy whom these two had in their charge were threefold: the importance of the Christian faith; the need to be absolutely truthful at all times; and the placing of duty before all other considerations. Of course, such lessons were taught to children in many families, but only rarely did they take root as strongly as they did in the mind of the young O'Connor. Because of the family's relatively reduced circumstances during these early years, he also learnt to be careful with money, especially in regard to his own expenses. Even when he became better off, he remained thrifty.

In May 1899, shortly before he was ten, Dick was sent to Tonbridge Castle preparatory school. His first letter home was written in a good, clear hand and was relatively cheerful, although he told his mother that on the first night 'I was awfully unhappy without you, though I try not to think about it.' His reports during his time at his 'prep' school, which moved in 1902 to the Towers, Crowthorne, were generally good, and his music was specially commended.

In 1903, Dick moved on to Wellington College at the age of thirteen years and nine months. His career there was not distinguished in any way, though he enjoyed his school days well enough and, in later years, was proud to become a Governor of Wellington. He also gave a bursary at the school for the use of sons of officers of his regiment. He played games with average skill and continued to play the piano well enough to receive excellent reports. Like many others who have done great things in life, the young O'Connor was a late developer. Thus it was not until he was twenty that signs of his unusual ability became noticed.

His tutor, or housemaster, at Wellington was not sufficiently perceptive to spot his true promise. As Dick said good-bye to him at the end of his last term, this man patronisingly made a joke about his future in the Army: 'Tell me when you become a General!' Typically, a letter with this information was in due course despatched to him in 1938 by one of the youngest Major Generals in the Army at that time!

It was just after he went to Wellington that his father died. Two years later a big change occurred in his life: Mrs O'Connor moved in to live with her parents in their London house at 88 Queensgate. Summers were spent in Scotland. In the very brief notes he wrote in old age about his childhood, O'Connor recorded that '88 Queensgate and Killundine now became my new homes, and I was blissfully happy.'[1]

The holidays at Killundine, and the companionship of his grandfather, old Sir John Morris, brought young Dick special joy. With the old man, he walked every Sunday to the Presbyterian Church in Morven, where an outstanding preacher called Donald Macfarlane made a lasting impression on him. When he had got to know Macfarlane really well, he often walked over the moors on Sunday evenings to have supper with him at his manse.

Another pleasure at Killundine was fishing, which remained something to be enjoyed for the rest of his life. An old ghillie who remembered O'Connor as a boy wrote to him during the Second World War: 'I often think of the happy days I had with the Morris family, we always looked forward to Sir John Morris coming down and how excited he used to get on catching a fish.'[2] On two occasions Sir John took his grandson to the Isle of Lewis to fish the famous Grimister river. At Killundine there was also grouse shooting to be enjoyed, walking-up over dogs, and stalking. Dick became an enthusiastic and proficient field sportsman.

It might be said that the young Dick O'Connor had an ideal start in life. He had the privilege of a good education and a loving home, without being in any way spoilt or given too good an opinion of himself, and he was allowed every chance to develop his own character and interests in the company of people of high quality.

2

From Sandhurst to the Regiment

Gentleman Cadet O'Connor joined the Royal Military College at Sandhurst, just a few miles from Wellington, in January 1908. He once again showed little sign of his future distinction as a soldier, and went through his eighteen months there without making any particular mark. In his day, cadets joined in January of one year and passed out in July of the following year, normally joining their regiments in September after a long leave. Only cavalry and infantry officers were trained at Sandhurst: artillery and engineers, and a few entrants for other corps, received what was probably a more thorough professional grounding at the Royal Military Academy at Woolwich.

The syllabus in force at Sandhurst at the time covered twelve subjects. One language had also to be studied. The twelve subjects were military administration, law, history, geography, tactics, engineering, signalling and sanitation, on the professional side, and in the purely physical area, drill, musketry, riding and gymnastics. The three language options were French, German and Hindustani: O'Connor chose German.[1] As he never spoke about his time at Sandhurst in later life, it is difficult to know what he thought about it. However, it is likely that he was an average cadet, who did well enough to be commissioned into a Scottish regiment as he wished, but made no effort to achieve special recognition. In fact, such efforts were not well regarded by the majority in those days—'pot-hunting' being considered very poor form—and as a normal, conventional young man, O'Connor would have shared the prevalent attitude in this respect. It can also be assumed that he enjoyed the riding and physical training in view of his known enthusiasm for both in the years that followed.

A year ahead of him, although two years older, was another cadet with whom he was to have much contact throughout the next forty years, and who frequently reappears in this story. Although it is impossible to tell whether they knew each other at Sandhurst, it is certain that the young O'Connor must have known *about* Gentleman Cadet, lately Cadet Lance Corporal, B L Montgomery, since the latter's reversion in rank was posted among College Orders on 29 January 1908, on the day the College opened after the Christmas break and O'Connor began his first term. It is also certain that Montgomery's offence, of setting light to a fellow cadet's shirt tails and causing him serious burns, was well known throughout the College, even though the victim never named his assailant.[2]

At the end of his time at Sandhurst, O'Connor passed out 38th in the order of merit, showing that he must have been reasonably industrious. As already mentioned, he was very anxious to join a Scottish regiment, and both on account of his love of Argyllshire and the fact that he had a cousin serving with the regiment, he had hoped for a vacancy in the Argyll and Sutherland Highlanders. However, although disappointed that there was not one open for him in that regiment, he was delighted to be gazetted to The Cameronians (Scottish Rifles), the 2nd Battalion of which he joined in Aldershot in October 1909.

The regiment which O'Connor joined was based on Glasgow and the county of Lanarkshire. It was a large organisation, consisting of a regimental depot in Hamilton; two regular battalions, one at home and one overseas; two Special Reserve battalions for holding reservists; and four battalions of the newly-created Territorial Army (TA), the successor to the old Militia and Volunteers, which had been formed the previous year.

All infantry regiments were now structured along similar lines, their territorial bases having been allotted to them and their names established under extensive reorganisation of the Army in 1881. Referred to as the Cardwell reforms, from the name of the Secretary of State for War who conceived them, though put into effect by his successor Childers, their essence lay in the grouping of regular infantry regiments into pairs, each pair thus combined forming a new single regiment of two battalions, based on a territorial area in which it would have its depot and from which it would find its recruits. In time it became clear that the great numbers of part-time soldiers serving in various militia and volunteer units in each county, and already in many cases affiliated to their county regiments, would be better placed if fully integrated into them and so formed into more cohesive bodies. This measure was implemented in 1908 by the formation of the Territorial Army.

This background is important, as the immense value that O'Connor placed on being a member of his regiment will often be mentioned. Before looking at his early years with the 2nd Battalion, and the people in it who did so much to guide and inspire him, the estrangement between the 1st and 2nd Battalions must be mentioned: a restrained hostility which was found in some other regiments as well, though rarely so pronounced.

The 1881 reforms had involved something of a forced marriage between the 26th Cameronian Regiment and the 90th Perthshire Light Infantry to form respectively the 1st and 2nd Battalions of The Cameronians (Scottish Rifles). The trouble sprang from the fact that the 90th considered themselves in every way vastly superior to the 26th. Garnet Wolseley who had joined the 90th in 1854 wrote of his fellow officers:

> They thought themselves socially superior to the ordinary regiments of the Line, which were always spoken of as 'grabbies'. Many of them were well connected, and some were well off. It was in every respect a home for gentlemen, and in that respect much above the great bulk of line regiments.[3]

For all ranks the amalgamation with a rather dull, heavy-footed, marching regiment like the 26th was most unpopular, as was the loss of territorial connection with Perthshire. Unfortunately the 26th were not all that impressed with the 90th; they were conscious of being a hundred years older, and having taken part in a great many more battles, in several of which they had particularly distinguished themselves. So, from the start, a state of undeclared war was established between the two battalions, which was reinforced by the 1st Battalion using the title The Cameronians and the 2nd calling themselves Scottish Rifles, and neither using the full name if possible. Over the years those who had served in one of the original regiments faded from the scene, and by 1909 little real difference between the 1st and 2nd Battalions could be discerned. In a rather silly way, however, the old rivalry was maintained for many years more though of no great importance to the more sensible members of the regiment.

The two regular battalions of each infantry regiment were so posted that one was stationed in Great Britain or Ireland and the other overseas. The home service battalion was given the responsibility of keeping the overseas one up to full strength by sending it periodic drafts of men, and it was accepted that, in doing so, its own strength might often be low. It was a system which lasted, apart from the First World War, up to 1939 and adequately fitted the Regular Army's primary imperial role.

When O'Connor joined the Scottish Rifles in Aldershot in 1909, it was the home service battalion, while the Cameronians were abroad in India, moving in December that year to South Africa. From Aldershot the Scottish Rifles were posted to Colchester in January 1910, and remained the home battalion for the next year and a half. During his time at Colchester O'Connor attended two courses. A signalling course, after which he was appointed Regimental Signals Officer, and a musketry course at the Small Arms School at Hythe in Kent, where he earned a 'Distinguished' grading. One of the advantages of becoming a signal officer was the fact that the appointment was a mounted one, and so he was given an official government charger to ride. Like most of his brother officers, O'Connor was a very keen horseman with a reputation for boldness in the hunting field and on the point-to-point course. There were some dozen chargers on the strength of each infantry battalion, and though allotted to specific officers for duty purposes, they could be ridden by others in various equestrian sports, all of which were much encouraged at the time. When the Scottish Rifles race was run at the point-to-point of the Essex and Suffolk hounds in March 1910, eleven officers faced the starter's flag, some on their own horses, some on chargers.

Although not a rich regiment, as they went in Edwardian days, it was necessary to have a private income of £100 a year at the very least, and preferably twice that amount, to serve in the Scottish Rifles. The immense wealth and power of Victorian Britain meant that her influential families had numerous children: as the Army was one of the careers considered suitable for their sons, such families filled the commissioned ranks almost entirely. Within the esoteric world of infantry and cavalry regiments, there were roughly understood levels of private means required for each. However, nearly all officers shared similar interests and backgrounds and had been educated at the major public schools, so they did the same things, but in various degrees of style, and at different levels of expense. Although not particularly well off as a young officer, for reasons made clear already, O'Connor with an allowance of £150 a year was able to do all the things he wanted, though it meant avoiding unnecessary expense and living abstemiously in the Officers' Mess.

Where he was particularly lucky in joining the Scottish Rifles was the presence of an above average number of intelligent and professionally enthusiastic officers. Too many regular officers, especially in the cavalry, were of the type described by the celebrated journalist C E Montague in his book *Disenchantment*, published in 1922, in which he attacked somewhat venomously the pre-1914 officer, claiming that: 'the fashion in sentiment in our Regular Army was to think hard work "bad form"; a subaltern was felt to be a bit of a scrub if he worried too much about discovering how to support an attack when he might be more spiritedly employed in playing polo.' Montague then differentiated between 'the average, staple article made by a sleek, snobbish, safe, wealth-governed England after her own image' and 'the pick, the saving few, the unconquerably sound and keen'. In the Scottish Rifles, and in many other regiments as well, considerably more than 'just a few' were in the latter category.[4]

During his first five years service, spent with his regiment from October 1909 to August 1914, the young O'Connor received a training in his profession, and developed an attitude towards it, which were to be of crucial importance during the rest of his service. Much of what he learnt was taught him, both directly and indirectly, by certain brother officers; and by the Warrant Officers and Sergeants of the battalion as well as by the men he commanded, whose respect and loyalty, as opposed to plain obedience, had to be earned. In the course of these five years of regimental soldiering, O'Connor matured and developed from the easily-forgotten schoolboy or cadet into a personality who, while still quiet and slightly diffident, certainly could not be overlooked.

Though the majority of the officers with whom he served in the Scottish Rifles were of high calibre, there were some dozen whose influence was specially important. Major George Carter-Campbell, Second in Command, set an example of strict obedience to the calls of duty. Surviving wounds at Neuve Chapelle in 1915, he went on to command the 51st Highland Division at the end of the First World War, only to die of cancer at a relatively early age in 1921. O'Connor was to attend his funeral and to record in his diary of that year, that Carter-Campbell was: 'a fine character, absolutely straight, and of extraordinary pluck to stick the War out, with this stress on him through it all. That alone would account for him being hard and even merciless, but always just.'[5]

8

The Adjutant from 1910 to 1912 was Lieutenant J C Stormonth Darling, with whom, as Signal Officer, O'Connor worked closely. A big, powerful man and a strict disciplinarian, Stormonth Darling both set and demanded high standards of turn-out and drill. Though not obsessed by such matters, O'Connor, throughout his service, gave them proper attention as an essential part of good soldiering. Of Stormonth Darling he recorded: 'I had great respect and admiration, bordering on affection, but I was greatly in awe of him.'[6]

In 1913 infantry battalions changed from having eight companies of around 100 men each to four companies of roughly double the size. The four companies then formed were commanded by Major E de L Hayes, 'A' Company; Captain E B Ferrers, 'B' Company; Major H C Ellis, 'C' Company; and Major H D W Lloyd, 'D' Company. All were capable and enthusiastic officers, and none was married, so devoting the greater part of their time and energy to the command of their companies. Between dawn and mid-day on 10 March 1915, at the Battle of Neuve Chapelle, the three Majors were to be killed at the head of their men, and Captain Ferrers was to be severely wounded.

More will be said about Ferrers in due course, but he was one of the most original characters ever to serve in the regiment—and one of the finest. His influence on O'Connor at this stage, and later, was immeasurable. Known for much of his life to everyone as 'Uncle', he was one of the relatively few officers to have joined the regiment from university; in his case Cambridge, where his father had at one time been Master of Gonville and Caius College. Of a ready wit and genuinely eccentric, Ferrers had the highest personal standards of honour and integrity.

A remarkable Glasgow-Irishman who had risen from the ranks was the Quartermaster, Captain—by the end of the War Lieutenant Colonel—Tommy Finn. He was, in O'Connor's own words: 'one of the finest QMs there have ever been in the Regiment'.[7] As Signal Officer O'Connor would have had more direct dealings with Finn than most junior officers, applying to him for items of specialised equipment for his signallers, and no doubt learning a great deal in the process of how a Quartermaster's department should be run.

Of the number of junior officers of unusual ability who were O'Connor's contemporaries, few survived the First World War. Among the outstanding ones who lost their lives were Lieutenant W B Gray-Buchanan, killed at Neuve Chapelle in 1915; Lieutenant W

J Kerr, died of wounds, 1915; Lieutenant and Adjutant W I Maunsell, killed 1915; Second Lieutenant C R H Stirling, killed in 1918 as a twenty-five-year-old Lieutenant Colonel commanding a battalion. Another eight of those with whom he served as a subaltern in the period before 1914 were also killed. These terrible losses were something he would never forget.

Two exceptional contemporaries who survived the War were Second Lieutenant J F Evetts, who rose in due course to be a Lieutenant General, and perhaps O'Connor's greatest friend in his life, Lieutenant A C L Stanley Clarke. Another entrant from university, Stanley Clarke came to the regiment from Winchester and Oxford, where he captained the University Soccer XI and started his long career of playing with the famous amateur club, the Corinthians. 'Clarkie', as he was known, was described by one of his officers when commanding a battalion at a later stage during the First World War as: 'a great leader and strong personality, steeped in regimental tradition'.[8]

The influence of his brother officers was not the only one shaping the attitude and conduct of the young O'Connor: he was to learn much from the Warrant Officers and Sergeants, both officially and unofficially, and from the junior non-commissioned officers and men over whom he was put in command.

The two Regimental Sergeant Majors (RSMs) of the Scottish Rifles in O'Connor's early days were Graham and Wood, the latter known as 'Tubby', and both were in due course commissioned as Quartermasters. Young officers stood in awe of a good RSM, who, though he treated them respectfully, was fully entitled to correct their faults and give them advice where necessary. On first arrival in the battalion, a subaltern spent much of his time with the soldiers who had joined at the same stage, all being drilled and taught weapon training together by Warrant Officers and Sergeants. In a rifle regiment the drill aspect was especially important for an officer newly arrived from Sandhurst. Those ponderous movements learnt from the Brigade of Guards instructors had to be turned into the quick action of a rifleman. In a Scottish regiment all subalterns were frequently paraded to learn highland dancing from the Pipe Major, usually early in the morning before breakfast. Cameron, the Pipe Major of the Scottish Rifles in O'Connor's time, was quite young, having transferred while the battalion was in Colchester from being a Corporal in the Cameron Highlanders to take up this appointment, which carried the rank of Sergeant. He was an outstanding piper, and must also have been quite an accomplished dancing instructor, for he certainly taught O'Connor to enjoy doing it well.

An officer of the pre-1914 Regular Army was very much set apart from the men he commanded: he was expected to know everything about them; to make their welfare one of his main concerns; to train them well and watch their progress carefully; and accept full responsibility for leading them successfully through any given task. But there was no familiarity with them. The officer was expected to be slightly distant, and the ordinary soldier approached him through the Sergeant. Despite this apparent gulf, his men could show a young officer what they thought of him in many small ways, and their level of efficiency reflected directly on him. Through the reactions of his subordinates, the young O'Connor learnt much of the art of command.

In September 1911 the Scottish Rifles sailed for Malta to become the overseas battalion of the regiment, while The Cameronians returned to Maryhill Barracks, Glasgow in March 1912, to take up their home service role, after eighteen years abroad in India and South Africa.

In Malta, the Scottish Rifles were part of a static brigade of five battalions commanded by a Brigadier General. Because of the shortage of space for field training, and also because of the heat in the summer, there was a pattern of activity in Malta different from that in most other stations. The winter was the main training period, though the scope was very limited, the summer months from May to October being mainly used for leave. The limited training facilities precluded exercises above company level, but the saving factor was the presence of good ranges, so that the standard of marksmanship in the battalion was very high. Most other aspects of individual training were well covered, and O'Connor was able to make his signallers thoroughly proficient. Writing about them nearly fifty years after he took over the Signal Platoon he wrote: 'I loved them all, and they were in my opinion the best signallers by far in the Brigade, but for some reason we had fewer signallers than any other battalion, though I don't know why we were given so few.'[9] The consternation with which O'Connor received a letter, while on leave in 1913, with serious reflections on his beloved platoon can therefore be imagined. Describing what happened, in the letter already quoted above, the sense of shock and outrage he must have felt is obvious in his words. The trouble started with Colonel C P H Carter, a commanding officer brought in from another regiment, of whom O'Connor recorded that 'we disliked him very much'. As a Brevet Colonel, Carter used to stand in for the Brigadier General when the latter was away from Malta. The letter which caused O'Connor such distress stated that:

> It was referred to in the Brigade report that 'The signallers of the 2nd Scottish Rifles were not up to the standard of the rest of the Brigade'. Actually we had done a so-called test with the rest of the Brigade signallers and every signaller who went through it was made first-class, so it was true to say that we had less first-class signallers than the others. But the test had been a complete farce, no one in fact was tested properly at all. Now this report was seen by Carter, when he was at Brigade answering for the General, and I was asked for my reasons in writing when I was home on leave. I wrote officially that our signallers were just as good as the remainder but that we had fewer (which I thought was obvious). I foolishly at the same time wrote to Maunsell [Stormonth Darling's successor as Adjutant] and said that the whole Brigade test was a swindle and explained how.

Matters took a more serious turn when Maunsell unwisely showed the letter to Carter, who sent it to the Brigadier General, who in his turn ordered O'Connor to return from leave and face a Court of Inquiry to investigate his allegations, which 'impugned the honour' of the Brigade Signalling Officer:

> I came back pretty miserable as you can imagine. The Court assembled and I was told to substantiate my charges. (I had no intention of making any charges at all, and only told the adjutant for his own information as I was a friend of his.) The Court of Enquiry went on for days, and I never suffered anything so awful. But to cut a very long story short, I was completely exonerated, and the Court ordered the test to be held again. In it, in spite of our smaller numbers, we were streets ahead of any other unit. We retained all our firsts, and the bulk of the other units was 2nd class! If things had not worked out like that I would have lost my commission.

Soon after this upsetting incident, O'Connor was himself appointed Signal Officer to the Malta brigade, a move which, before long, was to lead to a war appointment of considerable significance. For the rest of 1913 and most of 1914, however, he continued to enjoy life in Malta, especially the polo and racing which took up so much of his free time. Although appreciating the carefree life, O'Connor, like many of his contemporaries, felt certain that war with Germany was imminent. As he recorded later, throughout the early months of 1914 he talked constantly about this to his signallers and he trained them rigorously in their war-time duties.

3

The First World War

Although he was sad to leave the Scottish Rifles in August 1914 on his posting home to be Signal Officer of the 22nd Brigade in the 7th Division, O'Connor was at least getting nearer to the fighting than he would be in Malta. Along with most of the Army at that time he was certain that the war would be over quite soon, and was desperately anxious not to miss the chance of some active service. In the event, he was to have his full share before the long, devastating hostilities came to an end over four years later. Fortunately, he kept a diary throughout the War, and his mother retained the letters he wrote home. In addition, at a later date, he recorded his memories of the first weeks in Belgium and France.[1]

The divisional commander was Major General Thompson Capper whom O'Connor thought 'particularly good'. The division was made up of seasoned troops brought back to Britain from South Africa and the Mediterranean, and so was not difficult to form into an efficient organisation in a short time. The 22nd Brigade, based at Lyndhurst in Hampshire, was commanded by Brigadier General Lawford, in O'Connor's words, 'a wonderful man'.

On Sunday 6 October 1914, sudden orders were received to march to Southampton to embark for some unknown destination. On entering the city, they found that 'the crowds were in the streets, and broke into the ranks, embracing all and sundry'. When they had embarked they found that their destination was Zeebrugge, which the ship reached the following morning.

After disembarking they marched to Bruges then to Roulers, and finally to the Ypres sector where they joined up with the 1st Corps, which comprised the 1st and 2nd Divisions. 'Then began', O'Connor wrote many years later, though with obviously vivid memories of those days,

the first Battle of Ypres which culminated in the battle of Zandvoorde on 30 and 31 October. It was very hard fighting the whole time, and we were practically in the front line all the time. It was touch and go. One night we fell back through Ypres, but later turned round and advanced again.

The Divisional Commander came up to our small HQ one afternoon. The Brigadier and staff were out and I was the only representative—we were in a trench. On our right front were a few men in trenches of a number of different regiments. The Div Comdr told me to take shape of them and join in the counter-attack on Zandvoorde. I did what I was told, and we advanced by a series of short rushes being heavily fired at by a Bty of 6 guns. After each salvo we got up and dashed forward. During one of these rushes I tripped up and fell, badly straining my ankle. I did not worry about it at the time and continued our attack and eventually reached our objective, where we were joined by a number of men from the 1st Corps. It was now beginning to get dark and I thought there was nothing more for me to do. So I told the remnants of the men with me to try to rejoin their own regiments, and I, now very lame, tried to find my way to our HQ. I did eventually as we had moved to a small cottage. I got a warm welcome from the General and Staff. The General was concerned about my ankle and made me take off my boots and found it very swollen. He told me that I was to go to the Dressing Station the following morning to get it attended to. But when I tried to get my boot on I could not do it as it had swollen so much.

However, I was driven to a Casualty Clearing Station who would not even look at me, as they said they were too busy with the badly wounded and that I would have to go to another medical dressing station at Poperinghe. There, exactly the same thing happened. They had no time for me, and I was told I would be sent down the line by train to the hospital in Boulogne. The train started and some guns opened on it, but fortunately no one was hit. We arrived at Boulogne the following morning and were brought to the hospital. There were no beds and I was put with the other wounded on the floor. Attlee [the future Prime Minister] was one of the wounded.

O'Connor was then taken back to Dublin on a hospital ship. From there he made his way to Rugby, where his mother was staying with a sister. After a month, his ankle recovered, and he rejoined Headquarters 22nd Brigade near Fleurbaix.

From the 7th Division history the full strain of this first month in action can be appreciated.[2] In all, the division travelled some 100 miles. Although part of the journey from Bruges to Ghent was in a very uncomfortable train, most of the time was passed marching along muddy roads in incessant cold rain. When halted, no fires were allowed, for fear of disclosing the division's position to the Germans. By the end of the Ypres battles, the division was barely half its original size. Those who survived were exhausted. Since no reliefs had been possible, there had been no rest: the nights were used for carrying supplies, reorganising positions, and endless activities which prevented sleep, while the days were taken up with fighting. Apart from the action described in his own story, O'Connor's preoccupation was with keeping communications open between his brigade headquarters and the division. He found it impossible to take more than short 'cat-naps' at night, as it was during darkness that much of his work had to be carried out.[3]

Following his return to the 22nd Brigade on 7 December, he was constantly in action. However, he did witness two unusual occurrences, which he wrote about in his letters to his mother of 20 and 26 December 1914. The first was an unofficial truce between the British and Germans when they both came out of their trenches to bury their dead, and the second was the well-known truce on Christmas day. Of this O'Connor wrote later: 'The enemy opposite us were the Saxons, always the nicest of the Germans. The whole incident was spontaneous on both sides.' He also recorded that such doings were 'heavily frowned on by Army HQ'.[4]

At the end of December 1914 a new award was instituted, the Military Cross. O'Connor was one of the first recipients of this decoration, his name appearing in the *London Gazette* on 18 February 1915.[5] At about the same time, some of his signallers were also decorated, including his soldier servant Wyatt, who won the Distinguished Conduct Medal (DCM).

With the 22nd Brigade, O'Connor was involved in many of the major operations of 1915: Neuve Chapelle in March, where the brigade was in the flank of the main assault; Fromelles; Givenchy; and, in September, the Battle of Loos, where for a time he was reported missing.

In November 1915 he was promoted Captain and given command of the 7th Division Signal Company. The divisional history praised his organising ability and success in sorting out confused situations. Although he enjoyed his work and did it most conscientiously, he hankered all the time for command of a fighting company. He applied to return to a battalion of the regiment on several occasions, but without success.

He spent most of 1916 with the 7th Division Signal Company, and was involved in the Battle of the Somme in July. Later that year, he was promoted substantive Captain and temporary Major, and appointed Brigade Major of the 91st Brigade in the 7th Division.

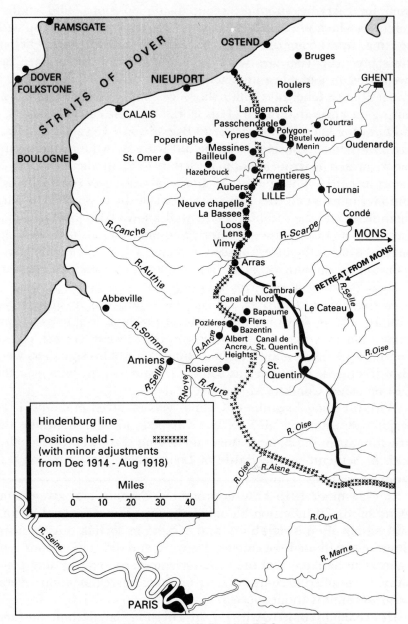

MAP 1. FRANCE AND FLANDERS 1914-1918

Legend:

Hindenburg line ——————

Positions held - ✕✕✕✕✕✕✕✕
(with minor adjustments
from Dec 1914 - Aug 1918)

Miles

0   10   20   30   40

Both he and the Brigade Commander were new, following a 'shake-up' of the brigade staff. For his commander, Brigadier General R H Cumming, who had also been his company commander at Sandhurst when he was a cadet, O'Connor had great respect. In addition he found in the headquarters a man who was to become a lasting friend, the Staff Captain, Owen Morshead, one of the few friends mentioned in the diaries by his Christian name. He appreciated Owen, who on return to civilian life after the War, became Librarian of the Pepys Library at Magdalene College, Cambridge, both for his intelligent company and his ability and efficiency as a staff officer. Just as Ferrers and other outstanding officers in the Scottish Rifles had given him an object lesson in the proper conduct of regimental duties, Cumming was to show him the right way to tackle the responsibilities of higher command. With an eye that missed no detail that was wrong, Cumming drove his battalions hard in action and when out of the line, realising the truth of the old saying, 'sweat saves blood'.

O'Connor came to admire Cumming for more than his attention to detail and insistence on rigorous training. He was equally impressed by his willingness to speak out against foolhardy plans emanating from corps or divisional headquarters. Cumming, as a proper soldier, would obey a direct command, but he did not assume that his obedience required silent acceptance of every suggested plan or scheme. He cared less for promotion and approval than he did for the lives of his men. In time, Cumming paid the penalty for his outspokenness and was sacked as commander of the 91st Brigade. By then O'Connor was not with him, but heard of his dismissal at second-hand. He regarded it as 'despicable' and wrote in his diary that Cumming had been made a 'scapegoat because he had the integrity to confront superiors and tell them an attack could not succeed on so short a notice——he's got a real devil as a divisional commander who thinks of nobody except himself'.[6]

In March 1917, he left the 91st and was transferred to be Brigade Major of the 185th Brigade in the neighbouring 62nd Division. He regarded his replacement at 91st Brigade with contempt and dislike, and so was most unhappy with this move to the 185th, which was both less efficient and less well trained than the 91st. The two things that cheered him up were the presence of his excellent soldier servant Wyatt, referred to in the diary at times as 'the faithful one', and the fact that the 91st were not far away, so that he was often in touch with them and able to see Owen.

The spring of 1917 saw plans being made for another 'big push'—a term much used in descriptions of the First World War—and in this case referring to the offensive which became known as the Battle of Arras. Both the French and the British were to be heavily involved in an assault which it was hoped once more would produce the final breakthrough. The Allied senior commanders believed that the Germans were weakening, evidence of which they assumed to be the enemy withdrawal to the Hindenburg line. The big offensive was planned to start on 9 April, and in the week leading up to it O'Connor found little time for food or sleep. On the night of 5 April—'another night with no sleep' as he wrote in his diary—the brigade pushed advanced posts forward to within 500 yards of the Hindenburg line. He wished to accompany the forward patrols to ensure all went well, but the Brigade Commander would not allow it, to O'Connor's considerable annoyance. On 8 April, the day before the offensive, he was unable to stir from the headquarters. Orders piled in upon orders. In his diary O'Connor confided: 'I have become like the French, who on principal never pay any attention to the first order, but always wait until the counter order to move.'[7] In the afternoon O'Connor exploded, and told the Brigadier General that he was sick of the confusion of orders and the lapse of elementary security. The frustrations of transfer to the 185th; his inability to get a fighting command; days without sleep; orders and counter orders; and not least a battery of eight-inch howitzers blazing away next to his headquarters, were telling on his composure. His outburst changed nothing, of course, but he felt a bit better for it. At 4 am on 9 April, he collapsed into fitful sleep, trusting that all had been done that could be done to make the brigade ready.

Before dawn, the massed formations of British, Canadian, Australian and New Zealand (ANZAC) infantry, supplemented by a few tanks, surged into no-man's land to assault the Hindenburg Line. In large measure Haig's forces were only a diversion to the French assault further south, as the commanders had calculated a breakthrough was more likely in the French sector. As it turned out, the British armies had better going in the opening hours of the attack. The 185th spent the early hours of 9 April waiting to follow up the first attack wave. While the headquarters staff waited for the word to move, they tried to follow the progress of the fight. At mid-morning they were elated by news that the Vimy Ridge had been taken. In the afternoon the 185th Brigade was ordered to prepare for an advance in conjunction with the Anzacs. Further word came that tanks would be brought up to assist both formations. The attacks would go forward at 4.30 am on 10 April. O'Connor struggled to get detailed orders out for each battalion commander, specifying objectives. The attack went forward as scheduled, but the Anzacs failed to move. There were good reasons for their advance being postponed, but information that it had been checked did not reach neighbouring formations in time. Unsupported, the 185th suffered heavy casualties and failed to secure all its objectives. O'Connor was furious. 'This is just the sort of thing they do in the damned Army,' he scrawled in his diary. 'Everyone was very sorry,' he added, 'but that does not bring good men back.'[8] Many good men were to perish in the days of fierce fighting which followed. Later on 10 April, news of a probable counter attack reached the headquarters. The Brigade Commander was away and O'Connor assumed command. He alerted the machine-gunners and the artillery, and warned the battalion commanders. The counter-attack did not materialise; instead the brigade was ordered over to the offensive. The battalions edged forward in the face of strong German resistance. The headquarters moved forward to the village of Ecoust. It was a 'beast of a place', made worse by sleet and snow and the heavy German barrage, and O'Connor set up an office in a muddy cellar. Advanced patrols prepared to push out ahead of the main force, but these were not required as the brigade received orders to stand by for relief. In fact, the entire offensive was stalling in the face of German counter-attacks along the whole front. The 185th had spent itself, and without more support on its flanks, any further advance was impossible.

The relief went badly. The relieving force arrived too soon and piled in upon the 185th. O'Connor's miserable shelter had to accommodate the whole of another staff, and no one could sleep. He was pleased to accompany his commander to a divisional staff meeting the next day, thankful to escape the confinement of his cellar. At the meeting they were astonished to be told that their relief was cancelled and that the brigade would attack the town of Bullecourt the next day. O'Connor described the news as 'wicked', especially since the brigade had been told to expect relief. It fell to him to break the news to the battalion commanders, who were outraged. For the next twelve hours he worked frantically to organise the attack. He hated the rush, knowing it would cost lives. At the last minute, the attack was postponed for twenty-four hours, and later was postponed indefinitely. A brief visit from Owen gave O'Connor the chance to vent his frustrations.

After a few more days, the 185th pulled back from Ecoust—the relief promised a week earlier came at last. Two thousand yards behind the front line the brigade settled into a training and refitting routine. They knew they could expect heavy fighting again soon, as the Allied commanders were determined to keep their Spring offensive alive. O'Connor assumed direct responsibility for training as the commander was again sick. Then he too began to experience a variety of ailments; headaches and nausea robbed him of appetite and rest and Wyatt despaired. These ailments lingered for several days until O'Connor happened to notice the orderlies scrubbing eating utensils with dirt and sand. He was appalled, as the ground around the headquarters was foul. He immediately ordered the orderlies to stop the practice and within a week he and the General had recovered. Another reason why he felt better was that word had been passed that a vacancy would soon exist for a battalion commander in the 7th Division. He hoped desperately to get this command, so much so that he asked his brigadier not to interfere should he be offered the position. O'Connor felt a certain guilt at wanting to leave the 185th. 'One ought not to think of oneself,' he wrote in his diary, 'but it is very hard not to.'[9]

Time for such musings was short. The offensive begun in April was continuing and on 1 May the 185th Brigade took part in a broad attack which failed, though he thought the 185th had done better than most brigades. Once again their objective was Bullecourt. Although the village was successfully taken by units of the brigade, it had to be vacated later due, once more, to lack of support on the flanks. Attacks followed apace and O'Connor was enraged that they were often launched with only a few hours' notice. The brigade was soon badly battered and had to be supplemented with units from other formations. The weeks of April and early May became a blur of barrage, attack, and counter-attack. On occasions O'Connor found himself under intense shell and machine-gun fire, and during lulls in the fighting, he reconnoitred the front whenever possible. Arriving back in the middle of the night, muddy and drenched from such excursions, he was ever grateful to find Wyatt waiting with a hot drink and food. A couple of hours sleep and the process was repeated.

Then, on 19 May, he was sent home on leave, taking Wyatt with him. Owen managed to get leave at the same time. The change from the grim conditions in the trenches to the comfort and security of his mother's home was a wonderful tonic, and he and Owen made the best of it. Returning to France he received two pieces of good news. On 1 June he heard that he had been awarded the DSO, but far more important in his view, he was also informed that he was promoted to temporary Lieutenant Colonel and given command of a battalion in the 7th Division, the 2nd Infantry Battalion of the Honourable Artillery Company, the HAC. He knew little about the HAC and its long traditions, nor about the battalion he was to take over, except that from now on it was to be his responsibility, and his alone. The prospect held no fears for him: it was the opportunity he had long yearned for. On 2 June 1917, some three months short of his twenty-eighth birthday, he left the 185th Brigade and rode a short distance to assume the position for which he felt he was now entirely prepared.

The battalion he found on his arrival was resting, and attempting to reorganise, behind the front line. 'Attempting' is the word because it was hardly functioning as a military unit. Something of the task facing the new youthful commanding officer, and the impact he made, was described over sixty years later in his obituary in the HAC journal:

> Lt-Colonel O'Connor was faced with problems which would have appalled an older and more experienced officer. The unit's strength was under 300, there was a shortage of every kind of specialist and the Battalion had just come through the trying experience of Bullecourt when all that had been left of it was 4 officers and 94 men.

The journal then quoted some comments written by a remarkably brave man who served under O'Connor at that time, Sergeant Major W J Bradley, DCM, MM:

> Since the arrival of the new CO, food improved considerably, and we had a good wet and dry canteen, but a new nightmare was introduced— Colonel's Inspection. Every time we were in Reserve it happened, and it was unbelievably thorough, even to the number of studs on the soles of our boots. All men on details had to parade with platoons which was a terrible shock for most of them, not having been inspected since they arrived in France. Although we did not like it at the time, it was a very good thing for morale and discipline. Colonel O'Connor made a great impact in the Battalion from which we all benefited and made us into a Battalion to be proud of.[10]

O'Connor himself wrote later that in his turn he 'learnt a tremendous lot all the eighteen months', he was with them, though their rather relaxed ideas on military discipline were a surprise to start with. A great help in putting the battalion back on the right lines was the Second in Command, Major Snape. There was some opposition to this appointment at brigade headquarters as Snape was a 'ranker' officer who had been a Sergeant Major for much of his service, and rankers were rarely given such appointments. However, O'Connor insisted that Snape was just the man he needed, and having got him, used his experience to the full in tightening up basic administration, particularly in improving dramatically standards of feeding and hygiene.

In a matter of weeks O'Connor had won the respect, even the affection, of the HAC and he was gratified when the officers of the battalion elected him to honorary membership of the Company. In July, O'Connor's brigadier inspected the battalion and pronounced the battalion in excellent shape. The brigadier was obviously impressed with the cleanliness and orderliness of the battalion, but O'Connor knew clean kit alone would win no battles. Consequently, he rehearsed his officers in the techniques of attack, and then officers and men carried out practice assaults at all levels from section to battalion, as well as receiving careful training in the correct methods of patrolling. Finally, cadres were run to train the specialists of which the battalion was so short.

The battalion was at the Front again at the end of June, and spent the next few months doing the usual periods in and out of the line without suffering serious casualties. Then in October 1917 the series of battles began which are known by the general title of Passchendaele. The first action, officially the Battle of Broodseinde, found the 7th Division back where it had been at the start of the war. Its objective was the Reutel–Broodseinde track, the approximate line held by the division in mid-October 1914. As the official history puts it: '... the battle of First Ypres was now being fought in reverse'.[11]

At this stage Bradley was a Corporal. He recalled later that on the afternoon of 8 October:

> ... we had a pleasant surprise which boosted morale tremendously. The Colonel and his runner crawled out to the front line to wish us all good luck in the attack to take place the next day. He was not his usual immaculate self but was plastered with mud, and as he shook hands with all and sundry I was surprised at the number of men he knew by name.[12]

Reutel was eventually captured, but the casualties sustained by the HAC amounted to eight officers and 49 men killed, 189 wounded, and 49 missing, almost all later reported killed. O'Connor would never forget these losses suffered in a frontal assault, and when in action again would always look for a way in from the flank against an enemy position. A death which caused him great personal distress came late in October when a 'heavy'—a big shell—killed Wyatt just as the battalion was coming out of the line.

Luckily for the HAC, Reutel was the 2nd Battalion's last battle in France. On 20 November 1917, it was moved with the rest of the 7th Division to the Italian front. Other divisions sent there were the 5th, 21st, 23rd, 41st and 48th.

Italy had entered the war in May of 1915. In June of that year the Italians, under the command of General Lug Cardona, launched the first in a series of offensives against the Austrians. The offensives, known as the Eleven Battles of the Isonzo, took place on a front which extended from Monfalcone on the Gulf of Venice to a point above Caporetto, roughly sixty miles north of Monfalcone. The battles were costly and inconclusive. Within a year's time the Italians had sustained in excess of 500,000 casualties; their territorial gains had been negligible. The only positive aspect of the Isonzo battles was that they had forced the Austrians to maintain a considerable number of divisions along the Austro-Italian border, thus denying Germany of much needed reinforcements.

Britain and France bolstered the Italian efforts with a substantial amount of war material, particularly machine-guns and artillery. The Germans, however, had been reluctant to aid their Austrian allies. Indeed, Germany had not declared war on Italy until August of 1916. It is not surprising that Germany had wished to avoid involvement on the Italian front, for her commitments on the Eastern and Western fronts had severely taxed her resources. It was not until the summer of 1917 that Germany was able to offer Austria any reinforcements. By October, seven German divisions had joined the Austrians. On 24 October, the German and Austrian forces initiated a major offensive, driving the Italians back to the Piave River. By early November, it had become apparent to the governments of France and Britain that Italy must have reinforcements.

The 7th Division travelled south through France to Marseilles, and then north-east through Genoa and Mantua to Lennago, where they detrained.[13] From here the HAC marched to Ramon, where the division went into billets. Occasional bombing by enemy aircraft was of little concern after the artillery bombardments suffered on the Western front.

O'Connor had a first close look at the Italian front when he took his company commanders on a reconnaissance of the Piave river on 13 January 1918. He considered the ground, broken by woods, ravines and streams, ideal for active offensive actions against the enemy, but his enthusiasm was not shared by his superiors, who adopted a purely defensive strategy at this stage. For many months the only action taken by the battalion was an occasional raid into 'no-man's land', while he himself frequently moved forward to reconnoitre the front.[14] The opportunity was not lost, however, to carry out a great deal of very rigorous training, with beneficial results to the battalion's efficiency.

Eventually an Allied offensive was planned and, on 20 October 1918, O'Connor was summoned to divisional headquarters and given orders that his battalion was to capture the upper half of the Grave di Papadopoli, a small island in the River Piave.[15] The importance of this operation lay in the fact that Papadopoli was the best point at which to ford the Piave and the Allied commanders would not move across the river until in control of at least half the island. Information about the enemy strength on the island was vague, and intelligence reports put the Austrian force there at three companies, supported by some artillery and machine-gun emplacements.[16] Close reconnaissance by O'Connor and other members of the battalion failed to establish the enemy strength more accurately, but later there were found to be five times more Austrians than originally estimated.

The 7th Division history gives a description of the island as it was in 1918:

> The Grave di Papadopoli was for the most part cultivated, being planted with vines and maize, and there was some scrub and brushwood in the uncultivated parts, while a dozen houses, mostly in ruins, were dotted about the SE portion. The defences consisted of two lines of trenches, one following roughly the bank of the main stream, the other some little distance in rear.... these lines contained several trench mortar emplacements, but by attacking from the NW corner, the trench lines could be taken in flank.[17]

The Papadopoli operation began on the night of 24 October shortly before eight o'clock. In all, O'Connor's force numbered about 800 men. These troops were ferried across to the island in large, flat-

24

bottomed boats which were skilfully handled by Italians. The first contingents of the attacking force reached the island without being detected and easily took the Austrian outposts along the shore. The Austrians, though taken unaware, soon responded with a heavy bombardment, causing some confusion among the landing formations. In spite of this barrage, all the British troops managed to disembark. After securing their landing sites, the British began to move down the island from its northernmost point.

O'Connor, his operational headquarters, and a small escort moved along the advancing front, making sure that the attack maintained momentum and coordination. Within a few hours, the upper half of the island was controlled by the British. The following day was spent in 'mopping up' the Austrian positions which had not fallen during the night operation. Impressed with O'Connor's swift and economical victory, the Allied commanders ordered him to take the lower half of the island. To assist in this operation, an additional two battalions were ordered to cross to Papadopoli.

On the night of 26 October, O'Connor launched his attack against the Austrian positions on the southern half of the island. The Austrians resisted the British advance with surprising determination and even mounted two simultaneous counter-attacks.[18] It soon became apparent to O'Connor that he was opposed by more than the remnants of three Austrian companies. Nevertheless, he continued to press the attack forward. At one point he and his group ran into a company of sixty Austrians in a 'strong point'. With hardly a moment's hesitation the small party drew their revolvers and rushed the Austrians. In the darkness and confusion they were able to make the surprised enemy surrender.

After fighting all night, the British still faced one pocket of determined resistance. A group of some 200 Austrians held a strong position in the southern corner of the island. Not only did the Austrians refuse to surrender, but they even called upon the British to lay down their arms.[19] O'Connor sent two Lewis guns to work round to the flanks of the Austrian position, and several bursts from the Lewis guns soon convinced the enemy of the hopelessness of their situation. One Austrian private crawled out of his defensive position and started towards the British, apparently with the intention of surrendering. Yet, after moving a few yards, he seemed to have second thoughts. O'Connor, sensing the private's consternation, called out in German and ordered him to come quickly to the British position, and the Austrian obeyed. In an effort to further demoralise the enemy, a group of prisoners, captured earlier, were paraded in front of their weakening comrades. This demonstration achieved the desired result and the Austrians capitulated.[20] The capture of Papadopoli set in motion the final offensive on the Italian front which resulted in Austria's capitulation on 3 November.[21]

The victory at Papadopoli was a remarkable success against a well-trained enemy. Although the Austrians gave in quite easily at the end of the operation, they offered stiff resistance throughout most of it. Success for the British sprang from the good training which they had received in the months preceding the battle, and from O'Connor's vigorous and aggressive leadership. Whenever the attack seemed to falter, he would appear on the scene at the right moment and get things moving again. Getting around the battle-field was not easy, especially in the dark. O'Connor and those with him ran, stumbled and crawled from position to position, not always certain that they were going the right way: but they got to the right places eventually, and the momentum of the assault was always maintained.[22]

The victory at Papadopoli attracted considerable attention. The Italian Government presented O'Connor with the Silver Medal for Valour, and he received a bar to his DSO. A report in *The Times* called the battle a singular success, and praised his gallantry throughout the operation.[23] He as usual was embarrassed by the recognition.

On 19 November, when hostilities had ceased on all fronts, O'Connor wrote to his mother, and started by telling her, 'I am so thankful you have been at last relieved of your anxiety.' He then went on to say how fortunate he himself had been to come through the whole war unscathed, in particular 'without being maimed. That was the only thing I dreaded.' There certainly appears to have been something miraculous about his survival through four years spent almost entirely in, or close to, the front line: he himself put it down, like the winning of his many decorations, to luck.

At the end of hostilities, the 2nd Battalion moved into Austria, and O'Connor became Officer Commanding British Troops in North Tyrol under the local Italian Army Commander, General Ugo Lani. It was a thoroughly enjoyable time, but it came to an end in March 1919 when the 2nd Battalion was disbanded, and O'Connor came home to join his regiment again.

4

The Post-war Years — 1919 to 1935

After the disbandment of the 2nd Battalion HAC, O'Connor reverted to his rank of Brevet Major to return to the 2nd Scottish Rifles as adjutant to Lieutenant Colonel Richard Oakley, who, in his turn, had come down the scale, having just surrendered his war-time rank of Brigadier General. This tour as adjutant was a remarkably short one of six months, a proportion of which was spent at sea on a troop-ship sailing out to India. It was a great joy to O'Connor to be back with the battalion he had left in 1914. Ferrers had returned to it as well, but few of the others from Malta days were still alive, many of them, as we have seen, having been killed in March 1915 at Neuve Chapelle. The reason for his tour of regimental duty being cut short so early was the receipt of an order posting him back to Britain to join the second post-war course at the Staff College, Camberley. Selection for the first two courses after the war, in 1919 and 1920, was made on the basis of reputations earned on active service with the usual requirement to pass an entrance examination being waived.

O'Connor's diary for 1920 opened with an entry on board a troop ship just reaching the Red Sea on the way home from India. Along with one or two other officers he had volunteered to work as a stoker in the engine room in order to keep himself fit on the journey: his fellow stokers belonging to the ship's crew he described as 'good enough fellows', but the engineer officer in charge was 'absolutely hopeless'. The rest of the ship's officers were put into the same category, while the elderly Colonel known as 'OC Ship', was 'a damned old ass and no good for anything'. At Suez, O'Connor left the troop-ship in disgust and paid for a private berth on a P and O liner to Marseilles, whence he travelled to Calais by train, and then home across the channel to arrive in London on 16 January. His mother and Christina were staying at Brown's Hotel. Of the latter he recorded, 'Christina is a gem and it is impossible to even consider life without her'; he was particularly conscious of her qualities as he had discovered she had just nursed his mother through a serious illness.

Before reporting to the Staff College on 22 January 1920, O'Connor took his mother and Christina to look at a house near Oxford which they were offered an opportunity to rent. Waterperry House at Wheatley, the property of Magdalen College, Oxford, was a splendid Georgian mansion in a large park. His diary entry for that day recorded: 'We both thought it a perfectly delightful house, only perfectly enormous, so unfortunately quite out of the question.' However, something must have occurred during the next three months, as by early May they had decided to take the house. On her birthday on 4 May, Mrs O'Connor moved into Waterperry, and stayed there for the next twelve years. Since the death of her father she had become a woman of some means, and while retaining many of her careful habits learnt in earlier, less affluent days, she was able to live at Waterperry in style, giving her son a home to which he could invite his friends to stay, and from which he could indulge in his love of hunting, point-to-point racing and shooting.

The Staff College year passed happily. He found most of the lectures interesting, and most afternoons he rode, or played hockey or cricket. As staff officers were still expected to be able to ride well in those days, they were given every encouragement to indulge in all branches of equitation, and during their time at Camberley were allotted government chargers, which were kept for them in the College stables. O'Connor also kept his own horse called 'Little Dick' in the same place, and was 'glad to have two good ones', as he wrote in his diary, since the mare provided through official channels proved a great success. He hunted both horses with the Staff College draghounds at Camberley, and also took them home to Waterperry when on leave.

Among the more important aspects of his time at the Staff College was the contact with officers who were to have significance in his later career. Chief instructor of his division was the future Field Marshal Sir John Dill, at the time a Brigadier General. Also on the directing staff (DS) were Lieutenant Colonel R H Osborne, with whom he had served on the 7th Division staff in the War, and another man with whom he was to be deeply involved twenty years later. His diary on 4 February recorded: 'Our first lecture this morning was by Lt. Col. Neame, the Sapper V.C., on Tanks.' Neame, who held the DSO as well as his VC, was the youngest member of the DS at the time and one of the best lecturers.

The names of six of O'Connor's fellow students on the course must be mentioned. Most important among them was Major B L Montgomery of the Royal Warwickshire Regiment. Others with whom he was to develop friendships which lasted into later years were Captain F E Hotblack, Lieutenant Colonel Victor Fortune, Major Kenneth McLeod, and Major B C T Paget. At the time he was also on friendly terms with Lieutenant Colonel R H Haining, but eighteen years later in Palestine there was to be less warmth between them.

In view of the immense range of experience of warfare among the students, many of whom had held higher rank during the War, and among whom only a handful had no decorations, the early post-war courses were run in a fairly relaxed manner. Much time was given to discussion as well as to lectures, and written work was not onerous. Easter leave was granted from 25 April to 22 May, but summer leave, which began on 8 August, was cut short after six weeks on 23 September when all officers were recalled to be detailed off for duties all around Britain in the event of a threatened coal strike. However, O'Connor had fitted in a lot in those six weeks. With his mother, an aunt, and Kenneth McLeod, he crossed the Channel and toured the old battlefields of the War. They travelled in his mother's car, a handsome vehicle, as shown in Plate 10, driven by a chauffeur called Munday.

Soon after returning to England from their French tour, he and his mother went up to the Highlands to stay with relations, first at Asknish on Loch Fyne, where he walked-up grouse and blackgame over dogs and fished the hill lochs for trout, and then to his beloved Killundine. The estate at Killundine was now owned by cousins of his grandmother's family, who had inherited it from her on her death, and he found a certain amount of family dissension between them. This, however, did not spoil his few days there. He visited many old friends among the local community, and had a day on the hill with a stalker called Willie, whom he had known since boyhood. The long day ended with the successful stalk of a heavy, ten-pointer stag.

Much of the time during his last months at the Staff College were spent on strike duty connected with the threatened miners' strike. His posting on this odd and rather unsatisfactory work was to an office in Lichfield, where, according to his diary, there was little to do other than wait for outbreaks of violence which never materialised. He took advantage of his spells on duty in the office to study military history, especially the Waterloo campaign. On two occasions, when not on call, he went to West Bromwich to see his late second-in-command in the HAC, Major Snape. Eventually the strike was called off, and on 4 November the students were all recalled to Camberley. Montgomery, who had been on duty farther north, collected O'Connor in his car and drove him to Waterperry, where they stayed the night before getting back to the Staff College the following afternoon. The diary records an incident on the first leg of their journey: 'We had an excellent run, except for the mishap of knocking over an old man who was leading a bull.... Montgomery brought the old man back to the farm, and brought another man out again, while I watched the bull at a safe distance.'

Every year at the Staff College, as the course nears its end, a major preoccupation of all the students is to discover what their next postings are going to be. Through Osborne, with whom he had tea on 19 November, O'Connor was given a clue to his own future:

> He told me in the strictest confidence that I had actually been given the job of GSO 3 of the 3rd Div. at Bulford, but that Aldershot Command were doing their best to get me sent to them instead as BM of the new Experimental Brigade. Cavan was going to do all he can, but the issue was very doubtful, so that is how the matter stands now. I am very afraid that it won't come off, as it is the best junior Staff appointment here.

The Earl of Cavan was GOC-in-C Southern Command. He had formed a very high opinion of O'Connor during the War when he had commanded the British contingent in Italy.

After a month's leave at Waterperry at the end of the course, which included plenty of social activity and hunting with the Bicester and South Oxfordshire hounds, O'Connor reported on 27 January 1921 to the headquarters of the 3rd Division at Bulford. The next day he wrote in his diary: 'I think it is a deadly place, and my job is also beneath contempt.' Fortunately it was not to last long. On 4 February, a letter from Osborne arrived to say 'I understand you have got the Experimental Brigade after all.' Three weeks later he was on his way from Bulford to Aldershot where he reported on 28 February. Next morning he met his new brigade commander,

Colonel H C Jackson. This was the moment in the history of the British Army when the rank of Brigadier General was abolished. Brigades consisting of three battalions instead of four, commanded by colonels, were instituted in order to keep in line with the three battalion regiments of the French and American armies. Later the rank of Brigadier was recreated, but without the extra word 'General' which had so incensed French Colonels commanding regiments during the war.

Of his first day with his new commander, with whom he was to serve for three years and establish a life-long friendship, O'Connor wrote in his diary on 1 March:

> Colonel Jackson seems very nice. He is tall and thin and has rather a long cadaverous face. He is a great man on a horse, and very keen that everyone should ride.... The Experimental Brigade is going to assemble on June 1st, and training will go on for two months and a half. The scope of the thing is very much in the air at present, and I think the programme will depend greatly on how much training the battalions have had up to date.

The Experimental Brigade, also known as the 5th Brigade, had three main tasks. As it included infantry, tanks and artillery, the first was to run exercises on behalf of the War Office testing procedures for the integration of these elements. Aircraft were sometimes involved as well. The second requirement was to lay on tactical and organisational demonstrations, which were visited by officers from all over Britain. The third task was the training in new techniques of those battalions sent to make up the brigade, which were changed every few months.

Though O'Connor greatly enjoyed his years with Jackson, who went on in time to become a full General, he did not find him easy to work for. In old age he recorded his verdict: 'He is one of my oldest friends in spite of the fact that having been his Brigade Major for two years, nothing would induce me to serve on his staff again. He is a most difficult man to serve.'[1] The main problem was Jackson's refusal to go into matters properly when first required to give instructions, but then to take great interest at the last minute, and often to insist on changes being made to orders which had already been sent out.

On 25 January 1924, O'Connor received an offer of promotion to substantive major in a vacancy in the Seaforth Highlanders. Although this accelerated promotion into another regiment would have helped him in his career as well as being financially beneficial, he turned it down, preferring to remain with his own regiment. By chance, three days later, on 28 January, there came a posting order detailing him for a job in the War Office, as a GSO 2. This appointment he resisted, as he was very anxious to return to regimental duty. He was urgently needed back in the regiment to help the new commanding officer of the 1st Battalion—The Cameronians—which had come to Aldershot in 1923, and was in need of a drastic 'pulling together'. This new commanding officer was his old friend Ferrers, who badly wanted O'Connor as his adjutant as he set about the task of restoring the battalion to a proper state of efficiency. Among the newly joined officers in The Cameronians in 1923 were two second lieutenants who were in time to become senior generals. One was George Collingwood, who appears again at several points in this book, and the other was Horatius Murray, better known by his nickname, 'Nap'. Nearly fifty years after these events took place, Murray wrote about Ferrers' impact on the battalion when he assumed command. His article in the regimental magazine, *The Covenanter*, began with a brief description of the new CO's character and previous career:

> Lieutenant Colonel E B Ferrers, DSO had joined the Regiment during the South African War and had remained a bachelor. Before the First World War he had commanded 'B' Company in the Second Battalion, then stationed in Malta, where all the Company Commanders were bachelors and all completely dedicated to the Regiment. This Battalion went to France towards the end of 1914 and in its first engagement suffered terrible casualties. One of the few officers to survive was our new Commanding Officer, but he had been so badly wounded that he could take little further part in the war. In 1919 he rejoined the 2nd Battalion and resumed command of his beloved 'B' Company, taking them to Kurdistan, Irak, and India. He was always actuated by the highest principles and was guided by them in all the decisions he made. The Regiment remained his first and last love and he had no use for any officer or other rank who thought otherwise. He was critical of any of those who, in his opinion, had been less active with the Regiment than they should have been during this war. Although he encouraged officers at all stages to become fully professional, he personally had no military ambitions outside of the Regiment. Needless to say, many feel short of his expectations and were condemned out of hand. He found means of making his feelings felt in his own inimitable way. He had a very highly developed sense of humour which was the delight of the Regiment and regimental officers elsewhere but which was apt to infuriate his seniors.

The reasons why The Cameronians were in such need of a major 'shake-up' were next explained:

> The Battalion had returned at the end of 1922 to the United Kingdom from a long tour of duty in Ireland during 'The Troubles'. In the early summer, the Commanding Officer had been promoted and was succeeded by another. The battalion must have been in poor order after Ireland, but the lack of continuity in command was most unfortunate. After the change in command, affairs seemed to lose direction with a lack of purpose. A heavy price was to be paid for this. The 2nd Division, in which the Battalion found itself, marched out of Aldershot on a hot summer's day on its way to the divisional camp in Sussex.
>
> The condition of the troops was so poor that they fell out on the line of march in dozens—a most humiliating experience for any regiment, particularly a rifle regiment. The immediate result was that the Commanding Officer was sent home and he retired from the service altogether some weeks later. This experience had a very bad effect upon the morale of the battalion and was one of the reasons why it was in such bad shape. It could well be that 'Uncle', as Ferrers was nick-named, realised the true state of affairs when he was appointed to command and decided that it provided for him a challenge which he could not resist. He was to command for the full four years of the appointment in spite of a considerable degree of unpopularity from many of his superiors, but during that time we who served under him learned how to restore a battalion to its full potential, to regain its self-respect and to participate, however humbly, in this transformation.

The assistance of a good adjutant was vital to Ferrers in this task of transformation, and no doubt O'Connor's experience of slightly similar conditions when he took over the 2nd Battalion HAC in 1917 was useful in many ways. Murray's article went on to tell of the methods by which all aspects of battalion training and administration were overhauled, and then mentioned the matter of responsibility:

> So far as the officers were concerned, when given some task or another, not one of us was in any doubt that we would be held personally responsible for all aspects of it and its full implications. How we set about it was our affair, but the outcome was to do with us, and there was no question of shared responsibility.[2]

What might be called a 'host' of future generals served with The Cameronians during Ferrers' years of command. As well as O'Connor, Collingwood and Murray there were another five who were to rise to eminence in the Second World War. Tom Riddell-Webster became a General; Sandy Galloway and Jack Evetts, Lieutenant Generals; and Douglas Graham and Eric Sixsmith, Major Generals. All, apart from the last named, had contacts with O'Connor when that war came.

When O'Connor made his move from the headquarters of the 5th Brigade to take up his post as adjutant of The Cameronians in October 1924, only a short journey was necessary as both were stationed in Aldershot. Given the task that faced him in helping Ferrers restore proper standards throughout the battalion, it was not a period for an adjutant to be relaxed. In correspondence with O'Connor a few years after the publication of the article quoted above, 'Nap' Murray pointed out to him that: 'Whether you are prepared to accept it or not, the fact remains that you were a somewhat frightening person. We were all told about the officer of the 2nd Battalion HAC who had fainted while being dealt with by you.'[3]

The tour as adjutant lasted for only ten months, but the battalion was well on the way to recovery by the time O'Connor was called away from the regiment to go, as a company commander, to the Royal Military College at Sandhurst. On 9 August 1925, Ferrers wrote him a touching letter, starting by saying how hard he had found it to say what he felt when they had parted the day before. Then, referring to O'Connor's surrender of his GSO 2 appointment in 1924 in order to come to The Cameronians, he wrote: 'But I cannot think that you have lost anything—a work done perfectly cannot fail to bring its own reward; and the appreciation of the whole regiment is in itself of no small value.'[4] His successor as adjutant was Sandy Galloway, who was also a 'somewhat frightening person', and nicknamed within the regiment as the 'PR', or 'perpetual rage'.

Of O'Connor's two years as a company commander at Sandhurst there is little account, either among his own papers or in the college journal, then known as *The Magazine and Record*. His first term was the Christmas term 1925, and for it he overlapped with his great friend Stanley Clarke, or 'Clarkie'. The latter had been a tremendous success during his tour, and had encouraged many high quality cadets to join the regiment. O'Connor worked hard to achieve similar results.

Throughout the two years that he was at the College, the most junior officer on the staff of his company was Captain M C

Dempsey, MC, of the Royal Berkshire Regiment, known by the slightly unfortunate nick-name 'Bimbo', the origins of which he would never disclose. At the time neither he nor O'Connor could have imagined how their roles would have changed twenty years later.

O'Connor kept up his equestrian interests, and there is a note among his papers saying 'Congratulations on winning your race', signed by all his company officers, including Dempsey. As a guess it was a race in the Staff College Drag point-to-point. It is interesting to note that the Christmas 1925 edition of *The Magazine and Record* carries a long article, reprinted from the issue of 1908, on the value of fox-hunting for officer training. Though this would arouse scorn in many circles over half a century later, there is a lot of truth in it, and certainly O'Connor himself would have agreed with it whole-heartedly.

His last term was the Michaelmas Term 1927, and the magazine dated that July includes a photograph of all the instructors on the steps of the old building at Sandhurst. O'Connor is next to 'Boy' Browning of the Grenadier Guards, who was then the College Adjutant. Once again his next posting was not to take him far, as he only moved through the grounds at Camberley to take up an appointment as an instructor at the Staff College. By now he had spent seven consecutive years in the area covered by Aldershot Command, an unusual fate for an infantry officer of the time, but one which suited him well. The main reason for this was the ease of travelling to Waterperry, only thirty-five miles away, and therefore both seeing his mother regularly, and enjoying the pleasures of the beautiful house and all that went with it. From the point of view of his military career he was also in what might be called the 'heart-land' of the Army in Britain throughout that time, and the excellent professional and social reputation he gained in this important part of the country greatly influenced his future advancement.

On the DS at the Staff College in 1927 were two officers who had been with him there as students seven years earlier—Montgomery and Paget. Among others whom he knew already were Pownall, who had served with him during the war in 2nd Battalion HAC, and 'Budget' Lloyd of the Coldstream Guards. All were Brevet, or acting Lieutenant Colonels.

The 62 students in 1927 were mostly captains and majors, with five lieutenants and one solitary Lieutenant Colonel. This was the Hon H R L G Alexander of the Irish Guards, the future Field

Marshal, known to all as just 'Alex'. Other names which would either become well known in future years, or have significance in O'Connor's life, were E H Barker, F H Berryman, of the Australian Staff Corps, A F P Christison, E E Dorman-Smith, O W H Leese, F R R Bucher and D N Wimberley. From the Royal Air Force, Wing Commander O T Boyd was a student while preparing to take up a post on the DS the following year.

In 1928 the incoming Junior Division included G C Bucknall, R L McCreery and G W R Templer, still only a Lieutenant. Two others whom he already knew well were Sandy Galloway and G H A MacMillan of the Argylls, nicknamed 'Babe', who had worked in his office in the Experimental Brigade headquarters as a 'staff learner'. Most important of all, was a young Captain in the Somerset Light Infantry, known to all as 'John' even though his initials were A F. Not only was the future Field Marshal Lord Harding of Petherton to be O'Connor's right hand man at the time of his triumph in the Desert in 1941, but he was also to become one of his greatest friends and admirers. Harding claimed in his later years that the two people who had the most influence on his own brilliant career, and from whom he learnt most, were Montgomery and O'Connor, and that the process of learning from them began at Camberley in 1928.[5]

Owl Pie, the Staff College magazine, provides little information about personalities serving in 1927 and 1928 to anyone not able to understand its oblique, esoteric references to them. Much of the issues for these years are devoted to rather heavy, 'insider' jokes and comic verses, and to recording social and sporting events. The Drag Hounds receive most attention, and several pages are devoted to their doings in each edition.

In a note about his time on the Directing Staff, O'Connor made a self-critical comment which is significant: 'I know I accept things too easily, and do not question authority and policy in the way I should.'[6] The significance of his remark lies in the fact that his later career shows that he took this to heart, and showed himself very ready to question authority and policy when he thought necessary, eventually to the detriment of his own career.

O'Connor left the Staff College in 1929 before the end of a full tour in order to attend a course at the Machine Gun School at Netheravon in Wiltshire. As a Brevet Lieutenant Colonel and late instructor at Camberley he was an unusual student on this course, normally attended by much more junior officers. The reason for his being sent there was his imminent return, once more, to regimental duty with The Cameronians. The 1st Battalion was about to leave Aldershot to go overseas in early 1930, and the 2nd Battalion, The Scottish Rifles, was preparing to return home to Scotland to take up the home duty role. O'Connor, in spite of ' is distinguished service, was still relatively junior on the regimental list, and so would be a company commander when he rejoined a battalion. His brevet rank gave him seniority in the Army only, not within his regiment. Since the Machine Gun Company was the most important, and the largest, he was naturally earmarked to command that, but before taking up his post had to learn all about the weapon on a course. The Vickers medium machine-gun was a .303, water-cooled gun capable of sustained fire for as long as its ammunition lasted, and remained in service with the British Army from before the First World War until the 1960s. Learning the value of machine-guns from the Germans in 1914, the British steadily increased the numbers allotted to infantry battalions, and by 1929 there were four platoons with six guns each in the company O'Connor was to take over.

The first overseas station for the Cameronians was Moascar, in Egypt, where the battalion arrived early in 1930 to join a brigade including battalions of the Wiltshire and the King's Liverpool regiments. Situated on the Suez Canal about seventy miles from Cairo, Moascar provided opportunities for numerous activities in which O'Connor happily took part. Sailing and swimming were enjoyed on the Great Bitter Lakes, and the marshes around them provided good duck shooting. A lot of polo was played, and there were visits to Cairo to take part in tournaments, and go to the races. Keen as always on games for the soldiers, he was especially enthusiastic about hockey, which was played on hard-packed sand at great speed, and was a game at which he personally excelled.

The Commanding Officer when the Battalion arrived in Egypt was Lieutenant Colonel H C Hyde-Smith, who was in the slightly incongruous position of being senior to O'Connor within the regiment, and therefore his superior in ordinary circumstances, while in the Army as a whole he was junior, due to O'Connor's brevet rank. Should the brigade commander be away, and a Cameronian officer be called for to stand in for him, O'Connor would have assumed the position over Hyde-Smith's head. Due to good sense on both sides this anomaly was not allowed to cause ill-feeling.

In December 1930, O'Connor was appointed Brigade Machine Gun officer and instructed to run a machine-gun concentration for the companies of the three battalions in the brigade. Camp was set up on the Sinai side of the Suez Canal in a desolate area where exercises with live ammunition were possible, and Anderson, O'Connor's excellent Company Sergeant Major, was put in charge of camp administration. During the twelve days of the concentration, from 8 to 10 December, a great deal of live firing was carried out, and two competitions were held. One was for turn-out and driving of the horsed transport still used to carry the machine-gun sections, and the other was for fire control. In the former, The Cameronians were second to the Wiltshires, but won the cup given as first prize in the latter. On 17 December the GOC Egypt, Lieutenant General Sir Peter Strickland, arrived to watch an attack scheme using live ammunition. O'Connor knew him from Aldershot days, when he had noted that 'he could be terrifying at times'. On this occasion he pronounced himself very satisfied with all he saw.

During 1931 O'Connor and another Cameronian officer drove in his car from Cairo to London on their annual leave. On the way they visited the Piave river, and crossed to the island of Papadopoli to inspect the scene of his battle thirteen years before. On one occasion he took local leave to go to Jerusalem to stay with Montgomery, at the time commanding a battalion of the Royal Warwickshire Regiment. Although his wife was with him, Monty himself lined up all the household staff, including the cook, every morning to give them their orders for the day; a practice which gave O'Connor considerable amusement.

In October 1931 the battalion sailed from Egypt to India under the command of Lieutenant Colonel Robin Money, who had just taken over from Hyde-Smith. Its station in India was Lucknow, which is well described in the second volume of *The History of The Cameronians (Scottish Rifles)*:

> Lucknow is an indifferent training area. The ground is flat and featureless, intensely cultivated and studded with villages in clumps of mango trees. Nevertheless, in spite of the region, the lack of up-to-date weapons and equipment, and outdated transport, shift was made to train all ranks for the modern war which seemed to be inevitable. The Rhineland had just been vacated, leaving Germany free to rearm and Adolf Hitler's name was becoming known outside Germany. In training, therefore, particular emphasis was placed on the tuition of leaders and the instruction of young officers and nco's.
>
> The first of January was a great day in India under the British Raj, since all garrisons paraded in strength to commemorate Queen Victoria's proclamation in 1877 which contained solemn pledges to the peoples of

India, scrupulously fulfilled. Year after year, therefore, the masses assembled to witness the 'Tamasha' and military display. An enormous concourse of people of all castes, was found serried on Lucknow airfield when the garrison arrived for the ceremonial parade on 1st of January 1932. The cries of vendors of betel-nuts and the hum of thousands of voices almost muffled the words of command of the officers. The firing of the *feu de joie* induced tumultuous applause and the march-past of the several Units to the music of massed bands and pipers transported the crowd to a state of ecstatic bliss. Unfortunately, when the Union Jack was unfurled at the appropriate time it was discovered to be upside down.[7]

Over Christmas and New Year 1931/32 O'Connor and other officers enjoyed several camping trips in the Lucknow district to shoot duck and snipe. Polo, cricket and hockey were soon in full swing again. Early in 1932, however, his thoroughly enjoyable two and a half years tour of regimental duty came to an end, and he once again found himself on board a troop-ship returning to London.

One of the most influential departments in the War Office, known today by the less attractive name MOD (Army), is that of the Director of Staff Duties. O'Connor's posting as GSO 2 in the section known as SD 1 made him the Director's most personal staff officer, and was what might well be called one of the 'plum' jobs in the Army for an aspiring, middle-ranking officer. His duties were mainly concerned with the Staff College, covering all aspects of the entrance examinations; nominations; the teaching policy and syllabus; and finally the placing of graduates in appointments at the end of each course. Though smaller than the directorates of Military Operations and Military Training, that of Staff Duties might be said to have held the reins of power through its control of appointments, and as O'Connor put forward recommendations to his Director on the employment of many of the brightest 'rising stars' of the Army he had a highly responsible job. Working under him as GSO 3 was another future General, then a Captain, called Harold Redman.

On Dick's posting to London, Mrs O'Connor left Waterperry House after twelve very happy years and moved into a flat in Alexandra Court, Queensgate, to provide a home for her son. It must have been a great wrench for them both to leave Oxfordshire, and Mrs O'Connor would have missed the enormous reception room on the first floor at Waterperry which she had used as her own bedroom, in itself the size of the London flat.[8] To keep himself fit, O'Connor ran in Hyde Park every morning before breakfast.

A friendship developed while he was in London which was to lead to one of the most important events of his life. This was with one Harry Macdonald, a member of the famous Indian cavalry regiment Probyn's Horse, and one of the few Indian Army officers at the War Office. Macdonald, who came from Skye, was married to a member of the family of Ross of Cromarty. His wife Sheila's sister Jean appeared back in Britain in 1933 after the break-up of an unhappy marriage to an American called Phelps, and through Macdonald, O'Connor met his future wife.

In October 1932 a difficult decision had been forced on O'Connor by the receipt of a posting order to command a battalion of the Oxfordshire and Buckinghamshire Light Infantry. Since he still thought that there was a good chance of commanding a battalion of The Cameronians (Scottish Rifles), he asked permission to decline the offer. The Director of Staff Duties, Sir Ivo Vesey, backed this refusal in a letter to the Military Secretary, General Clive, on 12 October, and two days later a letter was received in reply, giving permission for the command appointment to be turned down, and recording that the reasons were considered satisfactory. The next letter O'Connor received from Clive came two years later on 16 May 1934, notifying him that he had been selected to attend the ninth course at the Imperial Defence College assembling in mid-January 1935.[9]

The IDC, as it was known for many years before being given its current laborious title of Royal College of Defence Studies, had been opened in 1927 in London at 9 Buckingham Gate, with the role laid down in its charter of carrying out 'the training of a body of officers and civilian officials in the broadest aspects of imperial strategy, and the occasional examination of concrete problems of imperial defence'.[10] A staff of five officers from the three services, headed by a Major General, Rear Admiral or Air Vice Marshal, had the task of providing stimulating visits, lectures, and discussions for the students, as well as setting them problems to solve, and in the early days, papers to write, which at first were corrected and marked in Staff College style. This marking of written work was later dropped. The IDC had places for thirty students, allotted on the scale of British Services fifteen; Dominions ten; India two; and civil departments three. Dill had been one of the instructors on the original 1927 course, and students included Alanbrooke, or Brooke as he then was, Auchinleck and Haining: the last named had returned as Commandant in 1935 when O'Connor went to the college. Among the brief notes he made about his time at the IDC in later years, he mentioned an exercise which had been carried out on the defence of Singapore. It was in his opinion not a well run affair, but he recalled that within his group he, as the Japanese commander, 'easily got in' to the island. By chance a fellow student among those representing the defenders was the then Lieutenant Colonel A E Percival, who was to suffer disastrous defeat only seven years later as the man in charge of the real defence.

O'Connor enjoyed life in London, and living with his mother in her flat suited him well. His domestic arrangements, however, were due to change considerably during his year at the IDC. He had been gradually falling in love with Jean Phelps, and in September she was staying at Cromarty with her mother, Lady Ross. The IDC was due to pay a visit to HMS *Courageous* but this was suddenly cancelled. On 12 September a telegram arrived for Phelps, Cromarty: 'Courageous visit off. Could stay Saturday to Monday if convenient. Dick.' When he returned to London on the night train from Inverness on Monday, 16 September O'Connor was engaged to be married. The wedding took place on 21 December 1935. Jean's brother Geordie Ross, now Laird of Cromarty and head of the family, gave away his sister, and O'Connor's best man was 'Uncle' Ferrers. After a honeymoon spent partly in the house lent to them by Jean's half-sister, Pamela Phipps, and partly in Madeira, the newly married couple were on their way to India. O'Connor had not only found a wife, but also a step-son. Jamie Phelps, who later changed his name to O'Connor, was eight when his mother re-married, and at a preparatory school at Scaitcliffe, near Windsor. He did not, however, go out to India, but spent his holidays at Cromarty with his grandmother.

It had been in the middle of the IDC course that O'Connor's next posting to command, the Secunderabad Brigade in India, had been announced. Letters poured in to him with congratulations. Wavell, a Major General commanding 2nd Division in Aldershot, in a letter dated 26 June wrote of a brigade being 'a good command—the last really good command.'[11] The same day Sandy Galloway, a Lieutenant Colonel on the staff, and 'Bimbo' Dempsey, still a Major, sent their messages of congratulation as well. The news must have leaked out in India even before the official announcement in London, for a letter from Lucknow was despatched on the same date as the ones from the home addresses by O'Connor's former CSM Anderson, now Regimental Sergeant Major of the 1st Battalion: anyone who knows the East is aware of the efficiency of the 'contractor and char-wallah grapevine' as a conveyor of information! On behalf of the Sergeant's Mess, Anderson congratulated his late company commander on promotion to Brigadier, and expressed the sorrow of all the members that he would never command a Cameronian battalion.

On 20 September the posting to Secunderabad was changed to Peshawar. The background to this move will be described in the next chapter.

5

Commander, Peshawar Brigade, North-West Frontier, India

On 20 September 1935 O'Connor was informed that his posting to Secunderabad, which lies in South India near Hyderabad, had been altered to Peshawar, in the North-West Frontier Province, a much more attractive and exciting part of India. Soon afterwards, a War Office letter instructed him to sail out on 15 March 1936. At the end of October 1935 his late Director in his SD branch in the War Office, Sir Ivo Vesey, wrote from India, where he had become GOC-in-C Southern Command, to tell O'Connor how the change had been given his reluctant approval, though he regarded it as a good example of 'self-sacrifice' to lose such a good officer from his own command. Although Vesey thought it a sad loss to have O'Connor taken away from his area, the General into whose territory he was moved, Sir Kenneth Wigram of Northern Command, was not best pleased to have a British Army officer sent to command the Peshawar Brigade rather than an Indian Army man. There was a strong feeling among many officers of the Indian Service that only one of their own could successfully handle operations in the wilder part of the subcontinent, especially along the North-West Frontier. When O'Connor first met Wigram on his arrival in India he was conscious of a distinctly hostile reception, but fortunately a new Army Commander took over not long afterwards. This was General 'Daddy' Coleridge, a stout, genial man with a sharp brain, who quickly became a firm friend and supporter, and whom O'Connor thought 'excellent'. In the hierarchy of headquarters, there lay between the Peshawar Brigade and Northern Command that of the Peshawar District, the commander of which was Major General

Strettel, described by O'Connor as 'fat and vulgar', though he had no complaints about his military ability.

Arriving at Peshawar, O'Connor was met by the outgoing brigade commander, the newly promoted Major General Claude Auchinleck, who spent the next three weeks showing his successor round the whole of the brigade area, and passed on to him a mass of vital information about the local people. During this hand-over period a deep friendship grew up between the two men, which was to last another forty years and more. The help and advice given so freely at this stage by 'the Auk' enabled O'Connor to understand Indian soldiers more fully than most officers of the British Army, and to develop a great affection for them.

Among those serving under Auchinleck at the time, admiration for his qualities was mixed with respect rather than affection. Brigadier Freddie Noble, then a subaltern in the Highland Light Infantry, remembers him as 'austere and not very friendly'. 'Brigadier Dick', however, 'was, together with Jean his wife, like a breath of fresh air after the austere Auk. We all had the greatest respect and liking for them both, which I am sure was mutual. They both enjoyed hunting (the jackal) with the famous Peshawar Vale Hunt, and came out regularly on Thursday and Sunday mornings 6 am to 10 am. Dick came to many of our guest nights and parties, and he knew by name all the officers, most of the sergeants, and some of the jocks.'

The Peshawar Brigade headquarters were situated in the wired-off British cantonment lying alongside the large, sprawling native town of Peshawar. Also in the cantonment lived the Governor of the North-West Frontier Province (NWFP) with his staff, and General Strettel, the District Commander, with his. Sir George Cunningham was the Governor, and O'Connor admired him greatly.

O'Connor's new command included no less than five infantry battalions which were the largest component of the force. The British Army battalion was 2nd Highland Light Infantry, and the four Indian ones were 1/4th Bombay Grenadiers, 1/5th Mahratta Light Infantry, 4/15th Punjab Regiment, and 2/19th Hyderabad Regiment. There was also a regiment, or brigade as it was then known, of artillery, consisting of two Indian mountain batteries and a British medium battery; the 16th Indian Cavalry Regiment; and two light tank companies of the Royal Tank Corps. Headquarters Number 1 Indian Group and Number 20 Squadron RAF were under O'Connor's command as well. Support in the field of communications and supply was provided by the Peshawar District Signals, and by four companies of the Royal Indian Army Service Corps, two of these being mule companies for employment in the mountains.

The Peshawar Brigade had recently taken part in the Mohmand campaign, one of the many operations which took place throughout the days of the British Raj along the North-West Frontier. Reporting on it on 28 September 1935 *The Times* commented: 'Although no actual battle took place the operations were among the most notable which have been undertaken by the Indian Army in recent times.'[1] As so often happened in similar actions on the Frontier, the dissident tribesmen slipped away from their positions once the forces assembled against them were too big to confront successfully, and so lived to fight another day. Such small skirmishes as did take place during the Mohmand campaign were mainly fought by the Nowshera Brigade, whose territory lay east and north of Peshawar. The commander here was Brigadier The Hon Harold Alexander, later the famous 'Alex'. Although he and O'Connor were to be neighbours of a sort for the next two years, the latter reported little contact between them, though he did record of Alex that he was: 'not a man of great or original ideas, and I don't think unexpected situations would be welcome to him.'[2]

The military duties which O'Connor enjoyed most, and were fortunately his most important ones, were visits to and inspections of the units in the brigade. The further he had to travel and the steeper the hills to climb, the more pleasurable the trip. In the absence of General Strettel, on one occasion he acted as District Commander, and this necessitated going 100 miles north beyond his own brigade boundaries into the mountains of Chitral to the isolated station of the 1/11th Battalion Sikh Regiment at Drosh, commanded by the then Lieutenant Colonel John Smyth, VC. Later Smyth remembered how much O'Connor enjoyed being in the hill country, and how 'he revelled in the long treks by mountain paths'.[3]

In Peshawar, at Brigade Headquarters, there was the usual office work to be done, which O'Connor as a trained staff officer handled quickly and easily. There was also a certain amount of ceremonial to be carried out: big parades with many bands playing were admired by the Indians as much as by the British, and the splendour of the New Year's Day 'Proclamation' parades, which took place all over India, has already been described. O'Connor himself took a natural pleasure in the ceremonial aspect of his profession, insisting that it was well done, but without being obsessed with the minutiae of dress and drill.

The years in Peshawar were some of the happiest of O'Connor's life, and he wrote of them later as a 'wonderful time'. By the standards of the day his promotion to command an active brigade before his forty-seventh birthday was the sign that his 'star' was well on the ascendant in the Army. His job was demanding and rewarding, but gave him few serious worries. There was time and opportunity to indulge in many of the sports he most enjoyed, especially equestrian. Racing and polo went on for most of the year, and there was hunting with the Peshawar Vale hounds, of which he and Jean were keen followers, as already mentioned. The Indian newspaper *The Statesman* reported on 17 March 1937 the best day of the season for the Peshawar Vale, with a field of 71 and the brush of the jackal 'presented to Mrs O'Connor'.

It was in his domestic life, however that his happiness was most complete. From the start his marriage became the most significant thing in his life, and his letters to Jean, whenever they were parted in the following years show the depths of his love and trust. Their time together in Peshawar in the first years of marriage was therefore something to be remembered with special joy. The fact that they lived in a pleasant, spacious house with a host of servants, a beautiful garden and spectacular views in all directions helped to increase their delight in life.

A further pleasure was the presence within reasonable visiting distance of several friends and relations. Harry Macdonald and his wife Sheila, Jean O'Connor's sister, were at Risalpur where Macdonald was commanding the 1st Cavalry Brigade. At Kohat the Brigade Commander was Stuart Abbott, husband of Macdonald's youngest sister Marjorie, usually known as Cleodie. Kenneth McLeod was in an important post in the headquarters of the Northern Army at Rawalpindi. The four families, with their close relationships and strong Scottish connections were often referred to as 'the last tribal menace'. Menacing or not, for all of the 'tribe' it was a very happy time in their lives.

Also in India for part of the time that O'Connor was at Peshawar was Colonel Montgomery, an instructor at the Staff College at Quetta, 350 miles away along the frontier to the south west. It was a period in Monty's service when his future success was by no means assured: there were as many among his seniors who disliked or distrusted him as there were who appreciated his outstanding ability. On the other hand, apart from General Wigram, whose objections to his arrival sprang more from resentment that he was not of the Indian Army rather than anything personal, O'Connor was both liked and trusted at all levels, and was an officer expected by all to reach the very top of his profession.

Although the battalion was not a part of his own brigade, O'Connor was very pleased to meet up again with the Cameronians, who arrived at Landi Kotal, on the Khyber Pass, at much the same time as he arrived in Peshawar. The battalion was only there for a few months before moving down to Barrackpore in Bengal, near Calcutta, in November 1936, but during its stay at Landi Kotal O'Connor had a good chance to catch up with his many old friends. During the years 1935 to 1938 The Cameronians produced a remarkable polo team, which had major success in tournaments all over India, often beating cavalry regiments and teams from the Princely States. It also won the All-India Infantry Regimental cup one year, and was a finalist in another. In the words of the Regimental History:

> These successes—against Cavalry Regiments and well-known Indian teams, with unlimited numbers of good ponies—were not gained without much practice, hard work and abstinence from many of the other pleasures of life. The chief credit for this was due to Captain Collingwood, whose determination and tact in training and handling the team laid the foundation of its success.[4]

O'Connor already knew Collingwood well and when his next appointment came in 1938 he asked him to become his ADC. Collingwood was rather old for such a post, and was used more as a personal adviser, friend and staff officer than the more usual role of an ADC.

O'Connor's next appointment after Peshawar was as a Major General in command of 7th Infantry Division in Palestine. In fact he had returned to Britain in the summer of 1938 expecting to go to Taunton in Somerset to command 43rd (Wessex) Infantry Division, largely composed of Territorial Army units, which would have been domestically ideal but professionally unsatisfactory. The change to a more active command of regular troops in Palestine was notified in September 1938, caused by the worsening internal situation in the country, and a consequent build-up of military forces. Early in October O'Connor boarded the liner SS *Rawalpindi*, bound once more for the Middle East.

6

Commander, 7th Division and Military Governor of Jerusalem

It is a reflection of the overall lack of interest in Palestine and its problems in London, that no one had briefed O'Connor on the military and political situation before he set out to take up his new command. He had therefore only a vague understanding of the situation, and most of his knowledge had been gleaned from newspapers.[1]

From the day that Britain was given the League of Nations Mandate for Palestine and Transjordan on the breaking up of the Turkish Ottoman Empire after the First World War, the rival interests of Jews and Arabs were to be a constant cause of unrest. During many centuries of Turkish rule Palestine had been a backward province inhabited by a small, poverty-stricken population, partly Moslem and partly Christian, who scratched a bare living from the arid soil. Speaking Arabic, and calling themselves Arabs, they were of mixed racial strains. For hundreds of years only a relatively small number of devout Jews lived quietly in the hills of Northern Galilee, and in Tiberias by the Lake. These few Israelites were no threat to Turkish rule of the country, nor to Arab ownership of the land.

However, in Europe, in the latter half of the nineteenth century, there arose, in answer to the miserable existence of the ghettos and to generations of persecution and humiliation, the movement known as Zionism, seeking the return, on a large scale, of the Jewish people to the land that the Bible had told them was their own. There were already a few small and scattered Jewish communities, principally under the patronage of the great Baron de Rothschild, settled in Palestine; but a new dynamism was given to the movement, first by a succession of brutal pogroms in Czarist

48

Russia and second by the emergence of two brilliant and forceful leaders: Theodor Herzl, a spellbinding journalist from Vienna, and Chaim Weizmann, a distinguished scientist, born in Russia, educated in Germany and settled in Manchester. Weizmann's ardent and persuasive advocacy of the Zionist cause accorded with a mood of idealism in various influential members of Lloyd George's wartime Administration—the Prime Minister himself, Winston Churchill, Lord Milner and Arthur Balfour—and seemed to offer a way of consolidating British interests in the Middle East. These linked themes found a practical consummation, after months of discreet negotiations, in the issue, on 2 November 1917, of the historic document known as the Balfour Declaration, which stated that the British Government viewed with favour the establishment in Palestine of a national home for the Jews, and would use their best endeavours to promote that object, provided that nothing was done which might prejudice the civil and religious rights of existing non-Jewish communities in Palestine.[2]

While the Zionists regarded the Balfour declaration as a document giving them rights, in respect of the establishment of their 'national home', which were rather more extensive than perhaps originally intended, the Arabs had faith in another declaration of British origin. Their claims were as well documented as those of the Zionists. It had been an exchange of letters in 1915–16 between Sir Henry McMahon, British High Commissioner in Egypt, and the Sherif of Mecca that had set in motion the Arab rebellion, made famous in T E Lawrence's *Seven Pillars of Wisdom*, which was of such help to Allenby in his victorious campaign against the Turks. In these letters it had been promised that, on the defeat of the Turks, and the breaking up of the Ottoman Empire, Palestine would be put under Arab rule.

For thirty years these two contradicting promises were to be the cause of a bitter conflict of interest between the Arab and the Jewish communities, the populations of which were both increasing steadily. At times the conflict was latent; at others it exploded into bitter communal rioting, or resistance to the British Mandate, which had been bestowed on Britain by the League of Nations after the First World War. The reaction of the holders of this mandate was one of bewilderment and confusion. Successive governments allowed strategic and moral aims to become confused, and by frequent changes of policy made the task of the men responsible for law and order and good government in Palestine unnecessarily difficult.

Outbreaks of violence occurred in 1929, and again in 1933: the first inter-communal, the second largely anti-British.[3] 1933 was an ominous year as well, because Hitler's seizure of power in Germany, inaugurating his persecution of the Jews, caused a big rise in Jewish immigration into Palestine.

> In 1936 the Arabs reacted with a full-scale rebellion–guerrilla warfare against the British Administration and savage attacks on Jewish rural settlements. The small complement of British troops stationed in the country had to be heavily reinforced, and Lieutenant-General Sir John Dill was sent out to take command.... The first phase of the Arab rebellion lasted some six months, from April to October. The Jews remained on the defensive in the towns and countryside; a general Arab strike was called, under the direction of a body called the Arab High Committee, with the intention of forcing the British Government to suspend Jewish immigration; bands of Arab guerrillas were formed in the hill districts; attacks were launched on communications—the roads, railways, the telegraph wires and the oil pipeline to Haifa. The British Government sought the advice of Arab rulers outside Palestine, which did not prove helpful.
>
> The role of Dill's troops, after considerable reinforcement, began to shift from mere guarding of communications and installations to preparation for an offensive against the guerrillas. In May the British Government announced that a Royal Commission would be appointed 'to investigate the causes of unrest'.[4]

The Royal Commission worked quickly, but when its sensible recommendations came out in 1937, they satisfied neither side, and fresh violence erupted.

On 12 September 1937 Dill handed over command to Wavell, now a Major General. He did not stay long, passing on his burdens to Major General R Haining on 8 April 1938 and recording his feelings in two brief sentences:

> Dealing with the rebellion was a very unsatisfactory and intangible business, and I don't think I produced any better answers than anyone else. But I think I kept it within bounds and did as much as I could with the troops available.[5]

Haining soon found his hands full, as the Arab dissidents were no longer content with isolated acts of sabotage and occasional raids on Jewish settlements, but began to raid and ransack towns and district administrative headquarters. On 1 October 1938, a battle near Ramallah, ten miles north of Jerusalem, resulted in over 100

PLATE 1. O'Connor as a boy. A solemn but determined young face.

PLATE 2. At Camp with the Wellington College Officers Training Corps. (O'Connor (R) with bugle).

PLATE 3. The Riding School at the Royal Military College, Sandhurst. (Gentleman Cadet Richard O'Connor third from right).

PLATE 4. The Race Course, Malta. Before a Scottish Rifles regimental race. (Ferrers (L) stands beside O'Connor).

PLATE 5. Officers of the 2nd Scottish Rifles about to board the troopship for Malta in September 1911. (O'Connor fourth from left in the back row, his great friend Stanley Clarke is on his left. Stormonth–Darling, the Adjutant, is on the left of the middle row with Ferrers in the same row, immediately in front of O'Connor).

PLATE 6. 'Somewhere in France' 1914. O'Connor, as 22nd Brigade Signalling Officer, checks a field telephone.

PLATE 7. Tyrol 1919. O'Connor, in HAC uniform, with the Italian General Sani, Commander Allied Troops Austria.

PLATE 8. Staff College, Camberley, 1920. (O'Connor third row up, seventh from right. The officer with the dark, foxy face, fourth from the left in the same row, is Montgomery).

PLATE 9. Waterperry House.

PLATE 10. Visiting the battlefields in 1920. (Mrs O'Connor's car with (L to R) O'Connor in the driving seat; Aunt Vi; Mrs O'Connor and Munday, the chauffeur).

PLATE 11. Riding in a point-to-point in the 1920s.

PLATE 12. Staff College 1927. (Amongst the members of the Directing Staff, in the front row, O'Connor is fourth from the left and Montgomery third from the right. Amongst the students in the back row, easily identified by his Irish Guards buttons in two sets of four, is the future Field Marshal Earl Alexander of Tunis (the famous 'Alex'). On his right, with upturned, dark moustache is Dorman-Smith).

PLATE 13. Imperial Defence College 1935. (O'Connor, front row, two in from left. Centre: the Commandant, Major General Haining).

PLATE 14. With Sir George Cunningham, Governor of the North-West Provinces, and General Coleridge, Commander-in-Chief Northern Command, at a gathering of Indian Army veterans at Peshawar. (O'Connor in rear in grey top hat).

PLATE 15. New Year's Day 'Proclamation' parade in Peshawar, 1 January 1937. (O'Connor is the nearer of the two mounted figures on the extreme right. The 16th Cavalry, Indian Army, follow).

PLATE 16. Commander of the Peshawar Brigade 1938, shortly before leaving India.

PLATE 17. Jerusalem, late 1938. Major General Richard O'Connor with the Headquarters staff of the 7th Division. (Captain George Collingwood, his ADC is on the extreme left of the front row. Lieutenant Charles Mackinnon, another Scottish Rifleman, is third from the right in the second row. Lance Corporal C E Roberts, O'Connor's confidential clerk is second from the left, third row).

PLATE 18. Taking a short break. O'Connor and Collingwood on one of the many
reconnaissances they made around Jerusalem.

PLATE 19. Visiting a section of the Jerusalem-Tel Aviv railway. (General Haining left
foreground. O'Connor has a word with a railway official further back).

PLATE 20. Meeting Arab leaders in Palestine. (Mr Keith-Roach, the Commissioner for Jerusalem (R)). (*Squadron Leader C E Roberts*).

PLATE 21. Making a proclamation to the Arab leaders.

PLATE 22. Kasr-el-Nil Barracks. Cairo 1940. (*Squadron Leader C E Roberts*).

PLATE 23. The road into Mersa Matruh 1940. (*Squadron Leader C E Roberts*).

casualties. The next day, Arabs attacked the Jewish sector of Tiberias, killing nineteen inhabitants, including some children. On 5 October, the Government in London announced the despatch of four infantry battalions to Palestine, and a few days later ordered further reinforcements to be sent from India.

The 1938 rebellion was a generally popular movement, and was carried along primarily under its own momentum with little direction from any outside authority. In the face of the rebellion, civil authority vanished almost overnight in many districts, adding impetus to the insurrection. By early October, Beersheba, Bethlehem, Jericho and Ramallah had fallen to rebels, who now numbered more than 15,000.[6]

Jerusalem was rapidly becoming a city under siege. Lights in the city flickered on and off as power lines were routinely destroyed to Arab saboteurs, who even managed on several occasions to cut Jerusalem's communications with the outside world. Within the city itself, the sound of gunfire was becoming commonplace. Sniping and bomb throwing intensified almost by the hour. Mr Keith-Roach, the Commissioner for the Jerusalem district, narrowly escaped death when four bombs were hurled at his car.[7]

The rebels had smuggled large quantities of arms and ammunition into Jerusalem and had established a headquarters of sorts near the Mosque of Omar in Harem esh Sharif, an area which, because of its sacredness to the Moslem world, was untouchable by the British Army. Intelligence regarding the number of rebels within the city was vague, as it was virtually impossible to distinguish them from peaceful Arab citizens.

On 17 October, there were probably between 250 and 500 armed rebels in Jerusalem and they felt sufficiently strong to proclaim their control of the 'Old City'.[8] The rebellion had reached its climax.

On 16 October, the day before the rebel announcement, O'Connor arrived in Jerusalem. Soon after his arrival he met Haining and Sir Harold MacMichael, the High Commissioner, for his first official briefing on Palestine. It was apparent to O'Connor that relations between the High Commissioner and the Commander-in-Chief were strained. The difficulty rested primarily with Haining, who tended to be stiff and critical and seemed to think his authority should automatically override MacMichael's. O'Connor's attitude was different. He recognised and appreciated MacMichael's intelligence and experience and, from the first, he determined to establish a harmonious partnership with the High Commissioner. As a newcomer to Palestine, with little knowledge of the region and its problems, he badly needed, and wanted, the advice of the civil authorities.[9]

Though O'Connor had known Haining well at the Staff College in 1920, and had admired him when he was in charge of the IDC in 1935, he did not like the way he operated in Palestine. In later years he wrote very critically of Haining's attempt to have MacMichael unseated, which he was 'glad to say failed ignominiously'.[10]

O'Connor soon called a conference of his own, described in the narrative which he himself prepared on *Operations in Palestine 1938–39*:[11]

> As soon as I had discussed the general situation with all the Commanders, Mr Keith-Roach, and the Chief of Police it became quite clear that the country was in a state of extreme unrest bordering on anarchy. Bombs were being thrown and shooting was taking place particularly in the Old City of Jerusalem. Mines were being laid on many roads, trains were being derailed. Jaffa, Hebron and Gaza were more or less in the control of the rebels. The few troops available did their best in the circumstances. This consisted in raids by a mixed force of military and police on various towns and villages where suspects were picked up and sometimes arms were found. But these operations could not themselves solve the problem, therefore, on the arrival of reinforcements some more connected plan of campaign would have to be thought out, in which we must be sure that our priorities were correct.
>
> After much consultation and consideration of alternatives we decided on the following plan of campaign.
>
> First the Old City had to be re-occupied and law and order established as the first and most urgent measure.
>
> Second making safe the main roads, in particular the main road from Jerusalem to Jaffa and Tel Aviv.
>
> Third the re-opening of the railway from Jerusalem to Tel Aviv.
>
> Fourth, when convenient, and as a surprise, large scale raids, on the big cities, arresting 'Wanted' men and collecting arms.

On the following morning, O'Connor again conferred with Haining and MacMichael. During the course of their meeting, the High Commissioner informed him that he was to be named Military Governor of Jerusalem on 18 October; it was an important step, one which greatly simplified matters by allowing O'Connor to issue orders directly to the city's police and civil administrators. How matters then developed is recorded in his own words:

As I have said the first operation was to be the reoccupation of the Old City, and the planning for this started at once.

I had a good look at it from various points of vantage and it appeared to consist of a tangle of very narrow streets, lanes and byways bordered by a mass of houses and shops, the whole surrounded by a high perimeter wall with turrets at certain points, which commanded all parts of the Old City, and most important of all was the famous Mosque of Omar which from its tower dominated the whole area.

Another important factor was that the roofs of all the houses were flat, and projected outwards so that in some cases the width between the roofs on opposite sides of a street was only about 10 to 12 ft. This would make it quite possible for troops to operate on the roof tops, provided they could be protected. The only areas from which they appeared to be vulnerable were the turrets on the great wall and from the Mosque itself. So if the turrets were occupied with our Machine Gunners, they would not only remove all possibility of fire from them, but would be in an excellent position to discourage any interference by fire from the Mosque. A plan on these lines therefore seemed possible. What I was determined to avoid at all costs was getting the troops involved in the maze of small streets in which they would be vulnerable from all sides and might well suffer heavy casualties from snipers and bombs.

I put this plan to the various Commanders involved, and to my surprise it was received with no enthusiasm! The Commander of one famous Regiment protesting against it, as he thought his Battalion might well suffer 200 or 300 casualties. In spite of these apprehensions I was certain that there was no better alternative, and the plan was therefore adopted. This was in brief, first, the occupation of the turrets by the Machine Gunners of the Northumberland Fusiliers, with the task of protecting the whole operation. Next, occupation of the City to be carried out by a joint operation between the troops operating on the rooftops and those advancing up the streets thus enabling the police to search houses and pick up known rebels and suspects in comparative safety. As it turned out the operation was highly successful, and went off strictly in accordance with the plan, our troops suffering only one casualty on the second day.

I am very glad that no fire had to be opened against the Mosque, as this would cause no end of trouble in the Mohammedan world. I did take the precaution just before the operation was due to start, to inform the Mosque Authorities that any fire from the tower against our troops would be returned with heavy fire from a number of different points. Fortunately they were wise enough to take no action. There was actually a further enactment in the 'Emergency' laws which permitted troops to follow up suspect rebels into a Mosque. It was known as the 'Hot Pursuit' ruling and was used only on one or two occasions throughout the Campaign.

To me it seemed a fairly simple and straightforward operation, and looking back on it over the years I am still of that opinion. I think the very real apprehension felt by some Commanders was mainly due to their lack of experience in street fighting and to their general suspicion of any new form of tactics, which they had not seen tried out. In operations of this sort there is no doubt that regular, organised troops hold a great advantage over unorganised rebel forces. They hold the great factor of surprise as to the timing, and actual locality, to be attacked and in every way hold the initiative. They should, therefore, be successful, unless some quite unforeseen factor arises. In this case the operation gave us a good start and the High Commissioner expressed his great satisfaction that it should have been carried out with negligible casualties.

Since the outbreak of hostilities in 1936, the traffic on the Jaffa road had been a frequent target for rebels and bandits. The road's serpentine course amid the hills west of Jerusalem provided ample opportunities for ambush. This road, which linked Jerusalem and the port of Tel Aviv, was an important commercial route. In an effort to free the road from rebel interference, O'Connor established several posts, actually small temporary forts, on three sites which he selected shortly after the Jerusalem operation. From these vantage points, the roadway was observable for miles. O'Connor had seen the same sort of system in India on the Frontier, and it proved equally successful in Palestine.[12] Where the road ran through flat country he made the local Arab mayors or *hetmen* responsible for the safety of traffic which passed through their districts. He warned the mayors, usually in a personal interview, that if a convoy were attacked in their district, they would be held personally accountable. As an added precaution, he ordered the 11th Hussars, in their armoured cars, to patrol the road on a twenty-four hour basis. Before taking steps to secure the road, O'Connor consulted with the civil servants who administered the area and asked for their recommendations in dealing with the local population. In general, the civil administrators agreed that a show of force was helpful in deterring rebel activity. They endorsed his creation of forts and the patrolling of the Hussars, but they disagreed with the suggestion of holding local Arab leaders responsible for rebel activity. However, after discussing the matter with the High Commissioner, O'Connor decided to implement his intended plan, which quickly made an end to the rebel activity along the road.

Like the Jaffa road, the Jerusalem Railway carried much commercial traffic from Jerusalem to the coast. In addition it linked Southern Palestine with the trading centre of Lebanon. The rebels, recalling the skills they had learned from T E Lawrence, frequently mined the railway, thereby derailing trains and destroying tracks and rolling stock. As usual, O'Connor insisted on making a personal reconnaissance of the railway before formulating a plan to deal with the saboteurs.

As his own narrative shows, this turned out to be a more dangerous journey than anticipated:

> The Railway, like the road, ran through a hilly and difficult country, which laid it open to all sorts of attacks. I decided first to make a personal reconnaissance, which I considered would take two days. We started off, George Collingwood and myself, with a number of experts, suitably escorted by a platoon of the Black Watch. We encountered no difficulties and completed a useful day's work. The second day did not work out quite so well. My escort, that day, consisted of a platoon of the Worcesters, who seemed to be carrying too much equipment on their backs and did not look so agile as the platoon of the day before although a very good officer, whom I knew, was commanding them. Fairly soon after we started, we came upon a platoon of the Coldstream, who had had quite a little battle with a rebel force and said that a number of others had been seen one way or another.
>
> I suppose I should have put off the remainder of the reconnaissance for another day when things were quieter. But I decided nevertheless to go on and finish the job, as we had done two thirds of the dangerous hilly parts. But there were still some nasty places to pass through or get round before we were being met by our lorries. We had, however, arranged for an aeroplane to be in fairly constant observation and touch with us until we reached our destination.
>
> We continued our walk for some time without any incidents but having arrived at the end of a ravine, we did see men not very far off on our right flank who evidently intended to interfere with us. I ordered the platoon Commander to fire a few bursts of Bren Gun fire in their direction. It did not seem to have any great effect, and one of the guns was constantly developing faults. However, we went on, realising that as we went on down the ravine, the rebels would be able to shoot at us in certain places. This sort of running battle continued, with the Bren Guns only firing intermittently.

We had now reached the most dangerous part, where fire could be directed against us from both sides but, fortunately for us, we were only fired at from our right flank. Nevertheless, things were really beginning to get unpleasant when a man of the Worcesters was shot dead between George Collingwood and myself. The Worcester platoon was doing its best but was hampered by heavy equipment and their faulty Bren Guns.

For a time, firing continued on both sides and we were not making much progress. But just at this moment, we sighted a number of peasants at work in a field close by. These 'unfortunates' we collected and formed them round us as a protective screen. This proved most effective as the rebel fire lessened immediately, for fear of injuring their own people, and accordingly we were able to make much quicker progress protected by our reluctant civilian escort. Soon we came in sight of our rendezvous, which we reached without further incident.

Throughout, we were in wireless touch with our escorting aeroplane and, as a result of an XX call, three more aircraft came out to our assistance. This was the normal 'emergency' procedure, which worked very well.

It is true we completed the reconnaissance but I have always had the death of this young Worcester on my mind. The whole day's series of incidents showed how very important it was to have a very alert, lightly loaded escort with thoroughly tested guns. Had we had this I do not think we would have had much trouble. The emergency XX call procedure proved its worth.

The senior airman in Palestine at the time was Air Commodore Harris, to be better known in future years by the sobriquet 'Bomber'. His biography records that once the use of aircraft was appreciated by the Army, 'calls for assistance from us were by now incessant and their appreciation of its value unqualified'.[13]

Despite the unfortunate skirmish along the railway line, the reconnaissance patrol had succeeded in its objective. O'Connor had been able to study the railway and its relation to the countryside, which was rocky, barren and inundated with ravines, hills and shallow gorges. Wheeled vehicles were useless for patrolling in such terrain and there were no suitable sites for forts or observation posts. He decided he would charge local Arab leaders with the responsibility for the safety of the railway, in hope that they would deter saboteurs. Within weeks, mines were again being detonated along the railway. O'Connor, now busy with other operations, summoned the responsible Arab leaders to Jerusalem where he informed them that, from that time forward, they would each ride on a little trolley in front of every train. The Arab leaders were not dismayed by the new measure, indeed they looked upon it as something of a joke and apparently enjoyed their trolley rides.[14] Nor were the saboteurs confounded by the new plan; they simply began dynamiting the rear sections of the trains through the use of delayed charges and electric detonating devices. O'Connor responded by placing a prominent Arab in each car of every train travelling the railway. The mining stopped immediately.

Throughout November 1938, O'Connor organised and coordinated the operations to free the towns and districts of Southern Palestine from rebel control. Using the Jerusalem operation as a model, Ramallah, Jericho, and Haifa were soon wrested from rebel hands. The rebels rarely put up much of a fight, the success of the Jerusalem operation seems to have been a critical blow to their morale. Furthermore, the populace was rapidly losing interest in a rebellion which appeared futile in the face of a large and efficient military and police force.

Soon after O'Connor had arrived in Palestine, an old friend had to come out to command the 8th Division based in Haifa. The newly promoted Major General Montgomery took charge of operations in Northern Palestine, and was soon airing his views on the situation in his sector, and how to put it right. On 4 December 1938 Montgomery wrote a long report to the Deputy CIGS in the War Office, Lieutenant General Sir Ronald Adam. In it he told of his operations against the Arab rebels in the north, and explained the methods he was using. He mentioned that:

> I started off with this policy in the North and Dick O'Connor is doing much the same in the South. He and I are great personal friends and we are keeping in the closest touch.

Later in his report he had some comments to make on General Haining's headquarters, and the over centralisation that had been prevalent before his and O'Connor's arrival. Things were now different:

> Dick and I had to make it very clear that all this was to cease now that there were two divisional commanders to deal with instead of five infantry brigadiers. I had to do some very plain speaking on the subject!![15]

Besides his practical military responsibilities, O'Connor found much of his time consumed by political affairs. His influence and good will were much sought after, particularly by those groups and individuals who had a personal vendetta against the rebels. Delegations of both Arab and Jewish leaders were frequently ushered into his office to offer suggestions, complaints, or flattery to the Military Governor. On 1 December he received an important delegation from the Nashashabis, a prominent Arab family, who for generations had played an important role in Palestine's politics and religion. The Fakir Nashashabi, formerly the Mayor of Jerusalem, spoke for the delegation and invited O'Connor to address a pro-British rally sponsored by the Nashashabis. O'Connor gladly assented to the invitation and on 19 December he addressed more than 5,000 Arabs at Hebron, admonishing them to obey the laws and work towards a peaceful settlement of the country's political problems.[16] That 5,000 Arabs would gather for a pro-British rally was evidence that the rebellion's momentum was all but exhausted. Admittedly, there were bands of rebels which continued to raid Jewish settlements sporadically and attack British patrols and convoys. Occasionally, the rebels bombed British establishments; restaurants frequented by servicemen were a favourite target. O'Connor stopped this practice by placing prominent Arabs in the restaurants.[17] Any semblance of cohesion and organisation among the rebels—and there had never been much of either—was gone. At best, the disaffected Arabs could mount a strike or boycott in one of the towns. On 11 February 1939, such a boycott and work stoppage was initiated by the dissident Arabs in Jerusalem. O'Connor responded by ordering all participating shops closed after the strike for the same length of time they had remained closed during it. This tactic undoubtedly influenced many Arabs to abandon the strike weapon.

Just what the operations to pacify the country meant to ordinary citizens was recorded later in *The Scotsman* in 1942 by Dr Norman Maclean who was Minister of the Scots Church in Jerusalem at the time when the rebels were being brought under control:

> Far away East, in Jerusalem in 1939, General O'Connor became a heroic figure to Jew and Arab alike. Before his appointment as Military Governor of the Holy City, no man's life was safe. If you sat in a bus or stood at a counter, any moment a bomb might hurl through a window and explode. The congeries of huddled streets and lanes and ancient rookeries provided so ideal a refuge for criminals that no assassin was ever captured. The authorities were paralysed. But in a short time O'Connor worked a miracle. He could be seen any day standing at a corner, utterly unconcerned, with orderlies coming and going, giving their reports and

receiving commands. Outwardly he presented no resemblance to Wellington or Haig, and you might pass him without even noticing. Unless, of course, you came face to face, and he spoke to you. Then his eyes made you captive, for you felt yourself transparent before those piercing glances. And the rapidity of his answers left you breathless. One soldier explained his efficiency thus: 'He is the quickest in decision I ever met'. That, of course, is no explanation. For that rapidity of thought is only a symptom of the inner spirit. It was a wonderful deliverance, to awake one morning and feel that Jerusalem was as safe as Edinburgh, for General O'Connor had combed the criminals out of the huddled mazes as with a fine comb. Decisive action had ended the paralysis that left the city for months a prey to mass-murder.[18]

An equally interesting description of how O'Connor worked in Palestine has been written by C E Roberts who eventually retired from the Services as a Squadron Leader in the RAF Regiment, but in 1938 was a clerk in the Royal Army Service Corps. Due to his ability to take shorthand, he was appointed confidential clerk to O'Connor, and progressed in due course to become chief clerk in his headquarters during the later Desert Campaign.

On 29 September 1938, I was taken into a room at the Old Fast Hotel, a couple of hundred yards from the King David Hotel, but on the opposite side of the road. I faced a short of stature Major General and saluted. He rose and shook hands with me saying, 'Sit down, Corporal, and tell me about yourself'. He then explained his task in Palestine to me, ending with something like, 'We shall work together'. My mind said, 'This man has a difficult task on hand but he talks to me like a colleague and not as though I was one of the Army's small fry'. It occurred to me that I had a General for a Chief and that my 'small fry' days were over: he had that effect on me.

He was a little dynamo but good-humoured. Not everyone can dictate to a shorthand writer but he could, so that I wondered if he had received training in the art. To me he was a cultured man which pleased me because I was able to learn from him.

In Palestine I never saw him other than calm. When he gave orders to individuals he was, externally, just the same but one knew he was giving orders and not issuing requests.

When he moved about the Old City or countryside, he moved on speeding feet, his staff officers usually trailing after him. I did not usually accompany him on such journeys but before he left he would leave me with a spate of work which I completed and he would find in his 'IN' tray on return. He had only to sign and leave the rest to me.

As to his relationship with other officers, he never seemed impatient and never ill-tempered. His manner was that of a simple man as he stood amongst them with his head on one side, but I had the impression that he took it for granted that anything he said was so clearly put that the veriest simpleton would understand it.

At week-ends 'Dick' would ask me whether I'd mind doing his private correspondence along with the official. On Sunday afternoons I'd sit between Mrs O'Connor and 'Dick', out on their first floor verandah. She was the lady that I expected her to be and she, like he, treated me (by now, a Corporal!) as an honoured guest when in their house. A table was properly laid for me and tea unhurriedly served. So I was entrusted by them with their family affairs.

On Xmas Day 1938, the officers of the HQ played football against the other ranks and the former won, the final score being 2–1. It was a noble effort and appreciated by all. 'Dick' and George Collingwood were in the thick of the fray all the time. No quarter was sought or given. Physically, O'Connor was very fit, very much like a terrier.

In line with tradition, he was active as a waiter in helping serve up the Xmas dinner to the troops. He was always honest and fair, he asked honest questions and liked honest answers. He pondered on what people said to him, rank notwithstanding. I don't think people were always aware of his rank for he made no undue display of it and once one got to know him one warmed to him. He was a great man. I was very proud of my Chief.[19]

After the Arab revolt was brought under control, there was a period of calm. Then the British were threatened from a different direction. In early 1939, Chamberlain's government took steps to reconcile and reassure the Arab population of Palestine and thereby solidify Britain's relations with the Middle Eastern states. War was imminent and the Chiefs of Staff very much wanted the assistance, or at least the passive neutrality, of the Arab states. At the St James Conference, which convened in London in March, the Jewish delegates found the British disinclined to cater to Zionist aspirations. On the contrary, the British gave unmistakable signs of backing down from the Balfour Declaration. On 15 March, the British presented proposals to the Conference which clearly gave the Arab majority in Palestine the dominant political role. Even so, no official declaration of policy had yet been made, and the Jewish delegation returned to Palestine with the hope that Chamberlain's government might be induced to modify their stance prior to the release of an official statement.

The two months following the Conference were marked by a growing restiveness in the Jewish community, while many of the more radical Zionists exhibited an attitude of belligerence toward the Mandate's civil and military authorities. On 17 May, the British Government released its official policy statement on Palestine. Briefly stated, the policy called for the creation of an independent democratic state, organised on a federal model, and the cessation of Jewish immigration after five years. In other words, the Jews were to remain the minority in Palestine. The Jewish communities in Tel Aviv and Jerusalem reacted to the release of the White Paper by attacking government offices in both cities. On the following day, 4,000 Jews attended a protest rally in Jerusalem which was marked by emotional denunciations of the White Paper and occasional violence which culminated in the death of a British policeman. The Jewish leadership instituted a policy of active, but purportedly non-violent, resistance designed to harass the government and make implementation of the White Paper difficult or impossible.

O'Connor explained in his narrative the action he took when trouble with the Jews erupted:

> Throughout this trying period [of the Arab insurrection] the Jews had behaved very well. So when a serious riot suddenly broke out in the Jewish Quarter one afternoon everyone was taken by surprise. I cannot now remember the cause, but it did show how much more formidable the Jews were to deal with than the Arabs. As a result of this disturbance I had an interview with Mr Ben-Gurion at Government House and told him that we had been taking measures against the Arabs to keep law and order and to protect the Jews and that I should have to do the same to them if this should become necessary. In the meantime, I ordered a Curfew in the Jewish Quarter for a period each day. This quieted things down, partly because the International situation became so serious. At any rate, in all Sectors, both Jew and Arab ceased their hostile activities as the danger of War increased.

In the summer of 1939, an operation carried out by a company of the 2nd Battalion Black Watch went seriously wrong at a village called Halhul, lying between Jerusalem and Hebron. It was notorious for harbouring rebels, and it was suspected that many of the inhabitants had weapons hidden in their houses. When it was decided to take action against the village, instructions were given to Captain Neville Blair of 'B' company in an unusual fashion:

> One day I was hurriedly summoned to Brigade HQ, where the Brigadier himself gave me the orders. I was expressly forbidden to take any notes,

nor, I was told, would I get any written confirmatory orders. It was to be a completely secret operation, with nothing put down in writing. I presume the Brigade Major was present, but there was no one else present from my Battalion, not even my Commanding Officer. I forget now if I was authorised to tell him the details, but I believe that he was simply warned, perhaps by me, that the next day my company was to surround and search Halhul.[20]

Blair was told to surround the village at night, and then to search all the houses at dawn. Three compounds were to be set up, into which the occupants of each house would be taken after it had been searched. Women and children were to go into one, situated in the local school: the other two were for men. Those who surrendered weapons willingly went to a shady compound, while those who did not, were put into another in the full glare of the sun. In the sunny enclosure, the men were also limited to two cups of water a day. Though the search was completed in one day, Blair was ordered to keep these unfortunate men in their sun-trap for several more days. Daily he complained to his Commanding Officer about this increasingly inhuman treatment, but he was told that these were the orders of the local brigadier, and if he did not like them he had better send in his resignation.

To cut a long story short, on the night of the fifth day, five of the men in the sun-trap enclosure died of thirst. A hospital was immediately set up in the village, and steps were taken to restore life quickly to normal. However, an absolute furore soon broke out, and the press reported on the affair all around the world. O'Connor was horrified to hear what had happened, and reckoned 'had it not been for the imminent outbreak of war, that MPs in Parliament would have asked the High Commissioner some highly embarrassing questions'.[21]

In due course, a Court of Inquiry was convened to investigate the tragedy. As it progressed, the unfortunate Neville Blair began to feel that the evidence being given to the court was likely to lead to the blame for the disaster being laid on him, in spite of his efforts to tell his superiors that things had been going wrong. Somehow, O'Connor must have heard what was happening, because during the giving of evidence by the brigadier, which was very unfriendly to Blair, he suddenly walked into the room where the court was sitting. 'His entry', as Blair remembers, 'totally dominated the room.' He ordered the proceedings to be brought to a close immediately. He himself, he told the president, was the divisional commander, and as such the responsibility was his. When the brigadier tried to point out that O'Connor could not have known what was happening he was told in icy tones: 'That is my fault—and yours too.' Whatever the price to be paid for loyalty to his subordinates, O'Connor would pay it, rather than let unfairness occur. At the same time, no subordinate escaped his just wrath when necessary.

With the threat of war with Germany increasing throughout 1939, O'Connor's forces had been declining in numbers as the War Office siphoned troops from Palestine to bolster the Empire's defences elsewhere. He suddenly found himself with very little to do; for all practical purposes his active role in Palestinian affairs was at an end. In Jerusalem, he awaited the appointment to a new command. Haining had already returned to Britain and a new job, and Montgomery, his counterpart in the north of Palestine, had been given a divisional command in France. O'Connor must have wondered if he had somehow been forgotten.

7

Arrival in the Desert and First Actions Against the Italians

As the outbreak of war with Germany became imminent, the Headquarters of the 7th Division was moved, in August 1939, from Jerusalem to Egypt, where it occupied the Kasr-el-Nil barracks in Cairo. Charles Mackinnon, the young Cameronian subaltern who was camp commandant of the headquarters staff, remembers the officers being assembled for O'Connor to announce the declaration of war with Germany on 3 September. At 2 am the next morning, they entrained for their war station at Maaten Bagush, a lonely spot about 200 miles along the coast west of Alexandria. A few days were spent erecting tents and digging them in, while wondering if the Italians were going to declare war as well. When it became clear that they would not do so at this stage, the headquarters moved into more comfortable billets in the little coastal town of Mersa Matruh, another forty miles west.

The main task of the divisional headquarters was to take charge of the work on the defences and administrative build-up at Mersa Matruh, which was in the process of being established as the main base for desert operations in the future.

During this period, O'Connor took the opportunity to begin his study of the desert, and of the handling of armour when operating under desert conditions. In these studies he received much help from Major General 'Hobo' Hobart, the commander of what was then known as the Mobile Force, but would soon be redesignated the 7th Armoured Division. O'Connor is reputed to have described Hobart's force as 'the best trained division' he had ever known, but this standard had not been easily achieved. It had required all Hobart's formidable energy and ruthlessness to bring it about.

Some of the lessons which he had driven home to his officers and men—many of them newly converted from horsed cavalry to armour—had included the importance of rapid movement when widely dispersed; navigation and direction finding in the open desert devoid of any land-marks; and the importance of maintenance and endless attention to the mechanical condition of their vehicles. In November, Hobart left Egypt after an unfortunate row with his immediate superior, General Maitland Wilson, but by then O'Connor had seen a lot of him and learnt much from him.

In these early days, often referred to as the 'Phoney War', great care was taken to avoid upsetting the Italians in their Libyan colony across the Egyptian border. It was still hoped that Mussolini would not bring his country into the war on Hitler's side. Planning for this eventuality went on all the time, but was conducted in great secrecy to avoid precipitating any Italian reaction. Mackinnon remembers an occasion in December when a meeting between O'Connor and Wilson was held in an isolated hut near Maaten Bagush, to which the latter arrived alone in an unmarked car, having told his staff in Cairo that he was going away for a few days leave.

In April 1940, the headquarters of the 6th Division, as the 7th had been redesignated when the number '7' was given to the armoured division, returned to Palestine. After they had been there only two and a half months, the imminent collapse of France led Mussolini to declare war on the side of the Germans, whom he now felt to be assured of victory. Two days before this declaration, on 10 June 1940, O'Connor and his staff returned to Egypt and established a base once more at Maaten Bagush. Here, on 17 June, the day France made peace with Germany, he was confirmed as commander of the Western Desert Force, and promoted to the temporary rank of Lieutenant General.

At this time there was a good deal of 'top-brass' in Egypt, where peace-time standards of living still prevailed. Wavell, as Commander-in-Chief, Middle East, with his General Headquarters (GHQ) in Cairo, was O'Connor's ultimate superior. However, there was another commander immediately above him, General Maitland Wilson, always known, because of his bulk, as 'Jumbo', who commanded British Troops in Egypt, or BTE. His headquarters were also in Cairo. This top-heavy structure was not a problem during the lull which followed Italy's declaration of war, but once active operations were begun, would prove to be faulty. Chief staff officers in the two headquarters were Major General Arthur Smith at GHQ, and at BTE O'Connor's old friend and fellow Scottish Rifleman, Brigadier Sandy Galloway. The latter did much in due course to stop this clumsy surfeit of superior headquarters becoming too irksome to the Western Desert Force.

Before coming out to the Middle East in 1939, Wavell had written an appreciation of the tasks which he considered would face him as Commander-in-Chief. This included the requirement to plan, 'in conjunction with the other Services, not merely the defence of Egypt and our interests in the Middle East but such measures of offence as will enable us and our Allies to dominate the Mediterranean at the earliest possible moment; and thereafter to take the counter-offensive, against Germany in Eastern and S E Europe.'[1]

Mentioning 'Allies' when writing these words, Wavell was thinking of the French. However, when they signed the armistice on 17 June 1940, they not only ceased to be allies but became enemies in most of those areas where French colonial leaders accepted the Vichy government. Only a few joined the Free French and continued the war against the Axis powers. The British and Commonwealth forces in North Africa were now very much on their own.

From his earliest days at Maaten Bagush, O'Connor established excellent relations with the Royal Air Force and the Navy. The headquarters of 202 Group RAF, known as the Desert Air Force, was only a few hundred yards from his own, and he quickly got onto good terms with its commander, Air Commodore Collishaw.

On 11 June, the day after Italy came into the war, the first attack took place on their troops stationed along the frontier with Libya. On this frontier they had put up a 250 mile long fence, known as the 'Wire', some years before. It comprised three lines of barbed wire on poles with coils laid between them. The British armoured cars quickly learnt how to gap this obstacle, and the 11th Hussars had their first engagement with the Italians before their unfortunate troops in Libya had even been notified of the declaration of war. Fort Capuzzo, on the northern end of the Wire, just west of Sollum, was captured on 14 June with 220 prisoners; on the same day, some 70 miles to the south, Fort Maddalena also surrendered. Two days later, an Italian force of some 40 light and medium tanks and about 30 lorries full of infantry was surrounded and destroyed, with no British casualties, by squadrons of the 7th and 11th Hussars, supported by anti-tank guns of the Royal Horse Artillery, the RHA.

Roaming widely by day and night, offensive patrols gained a complete ascendancy throughout the wide areas of 'No Man's Land' along the Libyan frontier. The British avoided contact with the main Italian positions and concentrated on harassing communications, mobile columns and isolated posts. The enemy showed little inclination to match these activities, preferring to remain within static defensive positions. These sorties, however, presented one serious disadvantage—the wear and tear to the armoured vehicles, particularly tank tracks, caused by the extremely rough 'going' in the desert. Replacements were scarce and future major operations might be prejudiced if care was not taken to husband limited resources. The bulk of the armour was therefore pulled back to an area south of Matruh, where it would be well sited to attack the southern flank of the Italian army should an invasion of Egypt be launched along the coast road. Patrolling the frontier continued, but with armoured cars and lorry-borne infantry, with minimum tank support. To confuse the Italians, dummy tanks were put out in the desert to replace the ones withdrawn.

Also preserving the greatest economy of effort at this stage was the Desert Air Force. With little prospect of reinforcements or replacements, it was necessary to conserve aircraft for the possible major battle ahead for the defence of the Nile Valley. Bombing and reconnaissance flights were reduced to a minimum; luckily the Italian Air Force, in spite of great superiority in numbers of aircraft, was not particularly enterprising, though slightly more so than the army.

The three months of comparative calm after 10 June were used to full advantage by O'Connor himself to prepare for future operations, and he was constantly on the move, visiting units all over his extended command, from those at the Wire to the administrative units in the rear areas, of whose importance he was fully aware. Not only did these visits enable him to inspect and assess the quality of the troops under his command, while giving them guidance and impressing his personality on them—all vital aspects of the art of command—but the long journeys by staff car enabled him to study the ground over which he might one day have to fight. His desire to see everything for himself reflected the importance of personal reconnaissance which he had learnt in the First World War. On at least one occasion he even pushed on further than the line of his forward troops, the 11th Hussars informing their headquarters 'that one of their forward patrols had reported that General O'Connor had, in his staff car, come on the armoured car patrol from the west, i.e. from the enemy's direction'.[2]

An example of the impact his personality made on the men he visited is described in Major General David Lloyd Owen's book *The Desert my Dwelling Place*. The young Lloyd Owen was then commanding a company of the 1st Battalion Queen's Regiment in 16th Infantry Brigade, and was digging a defensive position in the area of Maaten Bagush when he was warned of the imminent arrival of the Western Desert Force commander:

> But I did not know much about General O'Connor. I had only met him once when we were both dining at Government House in Jerusalem, where I was staying with Sir Harold and Lady MacMichael. 'Good morning, Lloyd Owen', he said as he thrust out his hand to shake mine. There was a galaxy of brass hats in his wake. 'I see your men have dug some damned good positions. Tell them they've done well. The ground looks horribly hard. Are you sure that you can bring fire to bear all along the anti-tank ditch?'
>
> 'Yes, sir.'
>
> 'Good. I'm sure you know best. You're the chap who has got to fight this position. How are the men? Got any worries?'
>
> 'No, sir. They would like some beer if we could get it, but that's everyone's worry.'
>
> 'I'll see what I can do. Nice to see you again. I must be off now. Good-bye and good luck to you all.'
>
> Off he sailed amidst a fleet of accompanying Staff Officers. He was only with us for a few minutes but I felt that he had done me good; and I knew he had when an extra ration of beer came up that night.
>
> It was a tragedy when General O'Connor was captured later in the campaign for he was an inspiring leader and my story illustrates his human touch.[3]

The fall of France meant that the Italians in Libya had no further need to guard their western flank, and could move troops into Cyrenaica to prepare for the invasion of Egypt. O'Connor therefore had to ensure that strong defences were prepared, and plans laid for meeting this advance when it took place. The locations chosen for creating defensive positions were well back from the frontier at Matruh and along the Nagamish Nullah, with the second strongpoint, already mentioned above, further back at Maaten Bagush. The plan was to let the enemy come up to Matruh, merely harassing and delaying him without fighting a major battle, and then to launch the armoured division onto his flank from its position south

of Matruh. Not only was O'Connor preoccupied with these preparations, but his mind was also working out ideas for offensive action to
follow the anticipated defeat of the Italian invaders after a successful
outcome to the armoured attack.

In July 1940 he obtained the services of a temporary ADC from
the Royal Scots Greys, the twenty-two-year-old Earl Haig, son of
the Commander-in-Chief of the First World War.

> General O'Connor was at the station at Mersa Matruh to meet me and he
> at once made me feel at home. Small in stature, dressed in shorts, he
> displayed a personality which was vigorous and intense, and deeply
> serious. Behind the friendly facade lay an expression of grim determina-
> tion—of vigilance. He seemed like a horse which is eager and almost
> fretful. His eyes showed something of the deep feelings of his Presbyterian
> background.

It was of those eyes that Ronald Lewin wrote that 'they were a pure
and limpid blue; but in moments of decision they turned into pools
of ice'.[4]

Lord Haig's narrative continues:

> Without any small talk, he spoke with a temperament often tinged with
> anxiety and frustration. To be alone with such a man for hours on end
> driving through the desert would not be easy. On our arrival at Western
> Desert Force Headquarters at Maaten Bagush, I was taken to my tent,
> which was sandbagged, standing adjacent to the General's. I met
> Ingolsby, the General's batman, and Simons, his driver. Near us was 'A'
> Mess tent, where I met Brigadier Neil MacMicking and other staff
> officers who seemed to me immensely old—all of them senior officers over
> fifty years of age. Before dinner, the General took me across the dunes to
> the sea, where we left our towels and swam naked. Many long and tiring
> days of desert journeys were to end with this cool form of recreation, and
> often as we drove through the sand and heat we looked forward to the
> evening bathe, which became a ritual for all the soldiers, friend and foe
> alike, along the seashore. Further south was an area of harder desert land,
> which stretched between the coast and the Qattara Depression, and
> where vehicles would not get stuck in the sand. To the immediate eye, the
> ground seemed flat, but nevertheless was full of escarpments, of small
> undulations and hillocks which were of tactical importance. In the
> evening, when the sun was low, the desert, with its far horizons and
> scrubby vegetation, became strangely beautiful. The beauty of the
> evening light was accompanied by a cool breeze, and when we spent
> nights on our desert rounds we woke in the morning with our sleeping-
> bags damp in the dew. On these tours my duties consisted of organising
> the General's timetable and charting our course across the desert with the

aid of a compass and a map. Often I heaved a sigh of relief when the camp or rendezvous we were aiming at hoved in sight and I realised that we had reached our target.

We travelled in two cars. The General's car in front flying a red pennant was usually driven by himself or by me. Sometimes we transferred to the second car if our own car broke down because of overheating or a puncture.

A day's inspection might follow the course of the one described by Haig when:

> it was the ambulance train's turn to be inspected. The compartments were found to be dirty, the blankets were not disinfected and men were still in their boots. (All these deficiencies had been put right when the train was inspected a few days later). The General next spent some time examining the sinking of anti-tank mines and hedgehogs in the defences at Mersa Matruh, at Nagamish and at Daba. These could be important rear defences in the event of an enemy break-through.[5]

Sometimes General Wilson joined O'Connor on one of his tours, and Haig remembers that:

> I sat listening to the two of them together for long hours driving around the desert. Jumbo Wilson was a really cosy, chatty man and probably got General Dick to unbutton, which did him good. But I know he was no help to him when it came to moments of serious decision. Probably some help discussing where to sight small units—gun emplacements etc—rather like planning a pheasant shoot beforehand. Jumbo was rather like a nice, fat keeper![6]

The anticipated invasion of Egypt by the Italian army commanded by Marshal Graziani started on 13 September 1940. The British forces withdrew steadily as the enemy advanced, a thin screen of three battalions supported by artillery covering a twenty-mile front. One squadron of medium tanks backed them up, but was never called into use. The covering force pulled out of Sidi Barrani on 16 September, and the Italians entered the town. To the amusement of all, their radio announced this triumph by upgrading the solitary mosque, police post and handful of mud huts which in fact made up the place, into a city in which 'the trams were still running!'

After continuing some twelve miles past Sidi Barrani, the Italian advance came to a halt, having covered about 60 miles. During it they suffered some 3,500 casualties and 700 of their soldiers were taken prisoner: British casualties were about 160 of all types.

Having stopped, the Italians built a series of strongly fortified camps on a perimeter starting at El Maktila on the coast and then following an arc in a south-westerly direction to Sofafi, about 40 miles away. Each camp was surrounded by anti-tank obstacles and mines, and was garrisoned by the equivalent of an infantry brigade with tanks and artillery in support. Their weakness lay in the fact that they were too widely spaced to be mutually supporting.

Gradually it became obvious that the Italians did not intend to move further into Egypt for the time being; since they excelled in administration and engineering they wanted to establish well organised lines of communication before making a further advance. British plans for delivering the 'knock-out' blow as they approached Matruh were forgotten and, at all levels, commanders began thinking of carrying the offensive into enemy territory without first defeating them in the manner originally proposed.

Wavell's mind had started on this track even before Graziani's offensive was launched. On 11 September, he had sent a remarkably prescient note to Arthur Smith asking for a study to be made of the possibility of an offensive into Cyrenaica, which he envisaged taking place at the end of 1940 or early in 1941, following the defeat of the Italian invasion. In it he had written:

> In planning the operation, let us avoid as far as we can the slow ponderosity which is apt to characterise British operations.... We may therefore hope to be dealing with somewhat dispirited Italians, and to be able to take a certain degree of risk.[7]

Wilson and O'Connor were already thinking on the same lines. In the latter, Wavell had a subordinate whose qualities had nothing in them of 'slow ponderosity'. The genesis of the campaign which was to be given the name of Operation COMPASS was in Wavell's reflections, but its development followed easily through the co-operation of those others who were already well advanced with schemes of a similar nature. When Wavell sent a letter to Wilson on 20 October asking him to examine the possibility of securing a decisive success by attacking the enemy positions in the Sidi Barrani–Sofafi–Buq Buq triangle, he ordered that it should only be shown to Galloway at his own headquarters BTE, and in the Western Desert Force only to O'Connor and 'Dicky' O'Moore Creagh, commanding 7th Armoured Division. In it was born the concept of the 'five day raid', around which all the first plans were made, for Wavell wrote:

71

The operation I have in mind is a short and swift one, lasting four or five days at the most, and taking every advantage of the element of surprise.[8]

On 2 November 1940, Wavell followed his letter of 20 October with the only written directive for COMPASS, which began:

In continuation of my Personal and Most Secret letter of 20th October, I wish you to inform your *senior* commanders in the Western Desert as follows:

I have instructed Lieut-Gen O'Connor, through you, to prepare an offensive operation against the Italian forces in their present positions (if they do not continue their advance) to take place as soon as possible.

Another four paragraphs of general exhortation followed, including passing on the good wishes of Churchill and his promise of 'the resolute support of his Majesty's Government', and the letter ended:

One of our most powerful aids to victory will be surprise. Every means by which we can preserve secrecy and deceive the enemy must be studied. The plan and intentions must be confined till the last moment to as few persons as possible; and everyone must understand that the lives of his comrades and the success of the war may be imperilled by carelessness.[9]

The need of the Western Desert Force to make use of every possible advantage in launching its offensive can be seen when the balance of forces is explained. The Italian numerical preponderance was great, the whole of Graziani's force in North Africa amounting to 250,000 men, 1,400 guns, and 450 medium and light tanks. Roughly half this force made up his Fifth Army in Tripolitania, while the other half composed the Tenth Army in Cyrenaica and Egypt. O'Connor's Western Desert Force never contained more than 32,000 men.[10]

8

Planning the Five Day Raid

Wavell's secret instructions to Wilson and O'Connor on 20 October, for the raid he had in mind to last 'four or five days at the most', included suggestions in considerable detail as to the tactics which might be employed. He proposed that the attack should be a two-horned effort against each flank of the enemy's line: on the left, 7th Armoured Division, reinforced by infantry in trucks, would attack the Sofafi group of camps, while the 4th Indian Division would advance on the right along the coast road. This attack could be followed by a pincer movement by the two wings to cut off the Nibeiwa and Tummar camps. Wavell stressed the need for all troops to be mobile in vehicles, and pointed out the limitations imposed by restricted maintenance resources. Wilson went up to the desert to discuss these proposals with O'Connor, but neither thought highly of them.

It was at this stage that Anthony Eden, at the time Secretary of State for War, came out to Egypt. He travelled up to the Western Desert Force headquarters with Wilson on 23 October, and Haig remembers that

> 'A' Mess became heavy with top brass, and I was kept busy organising cars and aeroplanes and rendezvous. Mr Eden's mission was to examine the situation on the ground, and to make sure that every effort was being made both to defend the Nile and to plan an attack against the enemy.[1]

The objections to Wavell's plan of attack on the Italians were threefold. To attack Sofafi from the south would add fifty miles to any approach march; signal resources were too unreliable for the control of such widely separated wings; and air support was barely sufficient to cover one battle area, let alone two, thirty miles apart. Wilson returned to Cairo to present Wavell with O'Connor's

The Forgotten Victor

revised plan to pass through the gap in the enemy's defensive line at Bir Enba, south of Nibeiwa, and send the infantry division north towards the coast, taking the enemy camps in detail from behind, while the armoured division prevented counter attacks from Sofafi or the west. Wavell, who always had a taste for the unorthodox approach, approved this outline plan and work began in earnest to make the extensive preparations to put it into effect. Its originality is highlighted by Barclay:

> Any student who had produced such a solution at a Staff College exercise in peace would have been ridiculed by his fellows and very roughly handled by the Directing Staff. Yet it was the only method of obtaining the high degree of surprise if the offensive were to succeed.[2]

Apart from this method of obtaining tactical surprise, the other vital matter was security. To preserve secrecy, only a handful of officers were allowed to be 'in the know' while planning went on. At GHQ these were Wavell, his Chief of Staff Arthur Smith, and 'Chink' Dorman-Smith, the brigadier responsible for operations, while at HQ BTE these were Wilson, Galloway the BGS, and Harding, who had taken Galloway's place temporarily while he was ill. At O'Connor's own headquarters of the Western Desert Force, knowledge was limited to himself, his BGS, Hobday, his chief administrative officer Brigadier Nares, and the senior transport officer, Colonel Collings. Below Force headquarters, the two divisional commanders and their two senior staff officers were told, and then the information went no further beyond the level of brigade commanders and their brigade majors.

Among the main reasons for this preoccupation with secrecy was the fact that Cairo and Alexandria were full of agents and others working for the Italians, and there was always a chance that someone on leave in either place might inadvertently give something away which would be quickly passed on to Rome.

In view of the complications connected with moving two divisions forward from their main bases in the region of Matruh to concentration areas some eighty miles away behind the enemy positions, and also of actually assaulting the fortified camps, O'Connor decided that operations would have to be rehearsed.

To preserve secrecy, a rehearsal on 26 November 1940 was known as Training Exercise No. 1, and it was given out that Exercise No. 2 would be held in the second week of December. In fact this was destined to be 'the real thing'. Other measures, apart from restricting information on the plan to formation commanders and senior staff officers, included limiting written instructions to the minimum, and explaining the forming of forward supply dumps as a necessity for defensive purposes. Leave was not stopped until three days before the operation, and special hospital arrangements were only made at the last minute. The fighting units were not to be told until they had begun the final approach march that they were going into action. In the event some officers may have guessed that there was more afoot than mere training, but most junior ranks were not aware that No. 2 was anything other than an exercise until they were well on their way.

The rehearsal was valuable in ironing out problems in connection with the moonlight approach march as well as practising techniques for assaulting the camps. O'Connor's comments on Training Exercise No. 1 were that it 'went off well and proved most valuable'.[3] There seems to be some confusion about the rehearsal of the attack on the camp at Nibeiwa. Some authors describe the practice attack, which was made against the replica of Nibeiwa built in the desert near Mersa Matruh, as being a frontal assault based on a pamphlet called *The Division in Attack*, and claim that after this exercise the plans were considerably altered. O'Connor himself, however, stated in a letter many years later that, after the rehearsal: 'No change of any importance was made as a result. The main structure of the plan was settled a considerable time before, and in the operation that plan was carried out in its entirety.'[4] The truth is that there was never any change in the concept of attacking the camp from the west after sweeping through behind it, but merely an alteration in the method of conducting the actual assault after arrival in the forming-up position.

Instead of the conventional method of using an artillery bombardment followed by a combined infantry and armoured advance, it was decided to use the 'I' (for infantry), or 'Matilda', tanks of 7th Royal Tank Regiment in a surprise move, unsupported by artillery, down an unmined track into the north-west corner of Nibeiwa. Then the assaulting infantry were to come in behind the tanks, while other infantry would draw the defenders attention away to the east of the camp with heavy small-arms fire and pyrotechnics.

In a letter to Liddell-Hart after the war, O'Connor pointed out the axis of attack 'depended entirely on the latest photographs indicating the presence of minefields', and also that, since the fortified camps had all round defences, any approach could be called 'frontal'. In the same letter, he mentioned that the final method decided upon came out in a paper 'as if emanating from Headquarters BTE. I remember this well as Wavell later asked me whether I had any objection to the credit for the revised method of attack coming from BTE. I said I had none whatever.'[5] Clearly both he and Wavell were anxious to ensure that Jumbo Wilson and his headquarters were kept happy and did not feel left out of things.

Administrative preparations were, of course, vital. They were centred on the establishment of two forward supply dumps some thirty miles west of the Mersa Matruh to Siwa road. The men who had to bring the stores forward to these dumps, properly called Field Supply Depots No. 3 and No. 4, were too busy and too exhausted to bother about the unlikelihood of the official cover story, which pretended that they were being created as a reserve for defensive operations should the Italians advance again.

The date for operations to start was fixed for 9 December 1940. The troops were to begin moving forward to the west on 6 December, and the approach march proper was to start at dawn on 8 December. Both 7th Armoured Division and 4th Indian Division were to move south of the main escarpment, as there was better going and less dust would be raised.

The opening phase of the offensive was given the aim of destroying the Italian forces in the Nibeiwa and Tummar camps and then advancing north towards Sidi Barrani and Buq Buq, with the object of cutting off the enemy in Maktila and the town of Sidi Barrani.

Assistance from the other services was essential. The Royal Navy was to bombard Maktila, and the Royal Air Force had three tasks. First, it was to bomb enemy airfields on the night before the battle; second, it was to intercept enemy aircraft to protect the advancing troops and prevent their movements being spotted; and third, during the final move into position to the west of the camps, aircraft were to bomb the Italians and, at the same time, cover the noise of the approaching tanks with that of their own engines.

As a final preparation, a conference was held at GHQ in Cairo on 4 December 1940, shortly after which O'Connor moved forward to his battle headquarters.

9

An Outline of Operation
COMPASS

For ease of understanding, the desert campaign is covered in two chapters. This first short, purely factual one, gives the broad outline of the course of operations, illustrated with simple maps. In the long chapter that follows, General O'Connor's own actions and movements can be followed with a clear picture in mind of the separate stages of the campaign.

The Approach March

The approach march was carried out in two stages, the first concentration area being about ten miles west of the Mersa Matruh–Siwa road. This stage was completed by the evening of 7 December. The next day, a daylight move was made to another area some 40 miles further west. On the night of 8/9 December, the final approach was made in the dark, and by the early hours of 9 December, the 7th Armoured Division was lying south and west of Nibeiwa ready to prevent any interference from the enemy at Sofafi and Rabia, and poised to advance north towards Buq Buq as the situation developed. North of the 7th Armoured, and about five miles from Nibeiwa, was the 4th Indian Division, with the 11th Indian Brigade in the lead along with the heavy 'I' or 'Matilda' tanks of the 7th Royal Tank Regiment.

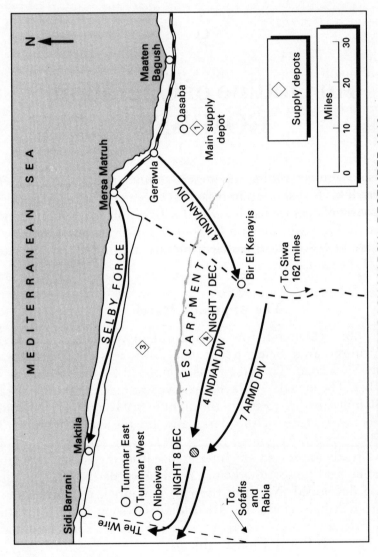

MEDITERRANEAN SEA

N

Sidi Barrani
Maktila
Tummar East
Tummar West
Nibeiwa
The Wire
NIGHT 8 DEC

To Sofafis and Rabia

7 ARMD DIV
4 INDIAN DIV
NIGHT 7 DEC

⟨4⟩

ESCARPMENT

⟨3⟩

SELBY FORCE

Mersa Matruh
Gerawla

4 INDIAN DIV

Bir El Kenayis

To Siwa 162 miles

Qasaba
⟨1⟩
Main supply depot

Maaten Bagush

◇ Supply depots

Miles
0   10   20   30

MAP 2. THE APPROACH MARCH - DECEMBER 1940

78

The Battle of Sidi Barrani—9 to 11 December 1940

Capture of the Fortified Camps

The attack on Nibeiwa achieved complete surprise. At 7.15 am the divisional artillery opened fire with 72 guns. This was immediately followed by an assault on the north-west corner of the camp by the 'Matilda' tanks, whose successful entry was followed by 'mopping-up' infantry. By about 10.30 am, the capture of Nibeiwa had been completed.

Attention was then turned to the Tummar camps. 7th Royal Tank Regiment rallied north of Nibeiwa and, as soon as the tanks had refuelled, advanced on Tummar West. The 5th Indian Infantry Brigade was carried to its position of assault, and the artillery moved forward. The course of the operation was much the same as at Nibeiwa, and in spite of various problems, the capture was more or less complete by dusk.

Other Activities on 9 December 1940

The two brigades of the 7th Armoured Division made good progress. The 4th Armoured Brigade and the 11th Hussars protected the western flank of the troops attacking Nibeiwa and the Tummar group, and then pushed patrols north across the road from Sidi Barrani to Sollum and on towards the sea. The motorised infantry of the Support Group prevented any interference from the enemy in the Sofafi area to the south.

The 7th Armoured Brigade was in reserve, covering the Enba gap. It was given orders to patrol to the west of the Sofafi stronghold to ensure that the garrison there did not escape.

To the north of all this activity was the mainly infantry 'Selby Force', drawn from the garrison of Mersa-Matruh, numbering about 1,750 men supported by a few light tanks and guns, and named after the brigadier who commanded it. Its job was to advance along the coast road and deal with the Italian base at Maktila. For several reasons, the progress of this column was slow, and it failed to prevent the Italian garrison escaping from Maktila.

Operation on 10 December 1940

On 10 December, 4th Indian Division continued its advance towards Sidi Barrani. During the morning, it bumped into a

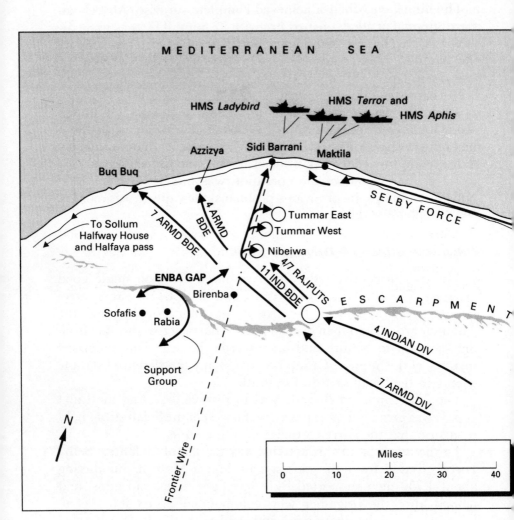

MAP 3. FIRST BATTLES

Blackshirt division, against which an attack was made by the 5th Indian and 16th British Brigades.

Selby Force on the coast road joined up with 6th Royal Tank Regiment of the 4th Armoured Brigade and a joint night attack in moonlight delayed the Italians who had got away from Maktila in their attempt to reach Sidi Barrani.

The 7th Armoured Division were ordered to carry out the second part of their task, and advance on Buq Buq as soon as Sidi Barrani was taken.

The efforts by the 8th Hussars, part of the 7th Armoured Brigade, to stop the retreat of the Italians from the Sofafi and Rabia strongholds were not successful. The garrisons of both slipped away during the night and next day reached the enemy encampment of Halfway House.

Operations on 11 December 1940

Information reached O'Connor early on the morning of 11 December to the effect that the 4th Indian Division was to be withdrawn from his command to go to the Sudan. Only the 16th British Brigade, which would be without supporting artillery and administrative back-up, was to be left in North Africa. The Indian Division completed the capture of Sidi Barrani during 11 December, and then were ordered to move back to the Delta as quickly as possible to conserve supplies at the front.

The 7th Armoured Brigade found a strong force of the 64th Catanzaro Division to the west of Buq Buq in a well-protected position between the coast road and the sea. After a fierce battle, in which the 3rd Hussars suffered badly at the hands of the Italian artillery, the bulk of the enemy force surrendered, though a few got away towards Sollum.

The results of these first battles were much more than had been expected. The count of captured prisoners and war material came to 38,300 officers and men, including four generals; 237 guns; 73 tanks; numerous lorries; and a vast amount of stores of all kinds.

The Approach to and Capture of Bardia— 12 December 1940 to 5 January 1941

The Approach

With the departure of the 4th Indian Division only the 7th Armoured Division was left to mop up the few remaining enemy detachments around Sidi Barrani, as well as to carry out the pursuit of those that had managed to make their escape towards the west. The 16th British Brigade was fully occupied with the guarding and escorting of the many thousands of Italian prisoners.

The orders to the armoured division were to push on to Sollum and Capuzzo, and later to cut the Bardia–Tobruk road. On the way they were to deal with the fortified camps at Halfway House and Halfaya, to which the garrisons of the Sofafi camp had managed to escape. During the night of 12/13 December, the troops in them slipped away and reached Fort Capuzzo, where they established another strong base. To the south, Sidi Omar still held out.

On the night of 13/14 December, the 4th Armoured Brigade moved north towards the Bardia–Tobruk road. The following day, 7th Armoured Brigade was sent to prevent those Italians who had collected in the Sollum–Capuzzo area withdrawing into the defences of Bardia. However, it failed in this task, as during the night of 15/16 December, the enemy succeeded in breaking out, and, by daylight, were safely into Bardia.

On 16 December, the 7th Brigade took the place of the 4th, which came south to an area between Capuzzo and Sidi Omar. It successfully attacked the latter base on 17 December. On 19 December, the Support Group was placed north of the Tobruk road to block a track running along the coast, and by the next day Bardia was completely cut off from the west.

While all these moves of the armour were in progress, the infantry formation which was to replace the 4th Indian Division was moving to join the Western Desert Force. This was the 6th Australian Division, consisting of the 16th, 17th and 19th Infantry Brigades.

The 16th British Brigade, less a battalion clearing the port of Sollum, was moved to the Bardia area to reconnoitre the defences, which were formidable, consisting of a deep anti-tank ditch, minefields, a great deal of wire, and well-sited concrete blockhouses.

It was decided that the attack on Bardia could not take place before 2 January 1941 due to the slow movement of the Australian

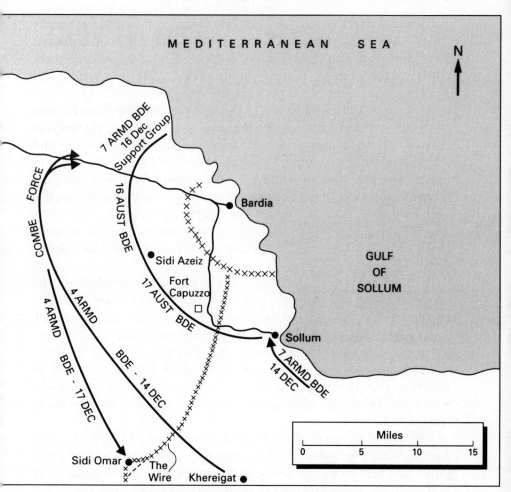

MEDITERRANEAN SEA

N

7 ARMD BDE
16 Dec
Support Group

COMBE FORCE

16 AUST BDE

Bardia

Sidi Azeiz

Fort
Capuzzo

17 AUST BDE

4 ARMD BDE

4 ARMD BDE - 14 DEC

4 ARMD BDE - 17 DEC

Sollum

GULF
OF
SOLLUM

7 ARMD BDE
14 DEC

Sidi Omar

The
Wire

Khereigat

Miles

0   5   10   15

MAP 4. THE APPROACH TO BARDIA

17th and 19th Brigades, and the never-ending problems of supply. On 1 January 1941, the Western Desert Force became known as XIII Corps.

The Battle of Bardia—3 to 5 January 1941

Unlike the tactics employed at Nibeiwa, the methods chosen by the 6th Australian Division to attack the strong defences at Bardia were devoid of the opportunity of surprise, and followed a more conventional pattern. Unfortunately only 22 Matilda tanks were runners, and these were concentrated in one sector. The tanks needed a way prepared for them through the minefields and across the wide anti-tank ditch, and this was a task that could only be carried out by infantry: it was therefore decided that the 16th Australian Brigade would be followed by the tanks. The infantry assault was preceded by a heavy concentration of artillery fire, after which sappers of the field companies came forward with the men of 16th Brigade to clear the mines, dig out the sharp sides of the ditch, and blow the wire away with 'Bangalore' torpedoes. Six suitable lanes were quickly made, through which the Matildas swiftly passed.

By the evening of 4 January, the defences had been cut in two, and on the morning of 5 January, large numbers of the enemy started to surrender. By the end of that day, resistance had almost ceased, apart from some enemy holding out in the central sector, who were not dealt with until the afternoon of 6 January.

On 5 January, while the clearing up of Bardia was still in progress, the 7th Armoured Division and 19th Australian Brigade, which had been kept back for the purpose, were on their way to cut off Tobruk.

The actual strength of the Bardia garrison was 41,000, of whom over 38,000 were captured, along with 33 coast defence and medium guns, 220 field guns, 26 heavy anti-aircraft guns, 40 light infantry guns, 146 anti-tank guns, more than 120 tanks, and over 700 lorries and soft vehicles. The Commonwealth casualties were around 500, mostly suffered by the Australians, in the rough proportion of three wounded to one killed.

The Advance to and Capture of Tobruk—
6 to 22 January 1941

The Advance 6 to 9 January 1941

By the time the last Italians had surrendered in Bardia on 6 January, the 7th Armoured Division, after sweeping through El Adem, was well on the way to cutting the western approaches to Tobruk. Close behind came the 19th Australian Brigade, which had been kept specially for this purpose, and on 7 January it reached the eastern sector of the Tobruk defences. By 9 January, the whole of the thirty-mile defensive line around Tobruk had been invested. The formations of XIII Corps were sited around these defences with the Support Group of 7th Armoured Division to the west, the 4th Armoured Brigade to the south-west, and the 6th Australian Division to the south and east, stretched from the Tobruk–El Adem road to the sea. The 7th Armoured Brigade was held in reserve to deal with any enemy advance towards Tobruk from the west, and was ready to press on after the capture of the base was completed.

The Assault on Tobruk—21 and 22 January 1941

At Tobruk, the outer perimeter was booby-trapped and mined, with an anti-tank ditch and concrete pill-boxes, but less strong than a main inner ring. However, the distance around the perimeter was greater than at Bardia, with fewer Italian troops in the garrison. So although the defensive siting may have been more formidable, requiring the attackers to break through two lines of well constructed defences, it was more lightly held. In addition, the fact that Bardia had been captured so recently, in spite of promises to hold out forever, did little to improve the morale of the defenders of Tobruk.

The most difficult part of the operation was the clearing of a route through the outer line of defences to enable the remaining Matilda tanks of 7th Royal Tank Regiment, now numbering only 14, to enter. The 16th Australian Brigade was given this task, with the divisional engineers carrying out the same tasks as at Bardia.

The assault was launched in darkness during the early hours of 21 January. The 19th Brigade came through to join the 16th. By mid-day, they had secured a bridgehead some four and a half miles deep into the south-east sector of the defences.

At dawn the next morning, 22 January, the whole of the 61st Division surrendered, and by the middle of the afternoon the battle was over. Some 25,000 prisoners were taken, with more than 200 guns, 87 tanks, and so many soft vehicles that nobody bothered to count them. The Commonwealth casualties were 400: 250 of them in the Australian Division.

As usual, the campaign plans were well laid for the next moves. The 7th Armoured Brigade was already probing west before the capture of Tobruk was completed.

The Advance to Derna and Mechili—22 January to 3 February 1941

The country which XIII Corps was now to enter would become only too familiar to Commonwealth soldiers during the next two years. From the barren sand and rock of the desert rose up the green, cultivated slopes of the Jebel Akhdar, with hills rising in places to 2,000 feet. West of Tobruk, the coastline bulged out into the Mediterranean, and the Jebel filled most of the bulge. At the further side of this prosperous area of Western Cyrenaica, which had been settled by many Italian colonists, lay the sizeable port of Benghazi, a valuable prize, if captured, for an army with so many supply problems. One either side of the Jebel ran two roads of great tactical importance. One ran close to the coast from Tobruk to Gazala, Tmimi, Martuba and Derna, and then turned south-west through the Jebel to Barce and Benghazi. The other started at El Adem and followed the southern edge of the Jebel, before turning south-west to Msus, Antelat, Agedabia and El Agheila. A branch track headed due west from Msus to Soluch, and from there west again to join the coast road south of Benghazi.

The Advance on the Coast Road

The elements of 7th Armoured Division on the coast road made contact with the enemy in the area of Martuba, some ten miles from Derna, and remained there until 19th Australian Brigade was ferried up on 24 January 1941. This brigade was ordered to capture Derna and the high ground around it as soon as possible; the Australian divisional headquarters and another brigade were to move up as soon as there was enough transport available; and the third Australian brigade was to garrison Tobruk and look after prisoners.

Resistance around Derna was fierce, and the Italians took full advantage of the steep hillsides, intercepted by wadis, to fight an infantry delaying action with considerable skill. Progress was slow but on 28 January Derna was captured.

The Advance to Mechili

On 23 January 1941, the 4th Armoured Brigade, with the 11th Hussars moving ahead, advanced to the area north-east of Mechili. Opposition was met from the occupants of the fort and the high ground to the north of it. The decision was made to prevent the garrison leaving their fortified position while extra artillery was brought forward. For various reasons, the armour did not properly cover the tracks leading away to the north and west of Mechili, and during the night of 26/27 January the Italians withdrew unmolested, though followed for a time by elements of 4th Armoured Brigade.

The Interim Period—27 January to 3 February 1941

During the last days of January, plans were made to capture Benghazi by a form of pincer movement. The Australian Division was to keep up the heaviest possible pressure on the enemy in the coastal area, while the 7th Armoured Division advanced from Mechili south-west to Msus.

These plans, intended to come into operation around 10 February, were never to materialise. Evidence started to come in that the Italians were withdrawing completely from Cyrenaica, the first intimation being a sudden slackening of resistance to the western movement of the Australians on 30 and 31 January after their capture of Derna. Air reconnaissance also showed that aircraft were abandoning the few remaining enemy aerodromes, and on 1 February, long columns of transport were spotted moving towards Barce. It rapidly became obvious that to forestall the possibility of a total Italian retreat from Cyrenaica would require much quicker action than that intended to start on 10 February: if the remaining elements of their Tenth Army were to be destroyed they could not be allowed to slip away before XIII Corps could cut them off.

In spite of the risks, it was decided that 7th Armoured Division must set off as quickly as possible to Msus, ideally on 2 or 3 February. The two big question-marks hanging over the operation were the doubtful mechanical condition of the tanks and other vehicles, and the problem of supplying the force with enough petrol as it made a 150-mile dash to the coast. Having decided that the gamble was worth it, the agreement of General Wavell, the Commander-in-Chief, was obtained. Wavell himself came forward to visit XIII Corps headquarters on 4 February, the day on which the armoured division set off on its perilous journey.

In the few days before 4 February, the 4th Armoured Brigade had been strengthened by taking over tanks from the 7th Brigade, the latter being reduced to only one armoured regiment.

The March to the Coast and the Battle of Beda Fomm—4 to 7 February 1941

The March to the Coast

The main body of the 7th Armoured Division was preceded by 'Combeforce', an advance guard of fast moving vehicles under the command of Lieutenant Colonel John Combe of the 11th Hussars. It consisted of armoured cars; field, anti-tank and light anti-aircraft artillery; and a battalion of motorised infantry from the Support Group in the form of the 2nd Battalion The Rifle Brigade. Leaving at dawn on 4 February, the armoured cars reached Msus by the afternoon, and then turned south to head for Antelat. The rest of 'Combeforce' had to move slower, and was not in Msus until early on 5 February. However, it made good progress after that, joining the armoured cars in Antelat during the morning. The whole force turned west and was in position astride the main road from Benghazi, at a point some 30 miles south of Ghemines, at approximately 1 pm. This remarkable feat had entailed covering 150 miles, much of the early section over appalling, unreconnoitred ground, in 30 hours, from 7 am on 4 February.

The 4th Armoured Brigade arrived in the Beda Fomm area between 5 and 6 pm on 5 February, and the divisional headquarters reached Antelat in the early hours of 6 February. 7th Armoured Brigade, now consisting of only 1st Royal Tanks (1 RTR), was held in the same area in reserve. The Support Group moved west from Msus towards Soluch, but met strong opposition around an old fort at Scleidima.

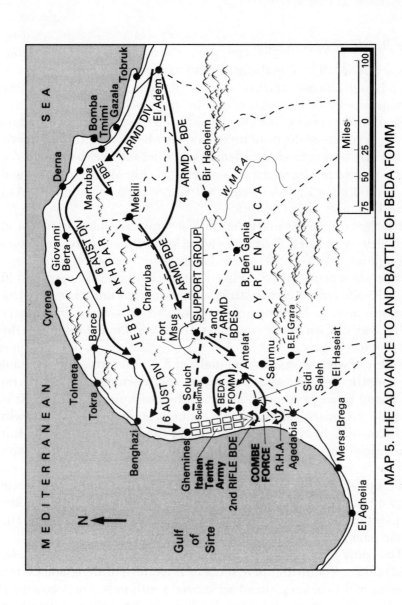

MAP 5. THE ADVANCE TO AND BATTLE OF BEDA FOMM

The switching of the axis of advance of 4th Armoured Brigade from the direction of Soluch down towards Beda Fomm was authorised at this stage.

The Battle of Beda Fomm

Very soon after 'Combeforce' had taken up its position on the main Benghazi road, the first column of the retreating enemy came unconcernedly driving down it. The surprise of finding a British force so unexpectedly blocking its way and the casualties caused by the accurate fire of the armoured cars, put the leading Italian troops off balance and no serious attempt was made to break through the all too thin screen formed by 'Combeforce'. The situation was much improved for the British when the 4th Armoured Brigade arrived at Beda Fomm at about 5.30 pm.

The next day, 6 February, fighting became very much fiercer, and both 4th Armoured Brigade and 'Combeforce' were in action throughout. Many tank battles took place, resulting in a large number of enemy M13s being destroyed, while 4th Armoured Brigade suffered many casualties as well, and at times ran very low in ammunition. The one regiment of 7th Armoured Brigade (1 RTR) was thrown into action at a critical point in the middle of the afternoon.

Fighting went on during the night of 6/7 February, and the final act was the heaviest attack of all on the morning of 7 February. A force of tanks penetrated as far as the headquarters of 2nd Rifle Brigade, on the seaward flank of 'Combeforce', before being brought to a halt with heavy losses, inflicted in the final phase by the last remaining anti-tank gun of the eight that had travelled with Combe.

This proved to be the end, though the sudden appearance of white flags of surrender all along the Italian columns so surprised the British that at first they suspected a trap. By 9 am, however, the whole enemy army had laid down their arms.

The only disappointed members of XIII Corps were the Australians. Following their successful capture of Benghazi on the evening of 6 February, they had started south to be ready to attack the rear of the enemy columns. By 2 pm on 7 February a complete brigade group had reached Ghemines, 30 miles south of Benghazi, only to find the battle was over. Had things not gone so well that morning, it might well have saved the day.

A Triumphal Conclusion

In a period of two months, XIII Corps, no more than two divisions strong, with a total strength of about 31,000 men, had advanced 500 miles, destroyed an Italian army of ten divisions, and captured some 130,000 prisoners, 400 tanks, about 850 guns, and thousands of lorries and other soft vehicles. The Commonwealth losses in men amounted to 500 killed, 1,373 wounded, and 55 missing. Losses of tanks were considerable, as much due to age and rough desert going as to enemy action.

Very shortly after the surrender of the Tenth Army at Beda Fomm on 7 February 1941, a squadron of the 11th Hussars, followed by the Support Group, was on its way south to Agedabia, where the garrison surrendered. The next day, two squadrons of the 11th were on the road to cover a further 60 miles to El Agheila, the fort and barracks on the border between Cyrenaica and Tripolitania. On 9 February, the armoured cars patrolled some ten miles on into Tripolitania.

10

General O'Connor's Conduct of the Campaign

At the start of COMPASS, John Harding, more correctly known in later years as Field Marshal Lord Harding of Petherton, was a Colonel attached to the headquarters of the Western Desert Force as Wavell's personal liaison officer. His task was 'to ensure that the triangular and awkward relationship, Wavell–Wilson–O'Connor, did not get its wires crossed and that all three knew what was in each others minds'.[1] During the campaign, on the departure to Cairo of the previous incumbent, Brigadier Hobday, with laryngitis and dysentery, he became O'Connor's Chief of Staff, or Brigadier General Staff (BGS) as the post was then known. Even after COMPASS ended, he stressed when talking about it that its success was entirely due to O'Connor. Wavell certainly instigated the enterprise and gave him support, and nobody was more conscious of this than O'Connor himself, but the real credit was his alone. Harding stressed his own debt to the lessons taught him by O'Connor in the desert when, forty years later, he gave the address at his memorial service:

> As I knew him in that campaign, Dick was my ideal of a commander in battle; always approachable and ready to listen, yet firm and decisive and always fair in his judgement of people and events; modest to a degree, shunning the limelight, and embarrassed by praise; calmly resolute and courageously determined. I can honestly say that such success as I have had in life is largely due to all I learnt from him and to his example.[2]

Throughout the course of the operations, the tactics to be used against the enemy were an important preoccupation of O'Connor's ever active mind, but even more pressing was the matter of supply.

He would have agreed wholeheartedly with the thesis propounded by his Commander-in-Chief in his lecture at Trinity College, Cambridge, just before the outbreak of war, that 'administration ... is the real crux of generalship'. In support of this Wavell quoted the words of Socrates, who began his comments on the subject: 'The general must know how to get his men their rations and every other kind of stores needed for war.'[3] Throughout the whole of his desert campaign, O'Connor would be occupied with the ceaseless struggle to provide those 'stores needed for war'.

The manner in which he tackled the problem developed from the setting up of Forward Supply Depots (FSDs), Numbers 3 and 4, so far in front of the main British positions that they were in 'no-mans land' between the rival forces. Of this bold but risky venture Brigadier Barclay suggests 'that it was a decision which very few commanders would have made'.[4] Fortunately, as he then goes on: 'General O'Connor's judgement in weighing the capabilities of his Italian opponents, and calculating the risks which could be taken invariably proved correct.' Fully conscious of the vital part they were playing, O'Connor frequently visited his administrative units to praise them and encourage them to even greater efforts.

The completion of 'Training Exercise No. 1' did not mean the end of training during the fortnight before 'Exercise No. 2'. Vehicles, especially the tanks, were restricted in movement to conserve fuel and track life, but the infantry were practised again and again in their roles. O'Connor constantly referred to the importance of training, and this included commanders and staffs, particularly in communications, as well as the fighting troops. His own experiences as a signals officer and staff officer in the First World War had shown him how wrong battles could go if staff work and communications were faulty.

A reflection of his own long study and practice of his profession is the brilliant report which he wrote on the campaign when he had become a prisoner of war. The story of how this was smuggled out comes in a later chapter. An essential quality in a great commander is the possession of a highly trained mind. O'Connor's narrative, which will be quoted frequently in this chapter, is astonishingly accurate for a document composed entirely from memory. It demonstrates his complete mastery of every stage of the campaign, and is a model of clarity.

Although the operation was planned as a five day raid, the possibility of extending it, if the first attacks were successful, was suggested in a signal from Churchill to Wavell on 26 November 1940, containing the sentence: 'If success is achieved, presume you have plans for exploiting it to the full.'[5] There is little doubt that Wavell must have had such ideas in mind, but it was not until 28 November that he told Wilson, in his last written directive before the operation, that this was now official policy. He wrote:

> I know that you have in mind and are planning the fullest possible exploitation of an initial success of 'Compass' operation. You and all commanders in the Western Desert may rest assured that the boldest action, whatever its results will have the support not only of myself but of the CIGS and of the War Cabinet at home.[6]

Though O'Connor was no doubt delighted at the prospect, and it can be assumed had himself given it more than a passing thought, the administrative difficulties once again loomed large. FSDs Nos. 3 and 4 held only five days' supplies. He wrote in his report:

> This it will be noted was in accordance with the Commander-in-Chief's original instructions, that the operation was to last five days. A few days before the operation started, a further order was received from GHQ to the effect that we were to be prepared administratively to exploit further. It was impossible with such short notice for the dumps to be increased, so all that could be done was to think out arrangements for bringing up supplies as quickly as possible after the battle had started.[7]

Throughout the preparatory phase, the security measures already described worked without a hitch. The troops still thought that Training Exercise No. 2 was simply what it was called until the last moment, but more surprisingly the 'cohorts' of journalists, the spies, and the miscellaneous agents in Cairo and Alexandria, had no inkling either. Even the Egyptian Prime Minister, Sirry, who prided himself on having 'sources who keep me informed of all that goes on', was to admit his ignorance in due course to Wavell and to congratulate him 'on being the first to keep a secret in Cairo'.[8]

On 4 December, a conference was held at GHQ in Cairo attended by Wilson, O'Connor, Harding, Galloway and Dorman-Smith. Following it, O'Connor moved back to Maaten Baggush, taking with him liaison officers from the Navy and RAF. It was decided that, when the offensive started, he would move forward to a suitable battle headquarters and that Wilson would come up to Maaten Baggush, accompanied by a liaison Officer from GHQ.

The co-operation of the Navy and RAF was essential for the

important tasks described earlier. The method by which this co-operation was ensured is described in O'Connor's report:

> As regards the system of command. I was to retain command of the actual troops taking part. General Wilson was to take over headquarters at Maaten Baggush, when I moved to my advanced headquarters. Air Commodore Collishaw, commanding No. 202 group RAF also remaining at his present headquarters at Maaten Baggush for the operations. General Wilson was therefore in a position to deal directly with Head-quarters RAF, Headquarters British Troops Egypt [his own main base] in Cairo, and the Navy through Alexandria.[9]

The system of command worked very smoothly throughout the whole campaign in relation to the other Services, but within the Army framework there were difficulties at a later stage, caused by its somewhat top-heavy nature.

To provide Collishaw with enough aircraft to play his vital part in the desert campaign was a major problem for the Air Officer Commanding-in-Chief, Air Marshal Longmore. 'Only by stripping air defences in the rest of his command to an alarming degree, could he manage to accept even a portion of the responsibilities which were to be asked of him.' By denuding Aden, the Sudan, and the Egyptian Delta of virtually all air cover he eventually contrived to provide two squadrons of Hurricanes and one of Gladiators as a fighter component of 48 aircraft. A bomber strength of 116 was raised, made up of three squadrons of Blenheims, three of Wellingtons and one of Bombays. Through an air liaison officer, an army/air component was placed directly under O'Connor's command. This consisted of two squadrons, with an extra flight, of mixed fighter and reconnaissance planes. These gave him essential and immediate information on enemy movements, and were of immense value to him both before and during the battle.[10]

The main cause of Longmore's struggle to find sufficient aircraft for Collishaw was his constant withdrawal of squadrons to send to Greece. As the 'shadow of Greece' hung over the whole of O'Connor's operations, and frequently affected the decisions of his superiors, it must be described in some detail.

The Tragic Greek Campaign

On 28 October 1940, Mussolini sent an ultimatum to the Greeks which was promptly rejected by President Metaxas. The Italian invasion which followed was fiercely resisted, and the Greeks drove the more numerous invaders back across their frontier, and a long distance into Albania. British air squadrons were quickly sent to assist their new ally against the Axis, but only ground troops to service the aircraft. This was the first loss of air power from the possible support of a desert campaign.

The success of the Greeks in defeating the Italians on their north-west frontier brought fears of attack by a much more formidable enemy lying to the north-east. The Germans had occupied Romania in October, and were preparing to enter Bulgaria. The danger that they might sweep south into Greece in support of their Italian allies became apparent, giving rise to differing emotions in London and Cairo. To Churchill, inspired by the Greek resistance, came thoughts of tackling the Germans in the Balkans, bringing Yugoslavia and Turkey into the war as well, and so attacking the 'soft-underbelly of the Axis'. To the Commanders-in-Chief in the Middle East it brought little but worry. The Royal Navy feared a threat to the port of Salonika and its control of the Eastern Mediterranean, while the Army and Royal Air Force foresaw even more strain on their slender resources of men and equipment in the event of action in Greece.

The possibility of despatching further troops to Greece was discussed from November 1940 onwards, with varying degrees of intensity. Its influence on O'Connor's movements was considerable. Throughout the campaign, his plans were always liable to dislocation by the withdrawal of men and equipment for Greece, or the threat to take them away. The effects were felt from the beginning: he recorded that 'certain squadrons of the RAF which were to have been available for the Western Desert were now deflected to Greece, similarly anti-aircraft batteries, which would have been of great value to us, were sent to the same destination'.[11] Much of the captured Italian transport was also sent off on the same route, though urgently needed by its captors. To put it mildly, the desert army could hardly look on the Greek venture with favour, even at an early stage. At the end of operations, as will be shown later, the result of sending help to the Greeks was as disastrous to O'Connor's corps as it was to the unfortunate force ordered to carry out the task. Its fate must be briefly related. As the probability of German intervention grew stronger during December 1940 and early January 1941, British preoccupation with Greece increased in proportion. On 13 January, Wavell flew to Athens and offered more

British troops, but General Metaxas refused to take them. When Metaxas suddenly died on 29 January his successor, Mr Koryzis, and the Commander-in-Chief, General Papagos, decided that they would ask for help if and when the Germans actually moved into Bulgaria. There is not room here to describe all the 'to-ings and fro-ings' that followed between London, Cairo, and Athens, while the question of the wisdom of the venture will be discussed later. The bare bones of the story are that the Germans entered Bulgaria on 25 February; Commonwealth troops sailed for Greece on 5 March; the Germans invaded on 6 April; and on 21 April after a gallant, but hopeless, short fight the decision was made to withdraw the Commonwealth troops. The withdrawal was carried out between 24 and 30 March: practically all the heavy equipment taken by the force was lost, and 12,000 of the 60,000 men sent were left behind as prisoners of war.

To return to the beginning of December 1940, O'Connor received his final official orders on the evening of 5 December, and gave out his own the following day. On Friday 6 December the approach march began.

The Approach March

By the evening of 7 December, all units had completed the first stage of their westward movement, and were in a concentration area. Although O'Connor had little to do himself in connection with this move, he had two major preoccupations. One was his usual concern with supply, the other was the forward thinking necessary to have a clear idea of the action he would take to follow up the successful capture of Sidi Barrani, so that it could be exploited to the full.

The daylight move to the next concentration area 15 miles from the Enba gap was risky. However, as O'Connor recorded, luck was on his side:

> Sunday, December 8th dawned with poor visibility, which fortunately for us tended to increase as the day went on. An enemy reconnaissance aircraft was, however, observed high up about noon. It was hoped that if anything peculiar had been noticed no action would result for another 48 hours. This actually was the case.[12]

Wilson had by now moved up to Maaten Baggush and, on the night of 7 December, O'Connor had moved his headquarters forward to a point, soon to be known as Piccadilly Circus. This lay on the top of the escarpment about 50 miles west of the Matruh–Siwa road, above and behind where his forces were concentrating in the plain below.

In the moonlight, for which the night of 8/9 December had been chosen, 'the last phase of the approach march was carried out without a hitch, all units taking up their allotted position by 1 a.m.'[13] O'Connor went on to praise the work of the staffs of 7th Armoured and 4th Indian Divisions, who had fitted so many tanks, guns and other vehicles into their correct positions around the Enba gap.

The First Battles—9–11 December 1940: Capture of the Fortified Camps

As soon as it was clear that the attacks on the camps had been launched successfully O'Connor was on the move.

> I had formed a small operational Headquarters at the junction of the Sidi Barrani–Enba track and the escarpment, and had driven down past Nibeiwa to Tummar, where I was lucky enough to meet General Beresford-Peirse, commanding the 4th Indian Division, just at the moment when the enemy counter-attack had been repulsed. He was able to give me the full situation, and I gave him personal orders to push on the next day to Sidi Barrani. I had no information of importance from the Matruh Column at that time.

> On my way to see General Beresford-Peirse I called in at Headquarters 7th Armoured Division and saw Brigadier Caunter, who was commanding in place of General Creagh, who was ill. I learned the latest news from him and was very pleased with the excellent progress made. The Armoured Division had carried out its instructions to the letter. The Support Group had been left to prevent any interference from the Sofafi Groups, whilst the 4th Armoured Brigade and the 11th Hussars were protecting the western flank of the troops attacking Nibeiwa and Tummar, and had pushed patrols across the Sidi Barrani–Sollum Road and on towards the sea.

> The 7th Armoured Brigade remained in Reserve covering the Enba gap. I ordered Brigadier Caunter to send a force to patrol round to the west of the Sofafi Group of encampments, as I wanted to ensure that the garrisons did not escape.

> I also suggested sending a responsible staff officer to the Headquarters 4th Indian Division who would be in a position to arrange any local points between the two Divisions, which was mutually agreed upon.[14]

In Correlli Barnett's words:

> The commanders now saw O'Connor for the first time in the role of a leader on the battlefield. The quietness, the deep thought had given way to bristling energy and crisp decision ... he ranged the battlefield in his staff car, the wound-up spring that kept the battle swiftly rolling.[15]

Operations on 10 December 1940

Two occurrences on 10 December were to spoil the pattern of complete success achieved in the opening phase. One was the advance of 16th British Infantry Brigade, getting ahead of its artillery support in the action against the Blackshirt Division on the outskirts of Sidi Barrani, and suffering a severe mauling; the other was the failure of the 8th Hussars to block the Italian escape routes from the Rabia and Sofafi camps, thus allowing the garrisons to slip away to the north during the night of 10 December.

O'Connor's annoyance at the failure of the 8th Hussars was intense, and reinforced his opinion that British armoured troops were not good enough at night work. This was a theme to which he would refer more than once again.

Throughout 10 December, reports on the progress of the operations were being sent back through Wilson at Maaten Baggush to Wavell in Cairo, and hence on to London in a succession of telegrams to Dill. Churchill, bursting with enthusiasm, allowed the wish to become father of the fact, and announced the arrival of troops on the shore near Buq Buq a day in advance of the actual achievement!

Events on 11 December 1940

The annoyance caused to O'Connor by the news of the escape of the Sofafi and Rabia garrisons was a small matter compared with the major blow received on the morning of 11 December. He decided to leave his own advanced headquarters early to visit General Beresford-Peirse, who was now based at a point two or three miles south of Sidi Barrani.

> Before starting, however, I received a most unwelcome piece of news, namely that the 4th Indian Division was to be withdrawn as early as possible for service in the Sudan. I had received no warning of this whatever, and consequently had made no plans to meet such a con-

tingency. Its withdrawal at this juncture would produce a difficult situation.[16]

The only person in Egypt, other than Wavell himself, who had known about the possibility of this move was Wilson, and he had been told in the strictest secrecy.

On 2 December, Wavell had held a meeting in Cairo at which were present General Platt and General Cunningham, commanders respectively of forces in the Sudan and Kenya. Platt was told that the 4th Italian Division would move to join him about the middle of December, the exact date depending on how the desert offensive progressed, and the availability of shipping.

Wavell planned to replace the Indian Division with the 6th Australian Division, one brigade as quickly as possible, and the others by the end of December. Because of the imprecise nature of the factors which would control the exact date of withdrawal, he knew that the decision would have to be made at short notice, and therefore the fewer who knew about it the better. He did not tell the Prime Minister what was in his mind, knowing the latter's penchant for giving not entirely wanted operational advice.

Before looking at the effect of this removal of the 4th Indian Division on O'Connor's immediate problems, there are conflicting views to examine about the correctness or otherwise of Wavell's strategy in this respect. His own reasoning was explained at the end of the war in a letter to O'Connor written on 27 June 1945:

> I am not quite sure whether you ever realised the necessity for the withdrawal of the 4th Indian Division immediately after Sidi Barrani. It was a matter of shipping; a convoy had come into Suez, and I could use some of the returning ships to carry part of the Division to Port Sudan, the only means by which I could get the Division complete in the Sudan by the time I had fixed as the latest favourable date for attacking the Italians ... with my limited resources I had to decide either to remain entirely on the defensive in the Sudan for some time to come, or to accept the delay in the pursuit in the Western Desert while the Australian Division relieved the Indian. My decision was a difficult one, but I am sure it was right.[17]

Others support this view, the general line of their reasoning being that the Indian Division was more suitably trained for Platt's operations from the Sudan into Abyssinia than the Australians, and would be more at home in the conditions likely to be encountered there. Furthermore, it must be remembered, as Lord Carver has pointed out, that

O'Connor's operation had been planned by Wavell as a limited one: to destroy the Italian army which had crossed the Libyan frontier in September, and was only expected to last five days. It would ensure that Wavell's main base in Egypt was made secure, while he dealt with the Italians in East Africa. Although the delay imposed by the change-over was frustrating to O'Connor, it is unlikely that it made any significant difference to the campaign.[18]

Other opinions have been voiced along the same lines. John Connell states in his biography of Wavell already quoted:

> since Major-General I G Mackay's 6th Australian Division replaced, brigade by brigade, the departing exultant (but much mystified) 4th Indian Division, there was no immediate ill effect on the conduct of the campaign, for all the troops involved had been thoroughly trained in desert warfare....[19]

Brigadier Barclay brings in both sides of the argument. He starts by saying:

> If we examine what actually happened as a result of this decision, it would seem that no great harm resulted. General O'Connor was not thereby denied a highly successful campaign. Within two months he had consummated his early victory by completely destroying an Italian army of ten Divisions, at a cost of less than 2,000 casualties. It is hardly conceivable that he could have improved on this performance whatever the circumstances. Looked at from this point of view, it would appear that General Wavell's decision—although it must have been a bitter blow to General O'Connor at the time—was a wise and courageous one when judged by events. He got his victory in North Africa—albeit three weeks later than it might have been—and he was also able to place the 4th Indian Division where he wanted it—in the Sudan.
>
> It is however, possible to take a different view in this highly controversial matter. It can be argued that if General O'Connor could have completed his campaign three weeks earlier—which would have been possible but for the withdrawal of this Division—it would have been easier to have persuaded the Government to permit the XIII Corps to continue the advance to Tripoli. It may be that this is so, but it is not certain. There are many indications that some time before this the Government had decided that it was only necessary to make Egypt 'safe' as a preliminary to an expedition to Greece. If this was the case, there was no point in advancing beyond Benghazi.[20]

In his own account of events, O'Connor wrote that the withdrawal produced a difficult situation, and then went on to explain that:

The situation in the battle area would become equally serious, as the 4th Indian Division transport was up to establishment and, by dumping stores of ammunition, had frequently been used for special purposes. This windfall would, therefore, no longer be available. The Reserve Mechanical Transport Companies also, which had done so well in the battle, had received casualties in men and vehicles, and were urgently required for bringing forward supplies, to replenish the dumps which had now fallen to two days reserve.

The situation was further greatly complicated by the large number of prisoners captured, now amounting to 20,000, who had all to be fed, watered, and guarded, and eventually brought back to Matruh. At the moment, however, there was no transport under my command available for ferrying purposes, and transport was required simultaneously for carrying back the 4th Indian Division, and the prisoners, and for carrying forward the 6th Australian Division. The situation, without a relief impending, from the administrative point of view was extremely difficult.[21]

These problems were to cause O'Connor many headaches in the following three weeks, but they did not deter him from moving on to the next phase, the advance to Bardia, immediately Sidi Barrani had been successfully captured. Some commentators have suggested that as he had fulfilled the requirements of the 'five-day raid' so completely, and had destroyed the Italian army which had invaded Egypt, he would have been within his rights to have withdrawn his troops to their start positions and 'rested on his laurels'. Apart from this being out of keeping with his own character, it would not have been allowed by Wavell, who, in his turn, was under constant pressure from Churchill to press on further. On 12 December, Wavell flew up to Wilson's headquarters and discussed plans with him and O'Connor, reporting back to London that evening;

Meanwhile mobile column of Armoured Division will advance to Sollum–Capuzzo and endeavour to get across Tobruk road and cut off Bardia. If Bardia falls quickly, though I think this is unlikely, I have instructed O'Connor that he can push on towards Tobruk up to the limit of endurance of vehicles and men....[22]

The Approach to and Capture of Bardia— 12 December 1940 to 5 January 1941

On 14 December, the Indian Division started on its way back to the Delta, having completed the capture of Sidi Barrani and spent a day helping to 'tidy-up' the battlefield. O'Connor was full of praise for 'the 4th Indian Division in general and General Beresford-Peirse in particular, whose drive and leadership was mainly responsible for the operations being brought so quickly to a successful conclusion'.[23]

On the night of 15/16 December, O'Connor was once again annoyed to find that units of 7th Armoured Brigade had allowed enemy troops to slip past them at night and reach the safety of the defences of Bardia. It took a long time for armoured regiments to break with the pre-war training which had frowned on night work for tanks, regarding the hours of darkness as sacrosanct for feeding men and maintaining and refuelling vehicles. O'Connor recorded his opinion of these customs:

> I feel that this question of preventing the movement of enemy columns at night must be tackled. I think the main difficulty arises from the fact that our training suggests that armoured units should not be used at night, and I have noted a distinct disinclination of tank units to be used in any such capacity. I have a strong feeling that the real objection is due to a lack of decentralization as regards maintenance and messing—in particular below a squadron basis. In the case of the 11th Hussars, I have met no disinclination. This unit decentralized its messing down to single cars, and was constantly employed at night.[24]

The Italian force in Bardia consisted of the 1st and 2nd Blackshirt Division, the 62nd Marmarica with some parts of the 63rd Cirene and 64th Catanzaro Divisions, and the original fortress troops along with the frontier guards from the wire. General Bergonzoli, known as 'Barba Elettrica' or 'Electric Whiskers' was in command, and, on being encouraged by Mussolini to stand faithfully to the last, at whatever cost, had replied: 'In Bardia we are and here we stay'. Although he had a dozen M13 tanks and many useless L3s as well, the main strength of his force lay in 300 medium and field guns, plus 100 light pieces, handled by artillerymen who, as always, were the finest of the Italian soldiers.

Wavell flew up from Cairo early on the morning of 16 December to see O'Connor and General Creagh, who was now back in command of 7th Armoured Division. That evening, he sent a signal to Dill in which the first paragraph explained the possible courses of action:

A P Wavell to CIGS.   16th December, 1940

> Immediate problem is how to deal with Bardia. We can (a) try to induce garrison to surrender, (b) cut it off from Tobruk and lay siege to it, (c) leave road to Tobruk open though under observation and if enemy withdraws by it attack him in the open.[25]

The enemy dispositions soon made it clear to O'Connor that Wavell's course (b) was necessary. At this stage, his tank strength had become much reduced. 7th Royal Tank Regiment had only 25 'Matildas' running, and the armoured division was down to 70 Cruiser and 120 light tanks. His narrative, which explains all the considerations he had had to take into account in great detail, demonstrates once again the extraordinary clarity of mind of a commander who could write it from memory in the most difficult circumstances well after the action had taken place. His long description of the planning stage, followed by a detailed account of the battle itself and its successful outcome, ends with the following paragraphs:

> It is interesting to compare the tactics employed in the Sidi Barrani battle and those at Bardia. In each case, the most important part was the entry of the 'I' Tanks within the perimeter. After that it was all fairly plain sailing. At Nibeiwa it was impossible to carry out an Infantry attack without surprise being given away, owing to the distance that both the Infantry and the Artillery were from their objective, so it was necessary for the tanks to precede the Infantry and force their way into the camp, at a point where patrol and photographic reconnaissance showed to be the most favourable area. This was successful, but with the loss of a number of tanks from mines. At Bardia, however, surprise, except in methods of attack, did not come into it. Also it was known to be strong—particularly the front line defences, which were concrete in many places, with a strong mine defence. The answer, therefore, appeared to be a successful Infantry attack against those defences, followed by the tanks passing over the anti-tank ditch and through a mine-cleared area across the perimeter. As soon as the area was selected, the Infantry attack was easy to arrange. The Infantry taking part was close up against its objective, and a very heavy concentration of guns could be put down on the area selected. The time, the area selected and the method of attack employed caused the surprise.

> Actually, the enemy was greatly surprised that the attack took place as early as it did, which fortunately enabled us to save much material, including water plant, from demolition.

> I was much struck by the excellence of the Staff of the 6th Australian Division and by the determination of its commander, Major General

Mackay. Throughout he showed himself to be the right man in the right place, and his Division thoroughly deserved its success.[26]

O'Connor had met Mackay at an earlier date in Palestine. He also knew the senior divisional staff officer, Colonel Berryman, from the days when the latter was a student at the Staff College in 1927. Important though these contacts were, his impact on the Australians went much deeper than mere surface goodwill. Some indication of the esteem in which he was held can be gauged from this extract from a letter written after the war by Gavin Long, the compiler of the Australian official war history:

> General O'Connor's comments are most encouraging; sometimes, I fear, over-kind. He himself, of course, won over the Australians as few others have done; perhaps, in World War II, as no other UK or Allied commander did. It is a great pity from our point of view that the association was so brief....

> General O'Connor's vignettes of the Senior Australians are most interesting—remarkable that he was able to see them so clearly in so short an acquaintance. The remarks about Mackay are specially interesting; but if General O'Connor had read the section on Greece he probably would not think that, over all, Mackay had been too faintly praised. It was only in Greece that those round Mackay realised the great qualities of mind and character possessed by their shy, bleak, sometimes fussy and pedantic commander; O'Connor saw them from the outset.[27]

On 1 January 1941, the Western Desert Force was renamed XIII Corps. At this stage, O'Connor was still under command of Wilson, who had by now moved back from Maaten Baggush to his proper headquarters in Cairo. He had, however, left an advanced headquarters at Baggush to assist in the control of XIII Corps' lines of communication. Although this did relieve O'Connor's staff of some problems, it created others. On more than one occasion, the wrong supplies came forward from the rear depots. Getting priorities right was essential when reserves in the forward areas were down to only two or three days requirements, and O'Connor emphasised several times that he alone knew the likely course of operations from day to day. He insisted that, in a fast moving campaign, control of priorities had to be in the hands of the corps commander.

Though excessive heat is the discomfort usually thought of in connection with the desert, it was very cold when the Australians launched their attack on Bardia on 3 January, and everyone was grateful for the recently issued sleeveless leather jerkins. In Barrie Pitt's words—the weather was vile.

> Records for the district are hard to come by, but local memory united in agreeing that the winter of 1940/1941 was the worst in recall. Rain fell in unremembered quantities, cold and with traces of sleet, filling the slit trenches with gritty slop and turning the powdered clay which had been mistaken for sand to glue; yet when the rain stopped and the icy wind continued, as it did all the time, it still managed to scrape up genuine sand to sting exposed hands and faces, and at times to turn the greyness into yellow fog.[28]

Following O'Connor's instructions, elements of the 7th Armoured Division were on their way towards Tobruk, even before the final surrender of all the defenders of Bardia.

The Advance to and Capture of Tobruk— 6 to 22 January 1941

As explained in the previous chapter, the long defensive perimeter around Tobruk was completely invested by 9 January 1941. Though he fretted at the delay, O'Connor realised that supply and transport difficulties prevented an immediate assault on the enemy. He set 20 January as the date for this to take place, though in the end it went in a day later.

During the two weeks that the troops on the ground were gathering the ammunition and equipment needed for the attack, and cobbling together their armoured vehicles once again, there was much telegraphic traffic between Wavell in Cairo and the Prime Minister and CIGS in London about strategic priorities. This was one of the periods of intense concern with possible operations in Greece, Churchill at this juncture being much in favour. He sent a minute to the Chief of Staffs Committee of 6 January:

> Although perhaps by luck and daring we may collect comparatively easily most delectable prizes on the Libyan shore, the massive importance of ... keeping the Greek front in being must weigh hourly with us.[29]

Wavell and Air Marshal Longmore were not, at this stage, in favour of dissipating their forces by sending men, aircraft and equipment to Greece, and were reluctant to carry out all the instructions reaching them from London. Ordered on 9 January by the Chief of the Air Staff to cut support to XIII Corps and send five squadrons of fighters and bombers to Greece, Longmore in fact sent two, as

Wavell notified the CIGS on 9 January in a telegram in which he insisted that:

> We must however continue our advance in Cyrenaica while we have Italians on the run and this will help Greeks indirectly more than sending small additional amount of transport that might be spared if we halted, quite apart from moral effect on our own and Italian troops of such action...'[30]

However, under pressure from Churchill, Wavell announced on 10 January that he would fly to Athens to see President Metaxas, probably on 13 or 14 January.

As already recounted, General Metaxas, the Prime Minister and virtual dictator of Greece, at this stage refused further offers of British support. So, for the time being, operations in the Desert once again became top priority in the Mediterranean theatre.

At some date before Wavell flew to Greece, O'Connor returned from the front to see him. In his own words:

> Sometime in the second week of January, I flew into Cairo and attended a conference at GHQ. General Wavell, the Air Officer Commander-in-Chief and Brigadier Galloway, the Brigadier, General Staff, British Troops in Egypt, being present. When asked what my proposals were after the fall of Tobruk, I said I considered the occupation of Mechili of great importance, as it immediately caused a threat to the enemy positions in the hilly coastal belt. General Wavell agreed and asked me to come and see him the next day. At this meeting he discussed with me the possibility of a raid on Benghazi, and asked me to study an 'appreciation' he had had prepared on the subject. I was very much in favour of an advance on Benghazi myself, but would have preferred it to have been of a more permanent character than a raid. However, I was delighted to think that there was a possibility of an attempt of some sort being made.[31]

Problems now arose over the command structure controlling XIII Corps. At the bottom of the difficulties was the large figure of General Maitland Wilson. Although he and O'Connor were old acquaintances, who had known and liked each other for twenty years or more, there is no doubt that 'Jumbo' Wilson's mind moved much slower than O'Connor's or Wavell's. The fact that his headquarters was interposed between Wavell's and XIII Corps was a constant source of friction, though O'Connor was always loyal to Wilson and wrote in his campaign narrative: 'General Wilson was also most helpful whenever I saw him, and I am very grateful to him for his sound advice.'[32] The only glimpse he would ever give of his truer feelings was a comment about Wilson many years later, when the latter had become a peer and had reached the highest rank in the Army: 'I dont really know why he ever became a Field-Marshal.'[33]

What brought matters to a head was confusion over the advance to Benghazi, coupled with the fact that Wavell was starting to by-pass Wilson's headquarters and deal with O'Connor direct.

Although he had told Wilson about the plans for Benghazi, O'Connor was much perplexed to receive instructions from head-quarters British Troops Egypt to the effect that no advance in that direction was to be considered. He took action swiftly:

> As this was completely at variance with what General Wavell had told me, I wired BTE for an explanation and received an answer that the Benghazi project was not being proceeded with. I wrote in and said that I should like to see the C-in-C on the subject, as I found it difficult to carry on with the different policies and I would like to know how I stood.[34]

Wavell, accompanied by Sandy Galloway from BTE, quickly flew up to Gambut to put matters straight with O'Connor. The latter was directed to prepare plans for an advance on Benghazi after the fall of Tobruk, and it was also decided that in future XIII Corps would operate directly under GHQ Middle East, cutting out Wilson's headquarters as a link in the claim of command. O'Connor recorded that 'This period of working directly under GHQ was the most effective and happiest time of my command.'[35]

It also made good sense to Wilson, who was already assembling equipment for the force which might have to be sent to Greece, and was fully occupied in making plans to meet that eventuality should it arise.

While the preparations for the assault on Tobruk continued—preparing gun positions, storing ammunition, and patrolling aggressively to confuse the garrison—a new factor emerged in the balance of forces in the Mediterranean theatre: the arrival of the German *Luftwaffe*. The Navy was to suffer most at the hands of this new adversary in the early days. On 10 January, units of *Fliegerkorps X* from its bases in Sicily severely mauled a British convoy near Malta. As far as XIII Corps' operations on land were concerned, the Germans had little effect, but their mine-laying from the air in the coastal area had a considerable nuisance value and made the use of supply ships somewhat precarious. This was unfortunate for the Royal Air Force, who had hoped to make better use of cargo ships to bring up bombs and petrol in bulk. On the other hand, the German preoccupation with operations over the sea left No 202 Group a free hand to continue its close support of the army, and its almost total destruction of the Italian *Regia Aeronantica*.[36]

The successful completion of the attack on Tobruk on 22 January brought generous praise from Churchill to Wavell.

Prime Minister to A P Wavell   23rd January, 1941

I again send you my most heartfelt congratulations on the third of the brilliant victories which have, in little more than six weeks, transformed the situation in the Middle East, and have sensibly affected the movement of the whole war.

The daring and scope of the original conception, the perfection of staff work and execution have raised the reputation of the British and Australian Army and its leadership, and will long be regarded as models of the military art.

Will you please convey those expressions in which the war cabinet and, I doubt not, Parliament would most cordially associate themselves to Air Chief Marshall Longmore and Air Commodore Collishaw and to Generals Wilson, O'Connor, Mackay and Creagh.

I shall be making a further statement on these lines before long.[37]

One of the major problems following this 'third brilliant victory' was the collection of a further 27,000 prisoners, bringing the total taken in the forty-five days since 9 December to over 100,000, or more than three times O'Connor's own strength at its peak. It would be a long time before his rear areas would be cleared of this burden.

Above all, Tobruk provided a base for the next advance westward towards Benghazi, the move which had been so much in O'Connor's mind since first discussed with Wavell:

For O'Connor was on edge with the desire to get on, to win final victory, before Greece and German intervention broke his run of success. This anxiety bred another—the anxiety over supply and transport that nagged at him continuously. Yet, by his energy and aggression and his gift of leadership, he kept the whole rickety, improvised campaign rolling forward on the heels of the demoralised Italians. It took everything he had to give. In his own words:

'There was really no time for any relaxation, other than sleeping, during this short campaign. I was constantly seeing and talking to the formation commanders, staff officers and officers of the services: talking to the fighting troops, or encouraging the administrative services to further efforts.'[38]

Being the man he was, he told nobody, apart from his immediate staff, that he was in considerable discomfort from a stomach complaint, nor did he let this prevent him driving himself as hard as he drove his corps. He told Roberts on one occasion that at times the discomfort made it hard to sleep, but that during such sleepless periods some of his best ideas came to him.

The Advance to Derna and Mechili— 22 January to 3 February 1941

The assessment of the remaining Italian strength in Cyrenaica after the fall of Tobruk was that there remained of General Tellera's Tenth Army the 60th Division, less a regiment, around Derna; an armoured brigade commanded by General Babini with 60 to 70 tanks at Mechili, along with the detached regiment from 60th Division; and the 17th and 27th Divisions further west. The dispersion was such that the separate elements of the Tenth Army invited destruction in detail.

O'Connor recorded in his own report that patrols of 7th Armoured Division had been sent out while Tobruk was under attack to probe as far as Gazala, Tmimi, and Bomba to the north, and south to Mechili, which was found to be strongly held.

Although the opening of the port of Tobruk would soon be a great help, the further west XIII Corps pushed, the more O'Connor's supply difficulties grew, and at this stage they were becoming acute. This no doubt prompted him to choose this point in his narrative to explain further the problems which faced his supply organisation, and also to praise those whose efforts just managed to overcome them:

I would like to say one word here on the magnificent work of the Transport Companies. Frequently new to the desert, they would nevertheless deliver their loads at the FSD, and return to the base for more—often a five days round journey. Of those I must make special mention of No. 4 New Zealand Reserve Mechanical Transport Company, whose work throughout the operations was outstanding. In front of the FSD the Divisional Supply Columns delivered to units, and I can say with certainty that I have never met a more efficient body of men than those in the 7th Armoured Division Royal Army Service Corps. They never failed the troops on any occasion, and in spite of every difficulty, such as execrable going and continual dust storms, their maintenance was kept up to a very high state of efficiency at all times, and this efficiency was fully appreciated by all the other units of the division, who depended on them for their supplies.[39]

In connection with the operational activities of the various formations under his command in the days immediately following the fall of Tobruk, O'Connor discovered the presence of a considerable enemy armoured force holding the fort near Mechili:

> As soon as I learned of the situation and the approximate position of this detachment of the enemy, I felt that by its isolated position it offered the possibility of defeat in detail, as it was out of supporting distance of the main position.
>
> I discussed the situation with General Creagh and told him what was in my mind, and impressed on him the necessity of preventing the enemy escaping.[40]

O'Connor was surprised to receive the report of A Squadron of the 11th Hussars on the night of 26 January that a column of Italian vehicles had been spotted in the foothills of the Jebel twenty-five miles north of Mechili. Surprise turned to anger when reports from 7th Armoured Brigade arrived on the morning of 27 January to say that Mechili was empty: all enemy troops had slipped away during the night and so evaded the units of 4th Armoured Brigade which had been given the task of stopping them.

General Creagh was very disappointed at the failure of his division, but pointed out the problems which partly accounted for it: bad maps, shortage of fuel, and the existence of a very steep wadi running north out of Mechili, which was at places impassable for armour.

O'Connor could not entirely accept these excuses, but returned to the charge made twice before, his assertion that there was a 'disinclination of armoured forces to take any action at night'. He pointed out: 'If the Italians were able to move their tanks away at night, I see no reason why we should not have been able to operate ours.'[41]

Caunter's 4th Armoured Brigade did attempt to pursue the Italians on 27 and 28 January through the wooded, rocky Jebel along a rough road not shown on any British map, but the bad going caused many breakdowns, and heavy rain turned the ground into red mud. On 29 January, the pursuit was called off, and the armour returned to Mechili.

The next day, O'Connor sent a letter to Creagh, which, although couched in relatively gentle terms, can have left him in no doubt as to the error of his ways. It began:

My dear Dickie,   H.Q. 13th Corps,
                                                                              30.1.41.

Thank you so much for your letter of yesterday. I am not going to impeach you I promise you, but I do want to find out how it is that the Armoured Division don't seem to be able to prevent people getting away when they make up their minds to try.

O'Connor then went on to remind him of the earlier occasions at Sofafi and Bardia, when the Italian garrisons had disappeared by night without hindrance. He continued:

Then this case, which has much more serious results, because it leaves in being and at large about 50 medium tanks, which will make it necessary for us to leave some of ours behind to neutralise them when we shall want them so badly elsewhere, and another serious aspect is that our few remaining cruisers will have been further strained by a fruitless pursuit over bad ground.

I absolutely understand your reasons for pursuing and I am sure that I should have done the same myself in your place, but it won't help our future operations.

In this connection you say that the Armoured Div. will be 'played out' after MECHILI. I'm afraid I can't agree. They will only be 'played out' when there are no more tanks that can move. It is no good failing in the object of our campaign with a reserve of tanks in hand.

No, Dickie you must do everything possible to get the largest number of tanks on the road by the 10th at latest, no relief of any sort will take place until the next operation is completed, and I know I can rely on you to do everything in your power to have the largest possible force ready to move by then. I will discuss the composition of the Force with you to-morrow, all being well.[42]

The same day, Dill signalled Wavell, no doubt under pressure from Churchill: 'Please tell me urgently when you hope to capture Benghazi.' For some reason the message was delayed, not reaching Cairo until mid-morning 30 January. Wavell replied immediately:

Situation in Cyrenaica obscure but owing escape of Italian troops from Mechili general plan needs adjustment. As rough forecast we may capture Benghazi about end of February, but this may be optimistic. Hope to give more accurate estimate next week when we know O'Connor's new plan.[43]

At this stage O'Connor made an 'appreciation of the situation'. The plan decided upon was for the Australians to keep up the pressure in the coastal area, while the armoured division advanced south-west from Mechili to Msus. If the enemy held Benghazi, the armour could move further west from Msus to Solluch, and then strike up from the south towards his defensive position. If, however, the Italians withdrew from Benghazi the armour could turn down towards Agadabia on the coast road and cut off their route to Tripoli. In either case, the move to Msus was the first step, which it was considered could not be carried out before 10 February at the earliest.

Within 7th Armoured Division, some reorganisation took place. It was due to be relieved in due course by the 2nd Armoured Division, newly arrived in the desert, on a gradual replacement basis, which it was hoped would begin about 7 February. After consultation with General Creagh, O'Connor gave instructions for the best cruisers and light tanks of 7th Armoured Brigade to be passed over to the 4th Brigade, reducing the 7th to a strength of only one regiment. It was intended, however, to reinforce it with the first of the regiments of the 2nd Armoured Division to arrive at Mechili. A squadron of the 2nd Division's reconnaissance regiment, the King's Dragoon Guards in armoured cars, had arrived ahead of the rest and had been attached to the 11th Hussars.

The Australians had been fighting hard around Derna from 24 to 28 January, where the Italians used, to good effect, the advantages given to them by the long, deep wadi running into the Jebel south of the town, which created a superb, natural defensive feature. Eventually, however, on 29 January, Derna was captured. The next day and the one following, 30 and 31 January, the Australians followed hard on the heels of the retreating enemy. Though this progress was constantly delayed by mines, pot-holed roads, and blown bridges, they did not meet any signs of proper defensive positions being prepared.

Reports began to come in to O'Connor's headquarters, now situated at Bomba, that planes were being withdrawn from the few airfields still in enemy hands. On the evening of 31 January, as it was becoming steadily more obvious that a major retreat from Cyrenaica was in progress, he conferred with his staff on the action to take. Present were Harding, Dorman-Smith, who had been sent up by Wavell to report personally on the situation, and the senior officers of the Corps headquarters. O'Connor's report explains the questions that had to be asked and the decisions that had to be made:

The questions were:

(i) Could we afford to await the arrival of reinforcements which now could not arrive before 10 February?

(ii) Could the Armoured Division be launched across 150 miles of unreconnoitred desert in view of its doubtful mechanical condition?

(iii) Would the administrative situation, already strained, be able to supply a column at this distance?

His answers were:

(i) could be answered at once in the negative

(ii) could be answered as easily; the Armoured Division would move as far as mechanically it was able

(iii) was more difficult. Because without petrol, vehicles will not move, and it was no use arriving on the Benghazi Road with no petrol, and the prospect of a battle. However, after deep consultation with, and encouragement to, the administrative staff, they were confident that it could be done.

> That was then enough, a warning order was immediately sent to the Armoured Division warning them to be prepared to move to Msus, move commencing if possible on the afternoon of the 2nd, or a latest early morning of the 3rd, movement to be as rapid as possible.[44]

On 1 February early morning reconnaissance flights reported long columns of enemy transport moving west between Giovanni Berta and Barce, confirming that a withdrawal, on a larger scale than anticipated, was well under way. O'Connor sent Dorman-Smith back by air the same day to obtain the Commander-in-Chief's authority to make the immediate, rapid advance to cut off the Italian retreat.

> Wavell saw him that same evening. As Dorman-Smith told the story, all expression drained from Wavell's countenance.... At the end he looked up. 'Tell Dick he can go on,' he said, 'and wish him luck from me. He has done well.'[45]

On 2 February Dorman-Smith arrived back at XIII Corps Headquarters with the good news. Though the warning order had given either 2 or 3 February for the start of the move to Msus, administrative reasons had put the date off until dawn on 4 February.

O'Connor moved his headquarters from Bomba to Mechili on

3 February. In Correlli Barnett's words: 'One of the epic marches of history was about to begin.'[46]

The March to the Coast and the Battle of Beda Fomm—4 to 7 February 1941

The story of the 'epic march' to the coast, and the fierce battle which followed, has already been related. O'Connor's own account demonstrates the importance to a commander of a trusted chief of staff such as Harding at such a crucial moment: one who is fully informed of his superior's intentions:

> I sent the BGS, Brigadier Harding, off by air to the Headquarters of the Australian Division, giving them the latest news of the operations and ordering them to push on as fast as possible in the direction of Benghazi, improvising transport to carry units forward, if necessary one at a time, both the Charuba tracks and the other two main roads to be used.
>
> Having done this, he then flew to a point near the Headquarters of the Armoured Division, and landed close by. He discussed the situation with General Creagh, who asked if he might move south-west from Msus instead of west to Solluch in view of the certainty now that the enemy was trying to evacuate Cyrenaica completely. Brigadier Harding said he knew my original intention had been Solluch, but that he was sure I would agree to anything General Creagh decided as a result of the latest news. As I could not hope to arrive at Armoured Divisional Headquarters before the afternoon, General Creagh very wisely decided to order the whole movement south-west, which was an absolutely correct decision, and one which I would have ordered myself had I been there. This decision was mainly responsible for cutting off the entire enemy force.[47]

While the armoured division was moving off on 4 February, O'Connor went back to Tmimi to meet Wavell, and explained his plans. Flying back to Cairo that evening, the latter was able to send a signal to London to say that XIII Corps should 'be at the gates of Benghazi in the next few days'. He also added that he had appointed Wilson to be Military Governor of Cyrenaica, leaving O'Connor in command of operations until the end of this phase of the campaign.[48] Dorman-Smith was left forward with O'Connor, as Wavell's representative from GHQ, and accompanied him everywhere throughout the next three crucial days.

The conditions faced by the armoured division as it struggled westward were described by Alan Moorehead:

The trucks were stacked to capacity, the men's drinking water cut down to the equivalent of about a glass a day, and the regulation halts for food and sleep reduced by half or more. There was only one order of the day. 'Get to the coast.'

The wind blew shrilly and bitterly at first. Then a storm of full gale force sprang up against the last convoys. While the forward units were often battling against fine sand that reduced visibility sometimes to nothing, those that followed on were faced with frozen rain that streamed down in front of the wind. Standing in their trucks like helmsmen, the commanders of vehicles had their fingers frozen clawlike around their compasses. Through day and night the long lines of tanks, armoured cars, Bren-gun carriers, trucks, ambulances and guns bumped onward. If a vehicle fell out, that was just too bad: its drivers had to mend it or jump aboard another vehicle and press on. The going was the worst the men had known after a year in the desert—bump over a two-foot boulder, down into a ditch, up over an ant-hill into another boulder—and so on hour after hour.[49]

O'Connor himself was determined to keep well forward:

Shortly after daylight on the 5th, I started off myself from my Headquarters at Mechili in my car, with an armoured car, both as escort and also to enable me to maintain wireless touch with the situation, and a second car belonging to Brigadier Dorman-Smith, who had been staying a few days at my Headquarters. Unfortunately, both the armoured car and the second car broke down in this stretch of bad going which I mentioned above. As it was essential I should get to the Armoured Division as soon as possible, I was forced to leave Captain Dent, my ADC, behind with the break-downs whilst Brigadier Dorman-Smith and I continued on our way in my car. In the afternoon, we arrived at Headquarters [7th] Armoured Division which was some ten miles east of Msus. After discussing the situation with General Creagh I wholeheartedly confirmed the change of direction, which he had ordered.

After failing to get in touch with my own Headquarters, which was on the move, I decided it would be better to remain for the present near the Armoured Divisional Headquarters, where I might be of some assistance.[50]

As they had driven forward, and O'Connor had seen the broken down tanks and other vehicles littered along the bumpy track, he gave Dorman-Smith a glimpse of the anxiety hidden beneath his usual composed exterior: 'My God, do you think it's going to be all right?'[51]

Not only did he share the discomforts of the march and the short rations with his men, but he drove himself even harder than he drove them:

> Throughout these final days O'Connor was always where he was most needed. His determination and his energy were formidable, surpassing even Rommel's. He covered huge distances, over atrocious terrain, and was able to keep personal control of his spearhead, the 7th Armoured Division, of his own HQ XIII Corps, and of the Australian Division; all were kept in play though widely separated from each other. During 5th and 6th February his presence at HQ 7th Armoured Division at Antelat prevented any recurrence of the Babini evasion at Mechili.[52]

The Australians in the north were faced with difficulties to be overcome on their route which were as bad as those met by the armoured division. The rain turned the countryside to a sea of mud and slush, and every few miles the roads were blown away by the retreating Italian engineers, or strewn with mines. However, as Alan Moorehead, who travelled with them, wrote: 'A kind of frenzy possessed the Australians now in their utter determination to have Benghazi at once.'[53] And on the evening of 6 February they achieved their object and entered the town as the battle raged on at Beda Fomm.

The action at Beda Fomm, as recounted by O'Connor, finished with a description of the battle-field after the Italian surrender:

> Much damage and considerable casualties had been caused by our guns and tanks, and I have seldom seen such a scene of wreckage and confusion as existed on the main Benghazi Road. Broken and overturned lorries; in some places guns, lorries and tanks in hopeless confusion. Elsewhere guns in action, and broken down M.13s all over the countryside, and everywhere masses of prisoners. Most of the enemy casualties were caused by direct hits from our guns on lorries. Most of the enemy tanks had dead men inside them. General Tellera, the Tenth Army Commander, was in one, lying seriously wounded. He died later during the day. A large number of generals and other senior officers were captured, including General Bergonzoli and General Babini.
>
> Our losses were extremely light, which in view of the continuous fighting over two days is remarkable.
>
> I think this may be termed a complete victory, as none of the enemy escaped.[54]

Although rightly claiming that a complete victory had been gained, O'Connor was more restrained in assessing his own achievement. Dorman-Smith, travelling with him to inspect the battlefield asked him what it felt like to be a completely successful commander. The reply he was given was both modest and wise: 'I would never consider a commander completely successful until he had restored the situation after a serious defeat and a long retreat.'[55]

Among the 25,000 prisoners taken were seven Generals. Alan Moorehead visited them in the farmhouse where they were held near Solluch:

> Pushing through the thousands of prisoners who stood about aimlessly in the mud, I went past the guards about the farmhouse door, and there, squatting in the unfurnished corridors or standing in the shoddy yard outside, were the captured generals, the brigadiers and the full colonels. In the yard outside, sitting in the back seat of a car with a rug wrapped round him, was Bergonzoli. He was ill; I stood outside and saluted him, and he opened the door and leaned forward to speak to me ... he was, a soft-spoken little man with a pinched swarthy face that had aged unbelievably since his great days in Spain. His famous *barba elettrica* was a neat, bristly beard parted in the centre. He wore a plain, undecorated green uniform. Among the fascist generals, he was certainly the bravest of the lot. One could not help perversely wishing that after so many risks and chances he had got away in the end.[56]

O'Connor also visited the captured Generals, speaking to them with his usual courtesy in Italian:

> 'I'm sorry you are so uncomfortable,' he apologised. 'We haven't had much time to make proper arrangements.'
>
> 'Thank you very much,' General Cona replied politely. 'We do realise you came here in a very great hurry.'[57]

The very last thought that must have been in O'Connor's mind was that he himself would be a prisoner exactly two months later.

Both the Royal Navy and the Royal Air Force had given enormous assistance during the campaign. The Navy's contribution was provided by bombarding enemy positions and installations from the sea, and by speedily opening the various ports as they were captured, which made such a difference in overcoming the supply difficulties.

The part paid by the Royal Air Force was recognised in O'Connor's own message of congratulations to No. 202 Group:

> Since the war began you have consistently attacked without intermission an enemy air force between five and ten times your strength, dealing him blow after blow, until finally he was driven out of the sky, and out of Libya, leaving hundreds of derelict air-craft on his aerodromes.

In his recent retreat from Tobruk you gave his ground troops no rest, bombing their concentrations, and carrying out low flying attacks on their MT columns.

In addition to the above you have co-operated to the full in carrying out our many requests for special bombardments, reconnaissances, and protection against enemy air action, and I would like to say how much all this had contributed to our success.[58]

No time was lost once the enemy had surrendered at Beda Fomm in pushing on towards the Libyan frontier. Armoured cars of the 11th Hussars were sent south towards Agedabia and El Agheila, and by the evening of 8 February regimental headquarters were at the latter place, with patrols out up to fifty miles along the coast road towards Sirte. Virtually no resistance was met at any point, though a few more prisoners were collected. XIII Corps was poised to follow the remnants of the demoralised enemy to Tripoli.

This, however, as is shown in the next chapter, was not to be allowed: the 'complete victory' was not to be followed up.

11

The End of the Campaign

O'Connor's Plans for Tripoli

One of the major tests by which a great military leader can be judged is his conduct of the pursuit of a beaten enemy. It is all too easy to rest after winning a victory, and history is full of examples of commanders who have paused at the end of a successful battle and later been forced to fight savagely to gain ground which they could have taken with ease a short while before, had they not allowed a defeated enemy time to reorganise. O'Connor had shown that he knew how to avoid such errors, and had conducted his pursuit with exemplary skill: as a senior Australian officer said to John Harding at the end of the campaign:

> Do you know what we call your general? The little white-haired terrier— because he never lets go?[1]

During the afternoon of 7 February 1941, O'Connor was turning his attention to the next possible moves westward: first to Sirte, 160 miles beyond El Agheila, and then to Tripoli. In the evening he sent off Dorman-Smith to travel to Wilson's headquarters at Barce to discuss the outline plan with him, and from there to go on to Cairo to obtain the go-ahead for a further advance from Wavell, as well as to give a full report of the events of the past few days. When Dorman-Smith reached Cairo on 12 February, he was shown in to see Wavell at 10 am. He found the maps of the desert gone from the walls of the Commander-in-Chief's office, and ones of Greece in their place.[2]

The possibility of a further advance by XIII Corps had in fact been given the coup de grace the previous night. On receipt of a signal from Wilson giving an indication of the scale of the victory at Beda Fomm, Wavell had immediately sounded out the War Cabinet in London:

The End of the Campaign

A P Wavell to CIGS   10 February 1941, 1900 hrs

Extent of Italian defeat at Benghazi makes it seem possible that Tripoli might yield to small force if despatched without undue delay. Am working out commitment involved but hesitate to advance further in view of Balkan situation unless you think capture of Tripoli might have favourable effect on attitude of French North Africa. Further advance will also involve naval and air commitments and we are already far stretched. Navy would hate having to feed us at Tripoli and Air Force to protect us. On other hand possession of this coast might be useful to both.

On the afternoon of 11 February he received a reply:

CIGS to A P Wavell   11 February 1941, 1445 hrs

This problem has been heavily discussed by Defence Committee last two days. I put it up. General feeling is that assistance to Greece and/or Turkey must come first apart from strain on Navy and RAF which advance to Tripoli would involve. Official wire will follow tonight.[3]

Dill made one final effort to raise the subject again at a War Cabinet meeting after dinner the same evening. His suggestions were not well received, as he told Major General Kennedy, the Director of Military Operations, on his return to the War Office after the meeting:

I gave it as my view that all the troops in Middle East are fully employed and that none are available for Greece. The Prime Minister lost his temper with me. I could see the blood coming up his great neck and his eyes began to flash. He said: 'What you need out there is a Court Martial and a firing squad. Wavell has 300,000 men, etc, etc.' I should have said, 'Whom do you want to shoot exactly?' but I did not think of it till afterwards.[4]

Churchill constantly badgered Wavell about the numbers of men he had under his command who were not in fighting formations. Although he had always been keenly interested in the development of modern weapons and vehicles he never quite understood the numbers of men required to supply and maintain them, especially over long distances in foreign countries.

While these decisions were being reached in London and Cairo, O'Connor, with is subordinate commanders and staff, now established in the Hotel d'Italia in Benghazi, were hopefully planning the advance towards Tripoli, in anticipation of shortly receiving the signal to go ahead. Explaining how he had sent his personal message through Wilson's headquarters to Wavell—the one taken by Dorman-Smith—O'Connor told in his narrative that he hoped the policy of a limited operation might be altered:

> There were undoubtedly grounds for reconsidering this policy. Previously, the most that could be hoped for was the capture of the Benghazi area with the Italian Army driven out of Cyrenaica. But now, as a result of the battle of Beda Fomm, the Italian Army had completely ceased to exist, and there was now no other organised army between Cyrenaica and Tripoli. All that there was thought to be in Tripolitania at this time was one incomplete Division with very little artillery. It is, therefore, fair to say that provided the enemy could be prevented from landing reinforcements, there would be little serious opposition to our advance. But no half hearted measures would be any good; nothing could ensure our success except a whole-hearted effort on the part of all three Services, with no other commitments of importance to detract from that effort.

> But unfortunately this was not to be. Notwithstanding this entirely new situation, a further advance had been decided against. The Government was not to be deflected from its policy. Within two days we saw the result of this policy being implemented. The first being the immediate withdrawal of the bulk of the Royal Air Force from Cyrenaica, leaving only about one squadron of 'fighters' in the whole area. The second the statement by the Navy that in view of their commitments elsewhere they were unable to spare the necessary 'sweepers' and other craft necessary to make Benghazi into a proper base port for Supplies.

> Nothing could therefore be done. An advance on Sirte without adequate air support was a great risk in view of the German Air Forces known to be able to operate in the area. Moreover, no advance on a large scale could be considered from the administrative point of view, unless Benghazi could be made into an advanced base port.[5]

In the years that followed, O'Connor often wondered whether he should have ignored higher authority after Beda Fomm and 'gone bust' for Tripoli on his own initiative without seeking Wavell's approval. As time went by, he became ever more convinced that he should have done so, and his letter to Kenneth Macksey, written in 1970, explains this opinion:

> Finally, there is the question of Tripoli. I was not concerned with Greece, but I was with Tripoli. With the knowledge I have today, I have no doubt we could have got there and maintained ourselves, living on Italian supplies in their large camps at Sirte and Tripoli.

Beda Fomm ended on the 7th February and no German landed for four days, and then only two small contingents. Hitler is reported to have said, 'Don't be like the British who failed to follow their victory and capture Tripoli.'

The question was should we have waited for orders or simply followed on without them. Actually, the whole strategical situation had changed in the course of a single day. Before Beda Fomm, the most that was hoped for was that the Italian 10th Army would be defeated and would presumably fall back in front of us towards Tripoli. What did happen was that the army was not only defeated, but liquidated, and nothing remained to fall back on Tripoli.... But on that afternoon, when the battle of Beda Fomm was over, a brigade of the 6th Australian Division, lorryborne, with supplies of petrol, was drawn up on the Benghazi and Sirte road, facing south, all ready to advance on Sirte and Tripoli. I have never really forgiven myself for not using them.[6]

The decision having been made against this possible extension of the campaign, there followed a rapid reorganisation of the Desert Army. By the middle of February, Commonwealth forces in Cyrenaica had been greatly reduced. 7th Armoured Division had returned to Egypt to rest and refit, being replaced by part of the 2nd Armoured Division, recently out from home. On 9 March, the splendid 6th Australian Division was withdrawn to prepare to go to Greece, and its place was taken by the 9th Australian Division, which was less experienced and not so well trained.

For a short time, Wilson remained Military Governor and Commander in Cyrenaica, and Headquarters I Australian Corps, under General Blamey, took over from XIII Corps, which was disbanded. O'Connor returned to Egypt to take over Wilson's old position as Commander of British Troops, Egypt (BTE).

The new arrangements were not to last for long, however. By 27 February, Wilson, with Blamey and I Australian Corps, were all on their way to Greece. Their fate has been briefly recounted already. The only officer left in the area to take command in Cyrenaica was Lieutenant General Philip Neame VC, of whom Wavell later wrote:

I did not know him well; he had had the 4th Indian Division and had then gone to Palestine to replace George Giffard. He was a Sapper, and had been an instructor at the Staff College [in 1920 when O'Connor was a student], and was the author of a book on strategy, so I accepted him as a skilful and educated soldier; and his VC was a guarantee of his fighting qualities. He was at this time a great friend of Dick O'Connor's for whose judgment I had much respect.[7]

Confusion surrounds the arguments put forward about the rights and wrongs of calling off the continuation of O'Connor's advance: confusion between operational and strategic considerations, between short- and long-term aims, between intended and fortuitous results, between known and guessed at enemy strengths and intentions. The arguments which have been put forward by different participants and commentators will be examined in the form of questions and answers.

Was the advance operationally possible?

Those who doubted the operational viability of extending the campaign included Wavell who later commented:

> Our own resources were not equal to the task. Our armoured vehicles were worn out by an advance of 500 miles; we had not enough mechanised transport to maintain even a small force for an advance of another 500 miles to Tripoli; and both in the air and on the sea we were still numerically inferior to the Italians alone, without any German reinforcement. It would have been an intolerable strain on the Navy to maintain a military and air force at Tripoli when even Benghazi could not be used as a port for lack of AA artillery and other resources.[8]

This point of view is shared by the late Field Marshal Lord Harding, who was even closer to the reality of the situation than Wavell. Lord Carver gives Harding's point of view in his book *Dilemmas of the Desert War*:

> O'Connor was deeply disappointed, and, while he was a prisoner of war and for long after, brooded on whether or not a golden opportunity was missed, which would have altered the whole course of the North African campaign and, incidentally, prevented him from having had to endure captivity. But his Brigadier General Staff, Harding, believed that, even if he had been allowed to send light forces on towards Tripoli, they would not have been able to stay there. The lack of air, naval and logistic support would have precluded it, and the Italians alone could have produced greatly superior force there.[9]

To set against these somewhat pessimistic attitudes there is not only that of O'Connor himself, who so clearly considered the operation feasible if given enough backing by the Navy and Air Force, but also the opinion of Rommel, who recorded that:

> On 8 February, leading troops of the British Army occupied El Agheila.... Graziani's army had virtually ceased to exist. All that

remained of it were a few lorries and hordes of unarmed soldiers in full flight to the west. If Wavell had now continued his advance into Tripolitania, no resistance worthy of the name could be mounted against him.... When a commander has won a decisive victory—and Wavell's victory over the Italians was devastating—it is generally wrong for him to be satisfied with too narrow a strategic aim. For that is the time to exploit success. It is during the pursuit, when the beaten enemy is still dispirited and disorganised, that most prisoners are made and most booty captured. Troops who on one day are flying in a wild panic to the rear, may, unless they are continually harried by the pursuer, very soon stand in battle again, freshly organised as fully effective fighting men.

The reason for giving up the pursuit is almost always the quartermaster's growing difficulty in spanning the lengthened supply routes with his available transport. As the commander usually pays great attention to his quartermaster and allows the latter's estimate of the supply possibilities to determine his strategic plan, it has become the habit for quartermaster staffs to complain at every difficulty, instead of getting on with the job and using their powers of improvisation, which indeed are frequently nil. But generally the commander meekly accepts the situation and shapes his actions accordingly.

When, after a great victory which has brought the destruction of the enemy, the pursuit is abandoned on the quartermaster's advice, history almost invariably finds the decision to be wrong and points to the tremendous chances which have been missed. In face of such a judgment there are, of course, always academic soldiers quick to produce statistics and precedents by people of little importance to prove it wrong. But events judge otherwise, for it has frequently happened in the past that a general of high intellectual powers has been defeated by a less intelligent but stronger willed adversary.

The best thing is for the commander himself to have a clear picture of the real potentialities of his supply organisation and to base all his demands on his own estimate. This will force the supply staffs to develop their initiative, and though they may grumble, they will as a result produce many times what they would have done left to themselves.[10]

O'Connor's old friend Brigadier Barclay, to whom was given the task of editing the narrative so often quoted in this book, gave his own opinion after a deep study of the campaign:

It has been said that, apart from the question of aid to Greece, the XIII Corps was not in a position to continue strenuous operations because of the fatigue of the troops and the condition of the equipment—particularly tanks. It would have been difficult to find anyone in a responsible position serving with the Corps at that time who would have subscribed to this view. Officers and men were 'itching' to go on and all were agreed that, with the spirit which animated the force at that time, all difficulties could have been overcome. There may have been good reasons for abandoning the North African offensive in favour of the Greek venture; but the condition of units of the XIII Corps was not one of them. They are to be found in the realm of politics and higher strategy which was entirely out of the local commander's hands, and very largely outside General Wavell's power to influence.[11]

On balance, it might be claimed that the optimists have the better case from the purely operational standpoint.

Was Tripoli a valuable strategic objective?

An outstandingly lucid exposition of the importance of Tripoli and the relative ease with which it might have been taken reached the War Cabinet, via the CIGS on 1 February 1941, though as Connell comments when quoting it:

> There is no evidence that this document ever received the careful and detailed study, either by the Chiefs of Staff or by the War Cabinet, which it merited.

It was written by Mr Leo Amery, then Secretary of State for India, based on his own wide experience and study of military history rather than on his current political appointment. Having started with some general comments on the importance of surprise, he went on to discuss the value of Tripoli as a base for Commonwealth forces, as well as the importance of denying it to the enemy. His final paragraph encapsulates the case he wished to make:

> To sum up then, my argument is that the advance to Tripoli should not be considered merely as the exploiting of Wavell's success in North Africa, but as the key to any future operations on a serious scale against Sicily, Sardinia, or in the Balkans. It might be the Open Sesame of the whole war and as an operation of surprise might completely disorganise the enemy's plans.[12]

This case put forward by Amery is extremely convincing. One can only surmise that the reason why it was not given much consideration was the fact that it appeared at a moment when Churchill's attention was so fixed on Greece, following the death of Metaxas only two days before on 29 January, and that its impact was lost due to unfortunate timing. A few days earlier or later it could have had more effect.

One thing that was certain was that the choice had to be Tripoli *or* Greece: there was no question of doing both. As already explained, the policy chosen was disastrous in the theatre, and it proved to be the same in North Africa. As well as defeat in Greece, the Commonwealth forces were flung out of Crete, which had been occupied in October 1940.

Can the decision to send a force to Greece be defended?

The 'follow-on effects' of the Greek venture were to have a considerable impact on O'Connor's life, and therefore the reasons for becoming involved in it must be looked at. The strangest aspect of the decision to undertake the Greek campaign comes out in the explanation of the way in which it was reached given by Wavell, after the war. In a lecture entitled 'The British Expedition to Greece, 1941', which was reprinted in *The Army Quarterly* in January 1950, he said that he wished to correct a statement which had been 'widely spread that the military leaders were forced into the Greek commitment against their will for political reasons'. He stated that was not true. Later in his talk he made the point that:

> The decision was that of the men on the spot, and the doubts came from London, where the Prime Minister and the Chiefs of Staff were apprehensive of a commitment so much more hazardous than that which they had approved ten days earlier. From the point of view of immediate advantage they were probably right and the men on the spot wrong; while as regards ultimate results, the men on the spot were, I think, right: *a curious reversal of the usual understanding*, that the men on the spot take a short-term view and those at a distance a long-term one.[13]

While a degree of humility is necessary on the part of a writer who makes comments, long after the event, on the decisions of great men faced with almost insuperable difficulties, Wavell's case as presented in his talk is hard to accept uncritically. In view of the fact that Churchill had already given Eden a glimpse of his unease about the risks of the Greek intervention, it certainly cannot be claimed that he was the main cause of the disaster. Back in February, before the first visit by Eden and the others, he had written:

Do not consider yourselves obligated to a Greek enterprise if in your hearts you feel it will be only another Norwegian fiasco. If no good plan can be made, please say so. But of course you know how valuable success would be.[14]

Wavell's reasons, as given in his lecture, for going on with the campaign in Greece, are not very convincing:

I think it may have been psychological and political considerations that tilted the balance in the end over the military dangers. To have withdrawn at this stage, on grounds which could not have been made public, would have been disastrous to our reputation in the USA and with other neutrals, would have ended all hope of Yugoslavia joining the Allies and would have shaken our ally Turkey. Our plan had been endorsed by the Dominion Governments whose troops were involved. And there were practical difficulties in any reversal of plan; the troops were on the move and a change would have caused confusion.

I was sure at the time, and I am sure still, in spite of what resulted, that the decision we took at our Embassy in Athens in that first week in March 1941, was the *only one consistent* with the political requirements of the moment, with military strategy and with our national honour.[15]

A valid point was made in the early stages of the deliberations of the Chiefs of Staff in London by Kennedy, the Director of Military Operations, though he was unable to persuade his superiors to take any notice of his opinions. He thought it wrong that the Cabinet had never asked for, nor received, a purely military appreciation of the situation from either the Chiefs of Staff or Wavell himself. He later wrote that 'all the service advice given on this problem had been coloured by political considerations—a very dangerous procedure'.[16]

Even more surprising is the evidence that Wavell was not only not asked, but seemed to be almost unwilling, to make a proper military appreciation. Barrie Pitt records that:

Wavell threw away O'Connor's victory by stripping Cyrenaica of its most experienced formations and sending them to Greece on a mission about which his own planning staff had the gravest doubts. Francis de Guingand was later to write how he and the Director of Military Intelligence, Brigadier Shearer, had put together papers showing both that Tripoli was within the grasp of O'Connor's force, and that, in view of the known resources and methods of the German Wehrmacht, the proposed expedition to Greece held little chance of success and every prospect of disaster.

The latter paper was returned to them with the single note, ' "War is an option of difficulties"—Wolfe. APW'—which, though apt, was to prove frustrating. Genius chooses the right options; and despite persistent post-war declarations, Wavell was not under overwhelming pressure from Churchill, and could have withstood Eden had he wished.[17]

Was it worth it in the long run?

Though Churchill had his doubts about the Greek enterprise at times, when the final decision to undertake it was made he gave it his full backing. Later he was to comment:

They said that I was wrong to go to Greece in 1940. But I didn't do it simply to save the Greeks. Of course, honour and all that came in. But I wanted to form a Balkan front. I wanted Yugoslavia, and I hoped for Turkey. That, with Greece, would have given us fifty divisions. A nut for the Germans to crack. Our intervention in Greece caused the revolution which drove out Prince 'Palsy'; and delayed the German invasion of Russia by six weeks. Vital weeks. So it was worth it. If you back a winner it doesn't really matter much what your reasons were at the time. They now say that I went to Greece for the wrong reasons. How do they know? The point is that it was worth it.[18]

In connection with the delaying of the German invasion of Russia, Wavell claimed that the weeks gained saved Moscow from falling in the winter of 1941. The Germans employed small forces in Greece and Yugoslavia, but they were mainly armoured, and they drove very long distances. Returning and reconditioning the armoured vehicles brought about the delay, though, as Wavell admitted, this 'cannot be claimed as a justification of our decision in March'.[19]

To reinforce this verdict there are the words of Jodl, one time Chief of Staff of the German Army, as reported by Field Marshal Smuts in 1946 in the presence of Harold Nicolson:

Jodl yesterday had stated that Germany had lost the war because she had been obliged to divert divisions to meet the British landing in Greece. That meant she lost six weeks. She lost time—and with time she lost Moscow, Stalingrad and the war.[20]

Assuming that the campaign in Greece was worthwhile in the long run, because of the 'spin-off' of assistance to Russia, there remains the question of whether, in the end, calling off the North African operations was to the advantage of the Allies. Those who support this argument maintain that the two years of further fighting backwards and forwards across North Africa forced the Germans and Italians to pour large forces into this theatre which the British and Americans were eventually able to destroy. It has also been contended that powerful Axis forces were diverted to Africa from more vital fronts, particularly Russia, and that in the end the invasion of Italy was facilitated.

In opposition to this theory it can be pointed out that the possession of Tripoli, had it been taken swiftly, would have enabled North Africa to be held with a relatively light garrison, releasing large forces to be used for operations in the Balkans or other parts of Europe. As it turned out, it was not until 1943 that the Eighth Army eventually entered Tripoli, and Montgomery was able to write on 10 February to Jean to give the good news, and to comment: 'How pleased Dick will be about it all, and how I wish he were here to share in our victory.'[21]

Further speculation on these issues in the end becomes sterile. History is replete with 'Ifs'. One of the most important ones in connection with this book is brought into focus in the epilogue: what would O'Connor have achieved *if* he had not been captured and spent nearly three years as a prisoner of war? How the disaster of his capture came about is the subject of the next chapter.

12

Capture

Although deeply disappointed at having to abandon the offensive, O'Connor was not entirely sorry to return to Cairo. Apart from his stomach complaint, he was exhausted. Not having seen him for two months, his wife was shocked by his thin and haggard appearance. As his new duties were not too arduous, he was able to rest and regain his strength. A particularly enjoyable interlude was a week's visit to Palestine to stay as guests of the High Commissioner and Lady MacMichael, which included a large party given in his honour.[1]

His services in his victorious campaign were rewarded by his being created a Knight Commander of the Order of the Bath (KCB), and so he and Jean became Sir Richard and Lady O'Connor.

On returning to Egypt, he set about the improvement of the defences of Alexandria and the Suez Canal. As he expected his appointment as GOC-in-Chief British Troops Egypt to last for some time, he and Jean moved into a house in Zamalek, a suburb of Cairo. It was a beautiful place, near the river and with a spacious garden. Shortly after they settled there, O'Connor made the all too prescient comment that it seemed 'too good to last'.[2]

The man who was shortly to upset O'Connor's life in a disastrous manner had arrived at Castel Benito airfield near Tripoli on 12 February 1941, and in Barrie Pitt's words had spent the following weeks:

> giving all who came into contact with him an exhibition of the extraordinary mental and physical energy which was to be the hallmark of his command. At this time, Rommel was just nine months short of his fiftieth birthday, a stocky, compact man with no excess flesh, lean features and

grey-blue eyes which generally sparkled with both humour and friendliness but which could crackle into blazing fury in an instant.

He had been informed of his new appointment by the Führer himself on the afternoon of February 6th (thus making that week one of the most significant in the history of the campaign) and despite the strict limitations placed upon his activities by the Commander in Chief of the Army, Generalfeldmarschall von Brauchitsch, during a subsequent interview, he was quite determined not only that the British advance must be held, but that it must also be thrown back at least as far as the Egyptian border, and preferably further.[3]

During March, a number of patrol clashes between Commonwealth and German light forces took place in the El Agheila area, and the Luftwaffe increased its activity, frequently bombing the port of Benghazi.

On 31 March, Rommel advanced on El Agheila. Meeting with unexpected success against weak and ill-organised British forces in the area, he decided to turn the operation which he had originally intended to be merely a reconnaissance in force, of limited scope, into a full-blooded attempt to recapture the whole of Cyrenaica.

Just how weak his force had become was well appreciated by O'Connor's unfortunate successor, General Neame. In his own report on 'Operations in Cyrenaica from 27 February 1941 until 7 April 1941', Neame devoted five of the ten foolscap pages to recording his unavailing efforts to make up some of his appalling deficiencies. Not only did he stress to GHQ in Cairo his shortage of all the equipment he needed, he also warned of German action. Of a visit to GHQ on 8 March he wrote that:

> I discussed the possibilities of a German attack, which was not regarded at GHQ at this date as probable, although I expressed the opinion that the Germans had not come to Libya for nothing and would not long rest content with a defensive role.[4]

In fact, nobody anticipated that Rommel would start his probing of the British positions so soon, nor that he would turn them into a full-scale advance with such speed. This applied to German and Italian senior headquarters as much as to the British.

Similarities between Rommel and O'Connor appear in the story of the brilliantly improvised German campaign. Each was outstandingly forceful and energetic; each was unusually farsighted and clever at judging an enemy's capabilities; above all, each was a bold commander willing to take calculated risks. As he pushed his troops forward into Cyrenaica, Rommel followed two of the routes which XIII Corps had come along so recently. He had more or less ignored his Italian superior, General Gariboldi, and he gave orders to Italians with as much freedom, if not confidence, as he did to Germans. Up the coastal road through Benghazi and Derna he sent the Italian Brescia Division, and along the track through Msus to Mechili were despatched the Italian Ariete Division and part of the 5th German Light Division.

The rest of the German 5th Division moved further south still, through unreconnoitred desert which the Italians told Rommel was virtually impassable: an opinion which he quickly proved, in his own car, to be totally erroneous.

The reactions of General Neame, and of General Gambier-Parry, commanding the newly-arrived, under-strength 2nd Armoured Division, to Rommel's advance were confused and apparently hesitant. Realising that this was the case, Wavell flew to Neame's headquarters at Barce on 2 April, where John Harding, who had remained in the desert as Neame's Brigadier General Staff, took an opportunity 'to talk to him personally and beg him to send O'Connor back to replace Neame'.[5]

Wavell himself had 'soon realised that Neame had lost control', but his criticism that he 'was making no effort to regain it by the only possible means, going forward personally' is not entirely fair. However, Wavell decided to send a message for O'Connor to come forward, and take over from Neame. Later O'Connor recorded:

> I cannot pretend I was happy at the thought of taking over command in the middle of a battle which was already lost.[6]

On the morning of 3 April, O'Connor left Cairo, taking with him John Combe, recently promoted to Brigadier from command of the 11th Hussars, and due to move the following day to take over a cavalry brigade in Palestine. Combe's own story of the events of the next four days gives a vivid picture of the sad disarray of Neame's command, which was explained to them by Wavell when they landed to join him at Barce. On the journey up, O'Connor had explained that he was taking Combe with him because of the latter's expert knowledge of the terrain and desert tactics. Combe 'thanked him profusely for what I considered a compliment, since I was not staff trained, and also because I was delighted to be active in desert work again.'[7]

Combe's narrative continues:

> At Barce, the C-in-C [Wavell] then had a lengthy conference with
> Generals Neame and O'Connor, whilst Brigadier John Shearer, head of
> Intelligence Staff, discussed with me the latest reports and situation.

> General O'Connor afterwards told me that whilst the C-in-C had agreed
> there should be no change and that he, O'Connor, was to remain, help
> and advise and to report to C-in-C direct.

How this situation arose must be explained. When Wavell told him
that he was to take over from Neame, O'Connor pointed out that he
did not know the divisions which now composed XIII Corps; that
they did not know him; and that there was little he could do at this
stage to improve on Neame's handling of the battle. He therefore
proposed that he should stay to help Neame for a few days, but not
assume command. Wavell accepted this as a sensible solution, but
O'Connor was later to regret it bitterly, and to describe it as 'the
worst proposal he had ever made'.[8]

Some extracts from Combe's narrative give a clear picture of the
progress of the next few disastrous days:

> My firm impression in the next days was that Neame looked to O'Connor
> for every decision and so remained in the background and willingly
> allowed O'Connor to make such decisions.

> In the next three days, wherever O'Connor went he was greeted with
> enthusiasm and as a saviour even at this late hour.

> On April 4, O'Connor and I set off to meet the GOC 2nd Armoured
> Division, Major General Gambier-Parry, whom I knew slightly. O'Con-
> nor asked him where his Division was and for a full picture. Gambier-
> Parry immediately said 'I would like to tell you the whole story from the
> start', but his very long-winded story of minor disasters, mishaps and the
> Armoured Brigade as far as I could understand never doing quite what
> was ordered and expected of it, took so long to relate that O'Connor had
> to interrupt and said 'Where are your Brigades now?' Whereon another
> long story ensued. Then to 'What is the actual position of the 3rd
> Armoured Brigade and how many tanks have they?' a further long story
> started and finally to 'What is the petrol and ammunition situation?' yet
> another story started.

> O'Connor then carefully explained Force's plan and directed that the
> whole Armoured Division must close in on Mechili area so as to guard the
> left flank and become the pivot for the whole of the general withdrawal on
> the coastal area and escarpment.

> We then said we would go on to Advanced Divisional Headquarters.

Capture

My own impression was that though Gambier-Parry had stated he clearly understood everything, I much doubted it would be done, because it was clear from his long story that he had no control, especially of the Armoured Brigade commander, Brigadier Rimington, and further I believe O'Connor was of the same mind, in fact we were both much shaken by the long-winded stories and apparent lack of sense of urgency and grip of the situation.

Advanced Divisional Headquarters were delighted to see O'Connor for whom it was obvious all had the greatest admiration and confidence that now things would be more coherent, with a steady plan from which there would be a more satisfactory outcome.

I listened whilst O'Connor, after certain enquiries, explained the whole plan to the GSOI, Colonel Younghusband, and I sat for some time afterwards and went through the whole thing again with him in detail. Colonel Younghusband told me of the Division's difficulties, and of his own in getting attention and decisions from his GOC.

Colonel Younghusband, though naturally tired, was clearly running his side well in spite of difficulties, accentuated by the lack of information from Brigades and the KDG [King's Dragoon Guards].

I was horrified by the paucity of information from the KDG and also the contradictions and discrepancies in their reports. From my own recent experience I knew only too well the constant flood of information that used to come in from squadrons and troops in touch with the enemy, all of which, after being sifted, was immediately passed to Higher Command, thus keeping Divisional Headquarters up to date. Whilst commenting thus, I must in fairness say that the KDG were new to the desert and their reconnaissance role.

When I left Divisional Headquarters, I was completely satisfied that Colonel Younghusband understood thoroughly Force's intentions and orders and also the vital necessity of 2nd Armoured Division becoming the pivot from the Mechili area and so blocking the open left flank. He agreed the lack of information of that desert flank was a serious weakness and anxiety and promised me that the KDG would be spread as wide as possible in that direction.

O'Connor and I had not been at all well impressed, in fact much to the contrary. The Division's difficulties and inexperience, shortage of men, ammunition and signal equipment, were all taken into account, but we came away feeling there was no real leader and driving force and that only Colonel Younghusband gave confidence. He at least, we assured ourselves, thoroughly understood the plan and the vital role of the 2nd Armoured Division.

Unfortunately, the situation rapidly deteriorated to the point where Younghusband's understanding of the plan made little difference. Two days later, on 6 April, a full-scale withdrawal was in progress. The Australian 9th Division, commanded by the highly competent General Morshead, carried out its rearward movement with considerable skill considering its lack of experience. The 2nd Armoured Division, on the other hand, more or less fell to pieces. These pieces were quickly picked up by Rommel, who included among them Gambier-Parry and his divisional headquarters. Unhappily for the British, he also collected, largely by luck, a much better prize.

By 6 April, XIII Corps headquarters had moved from Barce to Marawa. That afternoon it was decided to retire to Tmimi, and the bulk of the staff had left by 8 pm when the most senior officers and their personal attendants finally set out to join them. This party was carried in three vehicles: Neame's Lincoln Zephyr staff car in the front contained himself, O'Connor, Combe and his driver. Immediately following came a Ford 'utility' containing Neame's ADC, Captain The Earl of Ranfurly, a driver, and two batmen. Last in the line was a Chevrolet 'utility' with O'Connor's ADC, Captain John Dent in it, as well as a driver and most of the party's baggage and bedding. Fortunately for him, John Dent lost contact with the others about an hour later as the little convoy speeded past other vehicles moving in slow, congested columns towards the east.

O'Connor himself described the progress of the two leading cars ahead of Dent:

> However, after some delay we managed to turn off the main road to Derna on to the cross country track to Martuba, which Neame said he knew. We had a somewhat perilous drive part of the way by Neame taking the wheel to relieve his tired driver, who had been driving all day, as he went at a highly dangerous pace passing traffic all along the track! There was a bit of a moon, but quite a lot of dust, but in spite of this, after driving along for about ten miles, Combe caught sight of a sign board stuck on a petrol tin and suggested stopping to look at it, but Neame said there was no need to as he was sure he knew the road. After going two or three miles further, I felt by the position of the moon that we were going too far to the north, and on the three different occasions I said so, and on the last occasion persuaded Neame to stop, but he still maintained we were quite all right, as he said the road twisted about. The absence of traffic behind us was explained by the fact that we had passed it all! So we resumed our journey again, Neame having handed over the wheel to his driver, and all of us fell into a doze after the hard day we had had.[9]

In due course, these two staff cars came up with another long, slow-moving line of lorries and other vehicles. Once more they started to overtake, but eventually, not long before the moment of capture, they came to a halt in the middle of this column. Lord Ranfurly sat for a few minutes talking to the driver in his vehicle, who commented on some foreign language, which they heard being shouted further up the column, that it must be 'one of them Cypriots'—there being a number of Cypriots employed as drivers of administrative lorries. After a short while, Ranfurly got out and went forward to Neame's car, where he talked to Combe through the front passenger's window. The next thing he knew was a sub-machine gun being stuck in his ribs by a German soldier. This soldier moved on down the column, and he and Combe roused the two Generals in the back and told them to get down on the floor, hoping they might be able to slip out of the car and crawl away. Unfortunately more Germans arrived before this could be achieved, and the whole party was quickly taken prisoner. O'Connor did have time to hide a pistol inside his shirt, and Combe concealed a grenade in his clothes.

There was an element of bad luck in the way in which the capture occurred, in that the 3rd German Reconnaissance Battalion which made such a remarkable haul of prisoners was far further east than expected. However, this does not get away from the fact that it was a largely avoidable disaster for which O'Connor never ceased to blame both Neame and himself—Neame for refusing to listen when told he was going too far north instead of east, and himself for not insisting that they should go in the right direction, even though, as he wrote later:

> I must confess that the possibility of being on the wrong track did not really worry me very much, as I felt that we should strike the Derna–Tobruk road rather further west than Martuba, and I had no idea whatever that there was any chance of meeting a German force in that area.[10]

Harding set out on the journey to Tmimi about an hour after the Generals had left, and got there safely. Arriving shortly after midnight, it was not until daylight on 7 April that he became worried about the missing Generals, and sent out motor patrols to search for them. In their absence, he took responsibility for conducting the withdrawal of the British element towards Tobruk, while Morshead ensured that his Australians retired in an orderly fashion.

O'Connor considered he was well treated in the first few days of captivity, especially by the German commander at Tripoli, where the prisoners eventually arrived about 10 April. This officer invited them to dine, and expressed regret that Germany was fighting the British as opposed to being an ally. He was contemptuous of both the French and the Italians. From Tripoli the party of prisoners were flown to Rome, and from there taken to the camp described in the following chapter.

O'Connor and Combe hatched a plan to hijack the aeroplane, as they still had the pistol and the grenade. But due to a last minute alteration in their flight arrangements they were unable to attempt it—probably luckily for them and everyone else!

News of O'Connor's capture was received at first with incredulity, and then with sorrow and dismay, throughout the Army and the other services in North Africa. Especially sad to lose his most reliable and capable subordinate in the whole of his command was Wavell. Brigadier Freddie de Guingand, later well-known as Montgomery's Chief of Staff, was at the time serving at GHQ. In his book *Operation Victory* he told of Wavell's reaction to the news:

> The news of the capture of both Neame and O'Connor came as a real shock to the C-in-C, and I have never seen him so moved. As C-in-C he was bearing a very heavy load at this time, and to lose a close personal friend such as O'Connor was an added burden.[11]

On 14 April 1941 Wavell approached the CIGS in a signal to suggest that an offer should be made to the Italians to exchange any six of their captured generals for O'Connor. Some two weeks later Dill had to reply: 'Regret that COS [Chiefs of Staff] have considered your proposals for exchange of O'Connor and decided we cannot discriminate in favour of generals.'[12] Jean O'Connor kept hoping that something could be arranged, but a letter to her from Dill on 21 August confirmed the April decision, and a further plea to Anthony Eden the following year brought a final negative in his letter of 13 July 1942.[13]

The idea of attempting to get O'Connor back from the Italians also came to the mind of Wavell's successor, Auchinleck, who took over in Cairo on 21 June 1941. The trouble was that he thought about it too late, as he told O'Connor in a letter written a quarter of a century later:

Capture

I have for long been silently upbraiding myself for not having the wits or initiative to get Winston to spend twenty or fifty thousand pounds or more to buy you from the Italians so that you could have formed and raised the Eighth Army and finished Rommel in 1941! I mean this and it will remain a sorrow and admission of failure as long as I live![14]

13

The First Escape Attempts

This chapter and the one that follows are largely recorded in the words of General O'Connor himself and another remarkable man who wrote up his own escape story, Brigadier James Hargest CB, DSO, MC, the New Zealand author of a book entitled Farewell Campo 12.[1] *Because of this, the author's comments are in italics and slightly inset in the manner of this paragraph, while the material quoted from the escapees is shown as ordinary text.*

At first O'Connor, Neame and Combe were put into a senior officers camp near Sulmona, which lies about 75 miles roughly due east of Rome. Here they joined Air Vice Marshal Boyd, who had been captured when his plane was forced to land in Sicily while he was on his way to become second-in-command to Air Marshal Longmore in Cairo.[2]

Also a prisoner due to aircraft failure, who arrived about a week later, was the legendary figure of Major General Sir Adrian Carton de Wiart, VC, here described by Hargest:

Hargest

De Wiart was caught by bad luck also when on a flight from England to the Middle East. The plane in which he was a passenger came down in the sea near Derna and he was compelled to swim ashore, where he fell into the hands of the Italians. He is one of the most gallant men I have ever met, and one of the best comrades. His life story would read like a drama were it ever published, [*it later was*[3]] including, as it would, soldiering for Britain in South Africa before he was even a naturalized Briton; service in the Great War; where he lost an arm and an eye and won the Victoria Cross; service in Poland in the post-war troubles there, followed by twenty years living in the Pripet marshes in Poland, where it is said he was offered the crown. When this war began he was there still, and fought with the Poles against the Germans. Then he was sent to Narvik as the leader of the British Force, which was so outnumbered that it had to withdraw immediately. Thence towards the Middle East and capture.

The Italians arranged for the senior officers to be looked after by a staff of captured British non-commissioned officers and men, whose conduct is glowingly praised in O'Connor's story.

O'Connor

Very shortly after our arrival at Sulmona, the minds of some of us began to turn on possible means of escape. But owing to the very long distances to be traversed, and to our lack of money and civilian clothes, the outlook did not seem very hopeful, unless we were able to obtain some help from outside sources. I therefore decided to write to the War Office asking for help in the shape of money, clothes and passports, also if it would be possible for us to get in touch with some agent.

An opportunity to pass this letter out presented itself in June, 1941, during a visit of a party from the Vatican, which included a certain Monsignor O'Flaherty,[4] an Irishman. This gentleman was kind enough to take the letter, at considerable risk to himself, and to pass it to Colonel Fiske, US Military Attaché in Rome. It eventually found its way through US Channels to its destination, from which began the very successful efforts to assist us made by the special branch concerned at the War Office.

Shortly after this we had another piece of good fortune. The Italian Commandant of the Sulmona Prisoners' Camps allowed the visit one day of a certain officer from the junior officers' camp nearby. This officer had been taken prisoner during a Commando raid in Sicily. In the short period of his visit he was able to teach us a code which we were able to use with great success with the War Office for the whole of the rest of our captivity. As a result, we received and sent a number of important letters relating to escaping and other matters.

We now awaited the arrival of an answer from the War Office, and were overjoyed to hear during a visit from Colonel Fiske in August that the War Office had received my letter and had promised to help us.

During the six months in the camp at Sulmona, O'Connor wrote his long report on his desert campaign. It was through Colonel Fiske that it reached the outside world. On one of the US Attaché's visits O'Connor hid the manuscript under the seat of the lavatory next to the room in which the prisoners were gathered to meet

The Forgotten Victor

him. When introduced O'Connor said in a flat voice: 'Very good of you to come to see us—look under the lavatory seat.' The American gave every appearance of not having heard anything unusual, nor did the Italian officers standing nearby take any notice. Later, however, Fiske gave a nod to show that he had collected the documents.[5]

For O'Connor an unexpected result of being a prisoner was the creation of new friendships, the most important being with Adrian Carton de Wiart. Although he and O'Connor were in many ways complete opposites, they formed a bond between them which was to last many years after the war. Carton de Wiart wrote in his autobiography Happy Odyssey about his arrival at Sulmona, and the excitement it caused among the other inmates, going on to state: 'Straight away O'Connor and I paired off, and through adversity I found a very good friend.'[6]

Close bonds also developed between O'Connor and Hargest. The latter, who was a successful politician in civilian life in New Zealand, had every prospect of becoming Prime Minister after the war. He used to joke about this, and said that if it ever happened he would ask for O'Connor to be appointed Governor General.[7]

O'Connor

We moved to the Florence area early in September 1941. There we were accommodated in a Castle called Vincigliata. Escaping seemed likely to be initially more difficult, although the distances to the Swiss and French frontiers were 200 miles less than from Sulmona.

We were hoping for a visit from Colonel Fiske again, but he was constantly being put off by the Italian authorities, until the declaration of war by the US against the Axis Powers made any further visits impossible.

Nevertheless, by December 1941 we were beginning to receive coded letters from the War Office giving information and advice about escaping, and later books and games were received containing money and maps.

Before this, however, Carton de Wiart and myself and Boyd and Combe decided that we should try to walk to the French frontier. To this end, we started collecting food and the necessary clothing and rucksacks. Also we instituted a very vigorous course of training carrying packs up and down stairs, as well as rope climbing practice.

James Hargest arrived at Vincigliata on 13 March 1942, accompanied by three other captured Brigadiers: Stirling, late of the 13/18th Hussars; Miles, another

142

MAP 6. ITALY

The Forgotten Victor

New Zealander; and Armstrong, a South African. In his book he described the building known officially during the war as Campo Concentramento No. 12.

Hargest

The castle, for Vincigliata is a castle rather than a villa, stands on a rounded prominence high up on the hills above the city. Beyond it there is a slight hollow, then the hill goes on upward to other villas on other prominences, and eventually to a little mountain that we were to know so well later, Monte Fano.

To the west was a huge mass of rock several hundreds of feet higher than the castle, which we named the Quarries, and beyond that again Fiesole, the hill suburb of Florence. Below, on the other side, lies Settignano, beneath which runs the soft-flowing Arno on its course to Pisa and the sea.

The castle itself was built by an Englishman named Temple-Leader in the middle of the nineteenth century on the site of, and as a replica of, a medieval Florentine castle. It was an extraordinary design, with five stories above ground and two below, the latter slipping away downhill on the Florence side and the best bedrooms being underneath the formal garden with one side facing on to cloisters. The whole building was of solid stone with walls at least two and a half feet thick, and it was surrounded by an embrasured battlement from fifteen to thirty feet high, with two towers in the north-east and north-west corners. The architect had neglected every principle of health. The windows were small and few faced the sun, while the best positions seemed to be taken up either by passages or bathrooms. He had added to the general mix-up of spurious medievalism and insanitation a motley collection of statues and plaques mostly in white marble, building them into the walls in every spot he could find....

There were one or two pleasing features. One was the drive, which ran down from the main gate to the castle courtyard, ending abruptly at a low wall on top of a small potting shed. We called this 'The Stoep' in compliment to Armstrong, the South African. The other one was a flat area above the courtyard cloisters where one could sit and sun-bathe even in winter. From it we had a glorious view of Florence with its Duomo and steepled churches spread out below us like a plan.

The newcomers soon became involved in the escape business with the other enthusiasts already at Vincigliata. There was no doubt in Hargest's mind who was the keenest of them all.

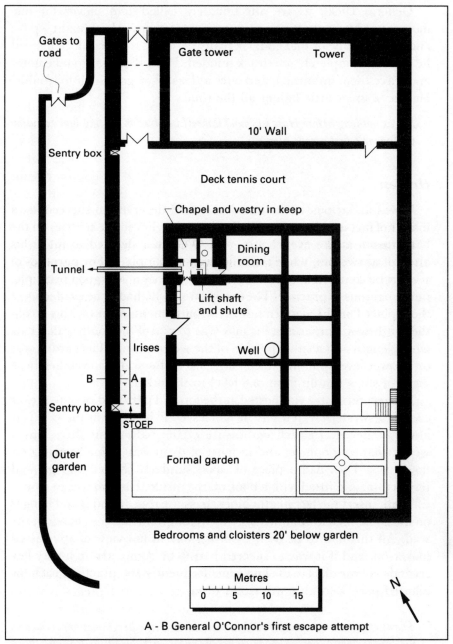

Gates to road

Gate tower

Tower

10' Wall

Sentry box

Deck tennis court

Chapel and vestry in keep

Tunnel

Dining room

Lift shaft and shute

Irises

Well

B — A

Sentry box

STOEP

Outer garden

Formal garden

Bedrooms and cloisters 20' below garden

Metres

0   5   10   15

N

A - B General O'Connor's first escape attempt

MAP 7. CASTELLO VINCIGLIATA, FLORENCE (LAYOUT)

Hargest

'General Dick', as we affectionately called him, never for one moment of his captivity gave up trying to escape. He thought, spoke and worked only for that end. He really deserved to succeed. In his zeal he became completely one-track minded. His failing was to take notes and leave them unburned, and once at least they got him into trouble. He was a great little fighter all the time.

It was not long before Hargest found himself involved in putting into execution O'Connor's first escape plan.

Hargest

It was audacious to the last degree and deserved to succeed; as a matter of fact it very nearly did. The guards relieved the sentries on the battlements at the even hours, and O'Connor decided to make his attempt at two pm, while the relief was taking place. For purposes of secrecy he confided in only a few of us, in theory a very good principle, but dangerous in practice. The two sentries who had to be evaded were those placed on the western side of the battlements. One had his box in the south-west corner and his task was to patrol the south wall for its whole length and a small portion of the western wall. The garden was on a lower level than the stoep and, to keep the wall an even height, a flight of steps ran up from one level to the other.

The second sentry was posted at the top and patrolled right to the far end of the western wall where he had a second box. It was there he was always relieved. In each embrasure of the battlement there was a wedge-shaped loophole, and in most of them was a small terra-cotta flower pot. Dick had a piece of wood similarly shaped and painted terra-cotta, and fitted with a hook on the inside. His aim was to mount the wall, insert the terra-cotta block, pass the rope round it and hang it on the hook, then lower himself away to the ground on the outside of the wall. All this had to be done in broad day in full view of any casual looker-on, and if it was to succeed had to be completed in a very few seconds. Those of us in the know met frequently and practised each his allotted part. Zero day was decided on.

The attempt had to be postponed, however, due to Brigadier Armstrong, who was not 'in the know', having made an arrangement with one of the Italian officers for that afternoon which precluded it. Thereafter all prisoners were kept fully informed of all escape plans, and no one abused this confidence at any stage.

146

The First Escape Attempts

The day finally arrived to try again. Brigadiers Miles and Combe were to throw O'Connor over the wall; Hargest was to give the word when the sentries were at the right places; and other officers had to move about to give the impression of their normal afternoon routine. O'Connor, in civilian clothes, came out with a pack on his back and sat on a bench between Miles and Combe, where the latter coiled a rope round his shoulder alpine fashion. At the crucial moment, with exactly 25 seconds in which everything had to happen, Hargest whispered: 'Go ahead, Sir.'

Smoothly and rapidly Miles and Combe stood up on the bench facing the wall with O'Connor between them. Each seized one of his legs and lifted him bodily up the face of the wall until he was able to grasp a wood post supporting the sentry's platform, when he drew himself clear on to the sentry walk itself. So far all was well. He was carrying the wooden block hooked to his belt and put his hand down to unhook it. It had become twisted in the ascent and he fumbled for perhaps two seconds; failing to release it he sprang like a cat into one of the embrasures and balanced himself there while he made another attempt to free the hook. This time he succeeded, and, pushing it into the loophole with one hand he passed the rope round with the other, hooked it and, lowering himself away, disappeared from sight. For one second I could see his fingers clasping the wall top, then they too went. All seemed well. 'He's away,' I reported.

Meantime the guard relief had passed on its way up the remaining forty paces to the last sentry box, obscuring O'Connor from the view of the sentry who stood half facing them. The relief completed, they went off, leaving him alone. He slung his rifle casually; then something must have attracted his attention. He came down towards us, quickening his stride.

I said to Miles: 'Go quickly and intercept him and keep his attention.' Miles did not understand at first, but then walked briskly along towards the man and met him still quite a distance from the point where the rope hung; but he had seen something and came on unslinging his rifle. When he leaned over the battlements and challenged we knew it was all up. He was a good fellow and not in the least excitable; he merely held the General covered while he called for assistance, which came in the form of some caribinieri who, storming down on O'Connor, threatened to bayonet him. I had discussed with him just such a happening and suggested that if it were possible he should attempt to throw his pocket book containing his maps and money back over the wall. Sure enough, back it came, falling at the feet of Miles, who whisked it through the courtyard gate into the hands of O'Connor's servant, Collins. In a very few moments it was safely away.

The castle became like an overturned beehive. The Captain, a new man who had aroused our suspicions by his ingratiating manner, now showed his real colours. He became almost hysterical, venting his rage on the poor sentry, calling him vile names and locking him up for the night. Then he broke in on us in a most abusive way, accused several of us of being O'Connor's accomplices, and said that we were no gentlemen. Meantime the culprit had been brought back to his room after an exhaustive search and the subsequent confiscation of his pack, and made to remain there for the night.

There was one nice moment when one of the Italian officers, Lieutenant Ricciardi, a general favourite with all of us and affectionately nicknamed 'Gussie', put his head into the drawing-room where we were assembled and said: 'The General is quite all right.' We appreciated his action immensely. He had been with the camp since its inception and knew us all, indeed he was more English than Italian in outlook, though never once did he turn aside from his duty to Italy. He was gay and kind and did much to make prison life as pleasant as possible, and officers and men alike were very fond of him. [Gussie worked with the British forces in Italy after the Armistice, and kept in touch with O'Connor for many years after the war.]

The upshot of the attempt was the arrival the next day of the area commander, a fine Italian officer called General Chiappe, who reversed the Captain's treatment of the sentry and gave him a present of five hundred lire for behaving like a gentleman, presumably in not firing on O'Connor. Then we were all assembled and informed that there was no use in attempting to escape. The castle was too strong and we would not escape from it alive, and even if we did there was no chance of reaching the frontier. O'Connor was sent to a fortress for thirty days' solitary confinement and the rest of the party did ten days in their rooms. There was a general overhaul of the Italian officers. The Captain, who had had the grace to apologize to Neame, was removed, as were Lieutenant Ricciardi and Visocchi, another good fellow who spoke English with a Scottish accent. They were considered too friendly, and were replaced by others not so well disposed, including one strongly Fascist lieutenant whom we suspected was a stooge placed by the General Staff.

The environs of the castle underwent a transformation. More and more lights were placed inside and outside the walls; new searchlights were mounted at each sentry box to be used to sweep the walls and the garden on the slightest noise. Eleven new strands of barbed wire were strung right round the battlements, placing the sentries in a kind of cage, and a new single-wire fence was placed a few feet out from the wall on the inside.

O'Connor was awarded one month's solitary confinement in a fortress away from Vincigliata. The way in which he described this period is evidence of the remarkable mental resources which he possessed, and which enabled him to endure his whole captivity so stoically, whatever its long term effects.

O'Connor

My month's confinement at Camp 5 was interesting and I quite enjoyed the change of scene. I was lodged in a cell from which it was only possible to see the sky by peering out of one of the two tiny windows. The electric light was insufficient to read at night. However, by sitting at the window it was possible to read by day, and the authorities eventually improved the lighting by night. The furniture consisted of a bed, table, chair, washstand and two chamber pots which had to be used for all purposes. Two hours' exercise was allowed daily on the battlements. My food was sent up from the main camp. No communication was permitted with any member of the camp, but I was able to carry on quite a satisfactory correspondence by writing on the inside of the lid of my mess tin. I cleaned my own cell and made my bed, but the slops were emptied once a day.

Actually I took plenty of exercise and was very fit, but was quite pleased when my sentence was over. I was escorted each way by a Colonel commanding an Infantry Regiment in Florence, a staff officer, and two Carabinieri. Both these officers treated me very well. The staff officer had been awarded a British Military Cross during the last war. [*World War One, in which O'Connor had been given his Italian Silver Medal for Valour.*]

I was delighted to see my friends again, and was also very pleased to find that they were already well on with another escape project.

As now attempts had been made to escape over the wall, by day and by night, there only remained *under* the wall—that is to say, a tunnel.

The great problem in every tunnel is the disposal of the spoil, and this had always given us much food for thought. Finally, it was decided to try and make an entrance into the chapel; sink a shaft to the requisite depth; and then tunnel outwards, hoping to pass immediately beneath the foundations of the outer wall. This locality had great advantages. The actual tunnel would be constructed from a point which involved the shortest possible route. The chapel was permanently closed, with its only entrance into the courtyard cemented up. This meant that once entrance had been effected, the work could be carried on with little fear of interruption, whilst, most important of all, the chapel and vestry could be used for the disposal of the spoil. The problem of effecting an entrance was a particularly difficult one, as any work on the wall would be so very hard to conceal. However, somebody suggested the ingenious plan of breaking through the wall at the back of the lift shown in the plan. The lift was electrically controlled, and was used to bring food up from the kitchen in the basement to the dining room immediately above on the ground floor. It was of an old pattern and was balanced by a pair of heavy weights. It could also be stopped midway, thus allowing the lift to be used as a platform. The spot selected to make the hole was at the back of the lift shaft on the dining room level. This could only be carried out when the lift was stopped midway between the two floors. A cover would also have to be made to conceal the hole.

The wall was found to be 18 inches thick and was composed of a sort of cement rubble. It was a tricky job as it was particularly difficult to work quietly. Special arrangements were made to make noises elsewhere to prevent the sentries becoming suspicious. However, it was finally successfully accomplished, and the first entry into the chapel was made. The drill for getting into the vestry was, first to lower the lift to half way, then to pull back the wooden cover, which was kept in its position by weights; a board was then put across through the hole and the workers had to push themselves through on their stomachs.

It was now possible to reconnoitre both the vestry and chapel. The former was a small room about 10 foot square, whilst the chapel, the ground floor of which was about 2 feet higher, was not less than 20 x 20 x 15 feet, so that there was plenty of room for the spoil.

A committee was formed to decide on the design for the tunnel. General Neame became chairman, and Boyd and the two New Zealanders formed the committee. The plan which finally emerged from their deliberations was that a shaft should be sunk against the outside wall of the vestry, 4' x 4' x 12'. This depth would, it was considered, be sufficient to enable the tunnel to pass under the outer wall of the vestry, but the general slope of the tunnel had still to be worked out, so as to make it deep enough to avoid striking the outer wall of the battlement, but not to be so deep as to miss the foundations completely, as it was intended that it should be finished by digging out an exit shaft straight up the outside face of the wall. Air Marshal Boyd was put in charge of the organisation of the work, which was to be carried out by Boyd himself, Combe, Hargest, Miles, Stirling, and Todhunter. Neame was to take charge of the general design of the tunnel and any points connected with its construction.

When I arrived back on October 1st I found that the shaft from the vestry had reached a depth of three feet.

Hargest describes how control of the work in the tunnel was assumed by O'Connor on his return, though Neame remained in overall charge.

Hargest

At about the end of September O'Connor came back and took over the command of 'operations' so far as the actual work went. Teams were organized to remain on a permanent basis. He and Combe made one, Boyd and Miles another, Stirling and I a third. We decided to work two shifts daily if possible—one from seven till nine-thirty am and the other from two-fifteen to four-thirty pm. As we had made fairly severe calls on men as watchers—men who could not benefit from our success—we insisted that the morning watch would be taken by those of the six escapers who were not working. It meant that of those six, five were working or watching and one was resting. Because of his inability to work due to injuries from the last war, de Wiart insisted on watching both morning and afternoon during the whole period. He is one of the coolest men I have ever met; yet in the six months that followed there were times when even his nerves were frayed by the incessant strain.

At this point O'Connor pays tribute to those prisoners who supported the escapers in every way possible although they knew they would not be able to get away themselves. In particular he mentions Major General Gambier-Parry; Brigadiers Vaughan, Todhunter, and Armstrong the South African; and Neame's ADC, Captain The Earl of Ranfurly, who proved to be a highly skilled carpenter. Among the non-commissioned officers and men, he gives special praise to Sergeants Baxter and Bain; Trooper Stones of the 11th Hussars, his own servant; and Cunningham, a sailor. But he stresses that there were others not named, who 'could not have been better'.

O'Connor

There is not space to describe some of the near shaves we had, but there is no doubt that Generals as a class do not make good sentries! On more than one occasion we were surprised by finding Italian officers in the building. Originally, whenever there was a report of Italians entering the castle, the workers were ordered to get back to their rooms. This was always dangerous, particularly when the tunnel had increased in length, as it took some considerable time to get both workers out of the tunnel and shaft, through the hole at the back of the lift, into the dining room, then upstairs to their rooms. We therefore decided to risk keeping the workers in the vestry, simply warning them by the alarm signal to keep quiet, and be ready to come out only if the head watcher thought it necessary. This arrangement worked much better, and greatly reduced the risk of detection.

All this while, General Neame kept check on the design of the tunnel, and calculated the slope required from the bottom of the shaft.

To assist him the carpenters made him spirit levels and other instruments for measuring angles, and reconnaissance of wall heights was made whenever possible.

Work proceeded slowly but surely, our excavating tools being one or two iron bars, a trowel, and an ordinary kitchen carving knife. The soil met with in the shaft was fairly easy on the whole, with little rock, but getting harder as it became deeper. But as we began work in the tunnel proper the soil became much harder, and gradually rock began to appear, which increased as time went on. These rocks were often so large that, when excavated, they required two men to roll them along the tunnel to the base of the shaft, where they were hoisted by rope to the top. With particularly big rocks three men were sometimes required. Of our tools, the kitchen carving knife referred to above was by far the most effective. With this it was possible to work silently, loosening the soil all round the rocks, levering under them with an iron rod, until finally it was possible to move them. One or two officers were real experts at this job; Combe, who was my partner, was particularly good, and also I believe Boyd and Miles.

Each Sunday, before work commenced in the afternoon, the previous week's work used to be measured by General Neame and there was much speculation as to what the weekly 'run' would be. I think two feet nine inches was about the record for one week.

O'Connor then explained at some length the method of excavation. Put briefly, the tunnel had to be dug 36 feet until it passed under the outer wall, after which it was slanted upwards to the point where it would come out into the open. Six inches were left for excavation when the night of departure was decided upon. The pile of soil and rocks carried back to the vestry and chapel eventually reached two thirds of the way to the roof.

O'Connor

By the 25th March the work in the exit shaft had reached to within six inches of the surface, and it only remained, therefore, to choose a favourable night for the 'getaway' from the point of view of weather. We had discovered that the outside of the outer wall was illuminated in certain places, thus allowing any movement outside it to be seen by the sentries looking outwards over the wall. Rainy weather therefore was necessary to keep them in their boxes. But at that time of year rainy periods were few and far between, and we were prepared for a long and wearying wait. All that we had decided was that we should take the first favourable night.

During the six months spent in constructing the tunnel, various plans were being worked out by the escapees. Boyd, Combe, Hargest and Miles had all decided to try and reach Switzerland, by rail to Como, and thence across the frontier on foot. Carton de Wiart and myself, however, had for various reasons decided to walk to the neighbourhood of Tirano, crossing into Switzerland along the eastern arm of the salient some miles north of the town. These two methods required different preparations, since the travellers by rail required little food and light clothes, whereas Carton de Wiart and myself required at least 17 lbs of food, spare clothing, socks, rucksacks and maps. Furthermore, we required to be extremely fit and strong, so that we could carry a big weight and walk long distances over mountainous country.

For this purpose we had collected certain articles of civilian clothing, which had still remained undiscovered, including two good rucksacks.

We had all we wanted in the way of food, first by collecting and keeping all the chocolate we were sent and were allowed to draw. We had also a few tins of bully beef, soups, etc., collected by the successful efforts of Ranfurly, our PMC, and the cook, Horsey, who frequently managed to bluff our captors. Combe also had collected all that he required as regards food and clothing. Boyd, Hargest and Miles had nothing, but Miles proved himself an excellent tailor and made three good suits of special blanket material, sent out by the War Office. We were also reasonably well off for both maps and money, thanks to the great ingenuity of the War Office in the ways and means they found to send them out.

As regards Identity Cards, two only arrived from the War Office— one for Combe and one for myself. It was a great achievement to have got them through, and my only criticism was that they gave our home town as Bologna. This was in fact too near home, and if captured one's ignorance could quickly be discovered by cross-examination. I think towns in Italian Tyrol would have been much more suitable, as not only would it have been difficult to cross-examine us on a town unlikely to be known intimately by the Carabinieri of our district, but it would also have given a reason for our foreign accent.

General Carton de Wiart, however, had not received one; but we were lucky enough to have a brilliant copyist in General Gambier-Parry, who copied the original from the War Office so cleverly that they were not even suspected as false by the Italian Carabinieri. But we had to find also a photograph for attachment to the Identity Card, and this was found, after looking through various numbers of the 'Illustrazione', in the person of President Antonescu of Rumania!

General Gambier-Parry not only made cards for Carton de Wiart, but also for all the others requiring them, and also set up and pasted on cardboard various maps for me. He was outstandingly good at this work, and we all owe him a great debt of gratitude.

Practically all our belongings were now transferred to the chapel, although a certain reserve was still kept in other places. Before describing the actual 'getaway' and a brief account of our wanderings, I would like to make a few general remarks.

The account I have given so far is a mere statement of fact, and does not touch on the nerve strain and various crises which we went through on occasions; nor have I said much about the personalities involved. I feel, however, the account would not be complete without touching on that side of it.

There are always two points of view about escaping in a prison camp: firstly, those who consider it is their duty to try to escape, and, secondly, those who do not want to, or realise that not everyone can go, and consider that they are helping the cause most by staying behind. In the latter category were Stirling particularly, and also Todhunter, who continued to help with the work in the tunnel, after they knew that it would not be possible for them to go. Great credit is due to their attitude.

The escapers fully realised that their efforts were likely to result in increased restrictions and difficulties for the remainder, and it is impossible to speak too highly of the co-operation and help we had from those who knew they were to be left behind. The same applies to the servant staff. Their assistance and loyalty were beyond all praise.

As to the escapers, we were really a very happy family, although we all had many differences of opinion, which was natural enough on so large an issue. Neame was a really good Chairman, and helped the party round many awkward corners. His technical knowledge was invaluable, and the plan for the design and construction of the tunnel was mainly his. He took some very bold decisions, which invariably proved right.

Boyd also was extremely sound in his ideas, and very good with his hands, but unfortunately did not run very easily in harness with Neame; but no serious effects resulted. However, he got rather weary of the difficulties connected with the organisation of the work, and I took it over from him some time after my return. But he was an excellent worker, and a first class carpenter, and much credit for our ultimate success was due to his efforts.

Miles was rather wild and unbalanced, as brave as a lion, but in one way or another was always producing crises. As he was Boyd's partner, he managed to involve the latter in questions in which he would never have been mixed up otherwise. Hargest, on the other hand, was a tower of strength, and always had sound ideas. Combe was my partner, and was a splendid worker, and he and I generally agreed on most of the problems. Stirling throughout put up a gallant and unselfish show.

Carton de Wiart was always magnificent and a great example to old and young alike. Ranfurly gave us the greatest help, both by his carpentering efforts and his success in obtaining tinned food for us. He was also a good example of the best type of prisoner, being both unselfish and hardworking.

The only other points of interest connected with the preparations were the necessity for Carton de Wiart and myself to be fit in every way for our long and arduous walk to the frontier. Our training was spread over two or three months, and involved hours of pack drill with a heavy load on our back; interspersed with walking up and down stairs many times per day. I ended up a certain period of training for one of our earlier escapes by walking up and down stairs continuously for five hours carrying my load. This involved 75 journeys up and down, which in height added up to between 3,000 and 4,000 feet—a very boring performance! This form of exercise had to be carried out when no Italians were about, often when work was taking place and the watching was going on.

Should we be lucky enough to escape, various problems had now to be solved regarding the best methods of keeping our absence secret for as long as possible. The first was how it could be hidden from the Italian officer doing the night check. The solution we proposed was the substitution of dummies in our beds. The deception would be made easier by having our mosquito nets let down. This we did for a month or more before the completion of the tunnel in order to accustom our captors to the sight of them, in spite of the fact that there would be no mosquitos for at least another month!

The decision as to the suitability of the weather was to be made by General Neame. This decision was a difficult one, as, in the previous years of our captivity there had scarcely been a single evening really suitable after the beginning of April, so that if we missed an opportunity before that date another night might not occur. On the other hand an unsuitable night might prove fatal.

The weather this year (1943) during the last week in March seemed more than usually 'Set Fair', but on the 28th heavy rain began to fall during the morning, continuing until after tea, when to our disappointment it began to lessen, with a fairer outlook in prospect.

It now remained for General Neame to cast the dye, and after a final look at the weather he decided that it was not suitable. A feeling of depression followed this verdict as some thought that we were missing a real chance. But General Neame very properly stuck to his guns, and our disappointment proved shortlived, as the evening of the 30th turned out to be a much better one for our purpose.

Rain began rather later in the day, and by dusk there was little doubt of its continuance, so the decision was taken that the attempt should then be made.

The plan for getting out was as follows. The excavation of the last six inches was to be carried out by General Neame and Ranfurly, commencing at 8 pm. A camouflaged cover to the hole had been made, which was to be temporarily stowed in one of the passing places constructed in the tunnel. All our kit, which was hidden in the chapel, had to be collected and brought to our rooms for us to change into. The dummies, so carefully made by our servants, had also to be brought out of the chapel preparatory to putting them in our respective beds before the night check by the Italian officer. Our dinner had to be eaten, and, in the case of Carton de Wiart and myself, our rucksacks had finally to be packed. Watchers had to be mounted to give early warning of any Italian entering our portion of the castle, and to observe whether sentries continued to remain in their boxes. And, finally, fully dressed and equipped, we had to enter the tunnel. The moment for which we had been planning for the past six months had at last arrived. The watchers were mounted, and General Neame and Ranfurly went down the tunnel, while the rest of us ate our dinner. Immediately afterwards, we changed and reassembled in the dining room. There was one slight hitch in my personal arrangements, namely that when I came to collect my rucksack I found that rats had eaten two large holes in it. However, Stones, my servant, managed to patch it most efficiently in under half an hour.

Just at the moment when the message arrived from General Neame that the shaft was open and all was ready, an 'alarm' came from the watchers that an Italian officer had come through the door by the white wall, and was making for the main gate into the courtyard. It was then only a matter of seconds before he might come into the dining room. Something very like panic ensued for a few minutes; everyone made themselves scarce as quickly as they could, hardly daring to breathe. It really seemed too desperate if this unlucky visit was to wreck all our six months' labour. However all was well, as the intruder never came even as far as the courtyard.

From now on everything went according to plan. We got out one after the other, as arranged. I left my rucksack at the bottom of the exit shaft, and Carton de Wiart passed both his and mine up to me, and also the cover for the shaft, which was a wonderful bit of work by Ranfurly. I then, with Hargest, helped Carton de Wiart out, and we slipped on our rucksacks and tiptoed off into the shadow, where the rest of our party were lying concealed.

The lights on the outside of the walls, although not actually over the exit, produced a considerable lighting effect over the whole area—much like Piccadilly in peace time it seemed to us—and I was extremely glad to move on out of it. Hargest remained behind for a few minutes longer, fitting on the cover to the exit shaft and generally making things look shipshape. In a few minutes, however, we were all present at the RV. From there, the first half mile lay through a wood to a point where those going by train had to take the road to Florence, whilst Carton de Wiart and myself had to take a path in a north-easterly direction towards the Appenines. Little time was spent in farewells and we were all soon on our respective ways.

Carton de Wiart and I were out for just under one week before our recapture, having reached a point in the valley of the Po about 20 miles NE of Bologna. We walked all the first night, crossing the R. Sieve successfully, and then up the main road towards Bologna until it was light, when we hid and rested for three or four hours. We then turned on to side roads, making a considerable detour, but reaching the main pass nevertheless by about 1900 hours. Here we were lucky enough to get well looked after and fed in a farmhouse, having said we were Austrians on tour. We slept well in a cow shed, being fairly tired, having walked just about 33 miles since we started, with full rucksacks on our backs.

Our object was to cross the grand trunk Bologna–Milan road between Modena and Reggio, so we had to turn off the main Florence–Bologna road and go across country in a north-easterly direction. This was very hard walking, as it meant crossing transversely the various valleys, which ran eastwards down from the main Appenine ridge. Sometimes, we walked by day, whilst at other times we were forced to walk at night for security reasons.

On two separate nights we walked from 2100 hours one evening to about 1000 hours the following day, with only short halts. Some nights we got shelter, and others we did not. Sometimes we got food from the inhabitants, and always water by asking for it. Generally, they were friendly, and were always willing to help and chat. Our description as Austrian tourists did us well. Before our recapture we were only once stopped and asked to produce our Identity Cards, and somehow or other we got away with that, much to our surprise.

My oil compass (kindly lent me by Todhunter) and the maps supplied by the War Office did us excellently, and our navigation was such as to enable us to cross the Modena–Reggio road actually at the point we had originally hoped to do. Our food was excellent, and proved to be in just the correct proportions. We were a bit weary at times, but we could have got on easily to the frontier, as far as walking was concerned. I calculated that at the moment of recapture we had walked just about 150 miles in the seven days.

Our capture was unfortunate, but we had been lucky on other occasions, so we could not really complain. It happened about 1800 hours on the evening of the seventh day of our freedom. We had been resting all day, and were proposing to walk all night to the actual area of the River Po where we hoped we should discover ferries, or small bridges, and avoid the main bridges. Whereas the existing cover over all the Appenines was generally adequate, that in the flat valley of the Po was non-existent. The country in which we were then walking was perfectly flat, and traversed by a large number of second-class roads bounded by small hedges about two and a half feet high. Every yard of ground was cultivated up to the last inch.

We hoped that in one more day we should be out of this dangerous area.

We were walking along one of these country roads, when without warning we were overtaken by two Carabinieri on bicycles. They decided to talk, and shortly asked to see our Identity Cards. Even then, conversation for a few minutes went on all right. However, the

Sergeant, who was rather more difficult, began to cross-examine me about Bologna, which he knew and I did not, and very soon they became suspicious. If only our Identity Cards had been made out for Bolzano or Merano, I am sure we should have got away with it even then. But we were told we should have to go to a Police Station, so realising then that the game was up, we admitted who we were. As soon as they understood we were Generals we were treated very well, and almost made much of, and a horse and cart was provided to drive us to the Police Station. Shortly after our arrival there all the Carabinieri chiefs in Bologna turned up to see us, and we were fairly comfortably lodged in a cell for the night. The next morning we were sent off by rail to Florence, where we were met and taken over by an officer from Vincigliata, and were there searched again and finally locked up in our rooms, with Carabinieri posted outside the doors. So ended this attempt, which we enjoyed immensely, and were not too downcast by our failure.

Hargest and Miles got away to Switzerland, and thence to Spain, where unfortunately the latter died. Hargest in his book told of what happened to the others. Combe was captured in Milan, and for three days refused to give his identity. Eventually the Italians were prepared to shoot him as a spy, so he had to confess who he was. Boyd was recaptured leaving a goods train which had stopped in Como.

Hargest heard in due course what had happened in the castle after the six had got away, and told the story in his book.

Hargest

Back in the castle events moved smoothly for a far longer period than we had expected. The dummies in the beds deceived the officer making the one o'clock inspection. In fact, he swore afterwards that one of them spoke to him; but somehow he wasn't believed, and received a month's imprisonment for neglect of duty. The same punishment was meted out to the young officer who conducted the eleven o'clock check, though there were extenuating circumstances in his case. When he arrived Neame took him in for coffee, and while he was there all the others came in and passed to and fro with such frequency that he was satisfied we were all there. So much for good luck. Things were going so well that they decided to put the dummies back into bed once again. Then things began to go wrong.

For the first time since we had been there the big gate was opened to let through a cartload of farm manure. The driver found the ropes we had hidden close beside it. Strangely enough the find did not cause a stir and nothing was done about it immediately. All the time, the Captain must have been uneasy, and at about six o'clock he made a round outside the battlements accompanied by Micky, the mess dog, a huge part-St Bernard, a great favourite with all of us. The Captain passed right over the covered lid without noticing anything unusual; but our friend Micky stopped and began scratching. The officer went back and found the exposed board; he had only to reach down and remove it to discover the outlet.

Even then he was not unduly worried. He still thought he had just forestalled us. Young Lieutenant Solera, whom we all liked, was sent in to assemble the prisoners and, approaching Neame, he said smilingly:

'Do you know what Mussolini said, General? He said that the best general was the one who had his troops on the field fifteen minutes before his opponent.'

Neame looked innocent and uncomprehending, so Solera explained himself. When he discovered that fifty per cent of the senior officers had decamped he lost his composure.

The hunt was up with a vengeance. Generals and senior colonels arrived, the chapel was opened, and the awful mess revealed. Disciplinary action was taken at once. All the servants were sent off, and each would-be escapee, as he returned, was sent straight to his room for thirty days' solitary confinement. Boyd told me later that coming back after having been so nearly successful he found this punishment the hardest part to bear; he craved for someone with whom to talk it over.

O'Connor was more fortunate. At intervals he was allowed into his bathroom, the window of which overlooked a sunporch we had christened the Cocktail Bar. At pre-arranged times all the others sat there talking to him while the Carabinieri sat in the corridor guarding his door quite ignorant of the ruse.

The Italians did seem mightily impressed with our industry. A steady flow of high officials came to see for themselves. Workmen cleared away the soil from the chapel, poured cement down the shafts and retiled the porch; but relations between the prisoners and their guards were never quite the same again. The same could be said truthfully of the castle and its ruined doors.

That our escape gave the Germans some concern is evident from a report issued on April 1, 1943, by the German Air Force Signals:

On the evening of March 31, 1943, six captured British generals escaped from a prisoner of war camp near Florence. They speak German well. It is possible that they will try acts of sabotage during their escape and will appear in German or Italian uniforms or in civilian clothing for this purpose. Special attention will therefore be paid to unknown persons in German or Italian uniforms or in mufti; when such persons enter military establishments or headquarters their identity cards *must be produced.* Papers shown will be thoroughly examined to avoid deception by forgeries.

O'Connor described his own treatment on return to Vincigliata, paying tribute as he did on several occasions to an Italian officer whom he much admired, General Chiappe.

O'Connor

During this period, the recaptured escapees were brought back and, as previously stated, confined to their rooms. Boyd and Combe were interviewed by the Army Commander, General Caracciolo, and Carton de Wiart and myself by General Chiappe, the Commander of the 'Difese' in Florence. He was, as always, very courteous and kind, and shook me warmly by the hand and congratulated us on our effort. I thanked him, and later in conversation told him that an officer at Florence Station, who had previously been on the camp staff, had deliberately failed to salute us on our return, which I considered most discourteous! He said he would deal with the case, and we heard that the officer had been punished and removed from his appointment.

He then said he could not say just what would happen to us, as the matter was in the hands of the Army Commander, but 'Soldiers are always generous to soldiers,' he said. I said I thought if that was so things did not look too bad, and he agreed that this was so, but said that it might be that General Caracciolo[6] did not like the English very much. I asked why, and he said that there had been some little trouble between his family and the British at Naples at the beginning of the last century, when Nelson hanged one of his ancestors at the yard arm on his flagship. I agreed that, as a result, he might not look on us in a very friendly light!

Our punishments, however, were quite reasonable—all of us were given one month's solitary confinement in our rooms at the castle. This ended about the middle of May, but in the interval a new Commandant of the camp had been appointed, who made life as unpleasant as possible by every means, including fairly frequent searches of our kit and effects.

I thought, therefore, that the time had come when he and some others of the more unpopular Italian officers should be frightened. Accordingly, I wrote a letter to the British Government giving a full report on the officers of the Italian Camp Staff, and the Generals and Staffs of the Zone and Difese of Florence. I was very polite about the more senior Generals, and extremely rude about the officers whom I disliked, and in the case of these latter I added that reports on them had already reached the British Government, who would know how to deal with them after the war. I hid this paper where I thought it would be found during the next search, which in fact it was. This also caused some excitement, but I know that they could not get at me for it, as I had hidden it and presumably had not intended it to be found. Moreover, the senior officers with the good reports were so pleased with them that they readily forgave the rude remarks I made about the others. At any rate, shortly afterwards the Commandant was replaced.

14

Escape after the Italian Armistice

As in the previous chapter, the story of the final successful escape is told mainly in O'Connor's own words.

During the summer of 1943, the military situation continued to improve and rumours were rife that the Italians might back out of the war.

On the 7th September, 1943, we were all assembled together in the drawing-room when the Commandant came in and said that he had a communication to make to us. We waited breathless. The Commandant drew a paper out of his pocket and then said: 'I have to announce to you that an Armistice has been signed between the Allies and Italy.' He added that General Chiappe, the District Commander in Florence, said that for the moment we were to stay in Vincigliata and that he would let us know as soon as possible what we were to do. The Commandant then withdrew and left us in a wild state of excitement. We went on talking into the small hours, wondering what if anything had been decided for the British Prisoners of War. The next day, no news came and the Italian sentries were still on their beat. I was able, however, to give some money to the sentry who did not fire after I had got over the wall of our prison on my first attempted escape.

However, on the day following that, we were told that we were to be driven the next afternoon to see General Chiappe in his HQ. We packed all our kit in suitcases and got into such civilian clothes as we had, and started off for Florence. General Chiappe was very kind to us and said that he had written to the Commandant at Arrezzo telling him that we should be arriving. He could not say what would happen to us then, but told us at all costs to keep out of the way of the Germans. As he was talking, the telephone rang, which he answered. He said that the Germans were just about to enter the town from the north end. He bundled us into the lorry and sent us to the south station and told us to board the first train to Arrezzo. We got to the station. This included not only the officers, but also our British staff—batmen and cooks. There were a number of friendly Italians who traded clothes and shoes with some of us. They were particularly keen to get our shoes as the leather was so much better than the Italian. But we did not have much time for all this as, very shortly, a train came in for Arrezzo which we got into.

General Chiappe was a very brave and friendly Italian. When the Germans occupied Florence, he was sent to an SS Camp and I have been told that he eventually died in confinement, either as a result of torture or illness. He had always been a very good friend to us.

When we arrived at Arrezzo, we found we were very far from welcome, and we were the last people the local garrison wished to see. There is no doubt that they were just as much in the dark as we were. It was really quite understandable, as a few days before they were fighting us, and now they were told, without previous notice, that we were no longer the enemy, but the Germans. I expect they had a pretty shrewd idea that the Germans would not take this new phase lying down. They were formal, but civil. We were herded into a room and told to wait until they had decided what to do with us. If the Germans happened to arrive when we were in Arrezzo, we would undoubtedly be handed over to them.

After a couple of hours, they told us that they were going to provide us with two coaches to drive us up to a monastery in the Appenines, called Camaldoli. The monastery at Camaldoli is partly a religious building and partly a tourist centre. The monks [Dominicans] seemed quite pleased to see us and gave us adequate accommodation and food. We had not really grasped that the Germans might have heard of us, or, more likely, that fascist Italians might inform about us. However, we stayed there for three or four days, but found that people had become curious and, after consultation with the Prior, who knew who we were, he recommended that we should go to another monastery higher up the mountain, as it was much more secluded. It was only about two miles from Camaldoli and was called Eremo. It was there that the *Priore Generale* lived. However, one day before we left, two of us walked across to where the main road through the Appenines ran from Italy to the north, and no doubt was one of the main roads to Germany. We stopped before we got there and took up a hidden position nearby, where we could watch the road. We stayed for quite a long time and saw long convoys of German lorries and vans pass by, driving northwards with furniture and other articles—no doubt loot taken from the Italians. It was quite an eye-opener!

Our party at Eremo was greatly reduced in numbers. Some remained at Camaldoli a few days longer. Most of our batmen had broken up into small parties and had taken to the hills. I think the only ones to come to Eremo were Neame, Ranfurly, Boyd, Todhunter, Combe and myself.[1] The *Priore Generale* thought it would not be safe to stay permanently and had made arrangements for us to go and live in a very isolated hamlet, high up in the Appenines, called Segetheina. They also arranged all the necessary payment for our keep, which was very trusting of them.

We found that Segetheina consisted of only four or five cottages, perched on an eminence. Only tracks existed—no road for cars. The nearest forest road suitable for cars or vans lay a mile away, with a deep gorge in between. The only water supply for the village had to be carried by hand from the water in the bottom of the gorge. The fact that there was no road through the village made it much safer for us, as nothing could approach us by day without being seen.

We were lodged in the various cottages. John Combe and I at a cottage belonging to a very pleasant woman with a lame husband, who could not walk at all. We were given quite a good room, which we shared. Todhunter and Boyd were put in another cottage. Their host was an extremely nice man called Lorenzo Rossi who was the headman of the village. Neame and Ranfurly stayed at the house of a very disagreeable man, who owned a number of bee-hives. He did not seem to have much contact with the others. The Rossi family was large, with a number of children of both sexes (not fully house-trained!). One or two other relations stayed there too.

During that time we once or twice paid a visit to Eremo. On one occasion, I arrived late in the afternoon, in very bad weather. I was hoping that I might be able to get some day clothes from my suitcase which they had kindly hidden for me. After I had arrived, I asked if I might have it for a few minutes. One of the priests said he would guide me to it. We walked through a number of rooms genuflexing whenever we passed a cross or Image of the Virgin. Finally, we reached a room which was really a chapel with an altar. My guide led me up to the altar and pulled aside the altar cloth. Underneath lay all our suitcases in a row. My guide said 'The Germans would never think of looking for them there.' The monastery authorities were very kind to us, paying the peasants for keeping us and interesting themselves in our welfare all the time.

During this time food for everyone was scarce, and what there was not very exciting, but the people of the village would have shared their last scrap with the escaped prisoners.

One day a party of four anti-fascist Italians came to visit them, and all were in time to prove most helpful. They were Signors Nanni, Spazzoli and Spada, and Major Tilloy, and further mention will be made of them.

About the same time a young Italian called Vailate came to see them, and he volunteered to get through the German lines and take a message to General Alexander.

The party were forced to move from Segetheina when some Germans visited the village, fortunately while they were away from it. But the inhabitants were naturally frightened, and Lorenzo Rossi suggested that they should move to another village called Straubatenza and make contact with a man called Maurizzio, a miller. They reached their new refuge after a six mile journey over rough country.

I walked with Combe and we arrived at Straubatenza about 5 o'clock and were looking about for a billet when General Neame, who had been in front of us, came up to us. He said that he had just received a communication on behalf of General Alexander to say that a submarine would call at two points on two separate dates with the intention of picking us up. Only General Neame, Boyd and myself were mentioned.[2] This letter had been brought by Vailate who had gallantly crossed the German lines and got in touch with 8th Army Headquarters, and subsequently GHQ. He returned in a submarine with two English Officers who had bravely volunteered to come and help us. Ferguson and Spooner were their names. We felt very indebted to them for having done this, but actually they could not help us at all as they could speak only English, and were two more mouths to feed.

The first date given was only 3 or 4 days off and the first rendezvous was at Cattolica which was many miles away and so we had to make a plan to get moving at once. I cannot remember just how this was arranged—whether by Maurizzio or whether something was put about it in the message sent to Neame. However, the arrangement was that we were to find our way to another monastery, Verna by name, where we would pick up a guide and three bicycles.

Escape after the Italian Armistice

The party spent a cold night at a rendezvous from which they were to be collected the following morning, and did not sleep much.

However, we were all ready to start when Maurizzio arrived. It was a long way across the mountains, only tracks, and nearly twenty miles to walk. We arrived at Verna about 2 o'clock, having walked with scarcely a stop. The monks were kind to us and gave us something to eat which was most welcome. We were introduced to a nice Italian, Cagnazzo by name, who said that he was going to guide us to Cattolica. This would entail three days bicycling. He would guide us in a car and produced three bicycles for us—mine was a lady's!

So, after a meal, we started off and bicycled between twenty and thirty miles to a village where Cagnazzo said we were to stop for the night—so in about thirty-six hours we had walked twenty miles across mountains and bicycled about thirty miles. We must have been very fit to have done it. We thanked Maurizzio for guiding us and took leave of the monks. Cagnazzo proved a loyal friend and was with us off and on until we finally escaped. But much had to happen before that....

I think we bicycled another day with Cagnazzo preceding us in a car and stopping from time to time. This day passed without incident and again we had satisfactory billets.

The third day we were due to arrive at Cattolica, and that was the night the first submarine was expected.

This day's ride had one interesting incident. Cagnazzo had decided to go on to Cattolica in his car, but another guide was provided to ride about half a mile ahead of us and warn us of any danger on the road. After having bicycled a few miles we saw our guide riding back to us as hard as he could. He said he had come to warn us that the Germans were preparing a bridge for demolition, which lay in our path. Preparing a bridge for demolition means making a number of holes in the surface of the road, putting a charge in each hole, and finally filling it up. There would probably be a path left wide enough for bicycles to pass. We decided, therefore, that the guide should go first, and if all went well, we should follow at a reasonable interval. We were able to watch the guide apparently riding through with no difficulty. So I followed and rode up the bridge. There were about a dozen Germans working, and as I rode up I prepared to get off. But I was waved on by the NCO, whom I saluted, and rode over the bridge. The other two also crossed without incident. We joined up again, breathing a sigh of relief!

We only had a few more miles to go and were guided to a farm house where we were given something to eat. Just as we were starting our meal, the wireless started and, to our joy, we heard it in English. It gave out that the Allies had determined that the surrender of both Germany and Italy was to be unconditional. This profoundly depressed our Italian friends, who were sure that it would lengthen the war. They also thought it very hard that the Italians should receive the same harsh treatment as the Germans. For us to hear anything on the wireless at all was a wonderful experience. No Italian was allowed to listen to an English broadcast.

During the afternoon, we bicycled into Cattolica to Major Tilloy's house. It will be remembered that he was one of the men who visited us at Segetheina. He had some children and they were kept up at the top of the house as he was very apprehensive that they might say something which would give away the fact that he had strangers in the house. So we kept downstairs and spoke only in whispers.

What we were planning to do was to get on to the beach and take out one of the existing boats. When we got into the right position, to keep on signalling our position with a torch until answered by a submarine— when we were to be put on board and the boat jettisoned.

After a considerable struggle to push the boat out to sea they signalled for hours, but no submarine came. Major Tilloy was not too happy to see them return, but agreed to shelter them until the next morning.

So ended our first attempt. When we finally escaped, I made enquiries and found that the submarine never came after all as it had been wanted for some important mission elsewhere.

Spada now comes into the story. It will be remembered that he was one of our visitors at Segetheina with Signor Nanni. He appeared next morning and Neame, Boyd and I were to go with him on our bicycles. So we started off and bicycled most of the day, stopping for coffee at a cafe.

Spada arranged for the party to be given a hiding place in a cold, uncomfortable chapel on the estate of one Count Spina, whose contacts with the Fascists were not clear, but he was suspected of playing a double game with them. After ten miserable days and nights Spada took them off to make the journey to Forli: a night on the way in a comfortable house was a great treat after the miseries of the cold chapel.

We had to leave before dawn and sometime that day we were introduced to someone in the underground movement who proceeded to forge identification papers for each of us. They were beautifully done and mine was signed by the Italian Command Office. I was also given permission to sell vegetables to the German troops. Fortunately, I never required to use them, but they would have got through any German post provided no Italian was there. We ended that night in a little town called Forli—I believe the original home of Mussolini. We stayed at the house of Signor Utila, an Italian lawyer. Again starting early, we only went a short distance to Signor Spazzoli's villa where we spent seven days. Spazzoli was a charming man, large and friendly and looked rather like a gamekeeper. I think his wife and sister were in the house and he had two sons, who had already created a good deal of trouble for the Germans. They winkled a wounded prisoner out of hospital and later on took part in various affrays, in which sadly they both were killed. Spazzoli himself was later arrested and tried by the Germans and executed. This was after we had escaped. They were a brave and gallant family and this country should indeed be grateful to them. After the war, I went out and visited them, thinking that they might well be very bitter. It was quite the reverse. They were delighted to see us and said how proud they were that their family was able to help us.

23 November 1943 was the night for the next rendezvous with a submarine. The party bicycled to a farm north of Cervia, where they were fed, and cared for kindly. After dark came a long and exhausting walk over difficult terrain to the shore: then another failure to be met by a submarine: finally, a miserable struggle back to the farm from which they had set out earlier.

Our friends of the night before did not dare have us again and we were told to try and get in touch with a man called Sovera who ran a small hotel in Cervia. Someone kindly went to Cervia and got hold of him and he came out to meet us. We told him our plight and he said that he would fix us up somehow and would come back as soon as possible and let us know. He did come back in due course, saying that he had a billet for us. This was actually on the outskirts of Cervia. He said he would bring along food from his hotel. He told us that the villa immediately opposite us belonged to an Italian who, holding a high position in the journalistic world, was a lukewarm fascist. His wife was an Englishwoman.

We found our villa very comfortable and found that it belonged to General Graziani, my erstwhile opponent in the Desert!

We were told that there were no Germans in Cervia.

Sovera arrived with a wonderful box of food. As we had had nothing to eat since the night before, and a completely sleepless night, we were ravenously hungry and did full justice to our meal. We also managed to heat some water and had a bath. During the afternoon, the English lady opposite, Signora Tellesio, came and called on us and invited us to tea the following afternoon. We accepted very readily and found her charming and sympathetic. So we had two comfortable days and nights.

The next day, however, things began to happen. The first thing we noticed was a party of Germans on bicycles riding down the road past our villa. We immediately tidied everything up and noted how to get into the thick wood which fortunately ran quite close to the back of the villa. We next noticed Signora Tellesio come out of her own villa and talk to the leader of the German party. They went off towards the centre of the town and as soon as they were out of sight, she came and told us that they were a German billeting party which had been sent forward to find billets for some troops coming that afternoon. She said that they had asked her about billets and she had said that the best billeting area was in the other part of the town. She said, however, that no time was to be lost and that we must take our bicycles with us and hide in the thick wood. She would tell Sovera what we had done and where we had gone to, and that he would get in touch with us later on.

O'Connor, Neame and Boyd hid in the wood until Sovera collected them in the evening and took them to a farm in the country for the night. They were moved on again on the two succeeding nights. At one farm they met some partisans. It was clear that the arms dropped to them by the Allies were being stored for use in gaining power after the war and were not going to be used against the Germans.

However, on the afternoon following our third night in the farms, Sovera came on a bicycle to see us. Accompanying him was Signora Tellesio. They told us that we were going back to Cervia and Sovera said that he had a billet for Neame and myself with a hospital nurse. Boyd was being billeted in Sovera's own hotel, which was the German HQ! As before, we were not to go out during the hours of daylight. Our hostess, whose name was Ida, was always known as 'Ida of the Hospital'. Neame and I shared a large bed and were quite comfortable. As far as I remember, Sovera brought us a box of food each day. Before we left, Ida asked us to write our names under the bed. When I went to see Ida after the war, she proudly showed us our names.

I can't remember just how long we stayed this time at Cervia, but we were beginning to become desperate as we could not finalise any plans. Sovera, Cagnazzo and Spada had been in touch with various partisan groups and they all seemed ready to help, but in the end it never came to anything. I think it was mainly because the various groups were so jealous of each other that they always prevented their rivals from being successful—each group wanted the credit.

The trio then moved, with Sovera's help, much further south to Cinglie, a place where there were said to be no Germans. Unfortunately, the day before they arrived, the Germans had appeared, and been rough with the inhabitants. After being lodged one night in Cinglie they were advised to go back to their starting point.

Our guide did not recommend us going to Cervia but for the present to an inn not very far from Cattolica. We were determined to try and get hold of some sailor ourselves with a boat, who would be prepared to take us to somewhere behind the British lines. We thought it was no good getting someone to make the arrangements for us. We insisted on seeing the person ourselves. By great good luck someone was able to contact a captain of a trawler, working from Cattolica, and he arranged to come and talk to us at the inn.

He arrived and we liked the look of him and broached the subject of his sailing us in his boat down the Adriatic and to some port behind the British lines. He said it would cost money as he would have to take his family up to the mountains and they would require to live and that the whole venture would be fraught with danger. He suggested £800 to start with and something more if we reached our destination safely. We wondered if we could find any friend who would be prepared to advance the money. He said it would be difficult to arrange as the fishing boats which sailed from Cattolica all had to return there by nightfall. The harbour was in the hands of the Germans and they carried out an informal check of the boats before departure. Moreover, the crews had to leave their boats each evening to go home—going aboard again early the following morning. Now I cannot remember which of our friends advised us whom to approach for a loan but the man suggested was a Signore Arpesella. He lived at Riccione, not very far away, and not far from Cattolica. Our friend promised to get in touch with him at once. In fact he returned later that day to say that Signore Arpesella would like us to come to Riccione and discuss the matter with him.

We bicycled after dark and arrived at Riccione and were introduced to Signore Arpesella. He generously agreed to pay the captain the money if we gave him an IOU with an explanatory letter. The plan we decided on was that we should get into the harbour at Cattolica at dusk, just before the crew left their boats for the night; that we should then go down to the hold and spend the night there, battened down. The crew would start up in the ordinary way in the morning. We hoped that the Germans would not make a very careful inspection of the hold. The captain had said that there was another hazard as well, namely, that the Germans might send either an aircraft or a submarine to look for us if we did not return to Cattolica in the evening, as directed. We could do nothing about this and could only hope that we were not considered important enough for it to happen. The captain would have to settle with Signore Arpesella for the most favourable night and the latter would drive us to a point within walking distance of the harbour, where we would be met and guided to the boat.

We shared an HQ with the Germans. I suppose the idea being the nearer you are to them the safer you are! We naturally did not appear by day but used to go out after dark and one saw German soldiers walking about just like British and we took no notice of them whatever. I was much more alarmed at the possibility of meeting a fascist Italian. However, we found that the time hung heavily on our hands as we did not seem to be able to get a day fixed. It was always tomorrow, but nothing seemed to happen. We constantly plagued and pestered poor Arpesella to do something more and I suppose he was doing his best.

However, at long last the evening arrived. Signor Arpesella took us down the road towards Cattolica. Before we reached the town we got out and he bade us farewell and we picked up a guide who took us across country to near the harbour. As soon as we reached the harbour, the boat was quite close to us and we had simply to walk down some steps and go on board. At once we went below to the hold and were battened down. One or two others came on board; Ferguson and Spooner, a priest who I recognised as having been at Eremo, and a woman. I can't remember if Cagnazzo was one of the party or not. After a few minutes, the crew cleared off and everything was absolutely quiet and quite dark. We talked in a very low voice ourselves.

Here we were, under lock and key—a wonderful prize for the Germans. We did not really know our Captain. For all we knew, he might be double-crossing us. Selling us to the Germans and taking the £800 from Signor Arpesella. However, I did not think that he would let us down. But I was quite worried about the Germans inspecting the boat before she sailed. I can't say that it was an enjoyable night. The hold was very stuffy and smelling strongly of fish. I don't think many of us slept—I certainly didn't. Eventually, at about 7 o'clock in the morning, while it was still quite dark, we heard someone come aboard. We waited in great apprehension as to whether we had been betrayed. I was sure we had not been, as if we had, the Germans would have been told at once. But nobody came and saw us. There was a clanking of chains as the crew moved about and then, quite suddenly, the engine started. It was a motor engine and just ticked over. There was a good deal of loud talk and then we quietly got under way and headed towards the mouth of the harbour. As we moved through the mouth the shouting and acceleration became louder. But we took no notice and kept on our course. I never heard exactly what happened, but I think the harbour officials were getting excited as we had not been inspected.

One thing greatly in our favour was the weather—it was blowing a gale and raining hard, and the visibility was very poor. So it was impossible to see us from the shore and if it would only last until night, we had a good chance of not being picked up. That was the most important side of the picture. But I should never recommend my worst enemy to be shut up in a stuffy, smelly hold in a storm. We nearly all were sick, and sick, and sick. I can never remember feeling so awful. A kindly Italian gave me a pill to take, which made me much worse! It went on blowing well into the night and suddenly the wind fell and the clouds cleared away and the moon came out very bright. This was a dangerous time and we were very frightened of an aeroplane or a submarine looking for us. We were allowed to come up on deck, which was something. About midnight, we changed our course and turned south. This enabled us to see the battle line, guns firing from *both* sides. It was wonderful to see this from the sea and we began to feel much safer as we were approaching the British Zone (General Montgomery's 8th Army).

Gradually the dawn came and aeroplanes were flying over us. It was wonderful to see Allied squadrons in the air, flying off on some mission. In the distance now we could see a town with a fairly large harbour, Termoli by name. As we approached, a certain number of armed men came down to greet us as we came alongside, and immediately we set foot on the shore we were arrested. I said we were British Prisoners of War who had escaped and I asked to see the officer in charge.

He came in due course and I knew him, as he had been a 'learner' in my office when I had been Brigade Major. I have never seen anyone quite so astonished! He said 'It can't be', and I said it really was and called him by his name, 'Professor' Grant. It was a wonderful reunion and one which I shall always remember.

After these preliminaries we were taken to the mess and given an excellent breakfast and allowed to wash and shave; and at the same time GHQ and General Alexander were informed. He sent us a message inviting us to stay with him. So, after saying goodbye to the

'Professor' and thanking him for his hospitality, we started for Bari, which was General Alexander's HQ. To us it was a wonderful drive seeing British soldiers instead of German and being given news which we had not heard since we became prisoners. Everything interested us. Everything was new and unexpected. We had never heard of a jeep! Eventually we arrived, just in time for dinner and were greeted by Alex who said 'don't bother about not changing! Just wash if you want to— we have a few people dining who will be interested to see you.' Actually the 'few people' to meet us were General Eisenhower and his chief planning staff from Supreme HQ! They were on an official visit to Alex and his HQ.

O'Connor could never say enough in praise of the brave Italians who helped their escape.

It really started by General Chiappe letting us out of our prison camp and setting us on our way to Arrezzo with an explanatory letter. Even though the Italians at Arrezzo wanted to see the last of us as quickly as possible (and one can hardly blame them) they sent us up in coaches to Camaldoli. How much the Priore Generale did for us we can only guess—he got and paid for our accommodation at Segetheina, where we were made welcome by Lorenzo Rossi and some others. Then three of our visitors to Segetheina helped us afterwards. Major Tilloy helped us at Cattolica and Spada was our constant companion and guide for nearly a fortnight. Then there was the Spazzoli family, to whose gallantry we can never pay sufficient tribute.

How great this gallantry was is shown in the following extract from the letter Madam Spazzoli wrote to O'Connor after the end of the war:[3]

Out of five brothers, only one is still in life, Renato; and one sister is still in a concentration camp in Germany, where she was taken by the Nazis.

Just now falls the anniversary of the tragedy of our family. Tonino and Arturo were slayed by the Nazi-Fascists; the former after being tortured for thirteen days, the latter was hanged together with others in the main square of Forli like a common assassin.

You who could witness their doings, their fearless undertakings, may well understand our torment, our agony in losing them in such a tragical way, at a distance of one day one from the other, and how painful it is to be without them, live without them, without our beloved who were every-thing to us, the moral support of the family.

The son of the doctor at Cervia, thanks to God, came through all it all right.

We have now one hope, one desire, to see again, soon, all those who lived near our beloved brothers, who could appreciate their worth in the momentous period of life.

We wish you'll soon be back in Europe. In such a case we shall much appreciate your visit, as you promised us in those days, and live a few days in the self same house that housed you in the most perilous moments of your and our life.

O'Connor Continues

Cagnazzo, who guided us when we got bicycles and Sovera, again whom we can never repay. Also Arpesella who was prepared to pay on our behalf £800 and put us up until the moment of final departure; and of course Vailate (and I was nearly forgetting him) who took our letter to General Alexander through the 'Lines'.

I hope this will make it clear how much we owe to our Italian friends. After we escaped, GHQ in Italy paid all our debts and gave presents and help to all those who had helped us. Neame, Todhunter and myself have been out more than once to see our friends and they were really thrilled to see us. Some came to England, including Arpesella, and stayed with Neame and Todhunter. I went out to Segetheina and saw Rossi and the others and stayed with Sovera at his hotel and saw 'Ida of the hospital' and many others including what was left of the wonderful Spazzoli family. We did in fact do our best to repay the tremendous debt and it is quite true to say that without their help we could never have got away.

We were also very much indebted to Signora Tellesio, who persuaded the German billeting party in Cervia to look for billets in some other part of the town. If they had come into our villa, we would have been recaptured for certain. She came to England after the war and was ill. I think she had consumption and was in very low spirits when I went to see her and thank her for what she had done for us. I met Sovera after the war and he told me that she had her baby taken from her by the Germans and was told that if she did not give them information about Sovera she would never see her baby again. She did, in fact, yield to their threats, but who can really blame her in the circumstances? Sovera got warning, so no harm resulted.

Dinner with General Alexander and his guests was a wonderful experience after the long wanderings of the previous months. It was marred to some extent for O'Connor when he tripped in the dark on a foot scraper on the way back to his

175

quarters and fell against a stone balustrade, resulting in a cut above the bridge of his nose requiring nine stitches. Boyd was able to vouch for his sobriety when the accident occurred!

The next day I felt my poor nose very sore and must have looked a sight with it bandaged up. But it was wonderful, being free again, without the feeling that I might be recaptured any moment.

Alex showed us round and told us some of his plans. We were decked out in battle dress which felt very stiff and uncomfortable, but we got accustomed to it. The day was the 22nd of December—the 21st being my wedding anniversary. A telegram had been sent to the War Office informing our relatives of our safe arrival. Alex also said he would get us home by Xmas. We were to fly to Tunis that afternoon on the first stage of the journey.

So we said goodbye to him and thanked him for his hospitality and embarked on our 'plane. Everything was new and exciting and our journey across the Mediterranean was thrilling. We arrived about 4 o'clock at the aerodrome and were met by Air Chief Marshal Tedder, who took us off for some tea.

At this time, the Prime Minister was in Tunis, in bed convalescing from his bout of pneumonia. He had apparently sent a message to say that he wished to see us and that we were invited to dine at the mess at Supreme Command HQ, which was where the Prime Minister was staying.

Directly after dinner, we were ushered into the 'Great Man's' bedroom by Lord Moran. There he was, like an old Bhudda, sitting up in bed. The first thing he said to me was 'Why did you allow yourself to be taken prisoner?'—and then after a moment he said 'But you are forgiven.' He then went on talking to us for nearly an hour and a half, hardly pausing to take breath. As one can imagine, talking to anyone would be interesting, but talking to a Prime Minister—and at that, Churchill—was something out of this world. He really brought us completely up to date. There seemed to be nothing he did not tell us and we sat there completely spellbound. At last, Lord Moran came in and said we simply must go and so we went, after I suppose about the most wonderful evening of our lives.

The next day we flew to Algiers where Mr Macmillan kindly invited us to dinner, which was extremely interesting. That night it poured with rain and the aerodrome got flooded, and we were not able to get off the ground that day at all. However, General Galloway, an old friend, was commanding an Armoured Division in reserve in Algiers—he came and saw me and we had a long and interesting talk. There was so much to talk about.

However, the next day the weather was better and we managed to get off and flew to Marakesh in Morocco. This entailed flying over the High Atlas Mountains and, as the cabin was not pressurised, breathing became quite difficult. However, we landed safely and were told we were going to fly to England at about 11 o'clock that night. We had to keep out a long way out over the Bay of Biscay to avoid being picked up by German fighters.

They landed at Prestwick next morning, which was Christmas Day.

The first thing I did was to telephone my wife at Cromarty. I told her that I was to travel to London that night and she said she would take the train from Inverness to London and would arrive at Kings Cross about 9 o'clock. This was wonderful news.

We were to travel south in a train called the 'Ghost Train' as it was not scheduled and only carried special passengers. We had a good journey down and arrived at Euston quite early. I had to meet my wife at Kings Cross, but I thought I would have time to go to a surgery and get my nose re-dressed. The doctor said it was healing well and that he could take most of the dressing off and so make me a bit more presentable. I just had time to get to Kings Cross, in time to meet the train from Inverness. I saw my wife in the distance before she saw me. She had hardly changed at all and it was wonderful seeing her again, after nearly two and three quarter years since I said goodbye to her on the day I was sent up to the desert in April 1941. A long and bitter time, of which I hated every minute. I always hoped I might escape and I had every intention of trying, but our success was all due to the bravery of our Italian friends.

We stayed a few days in London, during which my mother and my old Nannie came up from Rugby, where they had been staying, to see me. My old Nannie, [Christina], who had been with us for 60 years, died in her sleep three nights after I had arrived. I think she died of joy.

My wife and I went to Cromarty for a week, which we enjoyed enormously, and saw Jamie, my step-son.

But we had to go south again as I had been given command of the 8th Corps under General Montgomery. I was delighted at the thought of being employed again so soon. I was very lucky.

This brings me to the end of this narrative, which had a happy ending.

15

The Effects of Capture and the Years as a Prisoner of War

O'Connor had expected to be wounded or killed at many times during his spells of active service in both World Wars, but he had never contemplated becoming a prisoner. He had even told Jean on one occasion that this was something that would never happen to him. Whatever the circumstances, for a soldier of any rank to be taken captive is always humiliating, and for a General of his standing it could only be regarded as a devastating experience.

Because of his reticence about those matters which deeply affected his personal feelings, O'Connor rarely spoke about the emotional impact of being taken prisoner. Once after the war, when visiting some of the Italians who had helped him during the final escape, the ADC travelling with him, Simon Phipps, asked him how he had stopped himself becoming overwhelmed by the disaster that had struck him. His answer was that he knew that he had to overcome his dejection at all costs, and the way he gave all his mind to planning escapes was his main way of fighting depression.[1] His situation was similar to that which caused Field Marshal Slim to write so memorably of his own emotions after the long retreat through Burma in 1942, though perhaps O'Connor's plight was even worse. Slim wrote of the bitterness of being a defeated general:

> In a dark hour he will turn in on himself and question the very foundations of his leadership and his manhood.
>
> And then he must stop! For, if he is ever to command in battle again he must shake off these regrets, and stamp on them, as they claw at his will and his self-confidence. He must beat off these attacks he delivers against himself, and cast out the doubts born of failure.[2]

PLATE 24. Halfaya Pass (generally known as 'Hellfire') 1940. (*Squadron Leader C E Roberts*).

PLATE 25. February 1941. Lady O'Connor, as she had just become following her husband's knighthood, in a boat on the Nile during O'Connor's brief return from the Desert before his capture (*The Lady Aldington*).

PLATE 27. With Generals Wavell and Mackay (R).

PLATE 28. Photographed at Sulmona by the Red Cross. ((L to R) Younghusband, O'Connor, Combe, Carton de Wiart, Todhunter, Gambier-Parry).

PLATE 29. The Castle of Vincigliata. (*Mrs Rosemary Tripp*).

PLATE 30. Seghatina, September 1943, taken during the final escape. ((L to R) Angelo Rossi, hands in pockets, Ranfurly, Coombe, Spazzoli, Neame, Bruno (surname unknown), Signor Nanni, Todhunter, O'Connor and Boyd).

PLATE 31. With the very gallant elder Spazzoli.

PLATE 32. Speaking to senior officers in Yorkshire soon after taking command of VIII Corps.

PLATE 33. The trio who finally got away together (Neame, O'Connor and Boyd).

PLATE 34. Shortly before D-day. With Major General Gordon MacMillan (the Babe) at the 15th (Scottish) Divisional games at Brighton in May 1944.

PLATE 35. Normandy July 1944. Winston Churchill and Montgomery seated in front of Army and Corps Commanders. ((L to R) Bucknall, Ritchie, O'Connor, Dempsey, Crocker, Simmonds and Chilton (Chief of Staff 2nd Army)).

Plate 36. With HM The King and Montgomery. Normandy 1944.

PLATE 37. September 1944. Near Nijmegen. ((L to R) Ritchie, O'Connor, Graham, Dempsey, Montgomery and Verney).

PLATE 38. At the Alaf Khan Kot Camp near Kohat, North-West Frontier of India, in late April 1945. O'Connor with Auchinleck. (*Rt Rev Simon Phipps*).

PLATE 39. As Colonel of the Cameronians (Scottish Rifles), greeting HM The Queen and HRH Prince Philip at Lanark 1952. O'Connor is wearing the full-dress uniform of the Regiment. A Guard of Honour and pipers from the nearby Regimental Depot can be seen in the background. Lord Clydesmuir, the Lord Lieutenant of Lanarkshire stands centre. (*Scottish Daily Express*).

PLATE 40. Led by Mr Irvine, Principal of St Andrew's University, Field Marshal Earl Wavell and General

PLATE 41. May 1964. As Lord High Commissioner to the General Assembly of the Church of Scotland, O'Connor comes to the bottom of the steps of the great Assembly Hall in Edinburgh. On his left is the Purse Bearer, Major (later Sir) Alastair Blair in the uniform of the Royal Company of Archers. The second Lady O'Connor, who he had married in the previous year, follows just behind him.

PLATE 42. 1971. In the procession from St Giles Cathedral, Edinburgh, to the Thistle Chapel on the occasion of his installation as a Knight of the Thistle, O'Connor is preceded by the Dean of the Thistle and

O'Connor was not exacly a defeated general, but he had been involved in a defeat, albeit not of his own making, and worse still was his fate as a prisoner. However capture has been brought about, this fate is always, as already mentioned, a shameful one, and for a man of O'Connor's temperament it must have been an almost over-whelming disaster, requiring the greatest effort of mind and spirit to prevent it destroying him.

That this effort to 'stamp on his regrets' was not easy is shown by letters written to Jean by Carton de Wiart on 23 May and 15 July 1941. In the May one, he mentioned that on his own arrival at Sulmona, about a week after O'Connor, he had found the latter very down in spirits, but that he was now improving. By mid-July he was able to tell Jean that her husband was much better and fitter, with only 'an occasional bad day we all have'.[3]

Physically, the time spent as a prisoner did O'Connor little harm. He was always a frugal eater, and the rations provided by the Italians were adequate for his needs, especially when backed by regular parcels through the Red Cross. In general, the Italians treated all their prisoners well, and the senior officers while at both Sulmona and Vincigliata were as decently fed and cared for as was possible for a country itself at war and suffering shortages of many kinds. His good physical condition was proved during the escape with Carton de Wiart, and again in the final journey south to freedom in the winter of 1943.

While O'Connor fought to 'cast out the doubts born of failure' from his mind, and devoted all his energies to planning and preparing for escapes, there were a number of people still enjoying their freedom in various parts of the Middle East and India who began to denigrate his achievements. Some were perhaps jealous of his great reputation: others were simply amazed that a man of his ability should have been involved in such a futile mishap as his capture appeared to have been. The way in which Neame's force had collapsed under Rommel's assault both shocked and frightened the Desert Army, and there were many, who did not know the full story, who criticised O'Connor for not having taken over and mastered the situation in the way expected of him. He became in fact one of the scapegoats of the affair, and his loyal friends and supporters were forced into taking action to preserve his good name. One who was particularly incensed at some of the unpleasant aspersions being cast on his great friend's good name was George Collingwood, who in November 1942 felt so strongly about the matter that he wrote to Wavell, who was by then Commander in Chief in India. Wavell replied to him at length:

New Delhi
10th Dec. 1942

My dear Collingwood,

I have just got your letter of Nov. 10 and am answering it at once since I am going away tomorrow for four or five days. Curiously enough, I sent off a letter to Dick this morning; I write to him periodically and hope he gets them. I am sorry to hear that he has been in close confinement; I was sure he would have a shot at escaping if he could and I am very sorry he has not got away.

I am distressed at what you say about his being blamed for what happened in Cyrenaica and for being captured. The following facts may be useful to you and to Jean if you have occasion to combat such talk.

Two long paragraphs followed about the conduct of Operation COMPASS, and then Wavell returns to the events of April 1941:

(c) After Cyrenaica had been captured, General Wilson took over control as Military Governor and Commander in Cyrenaica, and Dick went back to the Delta for a rest. He had not always been fit during the operations and it was often only his grit that kept him going. When General Wilson went to Greece I put General Neame in command in Cyrenaica, as I thought Dick required a longer period out of the desert. He was thus not in any way responsible for the tactical dispositions in Cyrenaica at the time of Rommel's counter-attack.

(d) Shortly before Rommel's counter-attack, I visited the front and did not like the tactical dispositions that had been made and ordered certain alterations; as soon as the counter-attack took place, I went up to Cyrenaica. I was not satisfied with the way things were being handled and sent a special wire to Egypt for Dick to come out and take charge. He arrived at once by air, though he was far from well at the time. I thus sent for him specially because things were going badly, but he had no responsibility at all for what did happen up till then.

(e) He was captured, I think, within 48 hours of his arrival in Cyrenaica, so that he had no time to influence the course of events. I know very little of the actual circumstances of his capture, whether he was in any way imprudent in remaining behind when the rest of his headquarters had gone on, I cannot say; but I am quite sure that the proper place for a general during a retirement is to remain with the rear troops [i.e. the units nearest the enemy] as long as he safely can. So far as I know the facts, I believe Dick was most unlucky in being captured.

(f) As soon as I learned of his capture I sent a wire to the War Office to ask if they would offer any five Italian generals who had been made prisoner by us, in exchange for Dick. The WO rather primly replied that they thought it would be unprecedented, or something to that effect. This can hardly be made public, but it is a fact.

I think the above should give you or Jean any material necessary for rebutting any allegations that Dick was in any way responsible for what happened in Cyrenaica. I don't think they can be published, at least certainly not without reference to the WO, and I think further reference to me; but I have no objection to you or Jean making use of the letter privately, to show what I thought, and think, of Dick. For instance you may, if you like, send the letter to Wigram[4] to see, and if he did make any disparaging remarks about Dick, I am quite certain he will withdraw them. I have accepted full responsibility for what happened in Cyrenaica in March and April 1941, in my reports home; I never thought specifically to say that Dick had no responsibility, since it was obvious to anyone who knew the facts.

I hope this will give you what you want. I have always felt desperately sorry about Dick, and for my responsibility for getting him captured. He was one of the most gallant, and would undoubtedly have been one of the most distinguished, generals of this war if he had not been so unlucky.[5]

The criticism repeated by O'Connor's detractors was not limited to him alone: the same treatment was given to all the generals who commanded in the Desert before the victory at El'Alamein in October 1942. To some extent this was fostered by Montgomery, who dismissed the efforts of some of those who had preceded him in the area with contempt, though he himself never put O'Connor in the same category as the others. But among many of the officers who arrived in Egypt, as the build-up of the Eighth Army progressed during 1942, there was a tendency to regard all efforts that had gone before as inefficient and unimaginative. With their own preponderance of men and equipment, they were unable to comprehend how much had been done by their forerunners, with only a fraction of the advantages which they themselves enjoyed by the time the battle of El'Alamein took place.

It was probably unavoidable that some damage should be done to O'Connor's reputation among those who did not know him by the events of the fateful three days between 3 and 6 April, but in time it became clear to most people how little he was to blame, and in due course his successful escape did much to restore his good name. It was also unavoidable, and this was more important still, that he should have lost touch with many developments in the techniques of warfare while he passed his time so far from a modern battlefield. A particularly serious disadvantage was missing the opportunity of gaining experience of German tactics, especially their methods of handling armour in conjunction with anti-tank gun screens.

From the moment when O'Connor arrived with Neame and Boyd at Alexander's headquarters at Bari on 21 December 1943, he impressed everyone with his fitness and vigour. Many years later, in a letter written about the same time as the one quoted in the prologue, Eisenhower told him: 'I think that the evening on which you returned to Alexander's head-quarters from an Italian prison is one of the most memorable of the entire Mediterranean campaign.'[6] Quickly the word spread that Dick O'Connor was free, and showing little ill-effect of his long captivity. No doubt the impression he made on Churchill, his family, and staff at Marrakesh reinforced this good news. Montgomery certainly heard similar reports very soon, and on 28 December 1943 wrote to Alanbrooke from Algiers. Paragraph 5 of his letter ran as follows:

> I suggest that O'Connor is the man to come out here and take over 8th Army. He had it before. He must have some leave and then get up to date, and then come out here to relieve Oliver Leese. Leese then returns to UK and takes the Second Army. What do you think of this?[7]

The answer was that Alanbrooke did not think a great deal of the suggestion, and that anyway before making any decision he wished to see O'Connor himself. An interview was arranged for early January 1944 and O'Connor, who considered Alanbrooke 'Our greatest soldier from every aspect', later told how it was conducted:

> His method of testing me was to see what my reactions were to some of his stories of his troubles with Churchill and the Joint Chiefs of Staff. I was thrilled at some of the things he told me, and asked many questions, which was no doubt what he wanted.[8]

A few days later O'Connor was appointed to the command of VIII Corps, and instructed to assume his new assignment on 21 January, so he must have passed Alanbrooke's tests with credit. Certainly the general opinion in military circles were those recorded by Pownall in his diary in June 1944, who wrote of O'Connor; 'I hear he is in great heart and unaffected by captivity.'[9] Clearly this was the impression he gave, and it was a wonderful reflection on the strength of his determination not to allow himself to be destroyed by imprisonment. However, to an observer able to look back over the whole of his life, there is a lingering doubt as to whether in truth he was completely 'unaffected by captivity'.

Lord Harding, who was so close to him throughout the Desert Campaign, and whose urgent pleading to Wavell was the main cause of O'Connor being brought up from Cairo on 3 April 1941, was not prepared to say much about the effect of captivity on his late commander. But he made the guarded comment: 'No man can be a prisoner for nearly three years and remain unaffected in some way.'[10] At the risk of having misunderstood the true situation, it appears to this author that after his return to duty in January 1944, O'Connor lacked some of his original fire and confidence. This will be discussed in the chapters which follow: the picture, however, is not too clear. For one thing his handling of his corps in battle was particularly good at the end of his time in north-west Europe, indicating that he merely had to catch up with tactical lessons missed during his captivity, rather than that he lacked his original 'spark'. Against this, it might be claimed that nearly three years as a prisoner had aged him at twice the rate which would have occurred had he remained free, and been stimulated and inspired by the challenge of great events. He became 55 in August 1944, which was distinctly old for the wartime command of a corps. If a guess is made that the stagnation inevitable in prison life meant that his mental approach to many problems was more that of a man of 60, it can be seen how great a struggle the first weeks in Normandy must have been for him.

Though these comments are pure conjecture, they may have truth in them. What is not conjecture is the fact that O'Connor's mastery of himself during his long, miserable days of captivity was a wonderful achievement. By his will-power and courage he overcame dark forces which could well have destroyed him, though it is difficult to believe that they left him entirely unaffected.

16

Command of VIII Corps in Normandy

Preparations for Invasion

VIII Corps, which had started the war in a static role in south-west England, had been moved in June 1943 to the north in order to be made into a largely armoured formation, and to be trained to take part in the invasion of Europe. The headquarters moved to Sand-hutton Hall near York on 1 June 1943, and by 20 June had 'assumed its final shape for active service—Guards and 11th Armoured Divisions, 15th (Scottish) Infantry Division, 6th Guards Tank Brigade, 8th AGRA and 2nd Household Cavalry Regiment as the Corps armoured car regiment.'[1] At that stage the commander was General Herbert Lumsden, who was succeeded in July 1943 by Sir Richard McCreery, who only stayed a month before being flown out to command X Corps in North Africa. His successor, John Harding, likewise spent only a short time with the Corps before being called away to Italy as Chief of Staff to Alexander. By the time O'Connor arrived to assume command on 21 January 1944 Major General Gordon MacMillan was in temporary charge, while also command-ing his own 15th (Scottish) Division.

It was exactly one calendar month after landing at Termoli—unshaven, stinking of fish and just recovering from violent seasick-ness—that O'Connor took up this new appointment. His first task was to get to know his own staff, and then to see as much as possible of the formations under his command.

His Chief of Staff, still known as BGS at Corps level in those days, was Sir Henry Floyd, Bt, a 15/19th Hussar who had left the Army for a time before the war to become Chairman of Christies, a post to which he returned as soon as it was over. He was a tower of strength to the new commander and became a good friend as well. The chief administrative officer, known as DA and QMG, was Brigadier E P Sewell who was to remain with the Corps throughout the rest of the war.

Four other brigadiers served in the headquarters: Matthew, nicknamed 'Hammer', the commander of the Royal Artillery; Sugden the chief engineer; Knowles the chief signal officer; and as head of the medical services, the remarkable H L Glyn Hughes who held both the DSO and MC and 'became a famous character not only in VIII Corps but throughout Second Army, for his abilities were by no means confined to the practice of healing the sick and wounded', to the extent that on many different occasions, in all sorts of quandaries, 'The cry was always "Send for the DDMS—he'll know the answer." '[2]

MacMillan, the commander of 15th (Scottish) Division who had been also acting as Corps Commander, was a man O'Connor greatly admired, and one with whom he kept in close contact long after the war was ended. One of the youngest Major Generals in the Army, the thirty-seven-year-old 'Pip' Roberts commanded 11th Armoured Division: he was to make it into the finest armoured division in the Army, and to prove himself the outstanding British armoured leader of the war. During operation COMPASS in the desert he had been Brigade Major of 4th Armoured Brigade. At the head of the Guards Armoured Division was Major General Allan Adair, a Grenadier, and 6th Guards Independent Tank Brigade was commanded by Brigadier Gerald Verney of the Irish Guards. Lieutenant Colonel Henry Abel Smith commanded 2nd Household Cavalry Regiment, whose armoured cars did invaluable service in due course in Normandy and beyond.

O'Connor had learnt the importance of the supply and maintenance services in the desert, but had not seen before the provision of these vital elements on such a massive scale as he now found on arrival in Yorkshire. As usual he spent much time with them to show how important he regarded their work.

In February 1944, the Corps was put through its paces in a particularly rigorous and testing exercise code-named 'Eagle', which had been prepared by Harding before he left for Italy. Carried out in almost Arctic weather conditions, and designed to employ all arms and services in as realistic a representation of winter campaigning as possible, the exercise gave O'Connor a chance to bring himself up-to-date to some extent with the latest techniques of armoured warfare in European conditions. It also provided his first main opportunity to see his own headquarters staff and his subordinate commanders in operation.

There were many visitors to Headquarters VIII Corps while it was in Yorkshire. Montgomery, newly appointed Commander-in-Chief 21 Army Group, arrived not long after O'Connor had taken over, and took the opportunity to talk to many different units at apparently simple parades, which were in fact most carefully prepared and stage-managed, and consequently most effective. Each ended with the troops being called in around a jeep on which Monty stood to make a short, confident speech, before sailing off in a large Rolls-Royce flying an outsize Union Jack.

Following this visit, O'Connor received a letter dated 19 February from Dempsey, commanding Second Army, which put him in an awkward predicament. It stated that Montgomery considered Adair to be lacking in drive, and not suitable for command of an armoured division, and that therefore an adverse report should be written on him so that he could be removed. Being the man he was, and less in awe of his old contemporary, Montgomery, than most, and certainly not of his one time subordinate Dempsey, O'Connor refused to do this, and stated bluntly that he would write no such report on any officer whose true abilities he had not yet had time to assess. In the event Adair proved a competent leader of his division throughout most of the ensuing campaign, and retained his appointment without further interference.[3]

On 23 March 1944, Their Majesties the King and Queen, with Princess Elizabeth, visited the Corps, followed just over a week later by the Prime Minister. His Private Secretary John Colville recorded in his diary:

> Fri, 31 March 1944. Left the train at Driffield. Inspected RASC and corps troops, to whom the PM made a speech, and then the Guards Armoured Division. Saw a tank display and the PM went for a ride in a Cromwell. General O'Connor (who was captured in N Africa and escaped when Italy fell), Sir Henry Floyd and Brigadier Matthew (CCRA) accompanied us everywhere.[4]

On 26 April a letter was despatched from Downing Street, signed by Churchill himself, referring to this visit and instructing O'Connor to report direct to the Prime Minister on certain matters which had been discussed during it. He was told to consult only one or two of his most senior officers and then should '... let me have privately your detailed comments, especially about the escape hatches'.[5] This presumably referred to the driver's hatches of waterproofed tanks and the problem of escape when a tank was immobilised whilst still wading in deep water.[6]

VIII Corps began to move south in preparation for the invasion on 14 April, and in due course the headquarters was established at Worth Priory near Crawley. During the previous week, O'Connor and Floyd had attended Montgomery's briefing on his plans for 'Overlord', given at his headquarters in St Paul's School to almost everyone prominent in Allied circles at the time.

VIII Corps Ashore—Operation Epsom

On 7 June, VIII Corps headquarters began to move slowly towards the coast, embarking in a landing Craft Tank (LCT) on 11 June, and landing in Normandy at Rivabella near the mouth of the River Orne the next evening. Here O'Connor and some of his operational staff, who had crossed the previous day, were waiting to meet them. It took some days to move the whole Corps across to France: 11th Armoured Division as an example travelled from the Thames, round the coast of Kent, to disembark on 13 and 14 June. Others were slower, and the delays became worse as the weather deteriorated in the ensuing days.

Soon after arrival of the headquarters, plans were discussed for the first operations to be undertaken by the Corps, which was gradually concentrating some six miles to the north-west of Caen. The failure of the Second Army to take Caen as intended in the first two days after D-Day on 6 June, had disrupted all anticipated movements in the British and Canadian invasion sector. Montgomery now wished to by-pass the town in order to encircle it. At first he considered the use of VIII Corps in an operation provisionally named 'Dreadnought', to make a break-out from the increasingly congested bridge-head to the east of the River Orne. When he came to VIII Corps Headquarters to discuss this plan, O'Connor told him of the difficulties of this course of action. On 19 June Montgomery wrote to him:

> I am grateful for the very clear exposition on the problems of the attack from the existing bridge-head east of the ORNE, and considered the problem after leaving you and told Bimbo to chuck it; 8 Corps instead to deliver its blow on the EVRECY flank.

When you have got your plans thought out for the new thrust line, do come and see me and explain them—or I will come and see you.[7]

In his directive to Dempsey and Bradley of the same date, he explained that:

Detailed examination of the problem has revealed that the difficulties of forming up 8 Corps in the bridge-head east of the R Orne, and of launching it from the bridge-head as the left wing of the pincer movement against Caen are very great. The enemy is strongly posted on that flank and certain preliminary operations would be necessary; these would take time and we do not want to wait longer than we can help.[8]

In fact a period of waiting became necessary, because the weather continued to prevent the arrival of the necessary men and material to reinforce the Corps. As Montgomery wrote on 20 June to his old friend General Simpson in the War Office: 'This weather is the very devil. A gale all day yesterday; the same today. Nothing can be unloaded. Lying in ships off the beaches is everything I need to resume the offensive with a bang.'[9] He now decided to mount a major offensive south-west of Caen, across the River Odon, to seize the high ground dominating the west bank of the River Orne. The offensive was given the code-name 'Epsom', and it was hoped to launch it on 23 June, but the bad weather forced a postponement, in particular to allow 15th (Scottish) Division to complete its strength with those elements which had been prevented from landing on time by the storms. Also requiring time to reach full strength was 43rd (Wessex) Division, which had been put under command of VIII Corps for the operation. As many of its tanks had not yet been landed, the Guards Armoured Division was not to take part, but two independent brigades were attached, 4th Armoured and 31st Tank and two squadrons of 'flail' tanks for mine clearing. To help with many anticipated engineer tasks, several specialist Royal Engineer units were also put under command.

'D' day for 'Epsom' was eventually settled for 26 June. On the 23rd, O'Connor gave a full briefing to all officers of the rank of lieutenant colonel and above at Corps headquarters. The written operation order confirming this briefing stated as the intention:

On D Day 8 Corps will break out of the existing bridge-head on the front of 3 Canadian Division with a view to the Corps crossing over:

(a)   The River Odon
(b)   The River Orne

so that at a subsequent date the Corps can be positioned on the high ground north-east of Bretteville-sur-Laize, thereby dominating the exits from Caen to the south.[10]

Opposing the Corps were some very determined enemy formations, who had taken full advantage of the weather which had delayed the Allied build-up to improve their own strong defensive positions. The German Odon sector was commanded by the formidable General Sepp Dietrich, founder of the Waffen SS and the one time commander of Hitler's personal bodyguard. The two SS Panzer divisions which comprised his corps, numbered 1 and 12. The latter, which bore the title Hitler Jugend was largely composed of youthful fanatics who fought with a ferocity unequalled by any other German troops. They were also provided with Panther and Tiger tanks which were superior in armour and hitting power to any on the Allied side, although in numbers of tanks the Allies were much the stronger. Finally, the terrain they were defending was ideal for their purpose, being described as follows in the Corps history:

> the country is definitely enclosed with limited vision and comparatively short fields of fire. Hedges and copses abound to the south, as far as the first major obstacle, the River Odon, which is a sluggish stream averaging twenty feet in width with flat shallow banks and lined for most of its course with trees and small thick woods, the clearance of which was to prove a troublesome matter.[11]

Beyond the Odon the ground is more open and undulating. It is dominated by a slight ridge, the highest point being called Hill 112. Although quite low, this is just high enough to overlook its surroundings. It was to be of considerable significance during 'Epsom', and the scene of very bitter fighting.

In support of the opening moves of the VIII Corps attack on 26 June, O'Connor had been allotted very considerable artillery support, both from his own resources and the corps on his flanks—I Corps on the left and XXX Corps on the right. He had also asked for and been promised massive support by the RAF. However, once again the weather was against him. An hour before midnight on 25 June he was notified by G (Air) Branch at Headquarters Second Army that the heavy bombers due to come over before dawn could not take off from airfields in England: to make matters worse, the medium bomber and fighter-bomber sorties were also cancelled early on 26 June because of the overcast conditions. All that was left of the planned air effort was fighter cover and limited air-to-ground

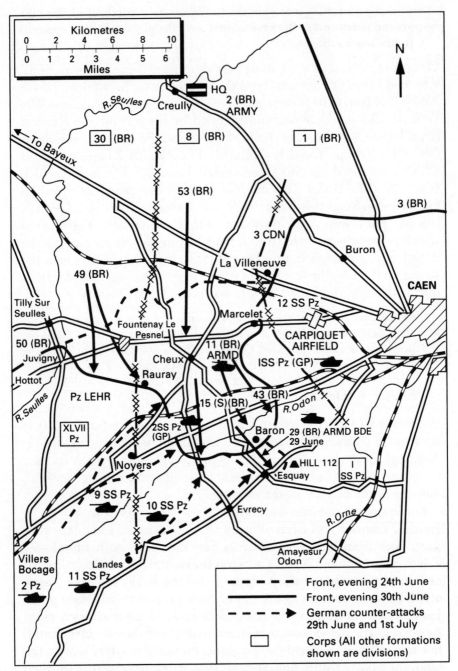

MAP 8. OPERATION EPSOM 26-30th JUNE 1944

support. This was of great value, but represented only a tiny proportion of the help that had been anticipated.

A further disappointment on that night of 25/26 June was the failure of XXX Corps on O'Connor's right flank to take a spur, round a village called Rauray. This overlooked the exposed ground across which 15th (Scottish) Division, leading VIII Corps advance, would have to move during the early stages of the battle. The plan was for the Scots to pass through the line held by 3rd Canadian Division and advance about five miles to establish crossings over the Odon river through which 11th Armoured Division would then pass before driving south-east to seize bridges over the Orne.

The VIII Corps history comments on 'certain salient features which should be borne in mind' about the design for 'Epsom':

1 It was the first operation undertaken by troops of VIII Corps and, for the vast majority of them, their first actual battle experience.

2 The plan was an ambitious one, involving an attack by an infantry division through which an armoured division was later to pass, against a resolute enemy in strongly prepared positions.

3 The objectives, several miles deep in enemy territory, were such that, if gained, the Corps would be in a very pronounced salient. Remembering the Commander in Chief's policy of endeavouring to attract as much enemy armour to this flank as possible and away from the Americans, the reaction of the enemy could be expected to be violent, and it was obvious that heavy fighting would ensue.

4 Deterioration in the weather limited the powerful air support which otherwise would have been at the disposal of VIII Corps.[12]

Only an outline can be given here of the heavy fighting which certainly ensued from soon after the first elements of 15th (Scottish) Division crossed the start line at 7.30 am on 26 June, with 9th Cameronians and 2nd Glasgow Highlanders the forward battalions of 46th Brigade, and 8th Royal Scots and 6th Royal Scots Fusiliers leading 44th Brigade. Following the massive artillery bombardment of 700 guns, the Scots moved quickly through cornfields for a short time, but soon found that the Germans had recovered quickly after the guns lifted and were defending fiercely the fortified villages and 'bocage' country which blocked the approach to the Odon river. After the villages of Cheux and St Mauvieu had been captured, though with heavy casualties, O'Connor decided to use 11th Armoured Division to attempt a thrust to the Odon bridges. The squadron leading 29th Armoured Brigade in this venture suffered severe casualties, as the enemy had fully recovered from the artillery barrage and the Scottish attacks, especially in the area south of Cheux. As recorded in 11th Armoured Division's history: 'It seemed that in accordance with a German defensive strategem ... he had been holding his forward positions in no very great strength; thus the barrage had not greatly injured him.'[13]

The first day of 'Epsom' ended in rain and mud with the British a mile short of the Odon river. The Germans were considerably worried by the advance of some four miles which had been made, and began the reinforcement of the sector which was eventually to see them committing elements of 1st, 9th and 10th SS Panzer Divisions in their efforts to check the British advance.

A German armoured counter-attack on the morning of 27 June was decisively beaten off, and later in the day the leading battalion of 227th Brigade, 2nd Argyll and Sutherland Highlanders, seized a bridge over the Odon near Tourmauville. As the History of the 15th (Scottish) Division records: 'Here, then, were the Argylls, across the Odon and deep in enemy-held country, but as yet unsupported.'[14]

The significance of this comment is that it points to the natural fear of those higher commanders, who were watching progress of the battle, of too deep and narrow an advance inviting the Germans to cut it off from a flank. Knowing from *Ultra* reports that two new Panzer divisions, 9th and 10th SS, were approaching the area Dempsey and O'Connor were anxious to strengthen and widen the bridge-head over the Odon before letting 11th Armoured Division push on a further six miles to the Orne river crossings. For this reason when the armour did move across the Tourmauville bridge on 28 June it only made a limited advance.

The afternoon of 29 June saw the start of a period during which 15th (Scottish) Division fought some of its most savage actions of the war, sustaining numerous German attacks from all directions during the following forty-eight hours.

On the morning of 29 June, 29th Armoured Brigade of 11th Armoured Division had taken Hill 112. To its surprise, and resentment, it was ordered to retire during the night to a position back across the Odon river. The bridge-head over the river was still to be held, however, by 15th (Scottish) and elements of 43rd (Wessex) Divisions, the latter having been sent up to reinforce the salient.

The withdrawal of the armour was probably a mistake, though understandable. Neither Dempsey nor O'Connor realised that the attacks on 29 June composed the major German counter-attack, which dwindled somewhat on the following day, although still inflicting severe damage to the British. Expecting even more furious assaults on 30 June, O'Connor's view was that '... the area around Point 112 and Point 113—though excellent for an armoured offensive, if it could have gone through with a bang—was no place for the 11th Armoured Division, with its insecure communications across the Odon, to "wait about" in'.[15]

General Paul Hausser, Commander of 2 SS Panzer Corps, spoke of the events of 29 June when interrogated later in England: of his own attack with 9th and 10th Panzer Divisions he said:

> It was scheduled to begin at seven o'clock in the morning, but hardly had the tanks assembled than they were attacked by fighter bombers. This disrupted the troops so much that the attack did not start again till two-thirty in the afternoon. But even then it could not get going. The murderous fire from naval guns in the Channel and the terrible British artillery destroyed the bulk of our attacking force in its assembly area. The few tanks that did manage to go forward, were easily stopped by the British anti-tank guns. In my opinion, the attack was prepared too quickly. I wanted to wait another two days but Hitler insisted that it be launched on 29 June.[16]

Although the pressure on the VIII Corps bridge-head eased on 30 June, the withdrawal of the armour from Point 112 allowed the Germans to recapture it, and later much vicious fighting would take place before it was again occupied by Allied troops. Though tactfully avoiding questioning the wisdom of the decision to withdraw 29th Brigade, the 11th Armoured Division history reflects that '... the general feeling that, in spite of tank losses, a further sweep southwards from Hill 112, coupled with the continual repulse of enemy attacks on the flanks, was well within its powers, was indicative of the high state of the division's morale'.[17]

Though the armoured division might well have been able to sweep south to the Orne bridges on 30 June, the ability of the infantry to support them would have been more questionable, due to the heavy losses they had sustained in some of the heaviest fighting of the whole campaign in north-west Europe. 15th (Scottish) Division were never to endure such savage German assaults again. In the five days of 'Epsom', the divisional casualties amounted to 130 officers and 2,590 other ranks—a total of 288 all ranks killed, 1,638 wounded and 794 missing, mainly captured. 'Of the total casualties that it was to suffer up to VE-Day, the Division had lost one quarter in these five days.'[18]

Montgomery was well aware of the need to conserve his limited manpower. Realising that the cost of continuing 'Epsom' in an attempt to reach the original objectives might be too great, he called off the offensive. Although it was certainly his intention from the start that German armour should be drawn into the Odon valley and away from the Americans to the west, it was also very much part of the aim to cross the Orne and encircle Caen. The failure to achieve this result led him to stress the importance of the defensive battle and the effect on the German armour rather than the encirclement of Caen, so turning the tale of a very limited victory into one of a major success. Also, in assessing the effectiveness of 'Epsom', the part played by the weather should not be forgotten. The unprecedentedly violent storms of 19 and 20 June caused the delays in launching it which, in their turn, allowed the Germans to build up such strong defences.

The various commanders received their congratulations on their conduct of operations from Montgomery, and in due course passed on their own messages to those below them. O'Connor's letter from Montgomery was full of praise:

TAC HEADQUARTERS
21 ARMY GROUP

My dear Dick   3 – 7 – 44
    I would like to congratulate you personally, and the whole of 8 Corps, on the very fine performance put up in your attack down to and over, the ODON valley. The whole Corps fought splendidly and displayed a grand offensive spirit; your contribution to the general plan of battle has been immense. Please tell all officers and men, from me, how well I think they have done and give them my best congratulations.
    I would like to send a special word of congratulations to your Chief of Staff, and the whole of Corps HQ; they handled the battle splendidly.
    Yours ever

B L Montgomery[19]

This first major action of VIII Corps was very different for O'Connor from the operations he had conducted with XIII Corps in the desert. The fact that he was able to handle the battle satisfactorily after so long an absence from high command, was a remarkable tribute to his intelligence and generalship, but it must at times have been a bewildering experience. Fortunately he had two outstanding divisional commanders in MacMillan and Roberts to lead his most heavily committed subordinate formations, and an excellent staff at his own headquarters, with a most able senior gunner in Brigadier Matthew to co-ordinate the immense fire-power granted to him. Although he had always enjoyed an independent role in the desert, at this stage in Normandy it must have been a relief to have both Montgomery and Dempsey close at hand to take many of the most important decisions.

Operations Windsor and Jupiter

Following the end of Operation 'Epsom' on 2 July 1944, the general picture in Normandy was that the Americans had taken Cherbourg and cleared the Cotentin peninsula, while the British had secured a strong bridge-head in the Caen area, though more restricted than originally planned, and were holding the main bulk of the German armour around it. Von Rundstedt, the German Commander-in-Chief, still expected an Allied landing in the Pas de Calais and held his 15 Army intact beyond the Seine to counter it. Before Von Rundstedt realised his mistake, Montgomery was anxious that the Americans should break out and swing east through Le Mans to the lower Seine and Paris. Second Army's task was to keep up the pressure in its sector to prevent any move of German forces, especially armour, away from the Villers-Bocage–Caen front to face the United States armies to its west.

In the VIII Corps sector 15th (Scottish) Division had been withdrawn to be rested and brought up to strength again, and its place in what was now referred to as the 'Scottish corridor' was held by troops of 53rd (Welsh) and 43rd (Wessex) Divisions, the former having been attached during the latter stages of 'Epsom', thereby bringing the total corps strength up to approximately 87,000 officers and men.[20] On 4 July, 43rd Division was involved in an attack north-east out of the corridor in support of operation 'Windsor', which was designed to enable 3rd Canadian Division to capture the airfield at Carpiquet.

43rd Division was given the main attacking role in the next corps operation as well, this one being codenamed 'Jupiter', with 'H' hour at 5 am on 10 July 1944. The aim was to seize Hill 112 and its surroundings, as well as the areas to the east towards the River Orne, with a view to the subsequent exploitation of the high ground to the south-west. It was now that really vicious and costly battles were fought for the possession of Hill 112. In the words of the Corps

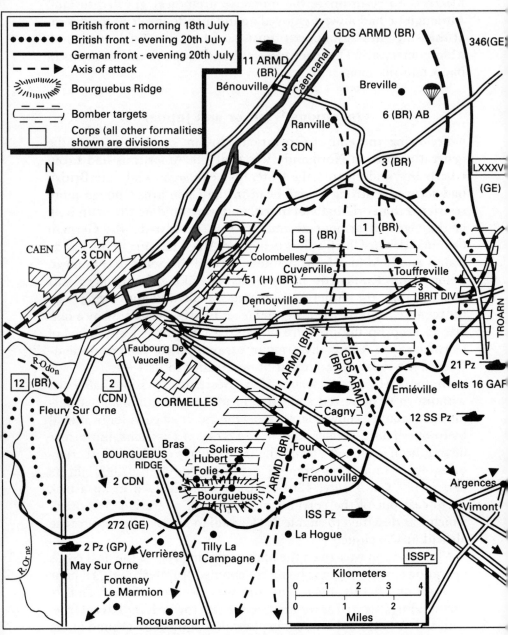

MAP 9. OPERATION GOODWOOD 18-20th JULY 1944

Legend:
- British front - morning 18th July
- British front - evening 20th July
- German front - evening 20th July
- Axis of attack
- Bourguebus Ridge
- Bomber targets
- Corps (all other formalities shown are divisions)

N

GDS ARMD (BR) 346(GE)

11 ARMD (BR)

Bénouville

Breville

Ranville

6 (BR) AB

3 CDN

3 (BR)

LXXXV (GE)

8 (BR)   1 (BR)

CAEN

3 CDN

Colombelles

Cuverville

Touffreville

51 (H) (BR)

3 BRIT DIV

Demouville

TROARN

Faubourg De Vaucelle

R.Odon

21 Pz

12 (BR)

2 (CDN)

Emiéville

elts 16 GAF

CORMELLES

Cagny

12 SS Pz

Fleury Sur Orne

Bras

Soliers

Four

BOURGUEBUS RIDGE

Hubert

Folie

Frenouville

Argences

2 CDN

Bourguebus

Vimont

272 (GE)

ISS Pz

La Hogue

2 Pz (GP)

Verrières

Tilly La Campagne

ISSPz

May Sur Orne

Fontenay Le Marmion

Kilometers
0 1 2 3 4

0 1 2
Miles

Rocquancourt

R.Orne

11 ARMD (BR)

GDS ARMD (BR)

7 ARMD (BR)

history, members of the 43rd Division 'held the northern side of the hill, the enemy in dug-in tanks remained masters of the southern half, and in between, the crest was a most effective no-man's land'.[21] It was also a 'hill of the dead', because the Germans in their counter-attacks suffered losses on the same scale as the British.

All units of 43rd (Wessex) Division taking part in 'Jupiter' were badly mauled. Although it was an effective operation in the sense of a battle of attrition, which the enemy could less afford than the British, its results were very limited, and exploitation to the south-west, planned to be undertaken by 4th Armoured Brigade, was never attempted.

On the final day, 12 July, activity on both sides was greatly reduced, and at 2 am on 13 July, the newly arrived XII Corps, commanded by Lieutenant General Neil Ritchie, took over the sector and VIII Corps moved back into reserve. (Ritchie had now been given a chance to prove himself once more as a field commander—a challenge to which he rose successfully in the months ahead. Early in 1942, he had been relieved of the command of the 8th Army in the Desert by General Auchinleck after the disaster of Gazala. It was generally felt that he had had rather a raw deal, having been ordered to assume that command from a senior staff appointment, having no previous command experience, even at Corps level.)

Throughout the first continuous period in the line during operations 'Epsom' and 'Jupiter', and to a small extent 'Windsor', the headquarters of VIII Corps worked smoothly under the capable direction of Sir Henry Floyd. It was well that it had settled down into a thoroughly efficient routine, because the five days in reserve following hand-over to XII Corps were to test its skills to the utmost.

Operation Goodwood

On 10 July Montgomery had issued a directive to Dempsey which stated:

> Second Army will retain the ability to operate with a strong armoured force east of the River Orne in the general area between Caen and Falaise.
>
> For this purpose a corps of three armoured divisions will be held in reserve, ready to be employed when ordered by me.
>
> The opportunity for the employment of this corps may be sudden and fleeting. Therefore, the study of the problems arising will begin at once.[22]

It was decided that O'Connor should command this corps. At 10 am on 13 July, Dempsey arrived at VIII Corps headquarters, accompanied by Crocker of I Corps and Simmonds of II Canadian Corps, to outline the pattern of the operation which was to be known as 'Goodwood'. O'Connor, who made strong but unavailing representations that Crocker, as the commander on the spot, should take his place, found that the composition of his force was to be purely armour and artillery. It was to consist of 11th and Guards Armoured Divisions and 8th AGRA from his original corps order of battle, with 7th Armoured Division added. 15th (Scottish) Division was taken away and put under command of XII Corps, to the considerable annoyance of MacMillan, who shortly afterwards wrote to O'Connor to point out the difficulties of operating under an unknown corps headquarters where staffs were not known to each other, and suggesting it was a pity to exercise 'corps flexibility at expense of its identity'. When O'Connor himself made a similar complaint to Montgomery at a later stage in the campaign he received a sharp rebuff: 'You must understand that there is no such thing in my set-up as a permanent composition for a Corps; Divisions are grouped in Corps as the battle situation demands, and this is a great battle winning factor.'[23]

Of all the operations in north-west Europe 'Goodwood' has aroused the most controversy. Much of this revolves around the question of what Montgomery intended it to achieve: so many differing theories have been put forward by his admirers and detractors—and he himself confused the situation as well—that the truth is hard to discover. It is hoped that the assessment finally made in this chapter will be near it.

The Operation Instruction produced by Dempsey on 13 July stated that VIII Corps would 'attack southwards and establish an armoured division in each of the following areas: Bretteville-sur-Laize, Vimont-Argence, Falaise'.[24]

Following Dempsey's conference on 13 July, detailed planning started at Headquarters VIII Corps and on the next morning, warning orders went out to the divisions. However, Dempsey returned on 15 July to give O'Connor a copy of the 'Notes on Second Army Operations 16 July–18 July' which he had just had passed to him by Montgomery. The notes gave Monty's slightly revised instructions for the coming operations. They are a good example of the value of brevity, but the really significant aspects are twofold. First, the stress on holding German armour on the Second Army

front, and second, the more limited objectives given to VIII
Corps.

1 Object of this operation

To engage the German armour in battle and 'write it down' to such an
extent that it is of no further value to the Germans as a basis of the battle.

To gain a good bridge-head over the River Orne through Caen, and thus
to improve our positions on the eastern flank.

Generally to destroy German equipment and personnel.

2 Effect of this operation on the Allied policy

We require the whole of the Cherbourg and Brittany peninsulas.

A victory on the eastern flank will help us to gain what we want on the
western flank.

But the eastern flank is a bastion on which the whole future of the
campaign in north-west Europe depends; it must remain a firm bastion; if
it becomes unstable the operations on the western flank would cease.

Therefore, while taking advantage of every opportunity to destroy the
enemy, we must be very careful to maintain our own balance and ensure a
firm base.

3 The enemy

There are a lot of enemy divisions in the area south-east of Caen:

21 Panzer Division
1 SS Panzer Division
12 SS Panzer Division
16 GAF Field Division
272 Infantry Division

Another one is coming and will be here this week-end.

4 Operations of 12 Corps and Canadian Corps— 16th and 17th July

Advantage must be taken of these to make the Germans think we are
going to break out across the Orne between Caen and Amaye.

5 Initial Operations 8 Corps

The three armoured divisions will be required to dominate the area
Bourguebus–Vimont–Bretteville, and to fight and destroy the enemy.

But the armoured cars should push far to the south towards Falaise, and
spread alarm and despondency, and discover 'the form'.

6 2 Canadian Corps

While para 5 is going on, the Canadians must capture Vaucelles, get through communications and establish themselves in a very firm bridge-head on the general line Fleury–Cormelles–Mondeville.

7 Later Operations 8 Corps

When 6 is done, then 8 Corps can 'crack about' as the situation demands.

But not before 6 is done.

8 To sum up for 8 Corps

Para 5
Para 7

Finally

Para 6 is vital.

B L MONTGOMERY
15–7–44[25]

These notes, written in Montgomery's own hand, appear to have been seen only by Dempsey and O'Connor. They were never passed to higher headquarters—Eisenhower's SHAEF. For some reason, the revised Second Army operation order, dated 17 July, which was based on these notes, did not reach SHAEF either.

Later on 15 July VIII Corps plans were firm and, at 3 am the next morning, operation orders were issued to all concerned. The 'Intention' paragraph stated:

> On 18 July, 8 Corps will debouch from the existing bridge-head east of the River Orne with a view to:
> (a) Dominating the area Bourguebus-Vimont-Bretteville-sur-Laize.
> (b) Destroying any enemy armour or other forces encountered en route to and in this area.
> (c) If conditions are favourable, subsequently exploiting to the south.[26]

These orders were initially given to the divisional commanders verbally by O'Connor, and then confirmed in written form by Floyd.

Due to the work that had to be done before an attack could be launched, the starting date was put off until 18 July, but even then there was little enough time. Whatever the difficulties in the ensuing preparations, the importance of acting quickly had to over-ride them. Only by launching one attack after another, without giving the enemy time to rest and collect together a strong reserve, could the Germans be held in the Second Army sector and there be successfully 'written down'. At this stage the campaign was inevitably a war of attrition: an enemy of the quality of the Germans could only be defeated in a bitter and relentless series of engagements with no time lost between them.

O'Connor had three main problems in planning 'Goodwood'. The first was the difficulty of achieving surprise, especially in view of the German retention of the Colombelles factory area, which gave them good observation over much of the Orne bridge-head. The second was the limited size of the bridge-head, which ordained that the break-out from it had to be launched on a long narrow front by only one division at a time. The third was the need for air support, springing from the small, elongated and crowded nature of the bridge-head, which necessitated artillery being held back to the west of the River Orne from where its range was too limited to support the armour in the assault of the Bourguebus ridge. Bombardment from the air was the alternative, but air support depended on the weather being suitable.

Since VIII Corps' activities were so controlled by the orders of Montgomery and Dempsey, and restricted by the nature of the area in which it had to operate, O'Connor and his staff were perhaps more concerned with the mechanics of 'Goodwood' than the philosophy of it. The amount of detailed staff work to be undertaken in the short time available before 18 July was enormous: although the Second Army staff did a lot of it, everything had to be co-ordinated between the two headquarters, and then instructions had to be passed down the long chain of command to the men on the ground. Every slip, every delay, might mean a loss of life when the battle started.

The first requirement was to get the armoured divisions to the start line. Because the River Orne and the Caen Canal ran next to each other they created a double water obstacle to be bridged. Since even with herculean efforts by the Royal Engineers only a certain number of bridges could be built, the routes forward for the vast range of armoured and other vehicles were limited by the availability of crossing places, leading to the need for immensely complicated movement tables. As the Orne bridge-head had been prepared, since its capture by 6 Airborne Division, later reinforced by 51 (Highland), to withstand expected German attacks, minefields had been laid around the perimeter. These now had to be taken up, and routes through them clearly marked. All these bridging and route clearing tasks undertaken by the Sappers were most ably controlled by Brigadier Sugden.

The second requirement was to arrange the artillery and air bombardment to support the armour as it crossed the start line. The artillery fire plan was evolved by Brigadier Matthew to cover each phase of the operation, though it could only be fully effective to the foot of the Bourguebus ridge because of limitations in range mentioned already. The Corps history gives a clear exposition of the problems as well as the extent of the air bombing programme:

Operation 'Goodwood' was to be assisted by an air effort on a larger scale than anything hitherto staged in direct support of ground forces, and the whole operation was made entirely dependent upon it. Thus, in the event of there being no air support available on the day in question, the attack would inevitably be postponed. This produced a number of problems and restrictions during the planning period, and certain counter-plans had to be allowed for in case there should be any delay. The main disadvantage was that it could not be known until only a very short while beforehand whether the state of the weather would permit flying, and thus the necessary preliminary concentrations of tanks and vehicles might become known to the enemy, unless they were very quickly dispersed—a difficult task under the circumstances.

The plan to employ such a large air force did not at first meet general approval. Previous experiences at Cassino, in Italy, and ten days earlier at Caen, had been disappointing. Enemy opposition had not been eliminated, whilst our own troops had been hampered by cratering and roads blocked by debris. However, the Commander-in-Chief requested General Eisenhower to agree to it and in addition to ask for assistance from the independent RAF Bomber Command of Air Chief Marshall Sir Arthur Harris, which was duly forthcoming. It was thus finally settled on the highest level that the RAF could, and would, provide the support asked for. Now, however, Corps Headquarters was to feel the lack of its air adviser, for no senior RAF officer was available to assist in choosing the targets to be bombed or the timing of the attacks. Everything had to be arranged with Headquarters Second Army, whence the GSO I (Intelligence) accompanied by the AOC 83 Group RAF flew to England for the necessary joint planning at the Headquarters of RAF Bomber Command.

It should be noted that the Operation Instruction shown to the staff at Bomber Command was the original one dated 13 July and not the revised one of 17 July based on Montgomery's notes.

The bomber aircraft allotted were from three different sources: 1,056 RAF Lancasters and Halifaxes to come over from 5.45 to 6.30 am; 482 medium bombers from 9 USAAF for 45 minutes from 7 am; and then 539 Flying Fortresses of 8 USAAF from 8.30 to 9 am. In addition 83 Group RAF, the tactical group based alongside Second Army, would carry out frequent air to ground sorties.

Although the massive bomber effort outlined above was more than might have been expected, it was not timed exactly as O'Connor would have wished:

> It will be noted that there was no bombing in the afternoon by the heavy bombers. General O'Connor, from the outset, had been most anxious to obtain a second heavy bombing effort at approximately 1500 hours on the day of the offensive, at which time it was estimated that the leading armour would be in a position to move forward to its final objectives. Thus in the minutes of the conference held by the Corps Commander at 1800 hours on 16 July, item 7 records the decision to hold the armour of 11th Armoured Division in the Cagny area until the second heavy bombing ceased, and then to direct it on to the Bourguebus to cause maximum destruction to the enemy. It was also known that at this point the limit of range of the medium artillery was being reached. Unfortunately, for reasons which were beyond the control of Corps Headquarters, the heavy bombers could not again be made available at his time.[27]

The third requirement was to ensure, through frequent visits and conferences, that all taking part in the battle had a thorough understanding of their orders, and were getting on satisfactorily with their preparatory work.

One commander not happy with his orders was Roberts, whose 11th Armoured Division, with 29th Armoured Brigade in the lead, was to be the first across the start line, followed by the Guards Armoured Division and then 7th Armoured Division. The axes of advance given to the three divisions put 11th Armoured on the right, Guards on the left towards Vimont, and 7th Armoured eventually between them, though it was given no precise role to begin with, but to be prepared to support either of the other two formations as necessary.

Roberts objected to two tasks given him by O'Connor: one was that of capturing two villages called Cuverville and Demouville to the right of his line of advance, lying two and three miles respectively from the start line, and the other was the taking of Cagny, which was on his left five miles away. To take Cuverville and Demouville Roberts was bound to use the infantry element of his division, 159th Brigade, which he wanted to keep as close to his leading armour as possible in the event of being held up by German defended localities, which could only be satisfactorily cleared out by infantry. To have this vital brigade left behind tackling villages which he reckoned should be by-passed by his men, and left to others to capture, upset Roberts considerably:

> Before the operation began he remonstrated with O'Connor that this mission ought to be assigned to the 51st Highland Division, who were to support the left flank of the Canadian advance down the east bank of the Orne during their attack to capture the Faubourg de Vaucelles. As Roberts later recounted the story, 'It meant that half the division was engaged on the front lines ... I not only spoke to Dick O'Connor about it but I wrote to him and said that this is a grave disadvantage to my division, and I was told that if I didn't like the plan because of my experience and so forth, then one of the other divisions could lead.' At the time Roberts never understood what he considered to be O'Connor's excessive caution, and it was only after the battle that he learned of Montgomery's 'Notes' which he believes was the reason.[28]

It will be remembered that these notes, recorded a few pages back, referred to the necessity for the eastern flank to 'remain a firm bastion'. Because of this, 51st Highland Division, holding the front through which 'Goodwood' was launched, had to remain in their trenches in case anything went wrong with the break-out—undoubtedly reflecting excessive caution. With this policy imposed on him from above, O'Connor was not in a position to relieve Roberts of the task of capturing Cuverville and Demouville, but he did agree to withdraw the order to capture Cagny as well:

> It was agreed that I would go to take Cuverville and Demouville but that I would only mask Cagny until the Guards (Armoured Division) came forward; and that was a very unfortunate decision because there was nothing in Cagny except four 88's ... and those four 88's knocked out our sixteen tanks which were masking Cagny until the Guards arrived. Knocked them all out in a matter of minutes. So I quite wrongly but perhaps understandably advised the Guards when they arrived that Cagny was strongly held. It took the Guards until 4 pm to enter the place.[29]

Roberts' preoccupation with trying to keep his infantry as close up with the leading armour as possible was well understood by O'Connor:

> In many ways, O'Connor was a general far ahead of his time. For example, before 'Goodwood' began he anticipated the need for the infantry to keep up with the tanks (his disagreement with Roberts notwithstanding) and at the same time be protected from small-arms fire

which made movement by lorry unsatisfactory. O'Connor found a solution by ordering that a number of the self-propelled gun-carriers of the artillery be turned over to the infantry for use as armoured personnel carriers. There were predictable howls of outrage at this temerity to violate the hidebound organizational structure of the army, and the order was soon countermanded by Dempsey, who was not convinced of its merit. O'Connor's protests to Dempsey fell on deaf ears....[30]

Many years later, he still felt that he should have pressed the matter more forcefully with Dempsey, who appears to have acted rather stupidly on this occasion. O'Connor's actual comment was: 'We could not provide enough of these self-propelled gun-carriages to carry all the lorried infantry, but we could have carried about two battalions, which, I am sure, would have been a great help to the advance. But unfortunately I was not allowed by higher authority to carry out the experiment.' He did not let the idea rest however. On 16 October 1944, he wrote to his old Cameronian friend Jack Evetts, now a Lieutenant General and a special military adviser to the Ministry of Supply, asking him to press for the development of an 'armoured carrier for the carriage of infantry into battle'.[31]

At the headquarters of both 21st Army Group and Second Army the strength of the German defences was not regarded lightly, but the intelligence staffs did not fully appreciate how deep and well designed they were. Nor did they realise the extent to which an attack in the area of Goodwood was expected by the enemy: 'Panzer Group West had anticipated the Goodwood offensive and had disposed the forces of 1 SS Panzer Corps and LXXXVI Corps in four defensive belts nearly ten miles deep, with a fifth as a reserve.'[32] The battle was not expected to be a walk-over, but great faith was put in the effect of the massive air bombardment to make its progress more successful than it turned out to be.

The BBC broadcast a report on the evening of 18 July from Chester Wilmot, describing how the RAF had made the first bombing sortie starting at 5.45 am that morning:

> In the half-light I stood on a hill on the east bank of the Orne, looking down on an open field at the foot of the hill. I could see the camouflaged shapes of tanks, hundreds of them—tanks that hadn't been there the night before, but now they were assembling to attack. And in the distance there was the sole surviving chimney of the great steel factory at Colombelles and the towers and buildings of the suburbs of Caen that the Germans still held.

Then I turned and looked out to sea ... the Lancasters and Halifaxes were beginning to darken the northern sky ... they came over the horizon in a black swarm. The markers dropped their target indicators and in a few seconds bombs were cascading down on the steel factory and the suburbs of Caen ... and on the German strongpoints on either flank of the line along which our tanks were to advance.

For forty-five minutes the procession of bombers came on unbroken and when they'd gone, the thunder of the guns swelled up and filled the air, as the artillery carried on the bombardment.[33]

During the next sortie, flown by 482 medium bombers from 9 USAAF from 7 am until 7.45 am, 29th Armoured Brigade moved out of the concentration area, through the gaps in the mine-fields, and down to the start line. The final wave of aircraft consisted of 539 Flying Fortresses from 8 USAAF dropping fragmentation bombs on enemy gun positions around Bourguebus. Of the 2,077 aircraft flown from England that morning, only 25 were lost: all were shot down by anti-aircraft guns, for no German planes at all came up in opposition.

The effect of the aerial bombardment, while in progress and for the first hour or two after it had ceased, was shattering. As the leading elements of 11th Armoured Division advanced for the first two miles they found Germans totally dazed and in some cases driven insane. The divisional history describes 'a waste land, five miles of utter devastation; the trees blasted, the buildings shattered, the air foul with the death-stench of cattle and horses'. But it also records 'that beyond and beside these fated areas the enemy waited behind his guns', and then after quite a short time 'even within the dead land itself he began to emerge blinkingly from his foxholes ready to sell his life dearly to our advancing troops'.[34]

The terrain over which those troops had to advance favoured the defender, rising gently up from where the attack was launched to the vital Bourguebus ridge, described in the VIII Corps history:

This elevated ground affords complete observation over almost the entire area of the advance, whilst the defenders had the benefit of long fields of fire and facilities for concealed movement in the woods and villages, of which they did not fail to take full advantage. Whilst therefore the country generally was by no means as enclosed as that fought over in 'Epsom', it still gave the enemy plenty of cover, particularly in the vicinity of the villages, enabling him to site his anti-tank weapons in cleverly hidden positions from which full use could be made of their superior range. The numerous villages, too, provide a series of mutually supporting strong points not more than 1,500 yards apart, which if garrisoned with resolute troops make a perfect natural defence line. The enemy therefore was not slow to adapt these as the backbone of his second defence zone.[35]

As well as the anti-tank and self-propelled guns, both 75 mm and 88 mm, which were well sited over the area, there were a good number of Tiger and Panther tanks for the Germans to employ both in static defence and for counter-attack if the opportunity offered. Constantly engaged by fierce opposition after the first two miles or so, 29th Armoured Brigade had advanced about seven miles when it stalled at mid-day on the slopes of the Bourguebus ridge. Reinforcement was essential, but could not be produced in enough strength, for reasons very clearly explained in the 11th Armoured divisional history:

> There now became evident a situation which more than any other single factor dislocated the plan of the operation. As has already been stated, the bridge-head west of the Orne was narrowly confined, and this limitation of space and hence also of roads was now seen to present a severe obstacle to the reinforcing columns upon whose prompt arrival the further stages of the battle depended. The debouchment from the bridge-head may be likened to the nozzle of a shower-bath fed by a pipe so small that the volume of water which can flow through it is sufficient only to serve two or three of the apertures, the rest remaining dry. The most essential feature of the 'Goodwood' plan was the deployment, in a short time and space only wide enough to ensure manoeuvre, of a very large number of armoured units. Only thus could the enemy's defences be saturated.

> But to achieve the saturation the shower-bath has got to work properly, and it didn't. During the morning the traffic congestion reached such proportions that the Guards were quite unable to make the expected advance on the 11th's left, and the preoccupation with this dangerous flank, where Cagny itself was a constant source of trouble, tied up a large number of tanks and hampered in consequence any progress that might have been possible towards the division's objectives to the south-west. Nor could the southward thrust be undertaken by the Seventh; for they in turn were held up behind the Guards and, in fact, their armoured brigade was still not across the Orne. So 29th [Brigade] unable to advance, hung on uncomfortably in their exposed positions.[36]

Realising that the initiative must not be lost, but also that his room for manoeuvre was hopelessly restricted by the congestion at the bridge-head and the continuing involvement of Roberts' infantry at Cuverville and Demouville, O'Connor called for a further saturation bombing attack on the Bourguebus ridge. His urgent request was turned down, though he was never told why.[37] Fortunately 83 Group RAF carried out repeated attacks with rocket-firing Typhoons, which did much to help when, in the early afternoon, Sepp Dietrich committed the Panther battalion of 1st SS Panzer Corps in a counter-attack against 29th Brigade.

> The German commander had not intended to commit the Panthers quite so soon, but once they had reached Bourguebus and made sudden contact with the advancing British armour it proved impossible to disengage. The remainder of the afternoon and evening of 18 July turned into the biggest tank battle of the entire campaign, a virtual shootout between the outnumbered but superior German Tigers and Panthers and the massed but more vulnerable British Shermans and Cromwells.[38]

O'Connor decided, having had his request for a major air strike rejected, to bring part of 7th Armoured Division forward to support 11th Armoured. At 1.50 pm he met Roberts and Erskine, commander of 7th Armoured, and a plan was made for a two-pronged attack against Hubert Folie and Bourguebus, with Roberts on the right and Erskine's 22nd Brigade on the left. In the event 5th Royal Tank Regiment, leading 22nd Brigade, had only reached the Caen to Troarn road by 3 pm and when it arrived close to the fighting at 5 pm it was too late to give much assistance to 29th Brigade. By the time the rest of 22nd Brigade arrived to attempt the thrust, directed earlier by O'Connor, the German resistance had stiffened and 29th Brigade had lost nearly half its tanks and was more or less spent. Roberts was *not* impressed by the efforts of the 22nd Brigade to come forward as they had been instructed!

The slowness of 7th Armoured Division in moving forward was felt at VIII Corps headquarters to be another example of its poor performance in Normandy: the famous 'Desert Rats', like the 51st (Highland) Division, lost much of their great reputation from their desert and Italian days when landed in north-west Europe. In discussing 'Goodwood' after the war, Major General Sir Percy Hobart, who was present at the battle both as commander of the specialist 79th Armoured Division and as an adviser on armoured tactics, gave it as his opinion that the only way to have overcome Erskine's excessive caution would have been to have had O'Connor alongside to spur him on.[39] Perhaps aware of his shortcomings, Erskine used attack as the method of conducting his own defence, and soon after 'Goodwood' ended wrote a letter on 21 July to O'Connor complaining about the staff work at VIII Corps headquarters: an odd, almost insubordinate, letter which can have done him little good.[40]

On the left flank the Guards Armoured Division was held up by fierce fighting around Cagny, which was not taken until 4 pm. By the end of the day they had only reached Frenouville, and were still two miles away from Vimont, their objective. Unfortunately this true situation was not part of a jubilant statement issued by Montgomery during the afternoon of 18 July which stated that they were 'in Vimont'. Other inaccuracies put 11th Armoured Division in Tilly la Campagne, over two miles south of their real location, and 7th Armoured, way beyond the actual positions of its strung out columns reaching back to the start-line, at La Hogue. There will be more to be said about this unfortunate signal later: it was to a great extent due to wishful thinking, following receipt of an optimistic situation report received at the end of the morning from Second Army, which included these words:

> At 0745 hours, 8 Corps, with one armoured division up, attacked southwards with infantry of 2 Canadian Corps and 1 Corps attacking on each flank. The armoured division moved very fast, and was followed rapidly by two more. By mid-day, strong armoured formations of 8 Corps had advanced nearly seven miles to the south and had broken through the main German defences.[41]

The rest of the course of 'Goodwood' can be described quickly. At mid-day on 19 July, O'Connor held a conference at the tactical headquarters of 11th Armoured Division, and gave orders for the three divisions to capture Bras and Hubert Folie on the right; le Poirier on the left, and Four and Bourguebus in the centre. 'This three pronged drive was completely successful, though as might be expected, Bourguebus proved the toughest nut to crack, and was not ultimately entered until the following morning.'[42] On 20 July, the Guards took Frenouville and beat off a German counter-attack from the east. During the afternoon, torrential rain turned the whole area into a sea of mud, with movement impossible except on metalled roads, and that evening the operation was brought to an end. II Canadian Corps took over the west of VIII Corps sector, and I Corps assumed responsibility for the east. Gradually VIII Corps was withdrawn into reserve to be prepared for further activities.

The conduct and results of 'Goodwood' need to be looked at from five different view-points: the intention; the effect of the bombing offensive; the results achieved; the tactical problems faced by O'Connor; and finally the controversy that followed the end of the operation.

Montgomery's notes demonstrate clearly that his purpose in launching 'Goodwood' was to engage the German armour, and destroy enemy equipment and men, so as to 'write down' its ability to influence Allied operations. It was also to obtain a good bridge-head over the Orne through Caen, which necessitated gaining control of the Bourguebus ridge to protect it. These were the main aims: they were entirely in keeping with Montgomery's often repeated strategic planning. If the advance went better than expected, a break-out towards Falaise would be a wonderful bonus. The confusion about its intention which has existed ever since 'Goodwood' ended was partly created by Montgomery himself, when, as already mentioned, he sent an erroneous signal home about the actions on the morning of 18 July, and then made matters worse still by repeating the errors in an evening press conference at which he afterwards admitted being too exultant, confessing later: 'I realise that now—in fact, I realised it pretty quickly afterwards.'[43] It was also, in part, caused by the request for the massive air strikes which preceded and followed 'H' hour on 18 July. Whether by accident or design, the impression was allowed to remain in the minds of the senior RAF and USAAF officers authorising the strikes that they presaged a more exciting battle than the one that really took place. The fact that planners at Bomber Command were shown Second Army's operation instructions dated 13 July rather than the revised ones of 17 July is also significant.

There were, in fact, three reasons for asking for this massive air support. First, because of the difficulty in covering the advance with artillery fire from behind the Orne, as the Bourguebus ridge was out of range of the gun positions. Second, because the German defensive system was known to be extremely strong and well sited. Third, because it was hoped that the devastation would be so great that the infantry would have a relatively easy job clearing out enemy strong points and thus reduce casualties: by this stage infantry manpower shortages were becoming a serious worry.

In fact, the air strikes were less effective than had been hoped, the main failure being missing so many gun positions on the Bourguebus ridge. The cratering caused by the bombing disrupted many possible routes forward, though the worst example of this was on the I Corps front to the left of the Guards Armoured. Finally, it would have been far better to have had only two strikes in the morning and a further one later in the day.

The results achieved by 'Goodwood' are often dismissed too lightly. The comments of an outstanding commander deeply involved in the fiercest of the fighting are particularly important. Here is Pip Roberts's verdict:

> But the real achievements of the operation are seldom mentioned. Apart from advancing six miles against strong opposition in 48 hours, by the end of the operation there were opposite 2nd Army front seven Panzer divisions, four heavy tank battalions (Tigers); opposite 1st American Army, there were two Panzer divisions, one Panzer Grenadier division (with no tanks), no heavy tanks (Tigers). Surely this must have played a significant part in achieving the American break-out? This, I always thought, and still do, was Monty's plan, and Goodwood contributed a great deal towards it. Exploitation to Falaise was just a nice idea if the miraculous happened.[44]

The many tactical problems which faced O'Connor before and during 'Goodwood' began with the short amount of time allowed for preparation after pulling out of 'Epsom' in the early hours of 13 July. Complicated movement plans were necessary to get the three armoured divisions into place, made even more difficult by the attempt to conceal the movement of tanks by using the short hours of darkness. The limited area of the Orne bridge-head produced endless headaches, especially in respect of the Royal Engineer tasks of bridging and mine-field cleaerance, which were on such a scale that help was needed from both I and II Canadian Corps on either flank. O'Connor must have also been extremely aggravated by Dempsey's refusal to let him use armoured gun carriers as infantry personnel carriers.

The limitations placed on O'Connor's freedom of action once the assault was under way sprang from Montgomery's insistence that the eastern flank 'must remain a firm bastion'. It has been suggested that:

> The boldness originally suggested in the 'Goodwood' plan seems to have been needlessly sacrificed by an overemphasis on security. Montgomery's mandate that O'Connor should give first priority to the security of his flanks was inconsistent with the premise that the three armoured divisions must strike quickly after the bombardment while the Germans were still disorganized. As General Roberts has pointed out, it was completely unrealistic to imagine that the Germans could have mounted any sort of

counterstroke after the awesome bombing and against the combined might of three attacking corps....

Neither Montgomery nor Dempsey seemed to have grasped the conflicting position in which they had placed O'Connor: on the one hand, security was overemphasized and on the other, O'Connor was told to get his armour forward quickly. Perhaps too much was anticipated from the bombardment, but O'Connor was forced to employ unsound tactics in an effort to accomplish a Herculean task. How different the outcome might have been had Dempsey ordered a combined tank-infantry thrust down the corridor to Bourguebus, where there would have been sufficient infantry available to deal with problems such as Cagny. What the British Army terms 'thrustfulness' had been absolutely essential on 18 July, and the spearhead of the 11th Armoured Division under the command of the most battle-experienced divisional commander in 21st Army Group was the perfect instrument to accomplish this, provided that the tanks and infantry were permitted to work in unison instead of being forced to accomplish entirely separate tasks.[45]

What, in Roberts's opinion, was 'the real set-back was the enemy gun position along the Bourguebus ridge. In all, there were 78 "88s", 12 heavy flak guns, 194 field guns, and 272 Nebelwerfers (8 barrelled mortars).'[46] The fact that these were scarcely touched by the bombing, as well as out of range of the Corps artillery, was more significant than any other consideration.

O'Connor was not personally involved in the controversy in high, Allied, military circles which followed the end of 'Goodwood': he was all too quickly struggling with some more knotty problems connected with 'Bluecoat', the next operation of VIII Corps. The furore which erupted at Eisenhower's headquarters, SHAEF, sprang from the belief there that a full-scale breakout on Second Army front was intended; a belief fuelled both by Montgomery's unfortunate signal and press conference on 18 July, as well as by the request for the heavy bombing before the operation, which might never have been provided unless the air chiefs expected more than a seven mile advance. In 1952 Tedder was to write to Liddell Hart:

There is no question to my mind but that we in SHAEF were quite clear that the intention of that Operation was to push right through to the South. We did in particular welcome the fact that O'Connor was given command of all the armour in view of his magnificent courage and leadership when he drove through to Beda Fomm and cleaned up the Italians in the Western Desert. Moreover a drive through to Falaise would at long last have begun to give us the airfield country south of Caen, which had been one of the original objectives.[47]

Liddell Hart's own comments were that Montgomery 'had not planned to break out on this flank, and was not banking on it. But he would have been foolish not to reckon with the possibility of a German collapse, under this massive blow, and exploit it if it occurred.'[48]

In fact his approach was thoroughly sound, but his obsession with showing that events always turned out just as he had predicted, especially in the north-west European campaign, prevented him admitting that he had been ready and hoping for the exploitation of 'Goodwood'. As a result, his already shaky relationship with Eisenhower and the senior staff at SHAEF was strained almost to breaking point, and there was even talk of his dismissal from his command. It was sad that such misunderstandings should have arisen just as Montgomery's plans for the defeat of the German armies in Normandy were about to come to fruition. Field Marshal Von Kluge, German Supreme Commander, wrote to Hitler on 21 July to explain that the orders given to him to 'stand fast at any price' would lead to 'the slow but sure annihilation of the force. In spite of intense efforts the moment has drawn near when the front, already so heavily strained, will break.' To his subordinate commanders Von Kluge could only give orders, in the event of no expedient to improve their position, to 'die honourably on the battlefield!'[49]

Operation Bluecoat

Following 'Goodwood' a few days rest—or relatively restful period compared with the days that had just passed and those that were to follow shortly—gave O'Connor the opportunity to give thought to the lessons of his first two major operations. One obvious matter to be put right in further battles, especially in thick 'bocage' country, was the integration of armour and infantry. Just before 'Bluecoat' started he talked to Roberts, who described how:

A few days later I saw General Dick O'Connor and he told me that we were going to operate on the right flank of Second Army, right in the middle of the bocage country. He said, and this was very relevant, that, 'You must be prepared for the very closest of tank-infantry co-operation on a troop/platoon basis.' I agreed entirely and so set to work at once to get this organised. It was my intention to have two brigades each containing two armoured regiments and two infantry battalions. Who commanded each group must be decided by the brigade commander and would, to some extent, depend on the type of operation.... In fact, this flexible arrangement remained till the end of hostilities and was highly satisfactory.[50]

The launch of the American operation 'Cobra', which would in due course sweep in from the Cotentin peninsula and drive the Germans right out of France, was planned for 24 July. It had a false start that day, however, as the majority of the 2,000 aircraft that arrived to make the preliminary bombardment had to return to base in England without dropping their bombs because heavy cloud had so restricted visibility over the target area. The next day the Americans were on the move, and the aircraft came in to lay a carpet of bombs across the US First Army front which virtually wiped out the one German armoured division, Panzer Lehr, which might have seriously hindered its advance. Montgomery had to keep up the pressure in the British and Canadian sector and so had ordered the newly constituted First Canadian Army to begin a major attack east of the River Orne on 23 July. In addition he noted that:

> ... there was no German armour facing the British, and therefore the situation was favourable for delivering a very heavy blow on the right wing of Second Army in the Caumont sector. If we could regroup speedily and launch a thrust in strength southwards from the Caumont area directed on Forêt l'Eveque and Beny Bocage, and ultimately to Vire, the effect would be to get behind the German forces which had been swung back to face west by the American break-through; any attempt by the enemy to pivot on the River Vire or in the area between Torigny and Caumont would thus be frustrated, as we should knock away the hinge. I, therefore, ordered Second British Army to regroup in order to deliver a strong offensive on these lines; not less than six divisions were to be employed, and the operation was to proceed with all possible speed. In the meantime, First Canadian Army and the remainder of Second Army were to maintain the maximum offensive activity on the rest of the front in order to pin the enemy opposition and wear it down.[51]

Also, on 23 July, as part of a move to extend the British sector westwards and release a US division to help Bradley, 15th (Scottish) had moved into the Caumont area and taken over a part of the front previously held by 5th US Division.

During preliminary discussions of the 'heavy blow' southwards from Caumont, the date fixed for striking it was to be 2 August.

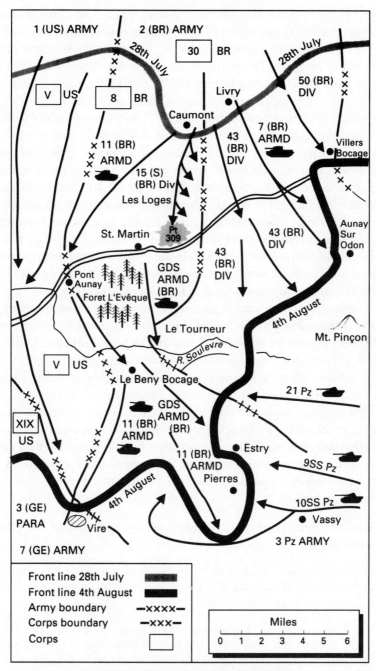

MAP 10. OPERATION BLUECOAT
VIII CORPS ADVANCE SOUTH FROM CAUMONT UP TO
EVENING OF 4th AUGUST 1944

However, the first two days of the American advance in the west met stiffer opposition than expected, and progress was slow. On 28 July, fearing that the Germans might start moving Panzer formations away from Second Army front towards the Americans, Montgomery brought the starting time for 'Bluecoat' forward to dawn on 30 July. The regrouping of the six divisions put 7th Armoured and 43rd and 50th infantry divisions under XXX Corps, while O'Connor was allotted the original formations which had trained together in VIII Corps before the invasion. Dempsey's Chief of Staff, Brigadier Chilton, explained these groupings at a conference at Second Army headquarters at 4.45 pm on 28 July, only 37 hours before the attack was to begin. The aims given were to retain enemy armour on the British and Canadian fronts; to prevent the enemy 'hinging' his forces on the high ground of Mont Pinçon (11 miles south-east of Caumont) and Point 309 (five miles south); and to retain a firm hold on the Caen bridge-head. XXX Corps was to be on the left of the advance, and VIII Corps on the right.

O'Connor gave verbal orders to divisional commanders as quickly as possible. These were confirmed by a written operation instruction signed by Floyd at 1 am on 29 July. Initially, the main task was to capture and hold Point 309: subsequent exploitation would follow. After preliminary air and artillery bombardments, 11th Armoured would move south from Caumont on the right and 15th (Scottish), supported by 6th Guards Tank Brigade, would advance on the left. To MacMillan, whose division was expected to have the hardest fighting during the first phase of 'Bluecoat', O'Connor wrote to encourage the Scots as well as to explain the speed at which the operation had to be organised.

His letter began:

> You are again being asked to carry out an operation of the greatest importance.
>
> As you know, the break-through on the American front has been most successful, and their armoured troops and infantry formations are striking southwards and westwards.
>
> The enemy is doing everything in his power to restrict the area of penetration by the Americans, but to do this successfully he must hinge his forces on some important feature of the ground, holding fast to this position, and being prepared to give ground slowly on his left flank.

Three paragraphs were then devoted to discussion of the best tactical methods for MacMillan to employ. Then the letter continued:

> After consideration of the above, and in view of the vital importance of the operation to the whole Allied plan, the Commander-in-Chief has decided that it is to be undertaken at the earliest possible moment.
>
> I fully realise how much is being asked of you, and what difficulties you will have to contend with, but I am sure they will be overcome in the same way as they have been overcome in the past. You have, in my opinion, the finest fighting record of any division in Normandy, and I do not feel that this task will be in any way beyond your powers.
>
> Will you please explain the situation to your officers and other ranks so that they may understand the reasons for speed and the vital issues which are at stake.
>
> I know they will respond as they have always done, and I am sure that their success will be the turning point in the campaign.
>
> (Signed) R N O'Connor
Lieutenant General
Commander 8 Corps[52]

In addition to all the usual preparations required before going into a major action, the Corps had the problem of arranging the movement of all the divisions and supporting arms into their new area. To give some idea of the complexity of this, the distances that the various formations had to travel were as follows: 6th Guards Tank Brigade—18 miles; 8th AGRA (Army Group Royal Artillery)—30; 11th Armoured Division—25; Corps headquarters—20; 2nd Household Cavalry Regiment—26; and Guards Armoured Division—45 miles. The tail element of the Corps was still nearly fifty miles away east of the River Orne when the attack began on 30 July. Some of the difficulties encountered on the way are described by Roberts:

> But first of all we had to get to the area, and this necessitated crossing the supply lines of both 12 and 30 Corps. Certain times were given us when we would have priority on the roads, but in fact no one else took any notice of them and we had particular trouble with some of 30 Corps, who professed to be quite unaware of any priority timings for us. Divisional HQ finally came to rest at 2100 hours on the 29th; Corps orders arrived at our HQ during the cross-country march, so that our orders to brigades arrived at around 0200 hours on 30th July and 'H' hour for the attack was 0655 hours. It was a scramble, but just worked. I had, of course, given verbal orders to the brigadiers.[53]

A comprehensive fire-plan for the artillery was organised by Brigadier Matthew with customary efficiency, and plans were made to employ a fleet of some 1,600 medium and heavy bombers of the RAF and 9 USAAF, 700 on XXX Corps front and the rest in support of VIII Corps. It was also agreed that a second bombing raid would be available in the afternoon on the Point 309 feature: in the event this proved to be of the greatest value.

The terrain over which the first phase of 'Bluecoat' was to be fought is well described in the history of the Guards Armoured Division:

> Caumont lies on an east-and-west ridge. Five miles to the south lies higher ground, culminating in Point 309, which is the north-west extension of the Mont Pinçon massif. Between the Caumont ridge and Point 309 is the 'Bocage' at its best, an area of many small woods interspersed with very small fields. The fields are separated by high banks, six foot and more, on the top of which are thick high hedges. There is but one road running south, not metalled, and in many places not wide enough for two-way traffic. The country is interlaced with very narrow deep lanes, which wander about in no very definite manner. Movement across country proved impossible for all vehicles except the Churchill tanks, and for infantry on foot it was a slow and laborious task. At this season the crops were at their highest and the trees and hedges were in full leaf. Even so, observation from both the Caumont ridge and Point 309 was quite good enough to enable movement to be detected.[54]

'Bluecoat', which O'Connor considered to be VIII Corps' best battle, and was certainly a particularly important one, was a prolonged and bitter struggle which tested the stamina of those taking part to the utmost.

At 6.55 am on 30 July, Cameronians and Gordons crossed 15th (Scottish) Division start-line, supported by tanks of 6th Guards Tank Brigade. By the early afternoon, leading elements of the division and its armour had advanced four miles to the foot of Point 309. It was then, at 3.55 pm, that the second air strike of the day took place, and the hill was heavily bombed by 9 USAAF. Realising that speed was vital in order to capture the hill before the enemy recovered from the shock of the bombing, MacMillan told Brigadier Verney, commanding the Guards Tank Brigade, to send one of his battalions straight up Point 309, and to use another one to follow, carrying infantry on the tanks. The gamble came off, the hill was captured and 4th Tank Coldstream Guards were congratulated two days later in a letter from O'Connor in which he wrote: 'No tank unit has ever been handled with greater dash and determination.'[55]

As already described, 11th Armoured Division was just able to reach its start-line on time after a long, frustrating night march. The main problem it had to face on 30 July, as well as the heat and dust, was clearing the heavily mined roads. Though progress was slow, by the evening the weary division had covered slightly less distance than the Scots, and was ready for a rest. However, as Roberts has recorded, 'firm orders came from the Corps Commander that we could not relax'.[56] As a result, 4th King's Shropshire Light Infantry were sent off in the dark, and following a remarkable night march, which was fortunately unopposed, by dawn on 31 July were astride the road outside the village of St Martin des Besaces, a mile west of Point 309. While the fighting to subdue the village was in progress a troop of 2nd Household Cavalry was carrying out a remarkable reconnaissance patrol.

Following a route south-west from St Martin, it passed through the wooded area known as the Forêt l'Eveque, along an undefended road which later turned out to be a boundary set by Von Kluge between his Seventh Army and Panzer Group West. Each army must have expected the other to guard it, but neither had. Two miles beyond the forest, an unmined and undefended bridge over the river Souleuvre was found. At 10.30 am, although at the limit of wireless range, the troop leader was just able to get a message back to his regimental headquarters, who passed it to Roberts. Half an hour later, at 11 am, the capture of St Martin des Besaces was completed and elements of 29th Armoured Brigade were despatched to make the five-mile journey to the Souleuvre river bridge. Due to confusion over boundaries and objectives with 5 US Corps on the right, there was some delay in reaching it.

At 2 pm, soon after O'Connor had heard the good news of the capture of St Martin and the seizure of the bridge, he issued a new directive to Roberts. This was to capture Pont Aunay, a village lying to the west of the Forêt l'Evêque near the boundary with the Americans, and also to occupy the high ground beyond the river Souleuvre known as Le Beny Bocage ridge. These tasks were to be carried out that night. The next day, 1 August, further bridges over the Souleuvre were to be opened. Finally, 2nd Household Cavalry were told that they must 'tonight patrol south with the utmost vigour in the direction of Vire. This task is also essential to the Allied plan.'[57] Vire lay another seven miles beyond the Souleuvre.

Due to the success of VIII Corps, as against the rather slow advance of XXX Corps on its left, O'Connor was now given the leading role in 'Bluecoat' and was allotted some of the XXX Corps objectives. Unfortunately, as the VIII Corps history records, although 'this was a highly satisfactory situation at the time, it was to sow the seeds of a big disappointment in store for the Corps three weeks later'.[58]

The rapidity of O'Connor's advance meant that he was creating a dangerous salient into enemy territory, with his left flank particularly exposed. For this reason he had to tie down 15th (Scottish) Division in protecting this flank until XXX Corps should catch up. He therefore brought forward the Guards Armoured Division on the afternoon of 31 July to take up the advance on the left of 11th Armoured.

Following the remarkably swift drive south during the first two days of 'Bluecoat', which took forward elements of VIII Corps almost 12 miles on from the start line, 1 August marked the start of a period during which the fighting grew steadily fiercer. The Germans reinforced the Seventh Army units opposing the Corps with 21st Panzer Division, followed by 9th and 10th SS Panzer Divisions. General George Patton's Third US Army was now passing through the gap south of Avranches and accelerating into its triumphal sweep to the Seine, so that VIII Corps' operations became what its history calls 'a measured driving-back process which was to help encircle and compress almost the entire German forces in Normandy into a small area between Falaise and Argentan known forever to history as the "Falaise Pocket"'.[59]

On 1 August, 11th Armoured Division cleared the Beny Bocage ridge and took the village, while on its left Guards Armoured started towards Estry on an axis soon found to be skilfully defended by 21st Panzer Division. Armoured cars of 2nd Household Cavalry penetrated as far as Vire, which at this stage was temporarily unoccupied by the enemy. However, as it lay in the US sector, the town was not entered. Throughout 2 August, the advance continued slowly, often checked by German counter-attacks. By 4 August, 11th Armoured Division had penetrated another six miles south from Le Beny Bocage, and was positioned on the high ground east of Vire known as Perrier Ridge. Leading elements of the Guards Armoured Division had covered some four miles of the route to Estry against strong opposition. O'Connor visited Roberts as his men moved onto Perrier Ridge, and agreed that the latter's plan to hold this high ground and wait for the Germans to attack it was correct. Having just had 3rd Infantry Division added to his command, O'Connor allotted a brigade from it to strengthen Roberts' position.

A considerable number of changes took place in the Corps command structure around the time that 'Bluecoat' was reaching its climax. Following the rather slow movement of XXX Corps at the start of the operation, General Bucknall was relieved of his command, as was Erskine of 7th Armoured Division. Bucknall's place was taken by the well-known figure of General Brian Horrocks, now recovered from a wound received in North Africa, while Brigadier Gerald Verney of 6th Guards Tank Brigade was posted across from VIII Corps to take over 7th Armoured. Then, on 4 August, 'Babe' MacMillan was wounded and 15th (Scottish) Division was taken over by Brigadier 'Tiny' Barber. Barber's brigade, in its turn, was taken over by 'Dickie' Villiers of 9th Cameronians—the good work of this excellently commanded battalion of his own regiment gave O'Connor much pleasure during the Normandy battles. The departure of MacMillan was a bad blow, and O'Connor wrote to his wife that evening:

> Babe is slightly wounded. It is a tragedy as he has been the mainstay of this party, and stands out head and shoulders above everyone else. He is one of the best, if not *the* best, commanders I have ever met, and commands the best lot out here. This is beyond dispute.
>
> I shall miss him as a friend, collaborator and adviser .... Most of the success out here has been the result of his initial efforts.

Another blow for O'Connor came not long afterwards when he heard that Jim Hargest had been killed. Following his escape from Vincigliata, Hargest had reached Britain after many exciting adventures and had then been appointed an observer in Normandy on behalf of the New Zealand Government. Quite by chance, his jeep was struck one evening by a stray shell: his country lost one of its finest men, and the O'Connors a good friend.

Knowing what an exhausting six days his division had endured up to 4 August, and realising that there were more to come, with no chance of respite, Roberts sent a message to his brigadiers and all commanding officers.

His first paragraph stated:

> I wish all ranks to know that during the present period of operations, tremendous demands will be made on their powers of endurance.

221

Although the enemy is resisting very stubbornly on our front, all men should realise that his endurance is equally, if not more, tested than ours. The main Allied plan is developing with the greatest success, and superhuman efforts now will not only save casualties later, but have every chance of bringing the war with Germany to an early conclusion.

He went on to say that he would 'only call upon troops to do the almost impossible and not the completely impossible', and then finished by pointing out:

It may be of interest, but perhaps not of comfort, to realise that the greatest enemy resistance at the present time is on 8 Corps front. By containing such enemy strength we are being of the utmost value to the remainder of the Army.

At 6 pm on 6 August, the Germans launched what was to be their last major attack against VIII Corps. Their error was to come in against the apex of a long salient which was so much more vulnerable on its flanks. Although there was some confusion at the start of the battle, as the brigade from 3rd Division was just relieving members of 11th Armoured at various points on the divisional front, all was soon under control. 'It was certainly the toughest battle we had in the campaign', recorded Roberts; 'both sides received heavy casualties, but the Germans had the heavier, largely because they were advancing and not dug-in, and we had the capability of putting down really concentrated gunfire from medium guns.'[60]

A Bitter Disappointment

The next day, 7 August, the pressure on Second Army eased, as the Germans made a desperate attempt to cut off the American spearheads now deep into France. Switching Panzer divisions away from the Vire sector, they attacked the US forces at Mortain. Desperately, Von Kluge tried to warn Hitler of the dangers of this effort. His warnings fell on deaf ears and, true to form, Hitler ordered him to reinforce his attacks, even when it was clear that they could only fail. On 8 August, Montgomery ordered a general advance to the Seine, with Third US Army carrying out a wide enveloping movement towards Paris, while the First US Army swung north from Alençon towards Argentan. The Mortain counter-stroke took the Germans deep into the trap which was now to be closed behind them through a major offensive by the First Canadian Army towards Falaise. Second Army was instructed to keep up the pressure at all points along its front: with victory so near there could be no relaxation.

The approach of victory, however, was to bring bitter disappointment to O'Connor and the members of his headquarters. As the collapse of the German armies in France came nearer, plans were made for the pursuit that would follow it, and it became clear that VIII Corps was going to be left out of this exciting phase of the campaign.

As Second Army began to pivot towards the east from the high ground held around Vire, and the Americans swung past to the south, VIII Corps was gradually squeezed out by the British XXX Corps on its left and the US 5th Corps on the right. Although still involved in directing 3rd Infantry Division and elements of 11th Armoured in a small operation, starting on 12 August and given the obvious name of 'Grouse', to capture the town of Flers, O'Connor began to have his command reduced on 14 August. First 11th Armoured Division passed under command of Horrocks in XXX Corps, and then 15th (Scottish) was switched to XII Corps. After the success with which he had conducted all phases of 'Bluecoat' it is understandable that O'Connor felt somewhat slighted by the situation which relegated his Corps to a back seat at such a moment of excitement: how his reactions grew more bitter later will come out in the next chapter.

However, in spite of being robbed of his period of glory, he remained on excellent terms with Montgomery, with whom he had dinner on 18 August. Later that night, he wrote a long letter to Jean, which shows how close he still was to his old friend at this stage. The letter began with mention of Jim Hargest:

> I went and saw Jim Hargest's grave today below Mt Pinçon, in a little cemetery recently made. Just a perfectly plain grave with a little wooden cross,
> Brig J Hargest
> N Z Forces
> Killed in action
> 12th Aug 1944
>
> The cross just the same as all the rest—very nice and simple. I managed to get a photo taken of it quite illegally, and if it turns out well do you recommend me sending it to his widow?
>
> I dined tonight with the chief [Montgomery]. He was in very good heart. Not the least bit cock-a-hoop about the battle—in fact very modest. Very

full of praise for the Americans, who have done magnificently. Having seen a good deal of them recently, I think there is a lot to be learnt from them. Their cooperation is excellent, and we both gave each other every possible assistance. I think this battle is working out very well indeed. And it is exactly in conformity with Monty's strategy from the start, which he expounded before he left England. Namely for us originally to draw the largest number of Divisions onto us to enable the Americans to break thro' to Brittany. This was essential both to enlarge the beachhead and to get the ports for the Americans.

They did their part magnificently. The next phase was pushing through all the American troops possible to work round the enemy's left flank, and so endeavour to push him onto the Seine.

Then the enemy himself took a hand in it by his counter offensive at Mortain with the object of reaching Avranches and cutting the Americans in two. He failed to do this and much more, because by doing it and failing he has not given time to his troops to get out before our outflanking movement and the advance from Falaise closed, or nearly closed, the gap. Now, as a result of that, he has two cordons to break thro'; one the close one between Falaise and Argentan, which is the result of his own delay in retiring, and the bigger but not less important one from Dreux towards Evreux, pushing him off onto a bridgeless Seine.

This latter cordon, but of course not the former, was foreseen by Monty all the time, and he often spoke to me about it. And now it looks like coming off. The enemy will get a fair amount of stuff out of the first cordon, and a certain amount eventually across the Seine in barges and ferries, but his losses will be enormous, and his Army will never be the same again. I don't see him stopping us for long anywhere. I hope I am not wrong, and I don't think I am. The greatest credit is due to Monty, which nothing that his detractors can say will affect in any way. He is a great tactician and the greatest leader of our time, and stands head and shoulders above everyone else.

I knew you would miss dear Jim [Hargest]. I feel we have been all so lucky to have known him. He was a very great man, and I am sorry he could not have lived to see some of his work progressing.[61]

17

Normandy to the River Maas

The capture of Flers by elements of 11th Armoured Division and 3rd Division on 16 August was the last battle of VIII Corps in France, apart from one or two minor 'mopping-up' tasks. By 20 August, the German resistance was at an end and the campaign in Normandy was over. O'Connor was left with only two divisions under command: Guards Armoured and 3rd Division. At this stage much greater opposition on the line of the River Seine was expected than actually materialised, and O'Connor was warned that he might be given the task of carrying out the assault river-crossing operation when it became necessary. On 21 August, he moved Corps Head-quarters to the vicinity of Flers, near which a practice bridging site had been established on a lake, and the two divisions were rehearsed in the techniques of crossing a major water obstacle against opposi-tion. It was soon clear, however, that the Seine was not held in the strength anticipated, and, on 24 August, the Guards Armoured Division was removed from O'Connor's command and posted to join 11th Armoured in Horrocks's XXX Corps, to take part in the heady race to Brussels and Antwerp, which was just getting under way.

Although what remained of VIII Corps was busily enough engaged on line of communication duties in France during the last week of August and the first days of September 1944, O'Connor became increasingly despondent as the time passed. After the success of 'Bluecoat' it was hard to see XXX Corps, which had been so much less effective during that hard-fought struggle, given the privilege of reaping all the rewards of the victory. There can be little doubt that Montgomery had decided that Horrocks, the newly arrived commander of XXX Corps (who had proved himself in the desert and in North Africa as a dynamic and charismatic leader), was the man to command the pursuit of the heavily defeated German armies and so had regrouped XXX Corps for that task. Horrocks, as a friend and admirer of O'Connor, realised the latter's feelings and wrote to him on 2 September: 'I can quite imagine how upset you must be at your corps being in reserve just at the moment.'[1]

Inevitably O'Connor began to wonder whether he was out of favour with Montgomery and Dempsey, and was being deliberately pushed towards the side-lines. Perhaps it was his age, or perhaps there were moves afoot to send him to India? Rumours that both Wavell and Auchinleck wanted him to go out there must have reached him, and he would have recalled a sentence in a letter from 'the Auk' earlier in the year: 'Perhaps we may see you out here again before the war is over. I hope we do.'[2] The letter he received from Montgomery, dated 4 September in reply to one of his own, demonstrates the extent to which these matters were troubling him:

Personal

TAC HEADQUARTERS
21 ARMY GROUP

4–9–44

My dear Dick,

I have your letter.
I know nothing of any appointment in India or anywhere else.
You have my complete confidence, and Bimbo's also. It is merely the march of events, and the very awkward maintenance situation, which made it necessary to drop a corps. But I think in a day or two you will find yourself up in the battle line again.[3]

The full extent of O'Connor's unhappiness at the situation came out in a letter to Jean which was posted on 7 September.

I can hardly bear reading that you and all my friends are thinking I am up when I am miles and miles behind. So sad and disappointing to have only the sticky part and none of the other. However, there it is, and it is the fortune of war and it is no good being unhappy about it. It sounds as if I had been demoted to the uninitiated, but that is not the case at all.

We have all had each others divisions constantly, there are very few I have not commanded at one time or another. Then the pace of the advance increased tremendously and the front being narrower, there was no possibility of us getting in until we got to the Seine. Here we would have been used, if there had been serious opposition to us getting over.

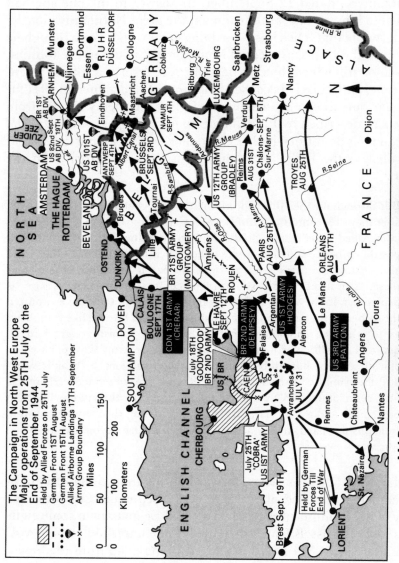

MAP 11. NORTH-WEST EUROPE. MAJOR OPERATIONS FROM 25th JULY - 30th SEPTEMBER 1944

There wasn't. Now it came a question of supplies and only Neil [Ritchie] and 'Hugh's double' [Horrocks] could be supplied.[4]

Jean must have been relieved to receive an encouraging letter from Montgomery, dated 12 September, in answer to the one she had written to him to congratulate him on the great Normandy victory. In it he wrote that 'Dick has been doing great work'. Even though he was given these reassurances of Montgomery's faith in his abilities, O'Connor still felt slighted at being kept in reserve at this momentous time, particularly because of the fame he had gained in 1941 for a similar pursuit of a beaten enemy. In fact the enemy was far from beaten, as described by Liddell Hart in his *History of the Second World War*, and it is doubtful whether O'Connor, in the circumstances that prevailed at the time, would have pushed any harder than the others:

> But throughout the Allied forces there was a general tendency to relax after they drove into Belgium. It was fostered from the top. Eisenhower's inter-Allied Intelligence Staff told him that the Germans could not possibly produce sufficient forces to hold their frontier defence line—and also assured the press 'we'll go right through it'. Eisenhower conveyed these assurances to his subordinate commanders—even as late as September 15, he wrote to Montgomery: 'We shall soon have captured the Ruhr and the Saar and the Frankfurt area, and I would like your views as to what we should do next.' A similar optimism reigned in all quarters.... John North in his history of the 21st Army Group, based on official sources, has aptly summed up the situation: 'a "war is won" attitude of mind ... prevailed among all ranks'. In consequence, there was little sense of urgency among commanders during the vital fortnight in September and a very natural inclination among the troops to abstain from pushing hard, and avoid getting killed, when everyone assumed that 'the war is over'.[5]

Gradually VIII Corps moved forward during that 'vital fortnight in September' mentioned above and, on 11 September, the advance party of the headquarters reached a small Belgian town some eight miles east of Brussels which delighted in the name of Erps Querps. Soon afterwards, 3rd Division started to move up from the Seine, and on 16 September 11th Armoured Division came under command again. It was at the time in contact with the enemy near the Meuse-Escaut canal: canals and rivers, an abundance of which dominated the flat landscape of the Low Countries, were to become the main barriers to the movement of Allied troops in the coming months. On the next day, 17 September, 4th Armoured Brigade was ordered forward and brought under command, and 1st Belgian Brigade also joined the Corps.

The significance of this date was that it was the first day of the operation of 21st Army Group code-named 'Market Garden', but much better known to the world at large as 'Arnhem'. Although there were considerable numbers of German troops in Holland north of the Meuse-Escaut canal, they were considered to be in such a thoroughly disorganised state that, though it proved to be over optimistic, a plan was made to take advantage of this by making a sudden, quick thrust right through to the German frontier. The official intention laid down by Montgomery was 'to place Second Army, including airborne forces, astride the Rivers Maas, Waal and Neder Rijn on the general axis Grave–Nijmegen–Arnhem, and to dominate the country between the Rhine and the Zuyder Zee, thus cutting off communications between Germany and Holland'.[6] The Allied Airborne Corps, consisting of two US divisions and one British, was to be dropped to seize the crossings over the Maas, Waal and Neder Rijn, while XXX Corps was to make a rapid dash of over sixty miles through Eindhoven, Grave and Nijmegen to reach the British Airborne Division at Arnhem. In support of Horrocks' XXX Corps, O'Connor with VIII Corps on the right, and Ritchie with XII Corps on the left, were given the task of broadening the base of Second Army's advance. With his corps dispersed over some 250 miles between the Seine and his leading formation, O'Connor was not at first ideally situated to carry out his role. However, by the evening of 18 September 3rd Division had arrived in the corps area as well as the two independent brigades. Also allotted to him that night was 50th (Northumbrian) Division, commanded by his brother Cameronian Major General Douglas Graham, a splendid fighting soldier much admired by Montgomery, who nick-named him 'the old war-horse'.

Rivers, Canals and Marshes—and Hard Fighting

The action during the next six days is difficult to describe without becoming as confusing as the maze of rivers and canals that criss-crossed the country to be fought over. Very briefly summarised, VIII Corps carried out a fighting advance of nearly fifty miles, and captured the two important Dutch towns of Helmond and Deurne lying east of Eindhoven, as well as forcing a crossing of the Zuid-

Willemsvaart canal before the enemy could establish strong positions behind such an ideal barrier for a prolonged defence. During the afternoon of 21 September, 11th Armoured Division fought a fierce battle with 107th Panzer Brigade, which had counterattacked from the north towards Eindhoven. In O'Connor's opinion, Roberts saved that important centre from being recaptured.

The type of fighting carried out at this period is well described by Roberts:

> Our military operations became quite different to anything we had met before. Now, the Germans consisted of a number of 'battle groups' bearing the name of their commanders; their divisions seemed to have broken up, but the groups still had a very high morale, particularly those of SS or Paratroops; they would often fight on without any officers. The country over which we were to fight was heavily 'canalised' and so, with these natural obstacles, little work was required to convert them into a strong line of defence very quickly. In Normandy we would start off an operation with a heavy artillery bombardment and sometimes with considerable air support, against well reconnoitred enemy positions. Now we came up against natural obstacles, sometimes fortified and sometimes not, but when held by the Germans they needed a lot of effort....
>
> In Normandy there was always real anxiety; if one made wrong decisions, if the front were penetrated by the Germans, if our line of communication was cut, the result could be catastrophic. Now mistakes or failures could only delay the end. Of course we wanted to finish the war as quickly as possible, but at what cost? Unless morale was high, we would not achieve our objectives; heavy casualties in a fruitless battle will not help morale. We must try to win our battles without heavy casualties; not very easy.[7]

Not only did the Germans put up an almost fanatical defence at many points, but they also launched frequent small counter-attacks. One of these came in on 22 September from the north-west behind the leading elements of XXX Corps to cut its main axis and seriously interrupt traffic moving forward. It became obvious that XXX Corps required assistance in the protection of its lines of communication and, at mid-day on 23 September, Dempsey held a conference at the headquarters of 101st US Airborne Division and put this division under O'Connor's command. At the same time 50th Division was ordered to move north to protect the American flank. That afternoon the American paratroopers successfully cleared XXX Corps' axis again. In the evening, O'Connor wrote to Jean, starting with comments on the weather: 'It is simply pelting.

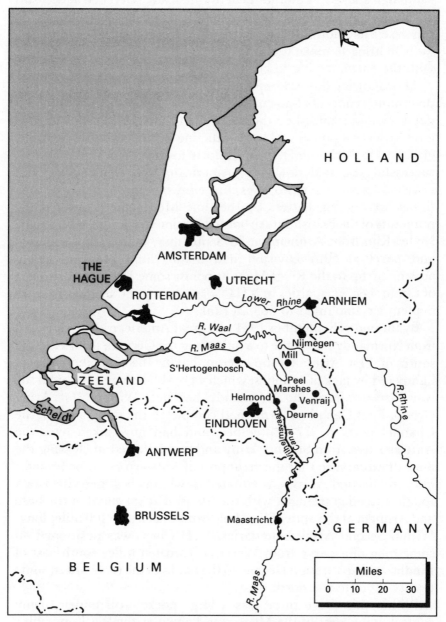

MAP 12. THE LOW COUNTRIES 1944-45

We certainly have had the worst weather ever met this last few days. It is really astonishing how few good days we have had since this campaign started.' Later in the letter he made reference to the 'sort of op which is called brilliant if it comes off and bad if it does not. In this case I had nothing to do with its inception but have had to do a lot of fighting to make it go.... We have had a lot of tough fighting with the enemy trying to cut the road.'

The following day, 24 September, the Germans made their most determined effort of all to cut XXX Corps' axis once more. By midday they had established themselves with tanks and self-propelled guns at several points and were inflicting severe casualties on units of 101st US Airborne Division. Efforts to shift them were not very successful and tied down the Americans and elements of 50th Division for the next two days, but elsewhere in VIII Corps area things were going better. By the time Montgomery ordered the remnants of the British 1st Airborne Division to withdraw across the Neder-Rijn from Arnhem on 25 September, both 11th Armoured and parts of 50th Division had made rapid progress north, advancing up to the River Maas at points some 15 miles north-east of Eindhoven. Casualties in VIII Corps during the six days from 19 September amounted to 663 all ranks.

By the end of September 1944, the great American sweep forward from Normandy had come to a halt along the German frontier to the south of 21st Army Group sector, having become increasingly hampered by lack of supplies, which were still being brought all the way forward from the Normandy beaches. Within 21st Army Group, First Canadian Army had completed the re-opening of the Channel ports by 17 September, and had now taken over the Antwerp area from Second Army and was involved in clearing the Scheldt estuary, so that the great port of Antwerp could be brought into use. Second Army was situated in what is best described as a rough, extended triangle, with the Meuse-Escaut canal at the base and Arnhem at the apex. The whole front was nearly 100 miles long. Within Second Army boundaries, VIII Corps was positioned on something of a curve from Weert, a town ten miles south-east of Eindhoven, up through Deurne to the banks of the river Maas, some twenty miles to the north-west.

Within this curve there was a large pocket still under enemy control, lying west of the Maas, and known as the 'Peel' marshes:

> The 'Peel' area is a large tract of reclaimed marshland extending along the west bank of the R Maas for about 20 miles on either side of Venlo.

Every field in it is surrounded by a deep dyke which drains off the water fairly efficiently in the summer, but in the winter or during a rainy season, the land rapidly reverts to type and the whole becomes once again a quagmire. One metalled road of poor quality leads across from Venlo through Meijel and Deurne to Helmond. In dry weather there are certain tracks but these disappear under water at the first shower of rain. In any event none are capable of standing up to heavy traffic, least of all tanks and military vehicles; later the utmost ingenuity had to be used in order to keep supplies going even in static warfare. It is perhaps the worst country in the world for armoured fighting for no tank dare leave the track, and one cleverly placed minefield can cause enormous delay.[8]

In the final days of September, 11th Armoured Division made several tentative thrusts against the Peel area, and in particular against a small town called Overloon in the woods on the outskirts of the marsh, but further efforts were called off when it became clear that the German positions were too strong for anything less than a deliberate attack. The possible ways of launching such a deliberate attack, in the strength necessary for success, were discussed at several meetings between Dempsey and O'Connor.

While these discussions were in progress, the boundary between Second Army and Ninth US Army on its southern flank had been readjusted, with the result that responsibility for the Peel area had been handed over to 7th US Armoured Division, enabling 11th Armoured Division to prepare for the major operation being planned by Dempsey. Roberts has described what then happened:

7th US Armoured Division were given the specific tasks of occupying Overloon and Venray. Major General Silvester, the divisional commander, came to visit me soon after his arrival. He quite clearly thought this task was easy, in spite of my warnings that the country was difficult and the enemy very determined. 'Oh!' he said, 'we'll turn on the heat and be down to Overloon in no time'. By 'turning on the heat' he meant that he would call up their escorting Thunderbolts on anything that held them up and they would be in Venray in no time. I wished them luck, but was not very hopeful. One of the troubles was that they had not experienced any positional fighting so far, but had arrived in time to assist in the 'gallop' across France. As the writer of the 23rd Hussars History explains: 'Their morale was rather higher than their skill'.... Suffice to say that after several days of fruitless fighting in which considerable casualties were incurred, the operation was discontinued.'[9]

While he made plans with Dempsey for 'Gatwick', as the next Second Army operation was provisionally code-named, O'Connor can have had little inkling of how significant a person Major General Lindsay Silvester would prove in his own life. In the end 'Gatwick' was called off: the idea had been for VIII Corps to storm the formidable German defences in the Reichswald forest, which lay across the River Maas at the head of the Siegfried line. It was eventually decided that such an assault was too hazardous, and attention was turned instead towards a less ambitious operation to be known as 'Constellation'. VIII Corps history explains the background:

> Whilst, thus, the larger plan was abandoned, it was both possible and desirable from the point of view of Second Army to clear up the Maas pocket. General Dempsey therefore gave instructions to this effect, and obtained the loan from Ninth US Army of 7 US Armoured Division which, together with 15 (Scottish) Division, was allotted to 8 Corps, so that for Operation 'Constellation,' as it was called, the Corps was to be a strong body of over 90,000 troops comprising the following formations:

> 7 US Armoured Division
> 11 Armoured Division
> 3 Infantry Division
> 15 (Scottish) Infantry Division
> 6 Guards Tank Brigade
> 1 Belgian Brigade.[10]

At the beginning of October, Corps headquarters was situated at Mill, a pleasant village three miles from the River Maas, and five from the German border and the Reichswald forest. A major change in the staff occurred in the first week of the month when Sir Harry Floyd was posted to Italy on promotion to Major General to become Chief of Staff to his old friend General Sir Richard McCreery, Commander of the Eighth Army. In his place came a brilliant young Brigadier called Victor Fitzgeorge-Balfour who had served in the Coldstream Guards in Palestine before the war. O'Connor wrote about him to Jean: 'Balfour is a very good chap, quite young, about 30 I should think. Coldstream Guards, aristocratic and Eton, etc, so Harry won't feel the job has been lowered! Good looking, which is good, as I should not call us a very handsome lot .... He got an MC which I put him up for a day or so before you arrived in Palestine in 1938—the time you got off with all those four oil kings, Minto's friends!?'[11] Though O'Connor missed Floyd, whom he had got to know very well and with whom he kept up a frequent correspondence in the following months, Balfour soon settled into his new post. In a letter to O'Connor after the war was over, Roberts was especially complimentary about him, mentioning that he was 'brilliant in his quick grasp of an enormous mass of detail'.[12] Balfour was young enough to be his new General's son and, like a son, he found the fifty-five year old O'Connor a little fussy over small matters and, although extremely pleasant to work for, less inspiring than Horrocks, on whose staff Balfour had previously been serving.

Operation Constellation

The German forces in the Maas pocket were to prove formidable adversaries:

> By the early part of October, the enemy west of the River Maas had not only been substantially reinforced but had clearly taken heart, both from the Allied reverse at Arnhem, and his own successful defence against 7 US Armoured Division. The Maas pocket itself was completely organised, with three divisions holding it, made up largely of paratroopers.... Moreover, the German High Command had not relied entirely upon the friendly offices of the terrible country over which the Allies were forced to advance, but had constructed two outer defence lines facing north west, and a third joining up with the major fortifications already encircling the bastion of Venlo. The reduction of the area had thus every possibility of being a slow, difficult and hazardous operation, and so it proved, though none foresaw that it would not finally be eliminated until the beginning of December.[13]

Operation 'Constellation' was the fourth and last of the major attacks to be launched under O'Connor's command in north-west Europe—the others being 'Epsom', 'Goodwood', and 'Bluecoat'—and it was the one for which he was given the greatest independence in the planning. Perhaps for this reason in Roberts' view, 'his handling of Constellation was the best he had shown in the campaign'.[14]

On 9 October, the enemy layout was plotted according to the most recent air photographs and brought to O'Connor to study, and he decided to take advantage of the fact that the major defences faced north-west. His plan was divided into four phases, the concept being to draw the bulk of the enemy northwards before a thrust came in from the south against the strong-point at Venlo. The initial three phases were planned to take the town of Venraij, and there to place the two armoured divisions in locations from which they would be able to carry out the fourth:

Finally the two armoured divisions and 15 (Scottish) Division were all to converge on Venlo. The greatest emphasis was laid throughout the preparations for 'Constellation' on concealing the eventual entry of the Scots into the contest. It was, moreover, felt by everyone at Corps headquarters, that in view of the appalling terrain, coupled with the extremely wet weather, the operation would be slow and difficult.[15]

Despite the fact that O'Connor had issued the strictest instructions on security at his verbal briefing of his divisional commanders and had explicitly forbidden that any approach should be made to the Belgian Brigade about the forthcoming move of 15th (Scottish) Division into the line, written orders to some forty addressees were issued by the staff of the division, thereby earning General Barber, the Divisional Commander, a considerable 'rocket'. 'My dear Tiny' began O'Connor's letter to him dated 14 October, continuing:

> You well know how fond I am of you all, but I can't but think you have handled this secrecy and security question very badly. After all I said about it, and the particular emphasis I laid on it, I feel that you can not have passed it properly to your subordinates.

The letter then went on to list specific faults, and particularly criticised the commander of the divisional artillery, the error of whose ways Barber was instructed to bring home to him immediately. O'Connor finished by pointing out that:

> I can't help feeling that you have, unwittingly I know, let me down, which can't be helped and doesn't matter much, but also your division, which matters a great deal.
>
> I am very sorry indeed to have had to criticise you in this way, but I feel very strongly about this, and felt that I could have trusted you in this more than almost anyone in the Corps.
>
> Let us hope that no damage is quite as bad as it seems.[16]

Operation 'Constellation' began at mid-day on 12 October 1944 with an assault by a brigade of 3rd Division in the Overloon area, strongly supported by Typhoons of 83 Group RAF and Marauders of the USAAF. Unfortunately, aircraft detailed to demolish the bridges over the Maas in Roermond and Venlo were diverted to another task further south in the US sector, and so the Germans were able to bring reinforcements across the river over these bridges which remained intact throughout the battle.

For the next three days, in appalling weather and over the most difficult terrain, 3rd Division and 11th Armoured gradually manoeuvred into position as O'Connor hoped they would, and drew the enemy northwards, as intended. The enemy were found to be 'first class infantry men brave and tenacious in their defence',[17] and attacks launched against them had to survive intense mortar concentrations as well as clear lavishly laid minefields.

By the morning of 16 October, elements of 3rd Division and 11th Armoured were ready to catch the Germans in a pincer movement around Venraij and 7th US Armoured, which had been 'demonstrating' on its front as part of the deception plan, was about to be launched into action. By the evening of that day, the whole enemy defence system was crumbling, and over 2,000 had been killed or captured. It was the moment for O'Connor to deliver the '*coup de grâce*'. At the very moment when orders were being given to 15th (Scottish) Division for this task, a telephone call from Second Army Headquarters ordered the immediate withdrawal of that division to a concentration area around Helmond, from whence they were about to be sent as soon as possible to take part in the final clearing of the Scheldt estuary. As the Corps' history records:

> Reviewing Operation 'Constellation', one cannot help feeling that here was a flawless plan spoiled in the very moment of its triumph, for the successive stages of introduction of the three divisions had had the effect desired and it is fair to suppose that if 15 (Scottish) Division had been allowed to carry out the tasks allotted, the whole Maas pocket would have folded up. However, the reason for the withdrawal of this division from 8 Corps was of the greatest importance and it is at least consoling to know that shortly afterwards the approaches to Antwerp were finally freed.[18]

Limited advances were made on 17 October, and Venraij itself was captured, as well as 500 more prisoners. However, without 15th (Scottish) Division, further movement in the Maas pocket was impossible and VIII Corps adopted defensive positions along its extended front of 69 miles. The same day O'Connor wrote to Harry Floyd in Italy to give him news of how 'Constellation' had turned out, expressing his disappointment in a fairly restrained manner, as he also did in a letter to Jean that evening, merely stating: 'It has been very sad not being able to finish it off. It will have to be done sometime without doubt.'

From Montgomery on 19 October came congratulations: 'I am delighted with the way you captured Venraij and the general progress you made.'[19]

An Uneasy Calm—The Germans Counter-attack

From 18 October there was a period of uneasy calm, during which it became increasingly clear that the Allied armies were going to be involved in a winter campaign before the war could be brought to an end; a particularly cheerless prospect for members of VIII Corps enduring the constant rain and cold in the gloomy environment of the Peel marshes. Across the Maas, they could see the Germans working on improving the defences on the east bank of the river, but apart from calling down air strikes and artillery concentrations they took no offensive action, as they were holding such a wide front with so few troops. How lightly the Corps front was held did not, however, escape the notice of Field Marshal von Rundstedt, now restored to command of the German armies in the west after his earlier dismissal in Normandy. He contrived to move into the area 47th Panzer Corps of two divisions almost unnoticed in the fog and limited visibility which had settled over the dismal countryside, and decided to attack the sector held by 7th US Armoured Division around the small town of Meijel, which lies south-east of Eindhoven, about eight miles from Venlo.

The main attack, which came, after a heavy artillery bombardment, in against Meijel at 7 am on 27 October, achieved complete surprise. This advantage, and also the poor visibility which prevented air attacks against them, were outweighed for the Germans by the difficulty in manoeuvring their heavy Tiger tanks except on the one road available across the marsh. Even so, they made a deep penetration on the first day into 7th US Armoured Division's defences, capturing the town of Meijel, and O'Connor quickly realised that the situation was serious. As the Americans were known to be short of artillery, the first reinforcement he sent to them was 25 Field Regiment RA, which was quickly in action on the morning of 28 October against a strong German attack westward from Meijel. The concentrated fire of this regiment prevented the enemy achieving more than a limited advance on that day.

On the afternoon of 28 October O'Connor asked Second Army for additional forces to help resist this dangerous German counter-attack. First to be ordered forward in this role was 15th (Scottish) Division; the reaction of the Jocks, who were enjoying unlimited hospitality in the Dutch town of Tilburg on the Scheldt, which they had just liberated, was not one of unbridled enthusiasm.

On the most crucial day of the battle, 29 October, it was once again concentrated artillery fire which decimated the attacking Germans. By that evening, the battle was really over, although fighting continued on a less hectic scale for nearly another week. 15th (Scottish) Division, back in the line in full strength by nightfall on 29 October, broke up various small German 'spoiling' attacks the next day. Other reinforcements soon arrived in VIII Corps' sector, including 53rd (Welsh) Division on 1 November, to relieve 7th US Armoured, and 4th Armoured Brigade. The Americans had suffered the highest losses during the repulse of this enemy counter-attack, but all involved reported casualties which were unacceptable at this stage of the war if they could possibly be avoided. In consequence, O'Connor was content with merely pushing the battered enemy back towards the Maas, leaving them in temporary possession of the town of Meijel until a proper operation could be organised to clear the whole Maas 'pocket'.

Finding Mill an awkward centre from which to direct operations, O'Connor decided to move Corps Headquarters further south on 2 November to a small, hospitable Dutch village called Mierloo, three miles from Helmond. Here it was to remain for the rest of the bitter winter of 1944–45, and it was from here that O'Connor controlled his last operation as Commander of VIII Corps.

Operation Nutcracker

Before the Allies built up their strength for the next major offensive, which was to take them to final victory in the Spring of 1945, Dempsey wanted the Maas pocket—the 'thorn in the flesh' of Second Army—finally eliminated. It was decided that this must be done slowly and in considerable strength, to ensure complete success with as few casualties as possible. XII Corps was to be involved as well as VIII Corps, and on 9 November considerable regrouping of formations took place. Operation 'Nutcracker', as the two corps effort was nick-named, began on 14 November, and started in Ritchie's area. Five days later, on 19 November, VIII Corps started to advance, and the task of clearing the Maas pocket was slowly completed. The Corps history describes the conditions:

> Little active opposition was offered by the Germans, but there were plenty of minefields and demolitions. The greatest hindrance of all, naturally, was the bad weather combined with the frightful country. Never before perhaps have troops successfully coped with such discomfort or so many difficulties, and that fighting was possible at all, was

very largely due to the patience and perseverance of the Royal Engineers, whose problems were enormous.[20]

Although VIII Corps' part in 'Nutcracker' was planned by O'Connor, he was not to control the final days of the operation. On 30 November he started to hand over command to Lieutenant General Sir Evelyn Barker, best known by his unfortunate nick-name 'Bubbles', and on 2 December he flew home to Britain, the day before all German positions on the west bank of the River Maas were finally obliterated.

A Matter of Honour

At this stage it is necessary to go back almost two months to the second day of operation 'Constellation', 13 October, on the occasion of a visit to VIII Corps headquarters by His Majesty King George VI. During the afternoon, three divisional commanders were invited to the headquarters to meet the King, and one of them was General Lindsay Silvester, of US 7th Armoured Division, who by this time had been under O'Connor's direct command for several days. Montgomery was accompanying the King, and he took the opportunity to talk to Silvester for a few minutes.

Unfortunately he was not at all impressed, and as he also considered Silvester to be too old for his job, he decided that he should be removed. After leaving VIII Corps with the King, Montgomery arranged matters with Eisenhower, but it was not until 18 October that O'Connor found out what was happening, causing him to write to Jean in some distress that evening:

A most upsetting thing has happened here. You gathered that I had a family of our cousins [Americans] with me now. The father is no Napoleon, but has been a 100% cooperator and his children have done successfully all the not very difficult things I asked them to do. He and I get on very well together, I like him immensely. Mike [Montgomery] and Baker [Bimbo] did not like his face and thought him no good, so Mike goes and tells Ike that he is no good, who as a result agreed to sack him forthwith. Can't you imagine what he will think of me? Complete underhand treachery, as I treated him all the time most cordially. He is like a big dog and just won't understand. But his family [his division] having trusted me completely will never do so again. So that is that. Just what action I am going to take I have not made up my mind, but in all probability I shall ask to be relieved of my command, which will undoubtedly be accepted, if I do, as I mean it.

You may, therefore, expect to see me in the course of a week or two.

It simply pelted last night and the going is quite frightful, so I have called this party off. A very good show spoiled by people changing their minds, and then a practically unceasing torrent since we started.[21]

Two days later he carried out his threat of asking to be relieved of his command in a letter to Dempsey:

Dear General,

I understand from the Commander-in-Chief that he has arranged with General Eisenhower for General Silvester, commanding 7th US Armoured Division, to be removed from his command at an early date.

Whilst completely understanding the Commander-in-Chief's point of view, I have felt that there are special circumstances in this case which would render it inadvisable to make any change—at any rate while the Division is serving under the command of Second British Army. These are as follows:-

(1) The Division has carried out successfully every task which it has been given by me.
(2) Its cooperation with these Headquarters has been whole-hearted in every way.
(3) The question of command as between Allies has always been a delicate one, and I have felt that the removal of General Silvester without any previous warning, in spite of his Division having carried out successfully all the tasks assigned to it, will have an extremely bad effect on the relations between the two Commands.

I did express this view to the Commander-in-Chief, but he felt neverthe-less that General Silvester must be removed.

With great regret therefore I would very respectfully ask that I might also be relieved of my command, as I feel that I shall have completely lost the confidence of the 7th US Armoured Division which I had previously held.[22]

The same day, 20 October, he wrote to Jean: 'I shall think they will have to accept my resignation and that I shall be back home in a few days. I don't suppose there is a chance of my getting anything else, so it will finish my so-called military career.'

For some reason the actual removal of Silvester took some time. On 22 October O'Connor still did not know if Silvester was aware of his fate, as shown in another letter to Jean:

My situation is as follows: Baker [Bimbo] will find out:-

(i)   Whether he (Silvester) has been told yet.

(ii) What wording was used.

(iii) What is the feeling in the Division about it.

If the reaction is bad, and they think that it has been an underhand show, which I think it has, then I won't stay. If they have had it put to them in a way that does not touch my honour, then I am prepared to stay.

Eventually he decided to withdraw his resignation, mainly due to the persuasion of Dempsey. In the account of the affair he made later O'Connor explained what happened after he visited Silvester and his division on 23 October:

I felt that the whole situation put us in a most unfair position, and on my return I again brought up the subject of relinquishing my command. The Army Commander begged me not to do so, on every ground. He said I was not responsible in any way and that should in fact be sufficient for my conscience. He suggested my sending him an appreciation of the work of 7 US Armd Div, of which I might send a copy to General Silvester, and he felt that might ease the situation. He said I could not be doing our own cause any good if I left, as there were not any good replacements that he knew of. I said that I considered I was quite easy to replace and that I had no great opinion of my capabilities. He said others did have, and I had in fact done splendidly. He asked me most strongly not to go, and thereby definitely upset the whole organisation and command out here at a time when the situation required that I should remain.[23]

In the event, Silvester remained in command of his division until the end of October, and did well in the fierce fighting to stem the German counter-attack of 27 October, as brought out in O'Connor's letter to Second Army when he was finally removed on the last day of the month:

To: Second Army
From: 8 Corps

As I understand that General Silvester is giving up command of 7 US Armd Div, I would like to express my deep appreciation of his whole-hearted co-operation, and also of his own dogged fighting qualities.

I wish further to express my admiration for the fine achievement of all ranks of 7 US Armd Div during the recent heavy enemy attacks in the MEIJEL area, where for two days they held up an enemy force superior in numbers by at least three to one, until other troops arrived in the area.

I consider the experience they have gained in the recent fighting will be of great value to them.[24]

It is necessary to explain the Silvester case at some length because it was to have an effect on O'Connor's own career on two occasions, and also his handling of it throws light onto his character and his judgement.

Although he mentioned in his letter to Jean on 22 October that he, Montgomery and Dempsey had 'the same mutual respect that we have had before for each other', it seems likely that the other two found his threat to resign at the least annoying. Although Dempsey persuaded him to stay, as just related, it appears likely that Montgomery's willingness to release him for a posting to India in early December was in part due to aggravation at his stance over Silvester, which was perhaps a slightly unnecessary fuss.

In his own description of these events, Roberts wrote that 'Dick O'Connor was one of the straightest and most honourable men I have ever met',[25] and this was part of the trouble. In fact, as he was to admit in the paper already quoted, which he wrote on 1 November setting out the whole case, Silvester 'as an experienced organiser and battle fighter was not of a very high standard'.[26]

While fully understanding and admiring O'Connor's determination that, as he wrote again on 24 October to Jean, 'I am not going to be concerned with stabbing him in the back', some doubt creeps in as to his wisdom in taking this stance. The fact that Silvester was clearly a brave man and a 'nice guy' seems to have affected his judgement: more than the qualities of 'a big dog' were required to command an armoured division in all phases of war against the German Army.

That Silvester was not an impressive divisional commander is borne out by the recollection of Field Marshal Lord Carver, who, as a 29-year-old brigadier in command in 4th Armoured Brigade, was placed under command of 7th US Armoured on 29 October. On that day he was present when O'Connor visited Silvester's headquarters and told him to remain on the defensive. Carver was then considerably concerned when he received orders to launch an attack into the boggy area across the canal in his sector, in which his tanks would be confined to roads raised above the marshy land. He rang up O'Connor's staff and asked that the Corps Commander should be told what was afoot. As a result, O'Connor came again to Silvester's headquarters and cancelled the attack. Silvester left next day, one of his staff commenting to Carver: 'Oh, he was an old time tank man: we knew he wouldn't last long!'[27]

A Posting to India

On 27 November 1944 O'Connor received his official posting order to take over from Lieutenant General Sir Mosely Mayne as GOC-in-C Eastern Army, India. That Montgomery was prepared to let him go away from Second Army has been accepted by some people as the equivalent of relieving him of his command, though the trouble taken by Dempsey to make him rescind his proposed resignation on 23 October hardly supports such a theory.

As to Montgomery's attitude, it is probable that if he had wanted to resist O'Connor's posting away from north-west Europe, he could have persuaded Alanbrooke that he should stay. However, the impetus for the posting to India undoubtedly came from the CIGS, who allowed no interference from any other source in the postings of senior army officers: his stern reminder of this fact to Mountbatten in the unfortunate affair of Leese and Slim is witness enough to its truth. With the offensive in Burma about to be launched, Eastern Command in India was a very important place. The main lines of communication to the Fourteenth Army front ran through the command area, and the task of ensuring that it was efficiently run was just as, if not more, important as operating against a German army which was certain to be defeated before long—though by no means as exciting.

With no way of ever knowing the whole story, it is fair to assume that Montgomery was not unduly worried at O'Connor's departure. Although, as Balfour remembers, both Montgomery and Dempsey always treated him with friendliness and respect, O'Connor's handling of his corps was thoroughly competent rather than brilliant, and the recent Silvester case had shown what a troublesome subordinate he could be where a matter of principle was concerned. Montgomery's letter to him about his departure is somewhat terse, and the impression cannot be avoided that he was perhaps relieved to pack off his old friend to pastures new without having to endure any unpleasantness.

My dear Dick,

I have arranged the following dates:

29 Nov: MacMillan joins 49 Div.
30 Nov: Barker goes to 8 Corps.
2 Dec: You leave 8 Corps.

Drive to my Tac HQ, to arrive at 10 am. I will be in, to say goodbye to you.

One of my ADCs will take you to my aeroplane which will take off at 1100 hrs for Gatwick.

You will see I have put back your departure to 2 Dec. I will arrange that a car, and a truck, meets you at Gatwick at 12.30 pm on 2 Dec.

Yours ever
Monty.

You will be a great loss here. But you are needed in India.

O'Connor's own reaction to his posting was of considerable sadness:

> In Nov 1944 Monty asked me to dine with him, and in the course of conversation told me that he had agreed to allow me to go to India as GOC-in-C Eastern Command with my Headquarters, Calcutta. It was very sad, and I was greatly distressed, leaving 8th Corps—the more so as I was given such proof of their confidence and affection, when I went round to say goodbye to the various units of the Corps. It was no doubt a young man's war, and perhaps I was getting too old for the job.[28]

That he had the affection of his own staff and the formations under his command cannot be doubted, but one or two did not have complete confidence in him. Roberts, eighteen years his junior, and having a vigorous, young 'rising star's' opinion of older men, felt that the orders given to 11th Armoured Division in the 'Goodwood' battle were faulty, and long after the war was over said that 'he believed that O'Connor did not understand the proper handling of armour on a European battlefield'.[29] Against this must be set Roberts' admiration for his conduct of operation 'Constellation', and Montgomery's congratulations on the capture of Venraij—and indeed on the earlier Normandy battles other than 'Goodwood'. In all these Normandy operations, O'Connor's scope for original action was very limited, and at 'Goodwood' he was placed under severe restrictions by his superior commanders, Montgomery and Dempsey. Furthermore, he was extremely tired after the long slog of 'Epsom' and the hurried preparations for 'Goodwood', and at this stage had not got his 'second wind'. Once he had got it, his performance improved again, but on the whole the comment in Max Hastings' book *Overlord* is fair in respect of the early stages: 'the evidence suggests that he never achieved the "grip" of VIII Corps which had so distinguished his command in the desert'.[30] In spite of this initial lack of drive after his long spell as a prisoner, his command of VIII Corps was carried out with more than adequate competence and he remained a greatly loved and admired personality.

18

Commands in India

To put the importance of O'Connor's appointment as General Officer Commanding in Chief Eastern Command into perspective, the curious and complicated command set-up in India and the surrounding countries must be briefly explained. At the time when Singapore fell in 1942 and the Japanese conquered Indonesia, Thailand and Burma, all British, Indian and Australian land forces in South-East Asia came under the overall command of the Commander-in-Chief, India, who was then Wavell. It became clear that such a wide-ranging area of responsibility was far too much for one man, and that part of it which lay outside the frontiers of India was put under the authority of a newly created South-East Asia Command (SEAC). At the head of SEAC, which became a tri-service organisation, a Supreme Commander, usually referred to as 'Supremo', was appointed with headquarters in Ceylon, as Sri Lanka was then known. The man selected to take up this post in 1943 was Admiral Lord Louis Mountbatten. Below Supremo in the hierarchy of SEAC were the individual service chiefs; in the case of the Army he was known as C-in-C Land Forces. The first officer to hold this post was General Sir George Giffard, who had been succeeded in 1944 by Lieutenant General Sir Oliver Leese, fresh from commanding the Eighth Army in Italy. Under him there were two armies: Twelfth Army was really an administrative body, better described as the Burma garrison, while Fourteenth Army, often calling itself 'the Forgotten Army', was the striking force which eventually drove the Japanese back out of Burma. At its head was that formidable General, 'Uncle Bill' Slim, the future Field Marshal and CIGS.

A glance at a map of India and northern Burma will quickly show that all the supplies required by the men facing the Japanese in

Burma had to pass through the area covered by the Eastern Command in India. For this reason it remained the most important of the four major commands in India as long as hostilities were in progress against the Japanese. It was essential that the man in charge of it had the full trust of the neighbouring C-in-C SEAC Land Forces, as well as the Burma Army Commanders under him, since so much of their success at fighting in a desolate area with limited natural resources depended on the supplies sent up from India. O'Connor realised the importance of his new responsibilities, but he did not relish being sent to a non-operational command.

On arrival in India in early January 1945, O'Connor was invited to stay with the Wavells at the Viceroy's House, New Delhi. From here he wrote a long letter to Jean on 12 January, and another the next day, with news of numerous people whom he had met. Apart from the Wavells themselves, he had met and been given a very warm welcome by Auchinleck, now his immediate superior as Commander-in-Chief, India. The Mountbattens stayed one night, and he liked them. Of Lady Mountbatten he recorded that, although she had been beautiful, 'she is far from that now and looks a bit haglike'. Lord Louis told him how his own name had been put forward in the previous June as one of the possible contenders for the position which was held by Oliver Leese. Because he already knew him, he chose Leese; also O'Connor was involved in Normandy, and could be less easily spared. This is borne out by the diary of Lieutenant General Sir Henry Pownall, who, as Mountbatten's Chief of Staff, was involved in the selection process, and wrote on 29 June 1944: 'Second choice would be O'Connor. He's engaged in battle in France with 8th Corps and again CIGS would not commit himself at all....'[1]

When he arrived at his new base in Calcutta, O'Connor was not much impressed. On 15 January he wrote to Jean: 'I have been here almost 30 hours. I think it is a depressingly awful job, but I will do my best. The house is too wee for words—very bare furniture, tiny garden and rather disappointing, and the servant question apparently insoluble.' His letters became more cheerful as her arrival to join him approached, and on 16 February he posted a letter, to catch her at Port Said on her way out from England, in which he told how he was 'counting the moments until you arrive'.

Though he might not regard his new job very highly, it was not in his character to tackle it with anything less than his full energy. He wrote to Montgomery expressing his disenchantment at the end of January, and received a reply dated 9 February:

> My dear Dick,
>
> I was delighted to hear from you. But I am sorry you are not too happy in your present job. You may like to know that Oliver Leese wrote and told me that he was delighted you had arrived to take charge behind him. I am sure you will do a grand job, and we must send good chaps to India and not only our duds.

In April Monty wrote again: 'You are doing great work in India; I hear that from all sides: including Archie Wavell, who came to see me last week.'[2] The high esteem in which O'Connor was held was underlined by his promotion on 17 April to the rank of full General.

During March there had been several meetings with Leese, whom O'Connor knew from his days as an instructor at Camberley when Leese had been a student there. Slim he also met, and tentative arrangements had been made with him for a visit in May to Rangoon, recently re-taken from the Japanese as Fourteenth Army pushed the enemy troops back through the territory so humiliatingly lost three years before. However, a surprising letter then reached him from Slim, dated 15 May, the second paragraph of which stated:

> I am sorry you could not come and have a quick look at Rangoon, but if you care to come within the next ten days or so I shall be delighted. After that I am afraid I shall not be in a position to invite you, as Oliver Leese has removed me from command of the Fourteenth Army. I need not tell you that this was a bit of a shock to me as I had had no inkling of his intentions in the matter, and I thought that the Army had done rather well. However that is a matter of which I am not the best judge, and so I have put in to go on pension, as I did not feel that in the circumstances I could accept command of the Burma garrison which was offered to me.

Although this is not the place to go into the details of how Leese became involved in trying to remove Slim and, instead, ended up being removed himself, nor to recount the story of Mountbatten's rather devious part in the affair, O'Connor's comment is worth mentioning. Many years later, recording how he might have been given Leese's job himself, he wrote that, '... I would have loved it, and I would never have tried to sack Slim.'[4] In July 1945, he received a letter from Montgomery who gave his view of the affair with his usual brevity: 'Oliver must have gone barmy.'[5]

With the end of the war with Japan in August 1945, the Eastern

Command ceased to be the most important in India, and the Northern, with its frontiers including Afghanistan, part of the Soviet Union, and China resumed once more its traditional place as the main focus of military interest in the sub-continent. Auchinleck was anxious to move O'Connor up to take over Northern Command, partly because of its renewed significance, and partly because it would bring him closer to his own headquarters in New Delhi. In the troubled times ahead, as India approached independence, Auchinleck was anxious to have his trusted friend nearer to him, as he would rely on his advice in many different situations. How difficult these situations had become has been explained by Major General S Shahid Hamid, who from 1 March 1946 to 25 August 1947 was the Auk's private secretary. (Then an officer of the old Indian Army, Hamid rose to his high rank later in Pakistan).

> When Germany and Japan surrendered, the problems of the C-in-C increased out of all proportion and he became, much to his disgust, a major political figure, second in importance only to the Viceroy himself, and found himself involved in a fierce political battle. Due to the impending political changes his main task was to keep the Indian Army in being and to prevent its involvement in any situation which might threaten effectiveness, morale and efficiency. He had to prepare its transition in status, its demobilization and rehabilitation. He had to decide the postwar composition of the Army, and the steps to be taken to nationalize the forces. Indian formations were still abroad and they had to be brought back. The British formations and units had to be repatriated and the future of the Gurkhas had to be decided.... The question of the Indian National Army trials loomed large and the Congress politicians were loudly accusing the regular army of being an army of mercenaries.

> The C-in-C's problems were further increased by HMG's insistence that India should provide the forces for the defence of South-East Asia, that the sea and air links should be secured and, above all, that India should be made to stay in the Commonwealth.[6]

Although O'Connor knew that he was to be moved from Calcutta by the end of August 1945, it was not until 1 November that he took over Northern Command, which, since it was an amalgamation (taking in the old Western Command), now covered a vast area roughly the same as that of modern Pakistan. His new headquarters were at Rawalpindi, roughly 100 miles from his happy pre-war station at Peshawar. He and Jean moved into the spacious Command House with few regrets at leaving Calcutta. At the end of the month, a new ADC arrived, Captain Simon Phipps of the Coldstream Guards, who was a nephew of Jean's. Phipps stayed with O'Connor for nearly two years, becoming his Military Assistant in his next appointment, and then leaving the Army to take Holy Orders. Eventually he became Bishop of Lincoln. As ADC, O'Connor found him 'witty, amusing and competent', and his company on the many long journeys they took together was much appreciated.

Within Northern Command, there were five Districts, each with a Major General in charge. As they were spread over 900 miles from Chitral down to Karachi there were many journeys to be undertaken in order to visit them all, mostly by air, and Phipps' record of the period shows O'Connor and he to have been constantly on the move. Between 15 and 28 January 1946, only three nights were spent at home in Rawalpindi. The other ten were passed in four widely separated locations: Karachi the furthest south and Saidon Sharif in the province of Swat, the furthest north, with Multan and Peshawar in between. One of the purposes of visiting Peshawar was to stay at Government House with the Governor, Sir George Cunningham. On hearing of Cunningham's death in 1963, O'Connor wrote a brief note on him.

> He was probably the greatest Governor of the NW Frontier Province and followed in the footsteps of many great men of the Indian Civil Service.
>
> He had great charm and was held in the deepest affection by all and not least by the turbulant tribesmen of the NW Frontier who were devoted to him. He spoke Urdu and Pushtu perfectly and was able to talk to everyone in their own language. He had wonderful judgement and he could be counted on to take the right decision.
>
> I met him first at Peshawar, when I came out to command the Brigade and then again after the war, when I came out to Rawal Pindi as Army Commander. He became one of my greatest friends and I saw a lot of him in peace, and was shocked by his sudden death.[7]

There were visits to the C-in-C's House in Delhi as well, and Auchinleck came on occasions into Northern Command territory. When this happened O'Connor would meet him, and Plate 38 shows them both at the Alaf Khan Kot Training Camp near Kohat, some 30 miles south of Peshawar. Not only did the C-in-C want to see O'Connor frequently, he also kept up a considerable correspondence with him. During the calendar month 6 November to 6 December 1945 he wrote four long letters to him. As Shahid Hamid noted in March 1946, during his early days as private secretary, 'the Auk always looked first to Dick O'Connor for advice when a tricky problem arose'.[8]

Perhaps the trickiest problem of all, and one which was the main subject matter of three out of the four letters mentioned above, concerned the Indian National Army, or INA. Its origins were in the activities of the man described here:

> The so-called Indian National Army, known in GHQ as the Japanese Indian Forces (JIF), was a product of the British Military disaster in the East and India's aspiration for independence. Subhas Chandra Bose was its creator. He was a Bengali who had topped the list in the Indian Civil Service entrance examination but later left the service to become a politician. Bose was elected President of the Indian National Congress in 1938 but, as he believed in the use of brute force to gain independence for India, he fell out with the more conservative Congressmen, including Gandhi, who in fact disliked him.
>
> In December, 1940, he stowed away in a Japanese ship from Hooghly to Yokohama and then found his way to Germany. There he tried to raise a Legion of 2000 men from Indian prisoners of war in German hands, but his efforts were poor and he did not find much sympathy or encouragement in Germany or Italy, as he and his troops refused to swear allegiance to Hitler or Mussolini. He wanted these countries to declare that India would be given Independence after the war, which they refused.[9]

Bose then moved to the Far East, and when Singapore fell in February 1942 a more fertile recruiting ground for the INA was found among the 60,000 Indian troops taken prisoner there, especially as the Japanese had quickly segregated them from their British officers.

In all, some 25,000 Indian officers and men joined the INA. Some of those who refused to do so were tortured, and all were brutally treated. As the INA was used extensively for guarding POWs, there were many cases of loyal soldiers being maltreated by fellow Indians who had gone over to the Japanese. The commanders of Japanese forces in the field were reluctant to use the INA, and when eventually ordered to do so from Tokyo, soon found their forebodings proved correct, as the Indians showed little interest in fighting when the going was hard. Since most had merely joined to have better conditions than would have been their lot in the prison camps, they were unwilling to be killed if given a chance to surrender. By 1945, the INA had become a farce, and in April was disbanded. Bose died later that year in an aeroplane crash on his way to Tokyo.

When the war against Japan ended in August 1945, there were found to be 23,278 Indian officers and men in custody who had been in the INA. Divided into categories of 'Whites', 'Greys' and 'Blacks', according to whether they had joined under compulsion, been luke-warm in support, or active members, all but a few 'Blacks' were quickly dealt with. The major problem was to know how to deal with the few, especially officers, who had not only joined the enemy but had abetted them in murders, and had also practised gross brutality against fellow POWs. Amongst the senior military men and government officials there was much heart-searching as to the right course of action. Wavell as Viceroy and Auchinleck as C-in-C were bombarded with advice. While virtually all were agreed that INA 'Blacks' *ought* to be punished, views diverged widely on the wisdom of doing so. One school of thought supported the 'punish and be damned' theory, while the other considered that the potential damage to British–Indian relations which would be caused by this action was such that no trials should take place.

O'Connor was a firm supporter of the former course, and along with nearly all British officers in India, and the majority of King's Commissioned and Viceroy's Commissioned Officers in the Indian Army, believed that a strong line had to be taken against the worst of the 'Blacks'. It was a matter, however, on which he differed greatly from his friend Cunningham, though he normally respected the latter's 'wonderful judgement'. In a letter to the Viceroy dated 27 November 1945, Cunningham set out a powerful case for abandoning the forthcoming INA trials, much as he disliked the idea of the wrong-doers going free. In his letter he mentioned that O'Connor did not agree with his proposal. It was a desperately difficult time for all in authority, made worse by somewhat unscrupulous use of the situation by various politicians, as explained by Shahid Hamid:

> However, the politicians had decided to exploit the situation, and in this GHQ unwittingly played into their hands. Instead of trying the culprits in the Field Areas, they were brought to the capital and placed in the Red Fort and were tried under a full blaze of publicity. To make matters worse, in one case a Hindu, a Sikh and a Muslim were picked and tried jointly, which unified the different parties and they adopted a common stand.

> The trial lasted from 3 November to 31 December 1945. It must be said that Auchinleck did not believe in 'trials in secret' and wanted to give the

accused the benefit of a full defence and access to their records. The charges against the accused were cast iron and Auchinleck wanted the public to be made aware of them. However, he misjudged the mood of the people and could not have chosen a worse time or place. It was a blunder. Nor did the Labour Government realise that it was becoming a 'political trial' and a trial of strength between them and the Congress. They thought they were holding another Nuremberg trial. When the trial caught the imagination of the people, Wavell, Auchinleck, and HMG did not know what to do and were anxious to get out of the mess somehow or other, but they were trapped. Auchinleck never fully recovered from this loss of prestige.[10]

Perhaps the last sentence is a little harsh, but certainly Auchinleck found himself in a true dilemma, which was solved by something of a compromise. The sentences passed on those found guilty in December were reduced on review, and further trials were quietly dropped.

Following the INA trials there were further incidents early in 1946 which gave cause for serious concern among senior officers of all services in India and the Far East. There was an apparently carefully co-ordinated mutiny of British airmen in the Royal Air Force, which erupted simultaneously in Egypt, India and Singapore. This was followed by a mutiny in the Royal Indian Air Force, and also by violent unrest in the Royal Indian Navy. In the latter case, the worst outbreak was in Bombay in February 1946, which took some time to bring under control, but there were also lesser mutinies in Calcutta and Karachi. All these events made it a worrying time for Auchinleck and the Army Commanders in India, who feared that trouble might spread to the Army. Fortunately, apart from two minor incidents, which were quickly dealt with, the Army remained unaffected.

In spite of the difficult times, O'Connor enjoyed his tour at Northern Command, and both Jean and he loved their house at Rawalpindi, even though their stay was marred for a short period when Jean was seriously ill with a thyroid deficiency. Thanks to a skilful diagnosis by Dr Hector Grierson, the station doctor, and to devoted nursing, she recovered quite quickly. O'Connor never realised how ill she had been, although it was a worrying time for him. The tour in India was not to last for long however. The first warning of impending change came in a letter, written on 26 January 1946, from Montgomery, who was due to become CIGS in the near future. He wrote: 'My own feeling is that you ought to come home to be the next Military Secretary. How does that strike you?'[11]

In the event O'Connor was given another job in the Army Council, that of Adjutant General, or AG. It was officially announced on 15 May 1946, on which day Auchinleck wrote that he was '... more sorry than I can say that you should be leaving India, and that we shall no longer be in partnership'. A letter from Wavell followed with his congratulations the following day, giving his view that AG '... is the most important job in the Army at the present time'.[12]

The O'Connors spent their last night in Rawalpindi on 27 May, and were the Auk's guests for the next night, in Delhi. On 30 May they set off by air from Karachi to fly slowly back to Britain via Iraq, Athens, and finally Trieste, where they spent a night with John Harding, now commanding the British element of the Allied force occupying the area.

19

Adjutant General to the Forces

The O'Connors arrived back in Britain on the evening of 4 June 1946. They were able to take a long spell of leave, and catch up with friends and relations in England and Scotland. O'Connor's mother, now over 80, was still alive and living at 39 Alexandra Court; she was thrilled at the prospect of her son being close at hand in London in his new job. For their own accommodation, the O'Connors were fortunate to be offered the opportunity to live in the house in Rutland Gate belonging to Dorothy Russell, widow of Brigadier Hugh Russell, the commander of 7th Armoured Brigade in the Western Desert campaign, who had later been tragically killed in an air crash. She and Jean had become very close friends in Cairo days, when Jean had moved into the Russell's house after O'Connor's capture in 1941.

In July, O'Connor took over his new appointment as Adjutant General to the Forces. In that capacity, he also became the Second Military Member of the Army Council, the body responsible to Parliament for the running of the Army. Chaired by the Secretary of State for War, the Council consisted of two further politicians, five Military Members and the Permanent Under Secretary of State for War—a civil servant who, as Accounting Officer, responsible to Parliament for the control of the money voted to the Department, was in a position of great influence and power.

When O'Connor first arrived, the Secretary of State was a grand old man called Jack Lawson, a former Durham miner who was later to be given a peerage and become Lord Lieutenant of his county.

The two other political posts were filled by Lord Nathan as Parliamentary Under Secretary, and F J Bellenger as Financial Secretary. Shortly after O'Connor's arrival a 'reshuffle' by the Prime Minister, Clement Attlee, saw Lawson replaced by Bellenger, and Nathan by Lord Pakenham, better known today as the Earl of Longford. Bellenger's place as Financial Secretary was taken by John Freeman, later High Commissioner in India and Ambassador to Washington, and also famous for his 'Face to Face' television interviews from 1959 to 1961.

The Permanent Under-Secretary of State for War (PUS) was Sir Eric Speed. Of Speed O'Connor wrote in later years that he himself 'never liked nor trusted him', though admitting that he was probably good at his job, and seemed to be liked by others. About Speed he also noted: 'Don't think he had much time for me.'[1]

The five military members of the Army Council, in descending order of precedence, were as follows:

1st Military Member The Chief of the Imperial General Staff (Montgomery)

2nd Military Member The Adjutant General to the Forces (O'Connor)

3rd Military Member The Quartermaster General (General Sir David Watson)

4th Military Member The Vice Chief of the Imperial General Staff (Lieutenant General Sir Frank Simpson)

5th Military Member The Deputy Chief of the Imperial General Staff (Lieutenant General Sir Sidney Kirkman)

His relationship with Montgomery as CIGS will unfold as the chapter progresses. Of the other military members, he was particularly fond of his old friend 'Simbo' Simpson, the VCIGS, an immensely level-headed and likeable man. About the time O'Connor joined the Army Council, another Cameronian was just leaving it to retire. This was Tom Riddell-Webster, who had borne the immense strains of being QMG for over four years since 1942.

Early on during his time at the War Office, O'Connor had his first brush with the politicians over a matter eventually sorted out by the CIGS. As described in his *Memoirs*, a person Montgomery calls a 'Junior Minister' behaved in a rather upsetting fashion:

> This one had planned an overseas tour, and he took it on himself to issue an order to the Adjutant General telling the latter to lay on the tour and

giving the most amazing instructions about how he was to be treated. The following are some extracts.

'I give advance warning that from time to time I shall see troops without officers being present.

My working day will be from 9 am to 6 pm.

I should like to lunch sometimes with officers, sometimes with other ranks.

I want no guards of honour, special parades, special meals.

This is to be treated as an order which I expect to be obeyed.

It will generally be desirable for me to meet as early as possible ... the C-in-C.

I shall listen to complaints on any military subject from any rank.

I wish Commands to be prepared to answer detailed questions.'

This order caused the father-and-mother of a row. The Adjutant General went to see the Secretary of State and tendered his resignation unless the letter was withdrawn; he then blew in to my office. My reactions were a mixture of anger and amusement. The letter was too silly to cause anger; it could only have been written in colossal ignorance or colossal conceit, and it seemed more charitable to accept the former. I saw the Secretary of State myself and made it clear to him that, quite apart from the other considerations of this case, on no account would any outside agent ever be allowed to address bodies of troops in the enforced absence of their officers. The letter was cancelled.[2]

O'Connor's responsibilities as AG included the recruitment, posting and demobilisation of all British officers and men at home and abroad, as well as their morale, discipline, welfare and education. The way in which the run-down of the Army was being handled in the aftermath of the war was extremely important, as well as politically sensitive, and was therefore a major preoccupation.

In August 1946, Montgomery gathered a vast concourse of very senior officers together for a conference on the future handling of the Army in modern war, based on the Staff College at Camberley. (Time was found for a little quiet showing off about the North-West European campaign as well.) Auchinleck came home from India to attend the conference, and the two Field Marshals presumably gave at least the appearance of cordial relations between them! Two days after the end of the conference O'Connor had a talk to Montgomery about his own responsibilities, and the next day the CIGS wrote him an exceptionally friendly letter:

My dear Dick,

Thank you for your letter: delivered at Euston. I am writing in the train at 60 miles an hour and it is not too easy!!

I am so glad you came round for a talk last night. There is much for us all to do. But we will do it all right, *between us*.

I think the big thing now is the problem of getting recruits for the Regular Army. We must not expect immediate results, we are suffering from the after effects of nearly six years of war and most people are fed up with being in the Army.

We shall get over this by putting our house in order and by slowly, but very surely, building up a first class show.

This will take time. We must not be disappointed if we do not get quick results; I reckon it will take about a year before we begin to see daylight.

Quick results are not possible; we must all understand this.

We shall get our results by building a very firm foundation, and then by adding to it carefully. We must not make mistakes in these early stages.

I have complete confidence in you as AG. That is why I brought you back from India; your experience, and sympathetic understanding of what the Army and the soldier needs, are exactly what is needed today.

The AG Branch is probably the most important in the Army today: as you say, we must put fighting soldiers into it.

For myself, I am not very knowledgeable about War Office procedure. I am more used to giving orders in the field!! If ever you feel that I am trespassing on your ground, I shall rely on you to let me know.

I do hope you will be able to read all this.

Your very old friend

Monty.[3]

Although Montgomery was certainly correct in saying that O'Connor's 'experience and sympathetic understanding' were exactly what the Army needed, his personality was not entirely suited to his appointment. Like many great soldiers he was politically unsophisticated, and his simple outlook and shining integrity were often a handicap when 'fighting his corner' amidst the intrigues of Whitehall. While he had enjoyed his three years at the War Office as

GSO 2 from 1932 to 1935, his return at an exalted rank eleven years later did not bring him the same happiness: in fact of the time spent in Whitehall, as opposed to visits away from London, he wrote that 'he hated every moment in the job'. His opinion of Bellenger was not high, though both Lord Pakenham and John Freeman he liked, and found able and helpful. However, the Labour Government was distinctly hostile towards many military traditions and attitudes, and there was a clear wish to reduce the power of officers to maintain discipline in the Army. Two suggestions put forward from the political side were fiercely, and successfully, resisted by O'Connor. One was that any soldier brought in front of his commanding officer on a charge should be able to call on a 'soldier's friend' to state his case: another was that junior officers at the platoon commander level should no longer be responsible for the discipline of their men. O'Connor felt that this political, 'anti-officer' bias was based on an out-dated conception of army life, which had changed enormously between 1939 and 1945, and he did everything in his power to put the record straight, and ensure that proper discipline was preserved. Both the Parliamentary Under-Secretaries understood his position, and tended to support him on occasions in opposition to their own party dogma. Freeman remembers that he looked up to O'Connor 'and held him in the highest respect as a man and, I hope, as something of a friend during the last period of his service'.[4]

One duty which the new AG felt had to be undertaken was to visit the far-flung stations still manned by British troops all around the world, in order to explain to the men, and their commanders, what was being done about the repatriation of those who had already served abroad for many years. To this end, plans were put in motion soon after his arrival in Whitehall for a tour of the Far East in 1947. In the meantime there were visits to be made nearer home: to bases in Britain in August and September 1946, and then over to Europe for practically the whole of October.

The first week was spent in Italy, visiting many of the Italians who had helped to guide O'Connor, Neame and Boyd to freedom two years before. 'Gussie' was visited in Florence, and then a trip was made out to the monastery at Camaldoli. Next O'Connor and Simon Phipps, who was now his Military Assistant and accompanied him on all his tours, moved south to stay in Sovera's hotel in Cervia, which was no longer troubled by the presence of the Wehrmacht! Here they were also able to make contact with Madam Teresa Spazzoli. Phipps was greatly struck by the warmth of the welcome given by these Italians who had risked so much, and in many cases suffered so much, to aid British escapers when virtually nothing could be done for them in return. The Italian trip ended with a visit to Trieste, staying again with John Harding at the Castello di Duino, and talks to the members of the British brigade serving there. After a few days in London on return from Italy, O'Connor travelled out to Germany to stay with General Sir Richard McCreery at the Headquarters of the British Army of the Rhine. He then spent ten days visiting British garrisons in Germany and Austria. In Vienna his base was the Villa Heinkel, the residence of the British GOC.

As 1946 drew to a close, two further main preoccupations of the Army Council were also in the province of the Adjutant General. The first was the requirement to persuade the Labour Government of the need to introduce National Service. Although it was generally realised that this was necessary if British international commitments were to be met, many ministers were reluctant to face the unpopular reactions to the introduction of peace-time conscription. In the end, the Bill to do so was passed, mainly through the influence of Attlee and Ernest Bevin. The second matter of concern for the Council was the necessity of reducing drastically the number of infantry battalions in the Army. It was decided that each regiment with two regular battalions would have to put one into 'suspended animation'—a polite euphemism for disbandment.

The Far East tour started on 12 January 1947. Fortunately, O'Connor recorded in later life the story of the two month trip, which is told here in his own words:

> We started off in a flying boat from Poole bound for Sydney. It took about 5 days flying. We stopped somewhere for each night.
>
> We came down first in Australia in Port Darwin—a very unpleasant hot spot. Then on to Sydney flying over Queensland with forest fires burning below us. It was very bumpy. It was very impressive alighting in Sydney harbour about 9 o'clock at night.
>
> We did not stay long in Sydney as we flew off the following afternoon to Melbourne, where I was staying with the Governor.
>
> We attended a party the first night given for me by Mr Casey [Casey had been Governor of Bengal when O'Connor was in Calcutta in 1945]. By some mischance I must have eaten a poisoned oyster and was very ill for the next four days, being kindly looked after by the Governor and staff.

All this unfortunately entirely spoiled my time in Melbourne, as it interrupted parties and conferences I had to attend. I was, however, able to call on the Caseys at home which I enjoyed. Also I saw Nell Evetts who was out in Australia with Jack. He was working on the Woomera rocket range. Our party consisted of Simon Phipps, my personal assistant and Cross our Pressman.

For the next part of the journey, Australia to Tokyo, we were given a 'Liberator' with an Australian pilot and navigator.

We stayed the first night on a small island in the Pacific which we had great difficulty in finding owing to bad visibility. [This was Morotai, manned by the Royal Australian Air Force.]

The next night was at Okinawa, which was occupied by the Americans. From there we flew straight into Tokyo, landing a few minutes after an earthquake but not a severe one!

I was tremendously impressed by General MacArthur. When I was in Tokyo he asked me to lunch. I enjoyed this as I sat next to him. But as I was going off he drew me aside and invited me to come to have a talk with him that evening. I was with him for a full hour, and I have seldom had a more interesting time. He spoke on a variety of subjects. Particularly on the Chinese Communist build up. He professed to being a great friend of Britain's and said he admired her enormously as a nation, which I am sure he meant. He also talked about the defences of Britain against a Russian onslaught. I was very sorry when the time came to say goodbye. I entirely agree with Alanbrooke's assessment of him. [Alanbrooke described him as the best soldier produced by any nation in World War Two.]

My time in Japan was spent in visiting units, HQs and the Ambassador, Sir Julian Gascoigne. I went down to the extreme south of the island to visit the Dominion and Indian troops who were still in occupation. I thought they might be fed up and expected some heckling, but actually I got cheered on two or three occasions at the end of my remarks. I stayed with General Cowan, who had once commanded the 17th Indian Division, whom I had always liked and admired. We flew off from South Japan on our flight to Hong Kong. It was one of the worst flights I have ever had. A storm raging, very bumpy and extremely cold. We arrived nearly two hours late. As the troops had been waiting for a considerable time I said I would talk to them straight away on disembarking. This I did with some success, as they were very friendly and appeared to have forgiven me for keeping them waiting.

I stayed two days with Gen Bobby Erskine, the Commander-in-Chief, and enjoyed looking round the City.

Our next visit was to Singapore and Malaya. We started off from Hong

Kong from the air strip which is very dangerous as it is directed at some high ground, which one has to be able to rise over in a very short time. We managed all right, but it was very unpleasant.

We came down in Indo-China on the way, but after refuelling we went on to Singapore. At Tokyo there had been a Guard of Honour of the Royal Welsh Fusiliers and at Singapore, Seaforths, I think. I can't remember where we stayed, but I know we looked at everything. At the conclusion of our visit we started off for Burma, visiting Sandy Galloway in north Malaya en route. We arrived at Rangoon and were met by General Briggs, whom I knew in the Desert. He was very good to us and we much enjoyed our stay.

The next hop was to India where we touched down at Calcutta. I was met there by Major Ian Murray of the Seaforth, who was staff officer for our tour in India. He did an excellent job of work. We stayed in India for nearly three weeks, and literally went all over it, mainly talking to British troops. We had our aeroplane and used to fly to our destination daily. We had very few days off.

In my tour I used to speak to the Officers and OR separately and I must have delivered at least 70 addresses. We stayed with the Viceroy [Wavell] on the occasion of his daughter Felicity's wedding, which, tragic to relate, coincided with the announcement of his dismissal by the Attlee Government.

We of course saw a lot of Auchinleck, the Commander-in-Chief, whom I always admired and had the greatest respect and affection for. The Viceroy himself was wonderful. He never complained. I know no one who has stood up to misfortune in the way he has.

This ended for me a very memorable tour. The next hop was home where we arrived early in March.[5]

Notes kept by Phipps show that in India they visited no less than nine stations: Calcutta, Madras, Bangalore, Bombay, Delhi, Lahore, Rawalpindi, Peshawar and Karachi. Phipps also has a slightly different recollection of the lunch at MacArthur's house in Tokyo. He remembers O'Connor deliberately sitting next to Mrs MacArthur rather than the General, knowing that he would have a better chance of being granted a private interview later in the day, if he had not already had a discussion at the table.

Other recollections of Phipps' include watching the film 'Wuthering Heights' at an open air film-show on Morotai island, the sights on the screen being in strange contrast to the surrounding palm trees swaying in the warm breeze. A slightly undignified arrival at the next stop, Okinawa, was caused by the pilot forgetting the time difference of one hour between Morotai and Okinawa, and signalling the wrong time of arrival to the American base. As a result the guard of honour was not waiting on the tarmac, so O'Connor and his party had to climb back into the aircraft to await its arrival before alighting again.

Not all meals on the trip were entirely satisfactory, and O'Connor's stay in Australia was to some extent blighted by the experience of the poisoned oyster, which he reported to Jean more fully in a letter dated 23 January 1947:

> I attended a meeting of the Australian Army Board which lasted about three hours and then I was to go on to a lunch given by the Chief of Staff. For the last half hour of the meeting I began to feel a bit funny and when I came to sit down to lunch I felt definitely sick. I ate no lunch and talked away and nearly got away with it, and only when I got back to GH [Government House] did I allow myself to be sick, which I was a couple of times. Then I went out to see Nell and was sick in her lavatory on arrival! She was a pet. I got back to Government House and was sick again and finally I took 2 Sulpho Granadine tablets, and this morning was much better. However, the Governor insisted on a Doctor coming and he gave me a most complete overhaul and pronounced me very fit, and I am feeling really quite all right only a little washed out. We are putting off our departure from tomorrow until Saturday, which means we don't make up our lost day. Tomorrow I have got a meeting or two and the next day I am off to the Caseys for the day and come back in the evening prior to embarking for Japan.
>
> Everyone here has been most welcoming and kind, and it is so annoying that I had that set back. I think I must have eaten something which disagreed with me at breakfast, as I could not have felt better on the two days after arrival. Simon has been angelic and I could not wish for a better companion or friend. I shall miss him no end, I fear.

Just before the tour had begun, the message had been sent out from the Adjutant General's Department to all commanding officers warning them of the big reductions about to be made in the infantry, and giving details of those battalions which were to be placed in 'suspended animation'. Among them was 1st Battalion The Cameronians (Scottish Rifles), then stationed in Malaya, which was to be broken up during February 1947. To the regrets sent with these orders to all regiments affected, O'Connor added an extra paragraph to Lieutenant Colonel K E M Brunker, commanding that battalion, with which he had last served himself in Lucknow in

1932: 'In addition to my official regrets conveyed to you and all ranks I would like to add my personal sympathy to you and all ranks of a battalion which has done so magnificently in the war.'[6]

Luckily there had been enough members of the 1st Battalion left in Malaya to provide a Guard of Honour for O'Connor when he passed through the country on his way from Singapore to Delhi, and he wrote a letter of appreciation to the Commanding Officer, of which the first paragraph read as follows:

> In case I don't see you, I would like to tell you what an outstanding Guard of Honour you paraded for me yesterday. It was quite first-class in every way, and I can't tell you how proud I felt.[7]

Not long after the end of the world tour, O'Connor said goodbye to Simon Phipps, who left the Army to train for ordination. In his place Mike Evetts, son of O'Connor's old friend Jack Evetts, and also a godson of 'Clarkie', became his MA. His tour of duty was not to last very long, however, as during the summer a very unhappy situation arose between Montgomery and O'Connor, which eventually drove the latter out of the Army into retirement. His own two narratives of the affair, one undated and the other written in about 1975, tell the story in full.[8] The account which follows is a combination of the two, but mainly extracted from the 1975 narrative, which runs as follows:

My departure from the War Office

Sometime in July 1947, Monty started off on a visit to the United States. I saw him off, and we discussed many things that we would do on his return. He was in excellent form and said a most friendly goodbye.

Sometime after he had been away, one afternoon when I was staying in a private house, I was called up from America by a lawyer, who said he represented General Silvester in an appeal, which was then being heard against his dismissal by General Bradley in France 1944, when he was in my Corps. I was asked whether I adhered to the letter I wrote to him at the time of his departure. In this, as I referred to earlier, I had said how sorry I was of the circumstances of his departure, and thanked him for all he had done for his division. The lawyer representing Silvester asked for permission to see Monty. This was granted, and he no doubt made it difficult and unpleasant as Monty had not been warned that he would be seeing him.

I am sure it must have been very embarassing for Monty, and I am very sorry it took place. But I felt I could not go back on my word.

About the same time there was a meeting of the Army Council in which one of the items on the agenda referred to the number of men being sent home for demobilization from the Far East. A certain number per month to be sent home was agreed to and had been promulgated by the Government. At this time owing to shortage of transport the Army Council decided to call this off. I argued that it would be very unfair to the men, and would lead to great discontent. I was, however, overruled and the decision was made to that effect.

I thought about this a lot and felt I could not be party to it, and so with great reluctance I submitted my resignation to the Secretary of State, Mr Bellenger. I received no reply to this and realised that he was going to discuss it with Monty before broaching it to me. Monty was shortly coming home and I noticed that the Secretary of State had arranged to see him directly on his return. I had arranged to see him on the following day.

When I met Monty I thought he would certainly support me. However, the contrary took place and he criticised me for my letter of resignation, saying as far as I can remember, that it was wrong and unnecessary. He went on further to say that he and the Secretary of State thought that I was not up to the job, and that I should go. He kept off the reason for my resignation and simply made it appear that the whole question was not that I had resigned, but that I had been dismissed. I wrote a further letter to him, saying that he had not in any way previously shown his lack of confidence in me, and that I had expected his support. I think this was a mistake and I should have simply said that the question of my dismissal did not arise, as I had resigned, but I was too shocked and hurt to think of this at the time. The result was (although I cannot vouch for this for certain, but I think it quite likely) that my letter of resignation had been destroyed, and that only the question of my competence had been dealt with.

I think I saw Monty again before I left the War Office, on ordinary business, and he again mentioned Silvester. But I was interested to see that they changed their decision about transporting men home from the Far East to the effect that owing to the shortages of transport the number would have to be limited to a trickle!

I heard afterwards that Monty had written round to ask members of the Army Council, what they thought of me! I quite realised that I was not a Whitehall man, nor was I a good AG on the office side, but I did a good deal on the practical side to help, and my long tour to Australia, the Far East and India did give a lot of satisfaction and confidence to a large number of people.

On 19 August 1947, under pressure from Montgomery, Bellenger, the Secretary of State, wrote to O'Connor to say: 'I feel that there is no course open to me but to accept your resignation.'[9] O'Connor's own story continues:

> I had to retire in about a month's time, which I felt most keenly. But there was nothing to be done about it. I did feel that Monty had been unfair and I did not speak to him for about two years. A reconciliation eventually was arranged through the good offices of Lieutenant General Sir George Collingwood who was a friend of mine, and had been approached by Monty on the subject. Monty did attempt to apologise as far as he was able to, as I think he really did feel sorry about it all.
>
> Looking back over the years, to be fair to Monty, I do think he was hardly tried over the Silvester case, and I can hardly blame him for what happened. However, if he had allowed me to remove Silvester in my way, by giving say a week to settle the whole thing, I am sure that I could have done so, and there would have been no trouble in any quarter.

It was a sad ending to a long and distinguished career as an active soldier, but it was by no means the end of a career of service to Queen and country, as the chapter that follows will show.

The friendship with Montgomery was restored gradually to normal. Discussing the war in North Africa with Montgomery in 1966, while helping him to prepare his book *The History of Warfare*, Anthony Brett-James recorded the Field Marshal saying:

> Do you know Dickie? Gweat friend of mine? For once I could say 'yes'. He had visited Sandhurst on two occasions to talk to members of the Napier Society, of which I had been secretary, and I had dined with O'Connor at Peter Young's house beforehand. I refrained from telling Monty that so many cadets had remarked, 'What a modest man!'[10]

20

The Last Years— 1947 to 1981

Leaving the Army at the age of 58, O'Connor was to live for a further 34 generally happy years, which was only three less than the number he had spent in military service. Throughout this time he was lucky enough to remain fully alert mentally, and for most of it to keep in good physical health. He involved himself in many activities, both civilian and military, and drove himself as hard as ever in carrying out anything he regarded as a duty.

As Jean's family was so prominent on the Black Isle, it was natural that it should be the area where they looked for a house to settle down permanently. They found Kincurdie House near the small town of Rosemarkie, lying on the coast some twelve miles from Inverness and nine from Cromarty. From the house there were fine views across the Beauly Firth to Fort George, which lies nearly opposite, and set just below it facing the sea was a splendid flower garden.

The pleasure of settling at Kincurdie was marred at the end of 1948 by the death of O'Connor's mother in November. She had come north to join Jean and her son in their new home soon after they moved in, but was not to remain with them long. Although she was in delicate health for some time before she died, she was only seriously ill for two days before the end. Many of the letters received from friends and relatives after her death mentioned how close she and her son had been, and also how lucky it was that she could have been with him and Jean when her last moments came. There were several reminders of happy days in Oxfordshire. Kenneth McLeod, now a retired general, wrote:

> For me, I shall always think of her and Waterperry in those happy years when we were at the Staff College and after it, when she was so good to us all when we stayed there. What a lovely time that was. Waterperry

radiated happiness, with your mother and Christina doing so much for all your friends!

It was not long before he was drawn back into military circles. In 1948 he was appointed Commandant of the Army Cadet Force in Scotland, a position which he held for eleven years up to 1959. His main task was to visit cadet units all over the country to give encouragement, particularly to the officers devoting their free time, without payment, to sustaining this important youth movement. He also needed to remind the army authorities at all times of the importance of the Army Cadet Force as a source of future soldiers as well as it being a good activity in its own right. This was not always easy, but his own enormous prestige, plus his experience of manpower problems gained while Adjutant General made his voice one that was listened to in circles where others could well have been ignored.

An important ally in this respect came to Scotland in 1949 when 'Babe' MacMillan, now Lieutenant General Sir Gordon, arrived in Edinburgh as GOC-in-C Scottish Command. Gogar Bank House, the MacMillan's official residence, became a frequent port of call when O'Connor had to come south to Edinburgh.

On 5 January 1951, a letter from Lieutenant General K G McLean, Military Secretary at the War Office, brought O'Connor particular pleasure. It asked him whether he was willing to succeed Tom Riddell-Webster as Colonel of The Cameronians (Scottish Rifles), and it was quickly answered in the affirmative. The regiment at that time consisted of the regular 1st Battalion stationed in Johore, Malaya; the 6/7th Territorial Battalion based on Glasgow and Lanarkshire; the Regimental Depot at Winston Barracks, Lanark; and detachments of Cameronian Cadets in the regimental area. In addition, an official affiliation had recently been arranged with the 7th Gurkha Rifles. To all these components, the new Colonel gave his full attention.

In February 1952, he flew out at his own expense to visit the 1st Battalion in Malaya. On arrival in Singapore, he was invited to stay first with John Harding, now C-in-C Far East Land Forces. Then he was taken to the small town of Segamat in north Johore, where battalion headquarters was situated. The regimental history describes his activities:

> In February 1952 the Colonel of the Regiment, General Sir Richard O'Connor, GCB, DSO, MC, flew out to Malaya to visit the 1st Battalion.

He followed an extremely full programme, which included visiting all the companies, various headquarters, the 1st and 2nd Battalions of the 7th Gurkha Rifles, and also his one-time ADC, Brigadier R G Collingwood, a Cameronian officer at the time commanding a brigade in Seremban. While staying in Kuala Lumpur with General R E Urquhart, the GOC, Malaya, he had a meeting with the newly arrived High Commissioner, General Sir Gerald Templer. Two of Britain's greatest soldiers were able to discuss the Emergency just as the latter was starting to embark on the work for which his name will always be famous—bringing under control a situation which at that moment seemed poised between failure and success.[1]

Later in 1952, he spent a September day at the Regimental Depot, touring all departments in the morning and taking a passing-out parade of recruits in the afternoon. He was in Lanark again on 29 June 1953 when Her Majesty the Queen visited the town during her tour of her kingdom after the Coronation in that year. The illustration, plate 39, shows him meeting Her Majesty wearing his regimental full dress, while a Guard of Honour commanded by Major Duncan Carter-Campbell, son of the officer who had influenced O'Connor so much as a young man, is drawn up behind. In 1954, he handed over the Colonelcy to Major General Douglas Graham, the gallant old 'war-horse' who had commanded 50 Division in North-West Europe. On his finishing his tour as Colonel of the Regiment, a tribute to him appeared in *The Covenanter*, the regimental magazine:

General O'Connor was an ardent Cameronian (Scottish Rifleman). His great ambition had always been to command one of the battalions of the regiment, but because his qualities outstripped the ordinary run of promotion, he was denied this privilege. It may not be generally known that he declined offers of accelerated promotion into two distinguished regular battalions of other regiments, thereby jeopardizing his subsequent career, in the hope that he might be allowed eventually to command a battalion of the Cameronians.

It was therefore most fitting, and no doubt a great consolation to him, that he should have been appointed Regimental Colonel at the close of his career. During his period as Colonel, all ranks in the Regular and Territorial units of the regiment will testify to the selfless service which he had rendered to us all, not least of which was to fly out to Malaya in 1951 to visit the 1st Battalion on operations. On his last official appearance, in July 1954, he flew to Belgium to visit the 6th/7th Battalion on their annual training. He spared no effort during his long and distinguished career to give service to the regiment, and in recording our gratitude and admiration, we wish him the best of luck in the future.[2]

While these military responsibilities were being given to O'Connor, civilian ones were coming his way as well. He became a Deputy Lieutenant for Ross and Cromarty in 1950, and a Justice of the Peace in 1952. Then in October 1955 a letter arrived from 10, Downing Street inviting him to become Lord Lieutenant for Ross and Cromarty. Following his acceptance his appointment was announced in the *London Gazette* on 8 November, and he held the post until 1964. In August 1956 he was involved in his first major Royal visit, when the Queen and several of her family visited the Isle of Lewis. There were several more times in the following years when he was to look after members of the Royal Family, both formally and informally, in his capacity as Lord Lieutenant, the final occasion being a major visit to the Highlands, by the Queen and the Duke of Edinburgh, just before his tour of duty finished in 1964.

In the post-war years, many newly retired senior officers of the three services took up directorships in commercial or industrial companies. Soon after he left the War Office in 1947, O'Connor was approached by Anthony Eden, now in opposition with the rest of his party, with a view to his becoming a director of Rio Tinto Zinc. Eden then put him in touch with the Chairman of the company, Mr A Rothschild, and several letters passed between them until O'Connor finally decided against taking up the offer.[3]

Throughout his retirement, he kept up a very considerable correspondence with a wide range of people. John Harding was constantly in touch, even during his busy time as CIGS from 1952 to 1955 and, once cordial relations had been re-established with Montgomery, he too wrote regularly on many different topics. Among others, Montgomery discussed the Suez crisis, declaring in a letter of 29 January 1957, 'Never in our history has anything been so thoroughly bungled!'[4] A frequent correspondent from another service was Admiral A B Cunningham, now ennobled as Viscount Cunningham of Hyndhope. Not all those to whom he wrote regularly were famous figures, however; in 1949 he caught up again with Roberts, his confidential clerk from Palestine and desert days, who had been commissioned during the war and finished his service as a Squadron Leader in the RAF Regiment. During the next 32 years, until his death, O'Connor wrote no less than 75 letters to Roberts, all of which the latter kept, covering a wide range of subjects, and showing an obvious genuine interest in all the doings reported to him by Roberts in his own letters.

As the 1950s came near to an end, a very black cloud began to overshadow the O'Connors' happy life at Kincurdie House when Jean developed cancer. She lingered for some time, but on 24 May 1959, she died at the age of 61. A memorial service was held on 3 June 1959 in St Andrew's Cathedral, Inverness. For O'Connor it was perhaps the worst blow of his life, even worse than being taken prisoner in 1941, and for a time he was desolated. Letters and messages of condolence poured in from all directions, including a personal telegram from the Queen. Many of the famous figures of the Second World War wrote; Montgomery had his own experience to underlie his sympathy; 'I can understand better than most what it means to lose one's wife. And I know how long it takes to recover. God bless you in your grief.'[5]

Letters from two of the doctors who had tended Jean in her two periods of serious illness in 1946 and 1959 are of special interest. Hector Grierson had been her doctor in Rawalpindi in the first instance, and he referred in his letter to the special relationship he had with her as a patient: 'I came to appreciate, when I thought she was very near to death then, her spiritual strength and integrity and her very deep devotion to your good self.' Doctor T N Mac Gregor, who operated on her not long before the end, told how 'Lady O'Connor was one of the bravest and most courageous women I have ever met. She knew of her condition from the first time I saw her, yet she begged me to keep it from you as she knew how it would upset you. You were ever in her thoughts and your happiness was uppermost in her mind.'[6]

One of the nicest of the many testimonials to Jean's character came from an old servant of the Ross family called Cathie Macaulay: 'Over twenty years ago when Lady O'Connor was getting married, old Bella McIntosh said to me "She's a proper lady, is my Miss Jean. A lady by birth and a lady by the goodness of her heart. Everyone loves her, but the folk that know her best love her most." What more can anyone say of someone who could give happiness to others, by just being herself?'[7]

Finally, among the letters came one from Dorothy Russell, which was perhaps the most significant of all. Apart from expressing her deep sympathy, and recording how much Jean was loved by everyone, she mentioned a visit to Kincurdie in July. That visit was followed by others during the next four years, and then in 1963 she married Dick and became the second Lady O'Connor. They both found great happiness in this late marriage, and lived together in complete harmony for the next eighteen years.

Quite soon after the wedding, the newly married Lady O'Connor found herself involved in a major public duty which at first appeared to be rather unnerving. Early in 1964, O'Connor was appointed by the Queen to be her Lord High Commissioner to the General Assembly of the Church of Scotland for that year. The significance of this appointment is explained in the brief history written by Sir Alastair Blair, who was Purse Bearer, or Chief of Staff, to various Commissioners in the 1960s.

> Once a year, in Edinburgh, the General Assembly of the Church of Scotland meets for a period of ten days—attended by about 700 Ministers and 700 Elders. This is the ultimate authority of the democratic church, and the representatives are elected locally—each Minister being a representative about one year in four and each Elder about one year in ten.

Blair's account goes on to explain how James VI of Scotland used to attend meetings of the Assembly in person until moving to London and becoming James I of England as well. Thereafter he exercised his right to be present by appointing a representative to do so, called The Lord High Commissioner. Every year since 1603 this appointment has been made, except when Her Majesty Queen Elizabeth II visited herself in 1969.

Blair's description ends with an explanation of the Commissioner's programme, and of the Purse Bearer's duties in making all the arrangements:

> The Lord High Commissioner's programme during the ten days is a full one, as, besides attending at least one session of the Assembly each day, and four Church Services in the first week, he visits Church organisations such as new Churches or Church Halls, Old People's Homes, Children's Homes, Church Canteens etc., as well as Hospitals, Universities, Schools and industrial undertakings. Then he entertains in Hollyrood Palace in a big way—four or five banquets of one hundred, one or two receptions of five hundred, a garden party of four thousand and a continually changing rota of VIP guests staying in the Palace overnight—up to ten arriving each day and departing the next.
>
> It is the Purse Bearer, with a staff of about four secretaries, who handles the details of all these different items of the programme in the closest consultation with the Lord High Commissioner. The planning starts each year in January, and the Purse Bearer finds that by the beginning of April

he is engaged on this full time until the close of the General Assembly at the end of May.[8]

During his ten days in office, the Lord High Commissioner is given Royal status, and he and his wife are referred to as 'Their Graces'; 'Your Grace' being the old Scots style of addressing the Sovereign.

Blair's personal record of O'Connor's tour of duty in May 1964 starts with a comment on Dorothy being unwell with 'flu at the time of his appointment, and also that she was understandably rather nervous about it to begin with. When the time came to take up residence in Hollyrood however, she carried out everything with great dignity and aplomb. Of her husband Blair comments:

> Of all my masters in the sixties' decade General Dick was by far the easiest to work for. He enjoyed ceremonial and he understood staff work. He drew a very clear line between the work he would do himself and the work he would delegate, and he never crossed that line. He knew the importance of timing. He kept his correspondence continually up to date. Within a month of his appointment he had provisionally fixed all the main items of his busy programme. A great soldier with a wonderful record, he was yet the gentlest of men, and hated hurting anybody by word or by deed.

Blair's account ends with a simple story which helps towards an understanding of how O'Connor's natural humility and kindness should never be confused with weakness:

> My other story is to show that although the General sailed along doing everything expected of him without even asking questions, he was nevertheless wide awake and never missed anything. When we arrived home after our long day at Cumbernauld, Their Graces had tea by themselves and did their Home-work for the evening—the last Banquet. In the middle of my tea, I was summoned to the presence, and was asked why the names of five different people that the General expected were not on the Banquet list. He remembered that in February or March he had put these names down for invitation: he realised that he had not seen them at any of the previous Banquets, and that this was the last one; why were they not on to-night's list? I could give him no answer, but asked time to consult the files. Jean Clark got these out at once and showed me the reason for the refusal given by each of these five people (absence abroad, illness, school leave out, etc). I took this information up to the General who was of course satisfied that neither I nor my secretaries had been in error, but did say, so gently, that if only I had reported these refusals to him at the time they came in, he would not now have had to ask his questions. I was lost in admiration of such a meticulous memory and such wonderful courtesy in his use of it.[9]

O'Connor had taken much pleasure in the fact that during his residence in Hollyrood the guard on the Palace, as well as the Guard of Honour at the opening of the Assembly, had been found by the 1st Battalion The Cameronians (Scottish Rifles). One of the guests whom he invited to stay at the Palace was Field Marshal Slim, who remembered the battalion well from the days when it had provided his personal bodyguard during the dark days of the retreat through Burma. This renewed close acquaintance with his old regiment made it all the more poignant for O'Connor when he heard only three years later that the 1st Battalion was to be disbanded. The final parade took place on 14 May 1968 on the same day and at the same place—Douglas in Lanarkshire—as the regiment had been raised in 1689. O'Connor was one of a party of twelve which led the long column of ex-servicemen who marched to the site of the disbandment immediately behind the regular battalion. The twelve were headed by George Collingwood, now Colonel of the Regiment, and apart from Lord Clydesmuir, Lord Lieutenant of the county and a Territorial Cameronian, they were all Generals. The sadness of all present was ameliorated by the excellence of the imaginative ceremony of disbandment which then took place.

One more great honour was to come O'Connor's way, and it was one which he found as exciting as it was unexpected. On 16 April 1971 the Queen's Private Secretary, Sir Michael Adeane, wrote to tell him that Her Majesty wished to create him a Knight of the Thistle, to take up one of the two places that had fallen vacant among the sixteen members to which the order is limited, other than Royalty. The Thistle is second only to the Order of the Garter among the orders of chivalry, and to become a member is an outstanding honour. It was an immediate and happy 'Agreed' that O'Connor replied by telegram to Adeane's letter, in accordance with the instructions as to how he should respond. With the Earl of Dalhousie, O'Connor was installed as a Knight by the Queen at a service held in the Thistle Chapel, which adjoins St Giles Cathedral, Edinburgh, on 3 July 1971. From that day, the letters 'KT' took precedence before the initials of all the other decorations which followed his name.

Mentioning his installation in a letter to Roberts, he stated that he thought himself very 'lucky' to be chosen as a Knight of the Thistle. Among his papers there are notes written on more than one occasion, on the matter of luck in connection with medals and decorations. He seemed almost embarrassed by his own remarkable collection of awards, especially those earned in the First World War, and constantly stressed how many other men had done braver things but had not received medals, because there was no one present to report their actions.

Throughout the remaining ten years of his life, O'Connor slowed down gradually, though he was a considerably more active octogenarian than most. The flow of correspondence continued, and he often answered at great length queries about his 1940–1941 campaign in the desert, which came to him from all over the world. In June 1976 a young American student, called Kenneth Startup, stayed at Kincurdie to receive help in the thesis he was writing on O'Connor's career. Like Alanbrooke and many other great soldiers, O'Connor 'always answered personal letters from high or low promptly', and 'believed in the swift and punctilious dispatch of business'.[10] Old friends kept in touch as well. In February 1977 Auchinleck wrote from Marrakesh to wish 'All the best to you—old and true friend', and also to make the comment 'Old age is hell! Especially when coupled with lack of money'.[11] Later that year came a letter from Horrocks, bewailing the failure to go on to Tripoli in February 1941. There was always something in the post.

In 1978 the O'Connors left Kincurdie House and moved permanently into Dorothy's London flat. It was a sad wrench leaving the Black Isle and all its happy associations, but they were finding the big house and garden almost a burden, and reluctantly decided to make life simpler by moving into a conveniently managed flat.

* * * * *

The end came quite suddenly in the Summer of 1981. In his old age, O'Connor was concerned that his memory was failing, so to keep it active he had developed the habit of writing down each evening all the things he had done during the day. On 1 June 1981, two months before his ninety-second birthday, he recorded all his activities as usual. Having walked to the Brompton Road he went up to Piccadilly by bus to visit the Royal Academy exhibition. Next he walked to the Ministry of Defence in Whitehall to discuss some matters connected with the Service of Thanksgiving for the life of Auchinleck due to take place on 5 June. He walked back to St James's Square to the Army and Navy Club to meet Dorothy for lunch, and then set off to walk to Westminster Abbey to check a detail connected with the Auk's service. On the way he felt rather tired, 'so picked a taxi and got home for £1.20, which was most expensive'. These were the last words he ever wrote. During that night he had a stroke which paralysed his left side. He remained in bed at home for a few days, and then was moved to Sister Agnes's, the King Edward VII Hospital for Officers. Shortly afterwards another major stroke followed, but such was his physical strength that he lived on in a state of coma for a further two weeks, before dying on 17 June.

Long obituaries appeared in the major newspapers, and telegrams and letters flooded in to Lady O'Connor. From Windsor Castle came one which read:

> I was greatly saddened to read of your husband's death. His distinguished wartime service is something for which we will all remain in his debt. Prince Philip and I send you our deepest sympathy.
>
> Elizabeth R.

Two memorial services were held, after a small family funeral. The first was in London at St Columba's Church of Scotland, Pont Street, on 15 July at which the address was given by Field Marshal Lord Harding. The second was held in St Giles' Cathedral, Edinburgh on 11 August 1981, and on this occasion George Collingwood made the address. He spoke of O'Connor's great desert campaign, of his remarkable escape attempts, and of his happy private life with his two 'wonderful partners in the home'. He then went on to say:

> So there is in a sense a picture of three different people. The dedicated soldier and brilliant fighting Commander, a prisoner of war exerting all his energies and taking great risks to escape and return to serve his Country, and the quiet, unassuming little country gentleman with the kindly smile and charming manners, who was a wonderful host and a wonderful guest, but of course it was one and the same person and the chief facets of his character were, I think, great courage and determination, an impelling sense of duty, loyalty, extreme personal modesty, kindness and generosity and a delightful sense of humour. I think the jokes he liked best were those against himself.

Epilogue

Looking back over O'Connor's long, active life, which spanned many of the most crucial and exciting moments in twentieth century history, the first fifty-one years show a pattern of steady advancement towards high rank and military distinction. Though his luck in surviving the First World War unscathed, in spite of his constant presence in the front line, verged on the miraculous, there is no cause to wonder whether events might have turned out differently. Then suddenly this pattern is shattered. The seven years from 1940 to 1947 are remarkable for the extraordinary changes in his fortune. Of these 'ups and downs', by far the most important was the transition from the triumphant victor of the desert campaign at Beda Fomm on 7 February 1941 to the helpless prisoner of war only two months later on 7 April. So crucial was this short period in O'Connor's life, and so far reaching its effect on his career, that there are certain questions which inevitably spring to mind in connection with it.

To start, there are two that concern decisions over which O'Connor had some control. Should he have sent the Australian division to Tripoli on his own authority on the afternoon of 7 February 1941, without reference to Cairo? Was he correct in suggesting to Wavell, on his recall to the Desert on 3 April, that he should not take over command from Neame but merely remain with him as an adviser for a day or two? These matters have been discussed already at some length in this book, and there is little more to be said about them, though, in respect of the first, Ronald Lewin has recorded that when he and O'Connor often 'discussed these considerations', the latter 'accepted intellectually' that the dash to Tripoli would not have been sustainable even though 'he could never quite rid himself of a haunting sense' that he should have made that bold advance.[1]

Then there are three questions which reflect mere conjecture and concern what might have followed had O'Connor not been captured on 7 April 1941. Would he have been given command of the Eighth Army when it was formed; if commanding that army, would he have

278

defeated Rommel; and finally, had he been successful in North Africa, did he have the ability to handle command at the army group level?

A tentative answer to the first and second of these three questions is to be found in Barclay's book *On Their Shoulders*:

> It is interesting to speculate on the likely course of events had O'Connor not been captured:- Would Rommel's original advance have been checked? Probably not: the course of events had been sealed before O'Connor reappeared in the Desert.

Would O'Connor have been given command of the Eighth Army? If so, would he have handled a large force of many divisions with the same skill as he handled a Corps of two divisions? The answer to the first part of the question is almost certainly 'Yes'. The second part is more difficult to answer. It is not unreasonable to think that he might have made a greater success of the 'Battleaxe' (mid-June 1941) and 'Crusader' (November and December 1941) battles. After that, much larger forces were involved and judgement becomes more speculative and we cannot judge with certainty how the campaign would have shaped under his leadership. Had the Battle of Alam Halfa (August–September 1942) and Alamein (October–November 1942) taken place, there is no evidence that O'Connor was not as capable of conducting these operations with the same skill as he had displayed in the Desert Campaign in the Winter of 1940–41. The chance German patrol on the night of 6 April 1941 not only deprived posterity of the opportunity to study the campaign 'O'Connor versus Rommel', it may also have delayed our victory in North Africa. It greatly influenced the careers of several British generals, and probably one American, whose names became famous in the latter years of the war.[2]

There are those, however, who have a more limited admiration for O'Connor's generalship, and are not convinced that his defeat of the Italian army, which rarely made a serious effort to disrupt his plans, deserves Correlli Barnett's summing up of COMPASS:

> It was a model campaign, opening with a set-piece battle of great originality and faultless execution, continuing with a relentless pursuit with improvised supply services, and ending with a daring strategic march and a battle of annihilation. Sidi Barrani, Bardia, Tobruk and Beda Fomm—their brilliance sparkles against the darkest setting of the war; hardly rivalled, never surpassed.[3]

They would suggest that many competent British generals could have conducted operations against such a half-hearted enemy with equal skill. Although such an opinion cannot be entirely dismissed,

279

and O'Connor in his own natural humility more than once pointed out this factor himself when he felt he was being too fulsomely praised, it misses the vital point, which is that he brought about a *total* destruction of the enemy Tenth Army. While there were many competent generals in the British Army at the time who could have defeated the Italians at each stage, there were few who could have made each of those stages follow the other with such rapidity and intensity that the annihilation of the enemy forces was achieved. This was the true measure of his success and is the explanation why it is not fanciful to put him in the same class as Rommel. Those who would deny him such a place are younger men who, if they served under him in the desert, were too junior to know him well, or if they saw him more closely in North West Europe, did so after his long spell as a prisoner of war.

In attempting to assess the quality of his generalship when he was at the height of his powers, reference must be made to the outstanding men who knew O'Connor intimately in those days before his capture. Interestingly, the names of two of them are quoted along with his own in Norman Dixon's fascinating book *On the Psychology of Military Incompetence*. At one point, discussing leaders with powerful and original minds, Dixon writes of '... such unequivocally great generals as Wavell, Auchinleck and O'Connor'. It will be recalled from earlier chapters that Wavell considered that O'Connor would have become 'one of the most distinguished generals of the war' if not taken prisoner, while Auchinleck long upbraided himself for not persuading Churchill 'to buy you from the Italians so you could have formed and raised the Eighth Army and finished Rommel in 1941!' The formidable Australian Prime Minister, Sir Robert Menzies, visiting his country's 6th Division in the Desert after Bardia, recorded in his autobiography *Afternoon Light*, 'General Richard O'Connor made an enormous impression on me ... he would have been one of the greatest military names in the history of the war.'

The most important verdict of all, however, is that of the man who was so close to O'Connor throughout the most testing days of the campaign: the man who shared his deepest thoughts and turned his plans into clear, readily comprehended orders. Of his brilliance at the moment of triumph at the end of COMPASS John Harding had no doubts. And of Harding's own judgement, as witnessed by his outstanding career in war and peace, there can be little doubt either. It was his opinion that O'Connor at the height of his powers was fully capable of assuming greater responsibilities than command of a corps, and his answer to the third question posed above would be 'Yes'. As he commented in a television programme in 1972 when the interviewer asked 'How great a loss was O'Connor's capture?'

> Oh! Very great indeed, he was a brilliant commander, he had what I would call the highest quality of command, that was to persuade or influence his subordinate commanders to suggest for themselves, that they should do what he wanted them to do ... he was quiet, modest, and not at all forceful but he *always* got his way.[4]

In attempting to understand how it was that he always got his way, and why it is reasonable to suppose that O'Connor's character and method of working was suited to those highest levels of command which his capture prevented him ever reaching, the following record of an interview he gave Ronald Lewin in 1968 is especially helpful:

> *His view of war.* He said that he would never tackle any situation if he had not been able to work out beforehand all the possibilities, including the worst. He said he was not a quick thinker; but by considering in advance every contingency, he was able to cope in action when the unexpected happened because he had thought it out in advance. He is a modest, neat, small, compact but clear-minded person: wholly self-confident. He was absolutely lucid about the way he ran a battle: you think the whole thing out in advance, the best and the worst, and when the worst happens you aren't surprised. He said he understood that a man like Rommel was different, that he could play off the cuff. He much appreciated Montgomery's capacity to think ahead to the next battle or the next battle but one. When he told me how he was switched from Palestine to take over the Western Desert Force on the eve of war, and how he was whipped up by Wavell to support Neame in the face of Rommel's first offensive, he spoke of each situation with absolute calm. In each case he was obviously ready to cope. Coolly and collectively. What impressed me about him was, emerging from this tiny gentle creature, a sense of complete certainty: he distilled confidence by a quiet certitude. I sensed that he was so sure of himself that his troops could be sure. Anywhere.[5]

While a study of O'Connor's eventful life would be incomplete without discussion of these topics, to speculate on them further would become a sterile exercise. His best epitaph is contained in the words of dedication at the front of the book *The Fire and the Rose* by his friend Arthur Bryant:

> *To Dick O'Connor who in the Western Desert, when Britain stood alone, took Time by the forelock.*

Appendix

Detailed Order of Battle of the Commonwealth and Italian Forces in 1940

The Commonwealth Force

The composition of the 35,000 strong Commonwealth force—this term will be employed hereafter though, at the time, Imperial would have been the designation more in use—was as follows:

HEADQUARTERS, WESTERN DESERT FORCE (XIII CORPS)

Commander:- Lieutenant General R N O'Connor
BGS:- Brigadier Rupert Hobday (succeeded by Brigadier John Harding, December 1940)
AQMG:- Brigadier E P Nares

Corps Troops
7th Royal Tank Regiment ('I' Tanks—'Matildas')
(Commander:- Lieutenant Colonel R Jerram)
1st RHA (25-prs)
3rd RHA (2-pr A Tk Guns) less two batteries
104th RHA (25-prs)
51st Field Regiment (25-prs)
7th Medium Regiment (6″ Hows and 6″ Guns)
64th Medium Regiment (4.5″ Guns)

HEADQUARTERS, 7TH ARMOURED DIVISION

Commander:- Major General M O'M Creagh ('Dicky')
GSO1:- Colonel C H Gairdner

4th Armoured Brigade

Commander:- Brigadier J A L Caunter ('Blood')
(Commanded 7th Armoured Division during the battle of Sidi Barrani)
7th Hussars
2nd Royal Tank Regiment
6th Royal Tank Regiment

7th Armoured Brigade

Commander:- Brigadier H E Russell (Hugh)
3rd Hussars
8th Hussars
1st Royal Tank Regiment

Support Group

Commander:- Brigadier W H E Gott ('Strafer')
1st King's Royal Rifle Corps
2nd Rifle Brigade

Divisional Troops

11th Hussars (Armoured Cars)
(Commander:- Lieut-Colonel J F B Combe, who also commanded an independent force known as 'Combe's Force' during *COMPASS*)
'M' Battery 3rd RHA (2-pr A Tk Guns)
2nd Field Squadron, RE
141st Field Park Troop, RE

Administrative Units

Nos 5, 58, 65 and 550 Companies, RASC
4th New Zealand Reserve Company
1st Supply Issue Section, RIASC
2/3rd Cavalry Field Ambulance
3/3rd Cavalry Field Ambulance

HEADQUARTERS, 4TH INDIAN DIVISION

Commander:- Major General N M de la P Beresford-Peirse
GSO1:- Colonel T W Rees

5th Indian Infantry Brigade

Commander:- Brigadier W L Lloyd
1st Royal Fusiliers

3/1st Punjab Regiment
4/6th Rajputana Rifles

11th Indian Infantry Brigade
Commander:- Brigadier R A Savory
2nd Queen's Own Cameron Highlanders
1/6th Rajputana Rifles
4/7th Rajput Regiment

16th British Infantry Brigade
Commander:- Brigadier C E N Lomax
1st Queen's Regiment
2nd Leicestershire Regiment
1st Argyll and Sutherland Highlanders

Divisional Troops
Central India Horse
One battery 3rd RHA (2-pr A Tk Guns)
1st Field Regiment, RA
25th Field Regiment, RA
31st Field Regiment, RA
1st Battalion, The Northumberland Fusiliers (Machine Gun Battalion)
4th Field Company, KGO Bengal Sappers and Miners
12th Field Company, QVO Madras Sappers and Miners
18th Field Company, Royal Bombay Sappers and Miners
21st Field Company, Royal Bombay Sappers and Miners
11th Field Park Company, QVO Madras Sappers and Miners

Administrative Units
4th Indian Divisional Troops Transport Company, RIASC
5th, 7th and 11th Indian Infantry Brigade Transport Companies, RIASC
14th Indian Field Ambulance
17th Indian Field Ambulance
19th Indian Field Ambulance

Mersa Matruh Garrison
Commander:- Brigadier A R Selby
3rd Battalion Coldstream Guards (detached as part of the covering screen in August and September)
1st Battalion South Staffordshire Regiment
1st Battalion Durham Light Infantry

1st Light A A Battery, RA
'A' Company 1st Battalion Cheshire Regiment

6th Australian Division

Finally, although not part of the Western Desert Force at the start of Operation Compass, mention must be made of this division which, as the story of the operation shows, replaced 4th Indian Division when it was withdrawn and played a major part in the successful outcome.

HEADQUARTERS, 6TH AUSTRALIAN DIVISION

Commander:- Major General I Mackay
GSO1:- Colonel F H Berryman

16th Australian Infantry Brigade
Commander:- Brigadier A S Allen
2/1st Battalion
2/2nd Battalion
2/3rd Battalion

17th Australian Infantry Brigade
Commander:- Brigadier S G Savige
2/5th Battalion
2/6th Battalion
2/7th Battalion

19th Australian Infantry Brigade
Commander:- Brigadier H C H Robertson
2/4th Battalion
2/8th Battalion
2/11th Battalion

Divisional Troops
6th Cavalry Regiment
1st Royal Northumberland Fusiliers (Machine Gun Battalion)—
    transferred from 4th Indian Division
2/1st Field Regiment, RAA (25-prs)
2/2nd Field Regiment, RAA (4.5″ Hows and 18-prs)
2/3rd Field Regiment, RAA (25-prs) (arrived January 1941)
Three Light AA Batteries RAA
2/1st Field Coy

2/2nd Field Coy
2/8th Field Coy

Administrative Units
2/1st Field Ambulance
2/2nd Field Ambulance

(The 6th Australian Division was deficient of many administrative units and was particularly short of transport, especially 2nd Line transport for bringing forward supplies, ammunition, petrol, water etc. Consequently their supply system was mostly on an improvised basis; but whatever the difficulties, they were always overcome by one means or another.)

Italian Forces

COMMANDER-IN-CHIEF
Commandante Superiore Maresciallo d'Armata Rodolto Graziani

TENTH ARMY
Generale d'Armata Gariboldi (until 17 November 1940)
Generale d'Armata Berti (until 23 December 1940)
Generale d'Armata Tellera (died of wounds 7 February 1941)

XXI CORPS—Generale di Corpo d'Armata Bergonzoli
(HQ Bardia)

1ST LIBYAN DIVISION (at Maktila)
2ND LIBYAN DIVISION (at Tummar)
4TH BLACKSHIRT DIVISION (at Sidi Barrani)
Maletti Group (at Nibeiwa)
63RD CIRENE DIVISION (at Rabia/Sofafi)
62ND MARMARICA DIVISION (along Escarpment between Sofafi and Halfaya)
64TH CATANZARO DIVISION (at Buq Buq)
1ST BLACKSHIRT DIVISION (at Bardia)
2ND BLACKSHIRT DIVISION (at Bardia)
Frontier Guard units and **Fortress** troops in Bardia

XXII CORPS—Generale di Corpo d'Armata Petassi Mannella
(HQ Tobruk)

61ST SIRTE DIVISION (in Tobruk)
Fortress troops and artillery in Tobruk

XX CORPS—Generale di Corpo d'Armata Cona (HQ Giovanni Berta)

60TH SABRATHA DIVISION (at Derna)
27TH BRESCIA DIVISION (at Slonta)
17TH PAVIA DIVISION (at Cirene)
Babini Armoured Brigade (at Mechili)

Note: Metropolitan Divisions such as Brescia and Pavia usually consisted of approximately 13,000 men; Libyan and Blackshirt Divisions of approximately 8,000. The total Italian strength was approximately 130,000.

Glossary of Abbreviations

AA	Anti-Aircraft
ADC	Aide-de-Camp
AG	Adjutant General
AGRA	Army Group Royal Artillery
ANZAC	Australian and New Zealand Army Corps (dates from the First World War when the two armies formed a single expeditionary force and used colloquially in the Second World War to refer to troops from those two countries)
AOC	Air Officer Commanding
BGS	Brigadier General staff
BM	Brigade Major
BTE	British Troops, Egypt
CB	Companion of the Order of the Bath
CCRA	Commander Corps Royal Artillery
CIGS	Chief of the Imperial General Staff
C-in-C	Commander in Chief
COS	Chiefs of Staff
CSM	Company Sergeant Major
DCM	Distinguished Conduct Medal
DS	Directing Staff (at the Staff College)
DSO	Distinguished Service Order
FSD	Forward Supply Depot
GAF	German Air force (term used by Allied forces to describe German Infantry Divisions formed within the Luftwaffe. Eg: 85 GAF Division)

G(Air)	General Staff branch dealing with air support and kindred matters
GCB	Knight Grand Cross of the Order of the Bath
GHQ	General Headquarters
GOC	General Officer Commanding (normally of a division)
GOC-in-C	General Officer Commanding in Chief (of an Army or equivalent command)
GSO	General Staff Officer (followed by 1, 2, or 3 according to grade. Eg: GSO 1)
HAC	Honourable Artillery Company
HMG	His Majesty's Government
HMS	His Majesty's Ship
HQ	Headquarters
IDC	Imperial Defence College
INA	Indian National Army
JIF	Japanese Indian Forces (alternative name for INA)
KCSI	Knight Commander of the Star of India
KCVO	Knight Commander of the Royal Victorian Order
KDG	King's Dragoon Guards
KT	Knight of the Thistle
LCT	Landing Craft, Tank
MA	Military Assistant
MC	Military Cross
MM	Military Medal
MOD	Ministry of Defence
MP	Member of Parliament
MT	Mechanised Transport
NCO	Non-Commissioned Officer
NWFP	North-West Frontier Province (of India)
PM	Prime Minister
POW	Prisoner of War

RAF	Royal Air Force
RASC	Royal Army Service Corps
RHA	Royal Horse Artillery
RMAS	Royal Military Academy Sandhurst (post-1945)
RMC	Royal Military College, Sandhurst (pre-1940)
RSM	Regimental Sergeant Major
SD	Staff Duties (as for SD1, staff branch No 1 in the SD Directorate of the War Office)
SEAC	South East Asia Command
SHAEF	Supreme Headquarters Allied Expeditionary Force
Sqn Ldr	Squadron Leader
SS	*Schutz Staffel* (used in connection with formation titles of the Waffen SS—the field element of Hitler's special force based upon his original bodyguard. Eg: 1 SS Panzer Corps)
TA	Territorial Army
Tac HQ	Tactical Headquarters
USAAF	United States Army Air Force
VC	Victoria Cross
VCIGS	Vice Chief of the Imperial General Staff

Notes

Prologue

1. O'Connor Papers, Liddell Hart Centre, Box 1/11–12, File 12.
2. O'Connor Papers, Liddell Hart Centre, Box 1/15–17, File 16.
3. Keegan, John. *The Mask of Command* (Cape, 1987), p. 143.
4. Barnett, C. *The Desert Generals*—author's Prologue to 1st Edition.

Chapter 1. Childhood and Schools

1. O'Connor Papers.
2. Letter in custody of Major J K Nairne on behalf of the family. Written 1 February 1944 by Charles Edworthy.

Chapter 2. From Sandhurst to the Regiment

1. Information given by Dr T A Heathcote, Curator RMAS Collection, in a letter to K Startup dated 9 April 1987.
2. This story is related in Nigel Hamilton's book *Monty, The Making of a General 1887–1942*, p. 48.
3. Wolseley, Field Marshal Viscount. *The Story of a Soldier's Life*.
4. Montague, C E. *Disenchantment* (Chatto and Windus, 1922).
5. O'Connor Diary, 23 December 1921.
6. O'Connor, letter to the Author, 26 September 1967.
7. O'Connor Diary, 19 May 1921.
8. Quoted in the Author's *Morale*, p. 26. (From a letter written to the Author in 1965.)
9. All that follows comes from the same letter to the Author of 26 September 1967 as at note 6 above.

Chapter 3. The First World War

1. The story of the first month of the War was written in 1972 and given to Major J K Nairne. His diaries are in the Liddell Hart Archives; the letters are in Major Nairne's custody on behalf of the family.
2. The first month of the war is covered in pp. 1–30 of *The Seventh Division 1914–1918* by C T Atkinson (London, 1927).
3. Information given to Kenneth Startup in an interview.
4. Notes given to Major Nairne.
5. Story, Colonel H H, MC. *History of The Cameronians (Scottish Rifles) 1910–1933* (published by the Regiment, 1961).
6. O'Connor Diary, 13 May 1917.
7. O'Connor Diary, 8 April 1917.
8. O'Connor Diary, 9 April 1917.
9. O'Connor Diary, 2 May 1917.

10. HAC Journal, August 1981.
11. Edmonds, Sir J. *Military Operations, France and Belgium 1917, Volume II* (HMSO, 1948), p. 312.
12. From recollections (recorded in 1970) of Sergeant Major Bradley, which are in Peter Liddle's '1914–1918 Personal Archives'.
13. Atkinson, *Seventh Division*, pp. 436–437.
14. Gould Walker, G. *The Honourable Artillery Company in the Great War* (London, 1930) p. 342.
15. Ibid., p. 344.
16. Ibid., p. 346 and Atkinson, p. 463.
17. Atkinson, p. 464.
18. Ibid., p. 467.
19. Gould Walker, p. 358.
20. Ibid., p. 359.
21. Atkinson, pp. 468–469.
22. O'Connor's own comments in an interview with Kenneth Startup.
23. Gould Walker, p. 361.

Chapter 4. The Post-war Years—1919 to 1935

1. O'Connor Papers, Box 1/15–17, File 16.
2. Murray, General Sir H. 'A Gaggle of Generals' in *The Covenanter*, 1971.
3. O'Connor Papers, Box 1/4–5.
4. Ibid.
5. Interview given to the Author in April 1988.
6. O'Connor Papers, Box 1/15–17, File 15.
7. Story, H H. *History of The Cameronians (Scottish Rifles), Volume II, 1910–1933*, p. 389.
8. Letter to the Author from C Havergall, 11 July 1988.
9. O'Connor Papers, Box 1/15–17, File 15.
10. *Owl Pie* (Staff College Magazine), 1927 edition.
11. O'Connor Papers, Box 1/4–5.

Chapter 5. Commander, Peshawar Brigade, North-West Frontier of India

1. *The Times*, 28 September 1935.
2. O'Connor Papers, Box 1/15–17.
3. *The Daily Record*, 10 September 1943.
4. Barclay, C N. *The History of The Cameronians (Scottish Rifles), Vol. III, 1933–1946* (Sifton Praed, 1947), p. 18.

Chapter 6. Commander 7th Division and Military Governor of Jerusalem

1. The information for this chapter comes from O'Connor's own writings as mentioned below, and from notes taken by Kenneth Startup during an interview in 1975, as well as from chapters in Startup's thesis.
2. Connell, John. *Wavell*, pp. 185–186.
3. *The Times*, 10 March and 8 November 1933.
4. Connell, p. 187.
5. Ibid., p. 197.
6. From Startup's notes.
7. *New York Times*, 12 October 1938.
8. *The Times*, 18 October 1938.
9. From Startup's interview with O'Connor.
10. O'Connor Papers, Box 1/15–17, File 16.

Notes

11. O'Connor's narrative is held among his papers at the Liddell Hart Centre, Box 5/2.
12. Startup interview.
13. Saward, D. *Bomber Harris* (Cassell, 1984).
14. O'Connor narrative, and Startup interview.
15. Hamilton, Nigel. *Monty: The Making of a General 1887–1942* (Hamish Hamilton, 1981), pp. 294–295.
16. *The Times*, London, 19 December 1938.
17. O'Connor Palestine narrative.
18. Maclean, Dr N. 'General Sir Richard O'Connor' in *The Scotsman*, 4 July 1942.
19. Letter from Squadron Leader C E Roberts, April 1988.
20. Information provided by Colonel Neville Blair in July 1988.
21. O'Connor narrative.

Chapter 7. Arrival in the Desert and First Actions Against the Italians

1. Connell, John. *Wavell: Scholar and Soldier* (Collins, 1964), p. 211.
2. Barnett, Correlli. *The Desert Generals* (Pan, 1983), p. 27.
3. Lloyd Owen, Major General David. *The Desert my Dwelling Place* (Cassell, 1957, and Arms and Armour Press, 1986), p. 26.
4. Lewin, Ronald. *The Chief* (Hutchinson, 1980), p. 50.
5. Unpublished manuscript kindly loaned by the Earl Haig.
6. Letter to the Author from Earl Haig.
7. Connell, p. 273.
8. Ibid., p. 278.
9. Ibid., p. 280.
10. Figures quoted from Barclay, C N. *Against Great Odds* (Sifton Praed, 1955), pp. 10–14.

Chapter 8. Planning the Five Day Raid

1. Earl Haig, unpublished autobiography.
2. Barclay, C N. *Against Great Odds*, p. 27.
3. O'Connor, quoted in Barclay, p. 24.
4. Letter from O'Connor to K Startup.
5. Letter from O'Connor to B H Liddell Hart dated 11 December 1946 (O'Connor Papers).

Chapter 10. General O'Connor's Conduct of the Campaign

O'Connor's original manuscript narrative, bound in leather, is among his papers in the Liddell Hart Archives (O'Connor 4/1–3). There are several other typescript copies in existence. Most references in this chapter are to extracts from the narrative in Brigadier C N Barclay's book *Against Great Odds* (Sifton Praed, 1955), and a few other easily available published sources.

1. Carver, Lord. *Harding of Petherton* (Weidenfeld and Nicolson, 1978).
2. The memorial service in London was held at St Columbia's Church, Pont Street, on 15 July 1981.
3. Wavell, *Soldiers and Soldiering* (Cape, 1953), p. 14.
4. Barclay, p. 25.
5. Connell, p. 285.
6. Connell, p. 286.
7. O'Connor narrative, quoted in Barclay, p. 26.
8. Connell, p. 291.
9. O'Connor, quoted in Barclay, p. 26.

10. Pitt, p. 88.
11. O'Connor, quoted in Barclay, p. 26.
12. O'Connor, quoted in Barclay, p. 31.
13. O'Connor, quoted in Barclay, p. 32.
14. O'Connor, quoted in Barclay, p. 34.
15. Barnett, p. 38.
16. O'Connor, quoted in Barclay, p. 36.
17. Letter from Wavell to O'Connor, quoted in Barclay, p. 38.
18. Carver, p. 17.
19. Connell, p. 296.
20. Barclay, pp. 82–83.
21. O'Connor, quoted by Barclay, pp. 36–37.
22. Connell, p. 295.
23. O'Connor, quoted by Barclay, p. 37.
24. Pitt, p. 124. Quoted from O'Connor.
25. Connell, p. 297.
26. O'Connor, quoted by Barclay, p. 44.
27. Letter of 7 December 1950 to Brigadier H B Latham, cabinet office, from Gavin Long, Canberra, who was writing Australian Official War History.
28. Pitt, p. 133.
29. Connell, p. 308. Quoted from Churchill, Vol. III.
30. Connell, p. 309.
31. Barclay, p. 53.
32. O'Connor, quoted in Pitt, p. 146.
33. O'Connor Papers, Box 1/15–17, File 16.
34. O'Connor, quoted in Pitt, p. 146.
35. O'Connor, quoted in Pitt, p. 147.
36. Guedalla, Philip. *Middle East 1940–42: A Study in Air Power* (Hodder and Stoughton, 1944).
37. Connell, p. 317.
38. Barnett, p. 49.
39. O'Connor, quoted in Barclay, p. 59.
40. O'Connor, quoted in Barclay, p. 60.
41. O'Connor, quoted in Pitt, p. 162.
42. O'Connor Papers, Box 1/4–5.
43. Connell, p. 320.
44. O'Connor, quoted in Barclay, pp. 64–65.
45. Connell, p. 321.
46. Barnett, p. 50.
47. O'Connor, quoted in Barclay, pp. 65–66.
48. Connell, p. 324.
49. Moorehead, A. *African Trilogy* (Hamish Hamilton, 1944), p. 111.
50. O'Connor, quoted in Barclay, p. 87.
51. Barnett, p. 55.
52. Connell, p. 325.
53. Moorehead, p. 106.
54. O'Connor, quoted in Barclay, pp. 67–69.
55. Quoted by Barnett at p. 58.
56. Moorehead, pp. 113–114.
57. Barnett, p. 59.
58. O'Connor, quoted in Guedalla, p. 103.

Chapter 11. The End of the Campaign

1. Quoted by Field Marshal Lord Harding in his address at O'Connor's Memorial Service, 15 July 1981.
2. Connell, p. 326 and Pitt, p. 193.
3. Connell, p. 327.

4. Connell, p. 328.
5. O'Connor, quoted in Barclay, pp. 71–74.
6. O'Connor Papers, Box 1/17–18. Letter to Kenneth Macksey, October 1970.
7. Connell, p. 383.
8. Wavell, 'The British Expedition to Greece', in *The Army Quarterly*, January 1950 (reprinted in Barclay, p. 102).
9. Harding's opinion is recorded in Carver, Field Marshal Lord, *Dilemmas of the Desert War* (Batsford, 1986), p. 18.
10. Rommell, Manfred and B H Liddell Hart (eds), *The Rommel Papers* (Collins, 1953), pp. 94, 96 and 97.
11. Barclay, p. 72.
12. Connell, pp. 321–323.
13. Wavell, reprinted in Barclay, p. 105.
14. Pitt, p. 219.
15. Wavell, reprinted in Barclay, p. 104.
16. Kennedy, Major General Sir John. *The Business of War*, p. 84. Quoted in Connell, p. 344.
17. Pitt, p. 312.
18. Boothby, Lord. *My Yesterday, Your To-morrow*. Quoted in Connell, p. 330.
19. Wavell, reprinted in Barclay, p. 107.
20. Recorded in an extract from Nicolson's *Diaries and Letters 1945–1962*, contained in O'Connor Papers, Box 3 (d,e,t,a).
21. O'Connor Papers, Box 1/5–6, File 5.

Chapter 12. Capture

1. Information given by O'Connor to Kenneth Startup in an interview in 1975.
2. From the same interview.
3. Pitt, p. 241.
4. Neame, Lieutenant General Sir Philip, VC, DSO. *Operations in Cyrenaica from 27 February 1941 until 7 April 1941*. This document is in the Churchill College Archives.
5. Carver, Field Marshal Lord. *Harding of Petherton* (Weidenfeld and Nicolson, 1978), p. 67.
6. Connell, p. 392, quoted from O'Connor's own campaign report.
7. Brigadier Combe's narrative is among the O'Connor papers at the Liddell Hart Centre.
8. From notes on an interview with O'Connor made by Ronald Lewin on 9 November 1977. Churchill College Archives, RLEW 4/1.
9. O'Connor Papers, File 3.
10. Ibid.
11. De Guingand, Major General E. *Operation Victory* (Hodder and Stoughton, 1947), p. 75.
12. Connell, p. 410.
13. Both Dill's and Eden's letters are in the O'Connor Papers, Box 1/5–6, File 6.
14. Letter from Field Marshal Sir Claude Auchinleck dated 3 September 1965. O'Connor Papers, Box 1/11–12, File 12.

Chapter 13. The First Escape Attempts

1. *Farewell Campo 12* was published by Michael Joseph in 1945. Inside the copy sent to O'Connor, Hargest's widow wrote: 'For General Dick and his wife as Jim wished.' Hargest, after successfully escaping through Spain and returning to UK, went out to Normandy in 1944 and was killed by a shell: the tragic loss of a great man. His son had been killed in early 1944.
2. Due to Boyd's ill-luck, the job went to Air Vice Marshal Tedder, who went on to higher things.
3. Carton de Wiart's remarkable life is told in *Happy Odyssey*, his autobiography published by Jonathan Cape in 1950.
4. Monsignor O'Flaherty helped many British prisoners to elude the Germans during the period described in the next chapter.

5. O'Connor told the story of this incident on various occasions.
6. Carton de Wiart, *Happy Odyssey*, p. 145.
7. O'Connor Papers, File 16.
8. A kinsman of General Caracciolo has provided some interesting information about his own assistance to escaping prisoners in 1943, and about Monsignor O'Flaherty. The ancestor hanged by Nelson was the Duke of Brianza. General Caracciolo belonged to a cadet branch of the ducal family.

Chapter 14. Escape After the Italian Armistice

1. Carton de Wiart left Vincigliata a few days earlier than the actual armistice, on a mission described in chapter XVII of *Happy Odyssey*, entitled '*Wings of a Dove*'.
2. Lord Ranfurly was left behind in the mountains, and was snowed in for the rest of the winter. He got away successfully in the Spring of 1944.
3. Madam Spazzoli's letter, dated 24 August 1945, was written from Forli: O'Connor Papers, Box 1/9–10, File 9.

Chapter 15. The Effects of Capture and the Years as a Prisoner of War

1. Interview with the Author in May 1988.
2. Slim, Field Marshal Viscount. *Defeat into Victory* (Cassell, 1955).
3. The two letters were posted through the Red Cross in Rome. O'Connor Papers, Box 1/5–6, File 6.
4. The reference to Wigram is presumably to the same General Wigram who was unfriendly to O'Connor in India in 1936.
5. The letter to Collingwood from Wavell is among Ronald Lewin's papers in Churchill College, Archives RLEW 4/6.
6. O'Connor Papers, Box 1/11–12, File 12.
7. Hamilton, Nigel. *Monty: Master of the Battlefield 1942–1944* (Hamish Hamilton, 1983), p. 476.
8. O'Connor Papers, Box 1/15–17, File 16. Notes on personalities.
9. Pownall Diaries, Vol. 2, p. 177.
10. Interview given to the Author in April 1988.

Chapter 16. Command of VIII Corps in Normandy

1. Jackson, Lieutenant Colonel G S. *Operations of Eighth Corps: Normandy to the Rhine* (St Clements Press, 1948), p. 7.
2. Ibid., p. 2.
3. O'Connor Papers, Box 1/9–10.
4. Colville, John. *The Fringes of Power* (Hodder and Stoughton, 1985), p. 480.
5. O'Connor Papers, Box 1/9–10.
6. This suggestion was made in an interview in May 1988 with General 'Pip' Roberts. No copy exists among O'Connor's papers of his reply to Churchill's letter.
7. O'Connor Papers, Box 1/9–10.
8. 21st Army Group Directive M-504, quoted in D'Este, Carlo. *Decision in Normandy*, p. 234.
9. Ibid., p. 237.
10. *Eighth Corps History*, p. 28.
11. Ibid., p. 29.
12. *Eighth Corps History*, p. 32.
13. *Taurus Pursuant: A History of the 11th Armoured Division* (privately published 1945), p. 14.
14. Martin, Lieutenant General H G. *The History of the Fifteenth Scottish Division 1939–1945* (Blackwood, 1948), p. 40.

15. Ibid., p. 50.
16. *Eighth Corps History*, p. 51.
17. *Taurus Pursuant*, p. 20.
18. Martin, p. 56.
19. O'Connor Papers, Box 1/7–8.
20. *Eighth Corps History*, p. 59.
21. Ibid., p. 63.
22. Ibid., p. 72.
23. O'Connor Papers, Box 1/7–8. Letter from MacMillan dated 21 July 1944, and one from Montgomery dated 4 September 1944.
24. Wilmot, Chester. *The Struggle for Europe* (Collins, 1952), p. 353.
25. *Eighth Corps History*, p. 80.
26. Ibid., p. 80.
27. Ibid., pp. 88–90.
28. D'Este, p. 373 (Roberts interview, 1980).
29. Ibid., p. 374.
30. Ibid., p. 389 (O'Connor interview, 1979).
31. O'Connor Papers, Box 1/7–8.
32. D'Este, p. 377.
33. *Eighth Corps History*, p. 93.
34. *Taurus Pursuant*, p. 24.
35. *Eighth Corps History*, p. 78.
36. *Taurus Pursuant*, p. 25.
37. D'Este, p. 379 (O'Connor interview, 1979).
38. Ibid., p. 379.
39. Notes for History, talk with General Hobart, 19 August 1947 (Liddell Hart Papers, King's College). Quoted by D'Este, p. 380. There is also a copy in the Lewin papers in Churchill College Archives (RLEW 2/1).
40. O'Connor Papers, Box 1/7–8. Letters from Erskine dated 21 July 1944.
41. *Eighth Corps History*, p. 96.
42. Ibid., p. 105.
43. Montgomery, Field Marshal Viscount. *Memoirs* (Collins, 1958), p. 257.
44. Roberts, Major General G P B. *From the Desert to the Baltic* (William Kimber, 1987), p. 184.
45. D'Este, p. 388.
46. Roberts, p. 184.
47. Letter from Tedder to Liddell Hart, 28 April 1952, in Liddell Hart Papers. Quoted in D'Este, p. 392.
48. Liddell Hart, *History of the Second World War* (Cassell, 1970), p. 556.
49. *Eighth Corps History*, p. 114.
50. Roberts, p. 184.
51. *Eighth Corps History*, p. 118 (Quoted from Montgomery, *Normandy to the Baltic*).
52. Ibid., p. 125.
53. Roberts, p. 185.
54. Verney, G L. *History of the Guards Armoured Division* (Hutchinson, 1955), p. 50.
55. Howard, M and Sparrow, J. *The Coldstream Guards 1920–1946* (Oxford Press, 1951), p. 305.
56. Roberts, p. 187.
57. *Eighth Corps History*, p. 132.
58. Ibid., p. 133.
59. Ibid., p. 135.
60. Roberts, p. 195.

Chapter 17. Normandy to the River Maas

1. O'Connor Papers, Box 1/7–8.
2. Ibid.
3. Ibid.
4. Ibid.

5. Liddell Hart, Sir Basil. *History of the Second World War* (Cassell, 1970), p. 567.
6. *Eighth Corps History*, p. 151.
7. Roberts, p. 214.
8. *Eighth Corps History*, p. 157.
9. Roberts, p. 219.
10. *Eighth Corps History*, p. 158.
11. O'Connor Papers, Box 1/7–8. Letter to Lady O'Connor of 13 October 1944.
12. Ibid. Letter from General Roberts to O'Connor dated 15 July 1945.
13. *Eighth Corps History*, p. 159.
14. Roberts, p. 220.
15. *Eighth Corps History*, p. 159.
16. O'Connor Papers, Box 1/7–8.
17. *Eighth Corps History*, p. 160.
18. Ibid., p. 161.
19. O'Connor Papers, Box 1/7–8.
20. *Eighth Corps History*, p. 164.
21. The letters quoted here to Lady O'Connor are in the possession of Major J K Nairne as custodian for the family.
22. O'Connor Papers, Box 1/7–8.
23. Ibid., Box 1/7–8.
24. Ibid., Box 1/7–8.
25. Roberts, p. 220.
26. O'Connor Papers, Box 1/7–8.
27. Letter from Field Marshal Lord Carver dated 6 August 1988.
28. From notes given to Major J K Nairne in answer to questions on the N W Europe campaign.
29. Hastings, Max. *Overlord* (Michael Joseph, 1984), p. 235.
30. Ibid., p. 235.

Chapter 18. Commands in India

1. Bond, B (Ed), *Chief of Staff: The Diaries of Lieutenant General Sir H Pownall*, Vol. 2, *1940–44* (Leo Cooper, 1974), p. 179.
2. O'Connor Papers, Box 1/7–8, File 8.
3. Ibid., Box 1/9–10, File 9.
4. Ibid., Box 1/15–16, File 16.
5. Ibid., Box 1/20–22, File 21.
6. Major General Shahid Hamid. *Disastrous Twilight* (Leo Cooper, 1986), p. 14.
7. O'Connor Papers, Box 1/15–17, File 16.
8. Told to the Author verbally in 1988.
9. Hamid, p. 15.
10. Ibid., p. 18.
11. O'Connor Papers, Box 1/9–10, File 9.
12. O'Connor Papers, Box 1/9–10, File 9.

Chapter 19. Adjutant General to the Forces

1. O'Connor Papers, Box 1/15–17, File 16.
2. Montgomery of Alamein, Field Marshal. *Memoirs* (Collins, 1958), p. 431.
3. O'Connor Papers, Box 1/9–10, File 10.
4. Letter from Rt Hon Professor John Freeman to the author dated 19 October 1988.
5. O'Connor Papers, Box 1/15–17, File 15.
6. Barclay, C N. *The History of The Cameronians (Scottish Rifles), Volume III* (Sifton Praed, 1947), p. 238.
7. Ibid., p. 240. After the disbandment, the 2nd Battalion, then serving in Gibraltar, assumed the title of 1st (see also Chapter 20, p. 274).
8. Both these narratives are in the possession of Major J K Nairne.

9. O'Connor Papers, Box 5/3.
10. Brett-James, A. *Conversations with Montgomery* (William Kimber, 1984), p. 91.

Chapter 20. The Last Years—1947 to 1981

1. Baynes, John. *The History of The Cameronians (Scottish Rifles), Volume IV* (Cassell, 1971), pp. 51–52.
2. From *The Covenanter*, Vol. 34, p. 56.
3. O'Connor Papers, Box 1/9–10, File 10.
4. Ibid., Box 1/11–12, File 11.
5. The letter from Montgomery is in a file among the personal papers in the possession of Major J K Nairne, as custodian for the family.
6. The two letters from the doctors are in the same collection.
7. Cathie Macaulay's letter was written to Jean's brother Donald Ross, and then passed by him to O'Connor.
8. Notes provided by Sir Alastair Blair, KCVO, TP, WS.
9. Extracts from Sir Alastair Blair's privately printed book *My Nine Years as Purse Bearer*.
10. Fraser, General Sir David. *Alanbrooke* (Collins, 1982), p. 204.
11. O'Connor Papers, Box 1/29–30, File 29.

Epilogue

1. Churchill College Archives, RLEW 7/6.
2. Barclay, Brigadier C N. *On Their Shoulders* (Faber, 1964), pp. 72–73.
3. Barnett, Correlli. *The Desert Generals* (Pan, 1983), p. 64.
4. Transcript of the 1972 Harding television interview is in the O'Connor Papers, Box 1/5–6, along with one of an interview with O'Connor himself at the same time.
5. Churchill College Archives, RLEW 7/6.

Bibliography

ATKINSON, C T. *The Seventh Division 1914–1918* (Murray, 1927).

BARCLAY, Brigadier C N. *History of The Cameronians (Scottish Rifles), Vol. III, 1933–1946* (Sifton Praed, 1947).
Against Great Odds (Sifton Praed, 1955).
On Their Shoulders (Faber, 1964).

BARNETT, Correlli. *The Desert Generals* (Allen and Unwin, 1960, and Pan, 1983).

BAYNES, Lieutenant Colonel Sir John. *Morale: A Study of Men and Courage* (Cassell, 1967, and Leo Cooper, 1987).
The History of The Cameronians (Scottish Rifles), Vol. IV, 1946–1968 (Cassell, 1971).

BELCHEM, Major General David. *Victory in Normandy* (Chatto & Windus, and Book Club Associates, 1981).

BELFIELD, E and ESSAME, Major General H. *The Battle for Normandy* (Pan, 1983).

BOND, Brian (Editor) Chief of Staff. *The Diaries of Lieutenant General Sir Henry Pownall, Vol. II, 1940–44* (Leo Cooper, 1974).

BRADLEY, General Omar N. *A Soldier's Story of the Allied Campaigns from Tunis to the Elbe* (Eyre and Spottiswoode, 1951).

BRETT-JAMES, A. *Conversations with Montgomery* (William Kimber, 1984).

CARTON DE WIART, Lieutenant General Sir Adrian, VC. *Happy Odyssey* (Pan, 1950).

CARVER, Field Marshal Lord. *Dilemmas of the Desert War: A New Look at the Libyan Campaign 1940–42* (Batsford, with the Imperial War Museum, 1986).
Harding of Petherton: Field Marshal (Weidenfeld and Nicolson, 1978).

CHEGWIDDEN, T S. 'The Imperial Defence College' in *Public Administration, 1947.*

CHURCHILL, Sir Winston. *The Grand Alliance*, Vol. III of *The Second World War* (Cassell, 1950).

COLVILLE, John. *The Fringes of Power: Downing Street Diaries 1939–1955* (Hodder and Stoughton, 1985).

CONNELL, John. *Wavell: Scholar and Soldier* (Collins, 1964).

DE GUINGAND, Major General Sir Francis. *Operation Victory* (Hodder and Stoughton, 1947).

Generals at War (Hodder and Stoughton, 1964).

D'ESTE, Carlo. *Decision in Normandy* (Collins, 1984).

DIXON, Norman. *On The Psychology of Military Incompetence* (Cape, 1976).

EDMONDS, Brigadier General Sir John. *History of the Great War: Military Operations, France and Belgium 1914* (Macmillan, 1933).

History of the Great War: Military Operations, France and Belgium, 1917, Vol. II (7 June to 10 November 1917) (HMSO, 1948).

EISENHOWER, General Dwight D. *Crusade in Europe* (Heinemann, 1948).

ELEVENTH ARMOURED DIVISION, Members of. *Taurus Pursuant: A History of the 11th Armoured Division* (privately printed, 1945).

ESSAME, Major General H. *The 43rd Wessex Division at War 1944–45* (Clowes, 1952).

FALLS, Cyril. *History of the Great War: Military Operations, France and Belgium 1917, Vol. I* (Macmillan, 1940).

FIRKINS, Peter. *The Australians in Nine Wars* (R Hale, 1972).

FRASER, General Sir David. *Alanbrooke* (Collins, 1982).

GILBERT, Martin. *The Road to Victory: Winston S Churchill 1941–1945* (Heinemann, 1986).

GODWIN-AUSTEN, A R. *The Staff and the Staff College* (Constable, 1927).

GRAY, Brigadier T I G. *The Imperial Defence College and the Royal College of Defence Studies (1927–1977)* (HMSO, 1977).

GUEDALLA, Philip. *Middle East 1940–1942: A Study in Air Power* (Hodder and Stoughton, 1944).

HAMID, Major General Shahid. *Disastrous Twilight: A Personal Record of the Partition of India* (Leo Cooper, 1986).

HAMILTON, Nigel. *Monty. The Making of a General 1887–1942* (Hamish Hamilton, 1981).

Monty. Master of the Battlefield 1942–1944 (Hamish Hamilton, 1983).

Monty. The Field Marshal 1944–1976 (Hamish Hamilton, 1986).

HARGEST, Brigadier James. *Farewell Campo 12* (Michael Joseph, 1945).

HASTINGS, Max. *Overlord* (Michael Joseph, 1984).

HER MAJESTY'S STATIONERY OFFICE (HMSO). *Destruction of an Army: The First Campaign in Libya September 1940 to February 1941* (printed 1941).

HORROCKS, Lieutenant General Sir Brian. *Corps Commander* (Sidgwick and Jackson, 1977).

HOWARD, M and SPARROW, J. *The Coldstream Guards 1920–1946* (Oxford University Press, 1951).

JACKSON, Lieutenant Colonel G S. *Operations of Eighth Corps: Normandy to the River Rhine* (St Clements Press, 1948).

JOSLEN, Lieutenant Colonel H F. *Orders of Battle—United Kingdom and Colonial Formations and Units in the Second World War 1939–45. Vols. I and II* (HMSO, 1960).

KEEGAN, John. *Six Armies in Normandy* (Cape, 1982).
The Mask of Command (Cape, 1987).

LEWIN, Ronald. *The Chief: Field Marshal Lord Wavell, Commander-in-Chief and Viceroy, 1939–1947* (Hutchinson, 1980).
Slim: The Standard Bearer (Leo Cooper, 1976).
The War on Land 1939–1945 (Hutchinson, 1969).

LIDDELL HART, Sir Basil. *The Liddell Hart Memoirs, Vol. I.* (Cassell, 1965).
The Tanks: Vol. 2, 1939–1945 (Cassell, 1959).
History of the Second World War (Cassell, 1970).
The Rommel Papers (Ed) (Collins, 1953).

LONG, Gavin. *To Benghazi* (Australian War Memorial, 1952).
Greece, Crete and Syria (Australian War Memorial, 1953).

MACKSEY, Kenneth. *Beda Fomm: The Classic Victory* (Pan/Ballantine, 1971).

MARTIN, Lieutenant General H G. *The History of the 15th Scottish Division 1939–1945* (Blackwood, 1948).

MONTGOMERY, Field Marshal Viscount. *Memoirs* (Collins, 1958).

MONTGOMERY, Lieutenant Colonel Brian. *A Field Marshal in the Family* (Constable, 1973).

MOOREHEAD, Alan. *African Trilogy* (Hamish Hamilton, 1944).

NICOLSON, Nigel. *Alex: The Life of Field Marshal Earl Alexander of Tunis* (Weidenfeld and Nicolson, 1973).

PITT, Barrie. *The Crucible of War I: Wavell's Command* (Cape, 1980, and Papermac, 1986).

PLAYFAIR, Major General I S O. *The Mediterranean and Middle East, Vol. I* (part of the official history of the Second World War. HMSO, 1954).

RICHARDSON, Major General Frank. *Fighting Spirit: Psychological Factors in War* (Leo Cooper, 1978).

ROBERTS, Major General G P B. *From the Desert to the Baltic* (William Kimber, 1987).

RYDER, Rowland. *Oliver Leese* (Hamish Hamilton, 1987).

SAWARD, Dudley. *'Bomber' Harris* (Cassell, 1984).

STEEL-BROWNLIE, Major W. *The Proud Trooper* (Collins, 1964).

STORY, Colonel H H. *History of the Cameronians (Scottish Rifles) 1910–1933, Vol. II* (published by the Regiment, 1961).

STEVENS, Lieutenant Colonel G R. *Fourth Indian Division* (McLaren and Son, 1948).

TEDDER, Marshal of the RAF Lord. *With Prejudice* (Cassell, 1966).

VERNEY, Major General G L. *The Guards Armoured Division* (Hutchinson, 1955).

WARNER, Philip. *Horrocks: The General who Led from the Front* (Hamish Hamilton, 1984).

WAVELL, Field Marshal Earl. *Soldiers and Soldiering* (Cape, 1953). *The Viceroy's Journal* (Oxford University Press, 1973).

WILMOT, Chester. *The Struggle for Europe* (Collins, 1952).

WILSON, Field Marshal Lord. *Eight Years Overseas* (Hutchinson, 1948).

WOOLLCOMBE, Robert. *The Campaigns of Wavell 1939–1943* (Cassell, 1959).

ZIEGLER, Philip. *Mountbatten* (Collins, 1985).

Index

305

Index

Boulogne 14

Bourguebus 199–203, 206–10, 212

Boyd, Air Vice Marshal O. T. 36, 140, 142, 150, 152, 153, 155, 159–61, 165, 166, 168, 170, 176, 182, 260

Bradley, Gen. Omar 265

Bradley, Sgt. Maj. W. J. 21, 22, 188, 214

Bras 209

von Brauchitsch, Generalfeldmarschall 132

Brett-James, Anthony 267

Bretteville-sur-Laize 189, 199, 200

Brigades:

British

3rd Armoured Bde 134, 135

4th Armoured Bde 79, 81, 82, 85, 87, 88, 90, 98, 111, 113, 185, 188, 197, 229, 239, 243

7th Armoured Bde 79, 81, 82, 85, 86, 88, 90, 98, 103, 111, 113, 256

22nd Armoured Bde 208

29th Armoured Bde 192, 193, 203, 206–8, 219

16th British Bde 81, 82

168th British Bde 82

1st Cavalry Bde 46

Experimental (5th Bde) 30, 31, 34, 36

6th Guards Independent Tank Bde 185

6th Guards Tank Bde 184, 216–18, 221, 234

16th Infantry Bde 68, 99

159th Infantry Bde 203

227th Infantry Bde 192

31st Tank Bde 188

44th Bde 191

46th Bde 191

22nd Bde 14, 15

91st Bde 15, 17

185th Bde 17–21

Australian

16th Infantry Bde 82, 84, 85

17th Infantry Bde 82, 84

19th Infantry Bde 82, 84–86

Belgian

1st Belgian Bde 229, 234, 236

Germany

107th Panzer Bde 230

India

5th Indian Bde 81

11th Indian Bde 77

5th Indian Infantry Bde 79

Nowshera Bde 45

Peshawar Bde 43, 44

Secunderabad Bde 41

Briggs, Gen. 263

British Government 49, 50, 61, 162

British Mandate 49, 61

Brittany 199, 224

Broodseinde, Battle of 22

Browning, Lt. Gen. 'Boy' 35

Bruges 13, 14

Brunker, Lt. Col. K. E. M. 264

Brussels 225, 228

Bryant, Arthur 281

Bucher, Gen. F. R. R. 36

Bucknall, Gen. G. C. 36, 221

Bulford 30

Bulgaria 96, 97

Bullecourt 19, 20

Buq Buq 71, 76, 77, 81, 99

Burma 244, 247–9, 263, 275

Caen 187–9, 194–7, 199, 201, 202, 205, 206, 208, 210, 213, 216

Cagnazzo 167, 170, 172, 175

Cagny 203, 204, 207, 209, 212

Cairo 37, 38, 64, 65, 73, 74, 92, 94, 95, 97, 99, 100, 103, 105, 106, 112, 115, 120, 121, 131–3, 138, 140, 183, 278

Caius College 9

Calais 28

Calcutta 47, 245, 248, 250, 254, 263

Camaldoli, Monastery 164, 165, 174, 260

Camberley, Staff College 27–30, 35, 36, 249, 258

Cambridge 9, 17

Cameron, Pipe-Major 10

Cameronian Cadets 269

Camp 5 149

Index

Campo Concentramento No. 12   144

Caporetto   23

Capper, Maj. Gen. Thompson   13

Capuzzo   82, 102

Caracciolo, Gen.   161

Cardona, Gen. Lug   23

Cardwell Reforms   5

Carpiquet   195

Carter, Col. C. P. H. (Brevet)   11, 12

Carter-Campbell, Maj. Duncan   270

Carter-Campbell, Maj. George   8

Carton-de-Wiart, Maj. Gen. Sir Adrian, VC   140, 142, 151, 153–7, 161, 179

Carver, Field Marshal Lord   ix, 100, 124, 243

Casey, Mr, Governor of Bengal   261, 262

Cassino   202

Castel Benito   131

Cattolica   166–8, 171, 172, 174

Caumont   214, 216, 218

Caunter, Brig.   98, 111

Cavan, Earl of   30

Cervia   169–71, 174, 175, 260

Ceylon   247

Chamberlain, Neville   60

Cheape, Colonel   1

Charuba   115

Cherbourg   195, 199

Cheux   191, 192

Chiappe, Gen.   148, 161, 163, 164, 174

Childers, Secy of State   5

Chilton, Brig.   216

China   250

Chitral   45, 251

Christison, Gen. A. F. P.   36

Churchill, Sir Winston   49, 72, 94, 96, 99, 102, 106, 107, 109, 112, 121, 127, 129, 139, 176, 182, 186, 280

Cinglie   171

Clark, Jean   274

Clarke, Lt. A. C. L. Stanley   10, 34

Clive, Gen.   40

Clydesmuir, Lord   275

Colchester   7, 10

Coleridge, Gen. 'Daddy'   43

Collingwood, Lt. Gen. Sir George   32, 33, 47, 55, 56, 60, 179, 267, 275, 277

Collings, Colonel   74

Collins, Tpr   148

Collishaw, Air Commodore   66, 95, 109

Colombelles   201, 205

Colville, John   186

Combe, Lt. Col. John   88, 90, 133, 134, 136–8, 140, 142, 147, 151–3, 155, 159, 161, 165

'Combeforce'   88, 90

Commands:

Aldershot   30

Eastern, India   244, 245, 247–9

Northern, India   43, 250, 251, 254

South-East Asia (SEAC)   247, 248

Southern   30

Como   153, 159

Cona, Gen.   118

Connell, John   101

Corinthians, The   10

Cormelles   200

Corps:

Britain

I Corps   197, 208, 209

VIII Corps   177, 182, 184, 186–9, 191, 193–201, 206, 208, 209, 212, 216, 218, 220, 222, 223, 225, 228, 229, 232, 234, 237–40, 244–6, 248

X Corps   184

XII Corps   197, 198, 223, 229, 239

XIII Corps (Western Desert Force)   xiii, 65, 66, 68, 69, , 71–74, 82, 84–88, 90–92, 101, 105–8, 110, 114, 115, 117, 119, 120, 123, 126, 133, 134, 136, 194, 281

XXX Corps   189, 191, 216, 218, 220, 221, 223, 225, 226, 229, 230, 232

Royal Army Service Corps   59

Royal Tank Corps   44

308

Index

Index

310

Index

Index

Index

Index

Index

Waterloo Campaign 30
Waterperry House 28, 30, 35, 39, 268
Watson, Gen. Sir David 257
War Office 31, 32, 57
Wavell, Field Marshal Sir Archibald xii, 41, 50, 65, 66, 71–74, 76, 88, 92–94, 96, 99–104, 106–9, 112–15, 120–9, 133, 134, 138, 180, 183, 226, 247–9, 253–5, 263, 278, 280, 281
Weert 232
Weizmann, Chaim 49
Wellington College 2, 4
Wellington, Duke of xiii, 59
West Bromwich 30
Western Desert 94, 96, 100, 212, 256
Wheatley 28
White Paper: Palestine 61
Wigram, Gen. Sir Kenneth 43, 47
Wilmot, Chester 205
Wilson, Gen. Maitland 65, 70, 71, 73, 74, 76, 92, 94, 95, 97, 99, 100, 102, 105, 107–9, 115, 120, 121, 123, 180

Wimberley, D. N., Capt. (later Gen.) 36
Winston Barracks 269
Wolseley, Garnet 6
Wood, Reg. Sgt. Maj. 10
Woolwich, Royal Military Academy 4
Worth Priory, Crawley 187
Wyatt, Pte 15, 17, 20

Yokohama 252
Yorkshire 185, 186
Young, Brig. Peter 266
Younghusband, Col. 135, 136
Ypres 13, 14, 22
Yugoslavia 96, 128, 129

Zamalek 131
Zandvoorde 13, 14
Zeebrugge 13
Zionism 48, 49, 60, 61
Zone of Florence 162
Zuid-Willemsvaat Canal 229
Zuyder Zee 229

S

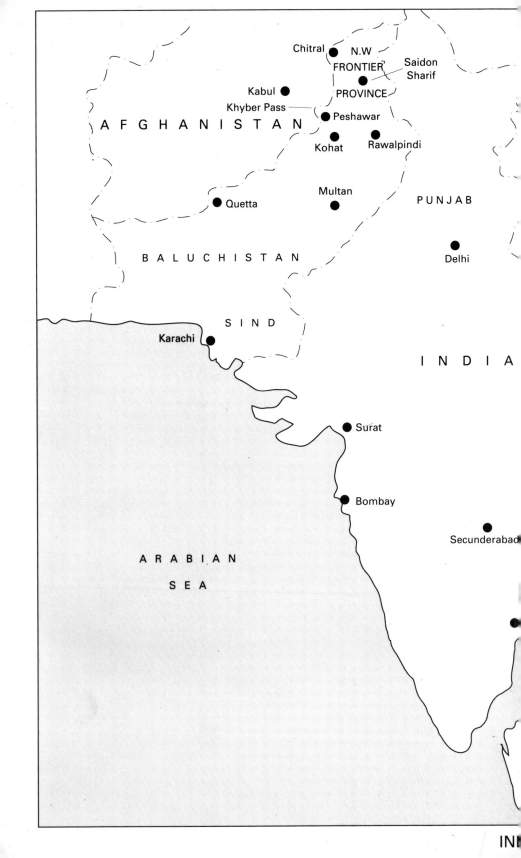